Beginners' Guide to Investment

D1465263

INVESTORS
CHRONICLE

Beginners' Guide to Investment

BERNARD GRAY

C

CENTURY
BUSINESS

First published in Great Britain in 1991 by
Business Books Limited
An imprint of Random Century Group Limited
20 Vauxhall Bridge Road, London SW1V 2SA

Second edition, revised and updated, 1993

Random Century Australia (Pty) Limited
20 Alfred Street, Milsons Point
Sydney, NSW 2061, Australia

Random Century New Zealand Limited
18 Poland Road, Glenfield
Auckland 10, New Zealand

Random Century South Africa (Pty) Limited
PO Box 337, Bergvlei, South Africa

Typeset by SX Composing Limited, Rayleigh, Essex

Printed in England by Clays Ltd, St Ives plc

A catalogue record for this book is available from the British
Library.

ISBN 0-7126-6026-7

Contents

Acknowledgements

A large number of people have very generously helped in the preparation of this book. The way in which so many people have given of their time, expertise and advice (when they had no need to do so) has been a real revelation.

In particular I would like to thank Andrew Radice and Ruth Sunderland for writing the Appendixes and other advice on taxation and investor protection. Thanks too to Stephen Lewis, Anthony Bailey and David Wighton for reading parts of the book and offering many useful observations and corrections. Many thanks to John Kegan for the help of the IC Studio, and to Jamie Wiles for producing such fantastic illustrations.

I am also very grateful to Michael Hughes of BZW for trawling through the manuscript; he courteously pointed out the flaws in some of my arguments, and helped me to strengthen my conclusions. My wife, Hazel McLean, not only put up with me whilst I was writing, but also offered many helpful comments. For this assistance, much thanks. Finally I would like to thank Gillian O'Connor, the Editor of the IC. Without her constant help, advice and support, I would never have finished this book.

The contribution made by these people was great; the mistakes remain mine.

B.G.
June 1991

Institutions as well as individuals have helped. Both the Stock Exchange and the Bank of England provided information readily, and many of the charts in the text were kindly provided by Datastream, the global information company. Thanks to all.

Preface

Sometimes beginners fear that the *Investors Chronicle* is for experts only. By the same token, the City is seen as an insiders' club, unwilling to share its secrets with the world. Both of these impressions are wrong.

The *Investors Chronicle* has a long history of encouraging novices to dip their toes into the water. One of the magazine's columnists, Stephen Lewis – a highly-regarded City economist – started to learn about the markets 20 years ago by reading the magazine. Every week the IC publishes an article for 'Absolute Beginners' which is one of the most popular features among newcomers and old hands alike. And behind all the hoopla of Big Bang, golden hellos, rocket scientists and swaps, most of what happens in the City is pure common sense.

So the first – and most important – point in this book is that beginners can understand investment. In fact it's not all that hard once the jargon has been stripped away.

'Beginners' Guide' tackles two questions. What happens in the City? And how can individuals decide what sort of investments are right for them? It uses simple, non-technical language to explain the issues, and presents charts, tables and diagrams to supplement the text. Each chapter concludes with an 'In a nutshell' summary which lists the major points made as an *aide memoire*.

The first section on '**The Markets**' describes the major markets operating in the City, their purpose, how they fit together as well as a little of their history. Besides putting decisions about investment into a wider context, it is also a general guide for the reader who simply wishes to understand what is going on in the City.

The second section, '**How to Invest**', explains how to choose a suitable investment from the many on offer. Different people have different needs and too often they put their money in the wrong place. Having provided some ground rules the section goes through different types of investment explaining how they work, and pointing out their merits and drawbacks.

Shares offer the greatest scope for the individual investor to make a killing or lose his shirt. The third section '**Companies**', examines the way shares work — what to look out for, what to avoid, what moves share prices, new issues and all the other ins and outs of the stockmarket. Although this section is more detailed than the others, it is just as easy to follow and uses simple real examples to guide beginners through.

Having made your fortune through investment, you will need an explanation of how to give some of it away to the taxman, so there is an appendix on tax — written by an accountant who is an expert on the subject. There is also a guide to investment regulation and the compensation schemes which protect investors from the unscrupulous or the foolish, as well as a directory to help you find a stockbroker.

Beginners' Guide explains from first principles the background to investment as well as how everything from unit trusts to takeover bids work. But each chapter is also designed to be intelligible in its own right. We hope it is useful to beginners and old sweats alike.

Introduction

At first sight the City is a diverse and confusing place. Bankers, brokers, market makers, salesmen, analysts, futures dealers, accountants, lawyers, insurance experts, entrepreneurs and a host of others all rush about doing very different jobs. Each group uses its own jargon, and to the outsider the only common factors are that they live in Surrey, drive expensive cars and are paid enormous salaries.

The City is a market for money

Of course that isn't the whole story. Members of each group are specialists in a particular field and the jargon lets them talk to each other in shorthand. But they are all part of a network which performs a single function. The City exists solely to funnel money from those who have it – call them lenders – to those who want it – borrowers.

The terms 'lender' and 'borrower' are a bit imprecise here. Sometimes the money 'lent' will never be repaid. But the principle is valid. Those who have money transfer it to those who want it in return for a rate of interest or a dividend.

Broadly, the savers are individuals who put money on one side for a rainy day or their retirement. The borrowers are companies who need cash to expand their business and governments who usually like to spend more than they can decently raise through taxes.

Because most individuals' savings are small and the amounts companies or governments wish to borrow large, the City often parcels savings up into usable amounts – a bit like a wholesaler who reaps economies of scale impossible for small retailers. In return for playing middleman between borrower and lender, the City charges a fee.

The complications arise because of the number of different ways the money can find its way from the saver to the borrower. People want to borrow or lend very different amounts for different lengths of time and are prepared to take very different risks. Agile City minds have come up with thousands of ways for getting money from lender to borrower – some of them very tortuous indeed. The main routes are explained in the section on 'The Markets' and those of particular use to individual savers under 'How to Invest'.

The second important point about this funnelling of money from individuals to companies and governments is that it is a market. Lenders want to earn as much as possible from their investment whilst taking the minimum of risk. Borrowers want to pay as little as possible to get the money they need. When you get a group of people competing to sell their wares at the highest price, and buyers hunting for a bargain, you have a market. In this case it is a market for money or a capital market.

In practice the City divides up into a number of different markets. These range from short-term money markets where banks borrow and lend to each other for three or six months, through long-term bond markets – like the Government bond market – where capital is invested for five or ten years, to share markets where companies borrow money which will never be repaid.

Within each market the price (or return on investment) is determined by the number of borrowers and lenders. As with any market, supply and demand are the controlling factors. If there are more lenders than borrowers the rate of return on investment will fall as money chases a home. If borrowers outnumber lenders the rate of interest will rise.

One recent example of this came from abroad. Even before Germany started to unify, the economy was growing so quickly that companies had to compete with each other for funds and interest rates rose. The demand for capital to rebuild East Germany after unification intensified the rise. As a result German interest rates

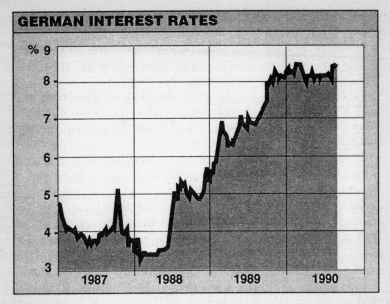

GERMAN INTEREST RATES

Fig 1 Demand for capital was rising in Germany even before unification, and as a result interest rates rose sharply.

almost trebled to attract the money needed.

Naturally enough, if one market looks more attractive than another investors will move between them seeking the most advantageous home for their money. So if bonds look more attractive than shares investors move out of shares and into bonds. As a result, the price of shares will fall and the price of bonds rise.

So the City can be seen as a clearing house for money where borrowers and lenders of all shapes and sizes come together to their mutual advantage. The price – or rate of return – of any particular investment is controlled by the laws of supply and demand. The City makes money by charging a fee every time someone borrows or lends (i.e. buys or sells an investment) and it has a useful sideline in advising on which investments look the most attractive.

Risk versus reward

But what makes one investment more attractive than another? The return on an investment is normally governed by two principles: first, the longer you are prepared to tie your money up, the greater the return you will get, and second, the greater the apparent risk that you will lose your capital, the greater the return you can demand on it.

These two rules mean that if an investor wants a safe home for money which he can get at instantly – like a bank deposit account for example – then he will probably only earn between five and ten per cent interest on his capital, depending on the overall level of interest rates. But someone prepared to invest money in a new company, where the risk of losing everything is high and there is little prospect of getting the capital out for years, is taking a big risk – and might earn a return of over 30 per cent for doing so.

Unfortunately these guidelines can only be rules of thumb. Other factors outweigh them from time to time. And it is important to remember that people can only estimate how risky an investment will be. Plenty of apparently safe, dependable investments have disappeared without trace, while occasionally apparent no-hopers have turned into winners.

Are markets efficient?

Some people argue that the operation of the market means that at any given time all of the information which is known about a particular investment is taken into account by the market and so capital is being allocated as efficiently as possible. On this theory the only thing left for an investor to decide is what level of risk is acceptable. 'The greater the risk, the higher the return.' The theory also implies that there is no way for investors to beat the odds – if the price of an investment changes it is because something unforeseen has happened.

That is almost certainly going too far. As the legendary

American investor Warren Buffett once remarked, 'It suits me that a lot of people are taught in business schools that there is no point in thinking.' Markets have fashions like anything else. Shares in computers, biotechnology, and waste disposal companies were all in – and then out of fashion during the 1980s. In each case the market anticipated that the business – and profits – of these companies would grow substantially. The most optimistic hopes went unfulfilled, so like the Grand Old Duke, the shares that had been marched to the top of the hill were marched down again.

This may all seem rather futile behaviour, and in some ways it is. But then it is very easy to judge events with hindsight. The problem comes because it was not at all obvious at the time that the hopes for biotechnology stocks were overdone. Financial markets are always looking forward, trying to anticipate what will happen next. Needless to say many of these guesses will be wrong – stockbrokers are not psychic – but it is always important to remember that markets are trying to discount what will happen up to 18 months ahead. If you think you have a smart idea as an investor, always ask yourself the question 'has someone else thought of it first?' If they have, you may be too late.

Some investors specialize in going the opposite way to the crowd, hoping to earn a better return than the sheep all heading in the other direction. Whilst taking a contrary view for the sake of it may seem a little perverse, simply following the market is no guarantee of safety either. Market fads are a bit like pyramid selling – you need to be in early if you are going to make a profit.

Between the 'efficient market' theorists and those who take a contrarian view, there is probably space for a canny investor to pick a winner. Financial markets may be roughly efficient most of the time, but sometimes they overlook things and they certainly over-react. One thing is certain – there is no shortage of investors trying to beat the system.

And small investors have one big advantage over the institutions – agility. The big pension funds and life insurance companies are like supertankers – it is difficult for them to switch direction quickly. But a small investor can theoretically sell everything with a single phone call. Sometimes that speed can be very useful indeed.

Routes from lender to borrower

If the City is a market for money which funnels small savings into large loans, what are the the main ways savers lend to borrowers? The great divide is between debt and equity.

Debt is easier to understand than equity, if only because it is familiar to all of us. Just like individuals, companies or governments borrow money for a fixed period of time, with a promise to pay it back plus interest.

For flexible short-term loans companies use overdrafts like the rest of us. When larger loans are needed for longer periods companies can go to the money market. This is the central market operated by the banks for borrowing and lending wholesale money. Most of the transactions here are between banks, which use the market to borrow or lend according to their needs or their view of interest rates. If a bank has too many deposits it can lend out its excess cash. Or if it has customers wanting a lot of loans which it cannot immediately meet from deposits, a bank borrows on the wholesale market.

Provided their credit is good enough, companies can borrow millions from the City. The two main ways for them to do this are to borrow money from the banks in the money market for periods of up to two years (sometimes up to five years) or to borrow long-term money from investors in the bond market. A simple example of a money market loan might be a company borrowing £5m for two years at 12 per cent and paying interest on the loan every six months.

In this case, the exact rate of interest paid depends on the balance between borrowers and lenders of two year money, and the credit rating of the firm. At some point the balance between borrowers and lenders might mean that the 'average' rate of interest on a two year loan between banks is 9 per cent (if more borrowers came into the market, the rate of interest would rise as demand outstripped supply, and vice versa). Because it is a good credit risk Shell might be able to borrow money at 0.5 per cent over the general level at which banks lend to each other – Shell gets its money at 9.5 per cent. (Banks, by the way, consider themselves a better credit risk than companies and so lend to each other at a lower rate.) But Nuts and Bolts Engineering might have to pay three per cent more than the general level because it is a new start up business – it pays 12 per cent. (For more details see chapter 4.)

Such loans are still only for relatively short periods of time, because banks are uncertain what will happen in fifteen or twenty years. Companies do go bust and banks with loans outstanding to them may not get their money back. But companies often want to borrow money for longer periods, so what's the answer? Larger companies (and governments) can borrow long-term money through the bond markets.

Bonds are just like loans – they pay interest and promise to repay the sum borrowed at the end of the loan. But they have an additional feature to make them attractive to investors – bonds can be bought and sold before the loan is due for repayment – in the jargon, they are negotiable. Investors who buy a bond are given a certificate which tells them the rate of interest the bond pays and the amount to be repaid at the end of the loan. If they need to get their money back before the company has promised to repay it, they can sell the bond in the market to other investors willing to buy.

These markets where bonds can be bought and sold are useful because they mean that investors need not have their money tied up for the full period of the loan – they have a way out if they need it. This extra feature means that bonds normally pay a slightly lower rate of interest than comparable loans. A £50m ten year loan to Shell might pay 10.5 per cent interest. But a ten year bond might only give a return of 10 per cent because investors have the comfort of knowing they can sell the bond if necessary.

One drawback to selling a bond early is that the

investor cannot be sure what it will fetch in the market. Although the return over the life of the bond is guaranteed, the return for selling early is not. Whilst interest rates may have been 10 per cent when our investor bought his bond, they will very probably vary over time. Investors in the market will only pay a market rate for a bond.

So beware: the fact that an investment can be bought and sold does not mean you are protected against loss. Only if a bond is held for the full period is its return guaranteed.

There are two main types of bond market. The government raises money through the gilt market (see chapter 2) and companies through the corporate bond market. Because bonds issued by the government are seen as safer than those issued by companies, they tend to pay a lower rate of interest.

So far, so straightforward. Debt in the City is like debt anywhere else – the sum borrowed has to be repaid on a certain date and interest paid in the meanwhile. The main refinement is that some debt can be bought and sold, it need not be held for the full term of the loan.

But equity is a very different beast. When an investor buys equity what he is really buying is ownership of something. Shares in companies are the most common form of equity and, as their name implies, when an investor buys a share, he is buying a share in the ownership of the company. That means that the investor owns a proportion of all of the company's assets – its buildings, stock etc. It also means that the investor is entitled to a share in any profits which the company might make. Because the shareholder is a part-owner of the business, he also has a vote on major decisions which the company might take.

All of which sounds very nice. The drawbacks to equity are that companies can make losses as well as profits and so the return to shareholders is not as predictable as with debt. Shareholders are also at the bottom of the heap if the company goes bust and is wound up. Everyone else who has lent money to the company will have his investment repaid (banks, bondholders and other creditors) before shareholders see a penny. Another factor making life more complicated is that shares are (almost) never repaid. Money lent to a company through shares is lent forever, and the only way out is for investors to sell the shares in the market.

Like bonds, shares are negotiable – they can be bought and sold in the stockmarket – so investors do not have to hang on to them forever. Although a lot of people like to buy shares when they are first issued, such events are relatively rare and so most shares are bought in the marketplace. Another consequence of the fact that shares are not repaid and company earnings go up and down is that shares are more difficult to value than bonds or loans. But their great plus is that they offer investors some protection against inflation, because the value of a company and the level of its profits tend to rise with inflation. In the short run bonds can look attractive to investors, but in the longer haul shares really come into their own.

When they have sorted out the basics like pensions, mortgages, cash reserves for emergencies and so on, private individuals should construct a portfolio of investments which is a mixture of both debt and equity (see chapter 7). Equity offers better protection from inflation and the chance of big gains, but debt is safer. Both debt and equity investments – and the markets where they are bought and sold – are discussed in much greater detail throughout the book. The point to remember now is that they are very different and that investors should spread their risk when constructing a 'portfolio' of investments. How they go about that is the subject of Section 2 of the book.

At this point it may be useful to draw another distinction. Not all of the transactions in the City funnel money directly between the small saver who is the lender and the company or government which borrows. If an investor who bought a bond when it was issued decides to sell it before it is repaid, then he will sell it in the market to another investor. The ownership of the bond has changed hands, but no new money has flowed between lenders and borrowers. One lender has merely replaced another.

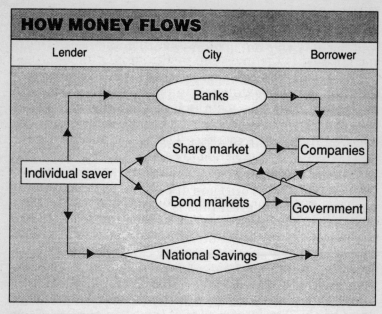

Fig 2 A simplified view of how money flows from individuals (who tend to be savers) to companies and governments (which are borrowers) in a purely domestic market. In practice international flows also play an important role.

This buying and selling without raising more money is big business. Most of the transactions in the share and bond markets are of this type. Critics say that this turnover is meaningless shuffling of paper because it does not directly raise money for those who need to borrow and encourages investors to chase short-term profits rather than invest for the long term. But the flexibility of the system helps money to be allocated efficiently and, since investors can sell if they want to, borrowers pay less for their capital than they would otherwise.

The process of selling new shares and bonds to investors is called the primary market; investors buy and sell existing shares and bonds in the secondary market. Most of the news about markets relates to secondary transactions — which are what cause share and bond prices to rise and fall.

Who's who

One other wrinkle which makes the City seem more complicated is the investing institutions. Although they are spoken of as powers in their own right, like the rest of the City they are middlemen in the funnelling of money. Institutions have two main functions – collecting money from small retail amounts into large wholesale lumps, and offering specialist expertise. They do make important decisions, but they are still only a link in the chain which runs from individual savers to company and government borrowers.

These institutions fall into two camps which very crudely could be called the 'debt group' and the 'equity group'. Most institutions will quibble with such a separation – debt experts will point out that they are also involved in equity and vice versa, but like most generalizations, it helps beginners see the wood for the trees.

The group which specializes in debt is led by the high street banks. The largest slice of their business is taking deposits from individuals and companies, and then lending it out again. They make money (their 'fee') by charging a higher rate of interest on loans than they pay out to depositors. Building societies are essentially specialist banks. Most of the lending they do is specifically mortgages on property.

Merchant banks are hardly banks at all – at least in the conventional sense. They lend very little money and don't really take deposits. Merchant banks are essentially financial consultants, advising companies on the best way to raise money, how to float on the stockmarket, how to make a takeover bid – or avoid one. Some also manage money for other people – charging fees for picking what they think will be the best investment in any field. Sometimes these banks, which specialize in securities, are known as investment banks.

The 'equity group' – as its name implies – mostly invests in shares. The two big guns in this field are pension funds and insurance companies. Both are investing money for much longer periods than banks. Most bank deposits or loans are made for perhaps a couple of years. But people save in pension funds or invest in life assurance for twenty or thirty years.

This long time-span makes a big difference to pension funds and insurance companies. Earning the highest rate of interest over three months is not so important to them. What counts is making sure that money they are given now will grow to protect investors against inflation over twenty years – so that when they come to collect, twenty-first century pensioners will have a decent income. This need to hedge against inflation in the long term makes them invest in shares. But aren't shares risky?

The great benefit that insurance companies and pension funds have is that they are big enough to spread their risks among a large number of shares. That means that although some of the companies whose shares they own will go belly-up, others will do well. Statistically they are safe. Indeed, the criticism is more often made of these institutions that they are all too similar. Big funds often merely mirror the market as a whole, and rather than trying to achieve outstanding performance, they are content to jog along at slightly better than average. Critics then say that if funds are only mirrors of the market, why do they need highly-paid advisers to run them?

Not all pension fund and insurance money is managed

WHO'S WHO AMONG THE INSTITUTIONS

Debt	Equity	Referees
Banks	Pension funds	Bank of England
Building Societies	Insurance Companies	International Stock Exchange
Merchant Banks		Securities and Investment Board

Fig 3 One view of the way the institutions stack up. Pension funds and life companies have long-term obligations, and tend to be most interested in shares. Banks and building societies have a shorter horizon and specialize in debt.

in house. Sometimes smaller funds, or larger groups seeking advice on specialist markets, subcontract handling of their investments to fund management groups. These groups are sometimes independent, or part of merchant banks, and they often also issue investments (such as unit trusts) directly to the public (see chapter 9).

Institutions are very important to the markets. The banks are major investors in bond markets, are the main force in currency markets and control the money market. Pension funds and insurance companies have large bond funds as well as owning around two-thirds of all shares in the UK. The decisions these groups make are critical for the markets.

But remember that they are only managers; the money they invest belongs to the man in the street. Some fund managers and private investors forget this – the fund managers get too big for their boots and the private investors too scared of the power of 'the Institutions'. One way of looking at it is that the private investor has merely contracted-out the management of some of his savings to his bank, insurance company and pension fund. The portion he retains to manage himself is a chance to pit his wits against the professionals. Often the results of that contest surprise both sides.

Standing outside the hurly-burly are the official institutions which hold the ring and see fair play. The Bank of England supervises the banks as well as the bond, money and currency markets; the Stock Exchange is responsible for the day-to-day management of the stockmarket and the Securities and Investment Board is the Government's watchdog enforcing the Financial Services Act (see Appendix B for more details), which is designed to protect investors from malpractice.

Before going on to consider the markets in more detail, let's recap on the main points in this introduction:

Introduction

IN A NUTSHELL

1. The City is a funnel for money between borrowers and lenders. Lenders are individuals with savings. Borrowers are companies and governments.

2. The City is also a market where buyers and sellers of different investments compete to get the best returns. Supply and demand dictate the price of investments.

3. The greater the expected risk of an investment, the greater the reward. The longer money is tied up, the better the return – usually.

4. Markets try to look ahead and take into account all the information they have. But sometimes they overreact or forget things.

5. The two main types of investment are debt and equity (shares). Investors should always spread their risk by having a mix of the two in a portfolio.

6. Debt can be overdrafts, longer term loans or bonds (which may be sold). It is less risky than equity, but offers limited reward.

7. Equity is part-ownership of a company. Owners share the profits and decisions of the business. It is riskier than debt, but offers long-term protection from inflation.

8. Not all transactions in the City funnel money directly from lenders to borrowers. In primary markets new money flows from lenders to borrowers; in secondary markets investors buy and sell existing investments among themselves.

9. Investment institutions are powerful middlemen
   which manage savers' money. Banks handle much
   of the debt investment, while pension funds and
   insurance companies have most of the equity.

Section One:
The Markets

Chapter 1
The Stockmarket

The Stock Exchange is the market which first comes to mind when people think of the City. Before the reforms of 1986 the crowded hexagons of the stockmarket floor symbolized the Square Mile; now trading rooms with brokers cooped like battery hens are one of television's favourite clichés. Yet the market for shares – or **equities** – is not the biggest in the City; these days other markets like foreign exchange and Eurobonds handle larger sums of money. So why is the stockmarket still regarded as the most important in London?

Partly because many people work for companies quoted on the Stock Exchange. These firms also make lots of news: takeover bids, new issues, financial scandals, profits doubled or halved – all make headlines. But the main reason for the interest is that the stockmarket frequently offers the individual his best chance to make money from investment. Building societies may offer a safe return, but choosing a deposit account is hardly a sexy occupation – picking a winning share is.

So what is the stockmarket, and how does it work? When an investor buys an equity he is really buying a share in the ownership of a company – he has a stake in all the company's assets, is entitled to some of the profits and has a vote on major decisions the company takes. The drawbacks to this exalted position are that businesses sometimes make losses; an investor's return from equity is not as predictable as from debt. And should the company go to the wall, shareholders are last in the repayment queue.

That said, most companies don't go bust. Equity investment also has the major benefit of a loose link to inflation in the long term – as the economy grows and inflation rises, a company's turnover, profits, assets (and so the value of its shares) all tend to rise. Since the war

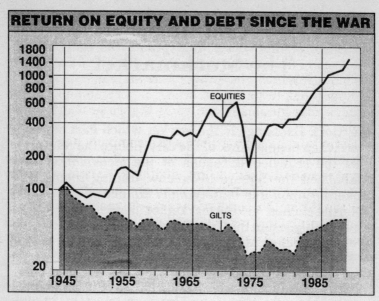

RETURN ON EQUITY AND DEBT SINCE THE WAR

Fig 1.1 In the long run investors have earned a better return from equities than bonds, but the ride can be bumpy. (Source: BZW.)

equities have given investors much better protection against inflation than debt such as bank deposits or gilts.

Companies are the 'borrowers' of equity money. Purists would object to the analogy since shares are not normally repaid. If a company borrows through a loan it expects, like any other borrower, to repay at an agreed date; equity, however, is 'borrowed' permanently – and that has important consequences for investors and the stockmarket.

Why sell your birthright?

Why do the original owners of companies give away their rights by borrowing equity capital? The most common reason is that a small company needs money to expand. Typically a company is started by a few people with some of their own cash and a bank loan. As the business expands the company needs money to invest in extra machinery, factories, offices and a host of other necessaries. Some of this comes from profits the company has made, more from further bank loans. But there is a limit to such borrowing. The problem with loans is that the company has to pay interest on them come hell or high water – and for small companies the water is often very high.

Borrowing by selling shares in a company has distinct advantages. For a start, the amount of income a share pays – usually called the **dividend** – is a variable proportion of the profits the company makes. So if times are tough, or the company wants to retain a lot of its profits to expand rapidly (common among young businesses) it simply pays out a small dividend, or even none at all. Dividend payments can also be much lower than the interest rate on loans because if the company's expansion is successful it becomes worth more – and its shares rise in value. *Investors accept lower payments from company dividends because they expect to make a capital gain from their shares as the company grows.* For a young expanding company borrowing equity can be more flexible than borrowing debt.

Equity has another benefit. People who have built up a successful small business can slap themselves on the back, name the company after themselves and point at a building saying 'that belongs to me' – but that doesn't buy them the yacht they want. Selling shares is a way for owners to release the fortune they have locked up in their company. That is true of some young entrepreneurs – the stockmarket has made many millionaires in the last decade – but it is also important to old family businesses. If a dynasty is failing, the last generation often sell shares in the company to release their investment.

Who buys the family silver?

Traditionally, small investors were the backbone of the equity market. They used their savings to buy shares –

effectively lending money to companies permanently.* For the most part these individuals used shares (and gilts) for long-term savings – buying when they were doing well to provide an income in future years.

Nowadays the pattern of long-term saving has changed. People rely on their contribution to pension schemes to provide an income in old age, and use life insurance as a means of long-term saving. Home owner-ship has become more important too – the rise in house prices since the second world war has provided many with a valuable tax-free asset for their old age.

These changing savings patterns have altered the ownership of the equity market substantially. Although individuals are still the ultimate lenders, much of the money they invest in shares is now handled by pension funds and insurance companies. Because a relatively small number of middlemen make the decisions about buying and selling large numbers of shares, they have become powerful, and companies direct much of their energy towards satisfying these institutions, without considering the original lenders of the money.

One other group of slightly less powerful middlemen who make decisions about small investors' money are the managers of the unit and investment trusts. Unlike gilts, which are all fairly similar (see chapter 2), each company is different. Some grow dramatically, others go broke. So it is important for investors to spread their money between a range of shares to reduce the risk of losing the lot. Both unit trusts and investment trusts offer a way to do this – investors can buy a trust which is itself a basket of shares**. These trusts are discussed more fully in chapter 9.

One important consequence of a company issuing shares to outsiders is that ownership and control of a company are split. Before the entrepreneur floats his

---

* The clever part of the deal was that the companies got a permanent loan, but the lenders were not tied in permanently since they could always sell their shares in the market.
** In fact there are unit trusts which invest in gilts – though why anyone would buy these is a mystery.

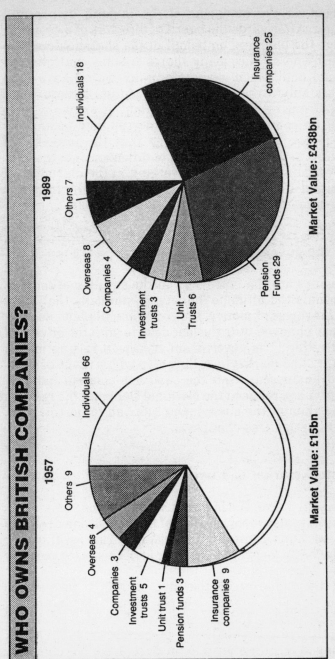

WHO OWNS BRITISH COMPANIES?

1957

Individuals 66

Others 9

Overseas 4

Companies 3

Investment trusts 5

Unit trust 1

Pension funds 3

Insurance companies 9

Market Value: £15bn

1989

Individuals 18

Others 7

Overseas 8

Companies 4

Investment trusts 3

Unit Trusts 6

Insurance companies 25

Pension Funds 29

Market Value: £438bn

Fig 1.2   The main feature of share ownership over the past 30 years has been the decline of individual investment and the rise of pension funds and life assurance as institutional investors. (Source: UBS Philips and Drew.)

business on the stockmarket, he is both owner and manager. Afterwards the board of directors of a company manage the business on behalf of the shareholders who are the owners. Since many shares are now controlled by financial middlemen, ownership and control have been divorced still further, because the eventual owners (those who put money into a pension fund, for example) have almost no contact with the businesses they technically own. Hence some people worry that the interests of company managers, financial middlemen and the ultimate owners of equity are diverging to the detriment of all. Britain and the United States seem to suffer from this problem much more than Germany and Japan.

Even the government has a share

Companies are the borrowers in the equity market, and individuals the ultimate lenders. Historically that other great borrower of money, the government, plays no part. This has changed over the last decade with the advent of privatization. The government has been raising money from the stockmarket by selling off a whole range of state-owned businesses. And the cash has come in handy – some of it has reduced the National Debt and the rest has cut the amount the government has had to borrow from the gilt market (see chapter 2).

The stockmarket is a two-way street

As we said above, the fact that shares are not repaid has important consequences. Most of the discussion of shares so far has concentrated on the original transfer of money from individual savers to companies – this is the **primary** or **new issue** market.

But the majority of the stockmarket's business is trading in second-hand shares. Most shares change hands regularly. And the fact that there is a market in which they can be bought is a precondition for investors agreeing to buy the shares in the first place. The company gets its 'perpetual loan' with the new issue, but because of the secondary market investors are not tied in for ever.

This market, where shares change hands like second-hand cars, occupies most of the stockmarket's attention; the amount of money companies raise through new issues is tiny compared to the secondary turnover of the Stock Exchange.

Is the City short-termist?

The trade in second-hand equities – with prices fluctuating according to supply and demand from investors – also creates an opportunity for speculators to buy shares, make a quick profit, and sell out again. Such speculators help by creating liquidity – the more people prepared to buy and sell shares, the easier an investor finds it to deal.

But some people allege that the speculative tail can start wagging the investment dog. Businesses are forced

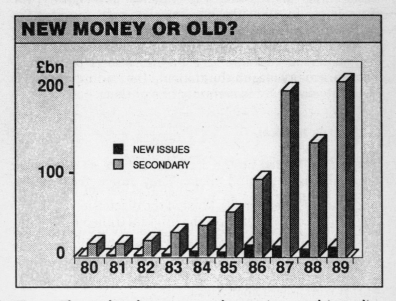

Fig 1.3 The stockmarket seems much more interested in trading existing shares than in raising new funds for companies. Without privatization the picture would look even worse.

to increase profits as fast as possible, regardless of any long-term damage to the firm in order to keep their share price high. Spending on essential long-range projects like research is discouraged. The counter argument to this is that increasing profits is always in a company's interest; that stockmarket winners like Glaxo spend a fortune on researching new drugs and that only those who cannot make the grade complain.

The debate is further complicated because one man's short-term speculator is often another's long-term investor. Pension funds and insurance companies hold portfolios of shares for long periods, but the performance of those who manage the money is scrutinized every quarter – and there is keen competition between managers to show a good profit on the shares they hold. Does that make them investors or speculators?

There is probably right on both sides of the wrangle. What is equally worrying, but less often discussed, is that far more people are employed buying, selling and researching shares than in raising new equity for companies. In 1989 the stockmarket only rounded up £12bn in new funds – including privatizations, whereas the Eurobond market (where new issues are very important) managed to raise £137bn in various currencies. There are many reasons for that, but the trading emphasis of the stockmarket is certainly one of them.

A diverse market

The shares traded on the stockmarket are as diverse as the companies behind them. They range from multibillion pound giants to tiddlers worth a few hundred thousand and from steel manufacturers to public relations firms – so sorting them into sensible groups is quite hard. But classifying companies is worthwhile because news affecting one company may also affect another firm in the same industry – for example most retailers will be hurt if consumers spend less.

Dividing companies up into groups of similar businesses is useful but fraught with difficulty because no two companies are exactly alike. And when twenty or more are grouped together, the differences between them are as great as the similarities. Nevertheless the **Financial Times-Actuaries** (FT-A) system groups the largest 800-odd companies quoted on the stockmarket into 35 sectors ranging from building materials to merchant banks. Some, such as the water companies, are fairly similar, others, like 'miscellaneous', are clearly rag-bags.

The Stock Exchange classifies companies in a number of different ways. First, the exchange divides itself into two – the **main market** and the **Unlisted Securities Market** or **USM**. The main market is the senior part of the Stock Exchange – one of the prerequisites for entry is that a company must have at least three years' worth of audited accounts. The Unlisted Securities Market was created in 1980 to allow younger companies to raise equity capital. Companies need only have a two year trading record to get onto the USM.

At the start of 1991 there were about 1,925 companies listed on the main market and 380 on the USM. There were also 540 foreign companies whose shares are traded on the London stockmarket. As a rule of thumb, main market companies are larger than those on the USM – but there are also exceptions: many small companies have been on the main market for years, while some USM companies have grown rapidly.

Shares are also classified by the Stock Exchange according to their liquidity – a useful guide to how easy it is for investors to buy and sell any particular share. In general, the larger a company, the more investors buy and sell its shares and the greater the number of stockmarket dealers who are prepared to quote dealing prices. The biggest companies – like Shell and British Telecom – which are easiest to deal in are called **blue chips** after the highest value chip in poker.

Putting companies in baskets

Because companies differ so much from each other, supply and demand for their shares will at least in part be dictated by how investors regard each individual company. As a result share prices often move independently of each other. At any given time, some will be going up, some down and others not moving at all. Which makes it difficult for investors to get a picture of what is happening to the stockmarket as a whole.

To overcome this problem baskets of shares have been designed to give investors a feel for what is happening to the market – these are known as share indexes. An index is purely a number which compares the value of companies in the basket now with their value at the starting date. Often an arbitrary value of 100 is assigned to the value of the companies at the start.

The oldest index in London is the Financial Times 30 share index. It is made up of 30 of the largest companies, picked from across a range of mainly industrial businesses, and it is calculated hourly whilst the market is open. When computers became widespread, more shares could be included and the index calculated faster. For most purposes the FT30 has been replaced by the Financial Times-Stock Exchange 100 index known as the **FT-SE 100**. 'Footsie' is a representative sample of 100 large companies, and is updated every minute* to give an indication of how blue chip companies are doing.

Investors can also get an idea of how different parts of the stockmarket have fared because each of the 35 FT-A sectors has its own index, published daily in the *Financial Times*. These are also aggregated together to produce the FT-A All Share index, which is somewhat inaptly named since it only represents the top 800-odd companies. Nonetheless it is the index containing the largest number of shares and is heavily used by investing institutions.

The Ancien Régime

The operations of the Stock Exchange were dramatically altered in 1986 by a set of reforms which are widely

---

* Some securities houses update the FT-SE 100 index continuously, to help them keep up with events. This is particularly useful in the futures market (see chapter 6).

known as 'Big Bang'. Before 1986 stockmarket members were split into two types. **Brokers** advised investors on which shares to buy; they had research departments which studied companies, analysed their business prospects and predicted profits. They also had departments which worked with merchant banks on the flotation of companies. Brokers charged their investment clients commission on a scale fixed by the Stock Exchange at a level where most brokers could make a pretty decent living.

Because brokers advised clients, they were not allowed to trade in shares; this was left to the **jobbers** who bought and sold shares on the floor of the Stock Exchange. Jobbers could only deal with investors through brokers and acted as a buffer at the core of the market. Often when one investor wanted to sell some shares, there might be no other investor willing to buy at that precise instant. The jobber filled the gap – buying the shares, and selling them on a little later when a willing buyer emerged. Jobbers made money by trying to buy shares slightly cheaper than they sold them, and also by owning shares they thought would rise in price.

Like speculators, jobbers provided liquidity to the market. They were particularly useful because they offered both to buy and to sell shares at the same time; jobbers offered a **two-way price** where they would buy – a **bid** – and where they would sell – an **offer**. Taking British Telecom as an example, a jobber might offer to buy the shares at 250p or sell them at 255p. The 5p difference is called the **bid-offer spread** and is the money a jobber hopes to make. The smaller the bid-offer spread, the more liquid the market; shares of large companies tend to have narrower bid-offer spreads than those of small firms. Jobbers used the spread as a defence: by widening the spread if the market became very volatile they asked a greater reward for trading in risky conditions.

One other peculiarity of the UK stockmarket, which as yet remains intact, is the payment system. Dealing is currently organized into two-week **accounts** which mostly run from a Monday to Friday the following week and all transactions are settled ten days after that. This has several advantages. First, if an investor or dealer has bought and then sold a share within the account it allows the two deals to be set against each other, so only the net profit or loss (plus commission) changes hands. The system offers administrative convenience, and allows speculators more scope.

Account dealing also means an investor can sell a share he does not own, hoping to buy it back within the account at a lower price. This is known as **short selling** and is a way of speculating against a share. The drawback of accounts is that deals are not settled for some time. Now that the **Taurus** plan for electronic share registers has collapsed, a lashed-together alternative to accounts is proposed. Institutions will initially move on to a ten-day rolling settlement period – where all deals are settled ten days after they are done. When a souped-up computer is ready they will move to five-day settlement and their share holdings will be recorded electronically. Private investors will have the option of dealing for longer periods but will have to agree it with their brokers and, guess what, it will cost more.

As with many old British institutions, the jobber/broker system was designed to separate conflicting interests by creating a group of independent advisers who were paid by commission. Brokers competed to provide the best advice and execute orders and jobbers vied for business through their prices. But competition was limited – brokers were an expensive cartel organized by the Stock Exchange and the jobbing system was slowly dwindling. Added to which both brokers and jobbers were mostly partnerships with very limited capital – they found it increasingly difficult to handle the large institutional orders which started to flow through the stockmarket in the 1980s.

Pressure for change came from financial institutions who felt the market did not meet their needs. The system (and commission structure) had been designed in a period when the private investor was king. Now powerful institutions found themselves incurring high costs to maintain a system which could not transact their business. The catalyst for change came for the Office of Fair Trading, which tried to take the Stock Exchange to court for its restrictive practices in 1983*. With that the Exchange agreed to reform, and the action was dropped.

Brave new world

Originally the Stock Exchange only agreed to abandon fixed commissions, and intended to keep brokers and jobbers separate. But this was considered impractical and it was agreed that firms of **market makers** would act as both jobber and broker. New groupings of **securities houses** – often incorporating jobbers, brokers and merchant banks formed. These giants were supposed to be the financial equivalent of supermarkets where companies could find everything they needed under one roof. The firm would buy and sell shares like a jobber in shares it had selected, act as a broker in others, advise clients, research companies, arrange new issues, deal for private clients and trade in other markets like Eurobonds and futures. For a while **one-stop shopping** became the City's favourite buzzword. Two of the largest of the securities houses are Warburg Securities – formed from merchant bank Warburg, stockbrokers Mullins and Rowe & Pitman and jobber Akroyd & Smithers – and BZW, which brought together Barclays Merchant Bank, broker de Zoete & Bevan and jobber Wedd Durlacher.

Another major change after Big Bang was the move away from the floor of the Stock Exchange. A new computerized system called Stock Exchange Automated Quotations (SEAQ) was developed where each market maker displayed his buying and selling price – the central computer collated all the prices for any share on to one screen. Because both customers and market makers could see the prices on the screen and who was offering them,

*It is perhaps ironic that the OFT (normally champion of the consumer) should prove the nemesis of the old stockbroking system. Under fixed commissions, small deals had effectively been subsidized by large ones, so private investors got an unfairly cheap service. Since Big Bang commissions for institutions have halved, whilst those for small investors have gone up – proving the adage that a free market is one where the big guy is free to sit on the little one.

there was no need for dealers to meet face to face. Indeed, using screens and telephones proved a lot more convenient. As a result market makers rapidly abandoned the floor in favour of hi-tech offices.

Institutional investors now have a choice of a large number of securities houses to deal through. Alternatively they can use an **agency broker** who acts much like an old-style stockbroker – advising on shares and trying to buy or sell for its client at the best possible price. The largest of these is the equity broking arm of James Capel (now owned by Hongkong & Shanghai bank) which is well regarded for its research into companies. Blue-blood broker Cazenove which specializes in new issues, has also eschewed the market making habit.

Small investors have fared less well than institutions. Many old broking firms ran private client sections, but most of the new conglomerates found these uneconomic. The private investor of modest means now has three choices. First, he can deal through a small country broker – some of which have carried over from the old market almost unchanged. Second, he can try one of the new chains of national brokers which are emerging as private client departments are amalgamated. Finally, there are the new computerized 'discount' brokers. Unlike the first two options, these brokers do not give advice on shares, they simply buy and sell them. Their advantage is that they are cheap. (For full details on brokers see Appendix C.)

Did somebody mention money?

The period between 1983 when change was agreed and 1986 when it happened was a Klondike gold rush for those in the stockmarket. Many UK banks and foreign firms wanted to buy into the previously closed world of British stockbroking, partially because it had been very profitable but also because two other trends were accelerating. First **securitization** – turning anything financial which wasn't screwed down into something that could be bought and sold – became popular. Then, as computers helped money flow freely around the world,

the links between different financial centres strength-
ened. For any serious financial firm two things appeared
vital – experience with negotiable securities and an
outpost in every important financial centre.

Stockbrokers provided a niche in London and equity
experience. The result was a beauty parade of international banks all desperate to pay as much as possible
for a few humble broking firms. With such high hopes,
disappointment could not be far behind. Too many big
competitors chasing too little business has meant heavy
losses. One management consultancy report put the costs
of the London equity market at £1bn a year – and
revenues at only £500m.

Low revenues are caused by competition. High costs
are due to firms paying large sums to hire scarce
experienced staff, and to cultural misunderstandings. As
small partnerships the old broking firms had tight control
on costs and could react quickly. But most of the new
securities houses are owned by large commercial banks
with bureaucratic natures; they initially threw money at
their new toys then, when losses mounted, tried to impose
management controls which were simply inappropriate
for a fast-moving business. It was a textbook case of how
not to enter an unknown industry.

As a result of the losses several large broking firms
have quit since 1986. Some famous names like Morgan
Grenfell have gone. There were other disappointments.
Securitization has not spread as rapidly as many hoped,
and the experience of London stockbrokers has not
necessarily proved useful in other markets. Companies
are also wary of one-stop shopping, and although markets
are becoming more interdependent, no firm has yet
emerged as a prime mover outside its home market.
Financial supermarkets may come – but they have not
arrived yet.

More unhappiness

Despite the low commissions they now pay, investing
institutions are not entirely chuffed with the new system.

They fear conflicts of interest in the new securities houses. Salesmen performing the role of brokers may recommend a company simply because their firm owns a lot of the shares. Or analysts may revise their view of a company's prospects and tell their market makers – the new-style jobbers – before they tell their clients. Perhaps worst of all, corporate financiers may let on to colleagues that a company intends to raise more money from the market – secret information likely to affect that company's share price.

All of these actions are forbidden and **Chinese Walls** are supposed to isolate different functions from each other. Nevertheless, investors and companies worry the rules may be broken. And several recent scandals suggest these fears are not entirely groundless.

Making the best of a mediocre job

The changes since Big Bang have not been entirely successful and issues like conflict of interest, high charges for small investors and a poor record for raising new capital are real worries. But some of the problems which have arisen are purely the result of bad management, and are not inherent defects of the system. Nor was the old market a model of virtue – insider trading was rife and the clubby nature of the Stock Exchange made it seem an institution run for the enjoyment of its members, rather than as a serious capital market. Whatever its faults, the new market, perhaps with some minor modifications, is here to stay.

We started out by saying that the stockmarket offered a prime opportunity for investors to make money. For that reason the third section of this book is devoted to the details of shares and companies – what moves share prices, new issues, takeover bids, company accounts and the like. This chapter only tries to give a flavour of the purpose and operation of the stockmarket. Before going on to look at gilts, let's summarize the stockmarket:

The stockmarket

IN A NUTSHELL

1. Equity is a share in ownership of a company. The return from shares can vary and investors may lose everything if a company folds. But equities do offer some protection from inflation.

2. Companies issue shares to raise funds for expansion. Individuals buy them, either directly or through pension funds, insurance companies or trusts.

3. Because shares are never repaid, a secondary market – where shares can be bought and sold – is essential. This attracts speculators. They add liquidity, but can distort the market.

4. Companies are very different from each other so to compare like with like, shares are grouped together into sectors of similar businesses.

5. Representative baskets of shares called stock indexes are used to indicate how share prices are moving. The FT-SE 100 index follows the largest companies, the FT-A All Share represents the wider market.

6. The stockmarket used to be split into brokers who advised investors and jobbers who bought and sold shares. Since Big Bang the two have been amalgamated into firms of market makers or securities houses.

7. Stock Exchange dealings are divided into accounts which normally last two weeks. Accounts help administration and liquidity and enable short selling. The system will probably change.

8. The Stock Exchange floor has been abandoned in favour of computerized dealing on SEAQ screens. These price screens can be seen by institutions and market makers.

9. Institutions have paid lower commissions since Big Bang, but private clients have paid more.

10. Intense competition and cultural clashes have meant heavy losses for securities firms since the reforms. Institutions also fear conflicts of interest in the new securities houses may lead to poor advice or dishonest dealings.

Chapter 2
The Gilt Market

Mr Micawber provided the briefest explanation of the gilt market: 'Annual income twenty pounds, annual expenditure nineteen nineteen six, result happiness. Annual income twenty pounds, annual expenditure twenty pounds, ought and six, result misery.' By that definition, most governments live in misery. In Britain (as elsewhere) politicians usually spend more on defence, health, welfare, education and roads than they think polite to raise through taxation.

In America this caused a real problem in the 1980s.* High defence costs and welfare programmes helped the federal government spend around $1,150bn in 1989, but big tax cuts in previous years meant that Washington only raised $1,000bn through taxes. So where did the missing $150bn come from?

One option for any government in this fix is to print the extra money it needs, since it has control of the printing presses. This used to happen quite a bit but is less popular now – it undermines the currency and can lead to runaway inflation. Another possibility is to borrow the money from banks, promising that tax revenues will be higher in future years. Latin American countries borrowed huge sums like this from international banks in the 1970s – an excess which is at the root of the endemic third world debt crisis.

Countries with more sophisticated financial markets like America and Britain have another choice – they can issue bonds which pay interest. In America these are called **US Treasury bonds** whilst in Britain they are

---

*What looked like a problem in the 1980s is turning into a calamity in the 1990s. Even though President Clinton is now trying to cut the deficit, it is still higher than it was in the 1980s. The deficit will be over $300bn in 1993; some $200bn of that is interest on outstanding debt.

known as **gilt-edged**. For governments, issuing bonds is cheaper than borrowing from banks for two reasons.

First, bonds can be sold directly to investors so there is no banking middleman to pay. Second, governments tend to be more creditworthy than banks – and less risk means a lower interest rate. Bonds also have the advantage that they give a government access to a wider range of lenders than simply relying on home-grown savers or banks. Much of America's huge deficit in the 1980s has been funded by Japanese savers buying American bonds.

Government overspending has been a habit for a long time so these annual deficits have rolled up into very large sums. In America the federal debt is heading rapidly over $3,000bn. Britain's **National Debt** is a more modest £210bn, and some £130bn is in gilt-edged. With the budget deficit running at £50bn a year, though, the total is rising fast.*

Gilts in theory

The classical explanation of the development of the gilt market is that wayward governments overspend and borrow the deficit from the gilt market. Every year there is a deficit and the National Debt grows. The gilt market snowballs because bonds are issued to pay for the current year's deficit and to replace any old gilts due for repayment. But provided the deficit is not growing too quickly, investors are fairly relaxed about this – they know HM Government is one of the safest investments around.

From one point of view, this snowballing of gilts is just piling up debts which future generations will have to pay. To counter this argument proponents of government debt say the money is used to invest in things like roads and schools which help make the country more productive. The more productive the country, the greater the tax revenue to pay off the borrowed money.

* To make gilts more attractive to investors, the government kindly exempts them from Capital Gains Tax.

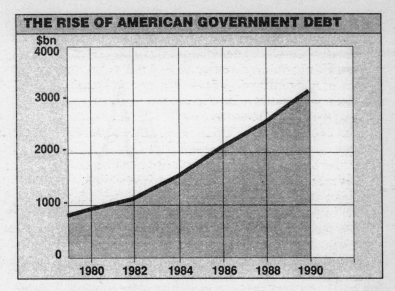

THE RISE OF AMERICAN GOVERNMENT DEBT

Fig 2.1 The rise in American government debt has been inexorable. The US now owes over $3,000bn, and problems with banks and thrifts (US building societies) mean that the annual deficit is still growing. Will there ever be a crunch?

There is a less attractive argument for ignoring growing government debt. Governments can remain relaxed about their debts because they know that inflation will eventually erode them – very much as homeowners know that increases in pay and inflating house prices cut their mortgage burden. So it is partly in the government's interest to let inflation rise – but government tolerance of inflation has a nasty side effect. Whilst reducing the burden of government debt, inflation also cuts the value of gilt investments. By accepting inflation, governments cheat the investors they have encouraged to buy bonds.

In the late 1980s the government used booming tax revenues and falling social security spending to repay debt. There was even loose talk of the entire National Debt being repaid by the turn of the century. Recession, higher government spending and rising unemployment have rapidly reversed that position. The government's deficit is currently £50bn a year, though the chancellor is

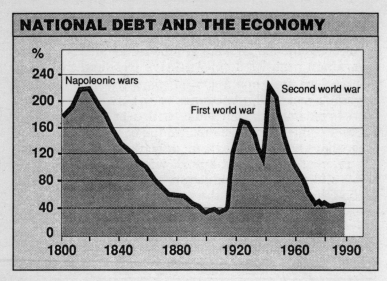

Fig 2.2 The National Debt as a proportion of the economy. Wars are worse than Labour governments for boosting the National Debt. Inflation has been the government's friend and the gilt investor's enemy. (Source: *The Economist*)

making efforts to cut this back. The gilt market is thus growing, making like much more comfortable for the gilts market makers.

The deficit is so large that there have been suggestions of a gilts funding crisis – the government is trying to borrow more than the entire cash inflow to institutional investors in 1993. So far that hasn't happened, perhaps because the banks and overseas investors have taken the strain.

What's out there?

Currently there are about 80 gilts issues outstanding, ranging in size from about £50m to over £6bn. These gilts have a wide range of repayment dates. Governments have issued gilts for different periods – some to be repaid (or **redeemed**) in two or three years, others which would not come home to roost for thirty years or more. As a result investors can choose for how long they wish to lend money to the government.

For convenience gilts are grouped into '**shorts**', which according to the FT definition have less than five years before they are repaid (seven years by the Bank of England's reckoning), '**mediums**' with between five and 15 years to redemption, and '**longs**' with over 15 years to run. There are also two specialist groups of bonds: '**undated**' which have no final repayment date (they just continue to pay interest) and '**index-linked**' where the interest payments and redemption values are tied to inflation. All can be bought and sold in the secondary market as some investors choose to sell their gilts and others wish to buy. There is quite a lot of activity in conventional gilts – shorts, mediums and longs – as professional investors switch between stocks. Turnover can reach £3.5bn a day.

How gilt returns vary

As interest rates rise and fall gilt prices move up and down to compensate so that the rate of return or **yield** of any gilt remains competitive with other investments. When gilt prices rise, the yield falls and vice versa. But an explanation of exactly why this is so can wait for chapter 8. The main point to grasp here is that gilt prices move in the market, just like share prices. However, one big difference between the two is that an investor knows a gilt will be redeemed at a fixed price on a known date, whereas shares have no such guarantee of repayment. That is one reason gilt prices do not move as wildly as share prices sometimes do.

The other point to bear in mind is that the prices of long gilts fluctuate more widely than those of short gilts. We can see why this is so by comparing a gilt yielding ten per cent with two years to redemption with one which has ten years to run also returning ten per cent. If interest rates suddenly jumped from 10 to 12 per cent, the prices of the gilts would have to fall. If they didn't, new investors would lose out on 2 per cent interest. Those holding the ten year gilt would lose far more – 2 per cent for an extra

eight years. So the price of the ten year gilt has to fall
further to compensate for this. For any move in interest
rates, the longer a gilt has to run, the more its price will
move.

Charts of the yield available from gilts of different
redemption dates are known as **yield curves**. In an ideal
world, the basic rule that the longer money is invested the
greater the return would apply: long gilts would give a
higher yield than shorts. Such a graph is called a 'normal'
yield curve. However, this pattern was not followed in
Britain in the 1980s as the government used high interest
rates to try to crush the inflation which had developed
over the previous decade. High short-term interest rates
meant high short gilt yields, but because inflation was
expected to fall, long gilts reflected a hope of lower
interest rates in the future. Since Britain left the ERM
there has been a more 'normal' yield curve. Yield curves
are also affected by the fact that different groups of
investors buy different types of gilt; demands for gilts can
vary between shorts, mediums and longs. When long gilts
are in strong demand their yield often falls below that of
short gilts.

Who buys gilts?

We know that the government issues gilts – it is the
borrower in this market – but who buys the gilts? Who
lends the money? Banks and building societies buy a lot
of gilts which have less than five years to redemption as a
convenient form of loan. Banks take deposits and make
loans, but sometimes they have more deposits than they
need. They have several options for putting this surplus
cash to work; one is to buy short gilts which can easily be
sold if need be. Gilts pay interest just like any other loan
and are backed by a good name – something which
always pleases a bank.

Long gilts are bought by those institutions which have
long-term commitments – the same insurance companies
and pension funds which buy shares. Just like individuals they want to invest in some debt as well as equity –

and long gilts fit their bill. Foreign investors can also be important buyers of long gilts when they choose to invest in the UK. Medium gilts are somewhat neglected because they don't meet most UK institutions' needs. The balance of supply and demand was further tipped against medium gilts because the 1970s Labour Government issued a lot of bonds which are currently classed as mediums. However the relative neglect has been eased because foreign investors have been buying, and UK institutions have been encouraged to hold mediums because of the recent shortage of long gilts.

Individuals buy gilts across the whole spectrum, depending on their needs. Quite a lot of the undated gilts like War Loan are owned by individuals who have held them for many years. Most of them have done very poorly from this investment.

The gilt market

Standing between the government and investors is the gilt market. This is the clearing house where buyers and sellers come together. It is both a primary market, where new issues of government debt are sold, and a secondary market where investors can buy and sell second-hand gilts among themselves. Reforms in recent years have not altered the purpose of the gilt market, but they have changed its operation substantially.

Like the market for shares, the gilt market was revolutionized by Big Bang. Before October 1986 wholesale trading in gilts was divided between jobbers who bought and sold gilts and brokers who advised investors. There were only two large gilt jobbers; they operated from stands or **pitches** on the floor of the Stock Exchange. Jobbers made money like second-hand car dealers, buying gilts and then quickly selling them on at a profit. A second source of income came from betting on movements of gilt prices. Because they owned a changing pool of gilts, jobbers manipulated their holdings to make sure they owned gilts which were likely to rise in price. Gilt brokers sitting in their City offices advised clients on which gilts to buy, and their representatives dealt with jobbers on the floor of the Exchange. Brokers charged commission on a scale fixed by the Stock Exchange.

In theory the old system offered advantages. Competition between jobbers was meant to ensure keen prices, and because brokers were paid to deal for the investor, they had an interest in ensuring their client got a good deal. But institutional investors were paying high commissions and competition had declined over the years. Old-style jobbers and brokers also had very limited capital, which meant the system found it difficult to cope with large orders.

The death-knell for the old system came because it was simply outdated. Commissions were fixed at levels which meant that large deals helped subsidize the cost of small transactions. This was fine so long as small investors were in the majority, but as investing institutions became more and more powerful, the situation altered. Professional investors were paying a high price for a system which did not meet their needs. Change was only a matter of time.

The new gilt market

Since 1986 the gilt market in Britain has operated along the same lines as the American Treasury bond market in New York. Instead of jobbers and brokers, new firms of **primary dealers** fulfil both functions. Operating from cavernous dealing rooms, they commit themselves to being prepared to buy or sell any gilt an investor may ask to deal in, quoting a price at which they are prepared to buy – a **bid** – and a selling price – an **offer** – in the issue. In return, primary dealers have the exclusive right to deal with the Bank of England. If the government wishes to buy or sell gilts in the secondary market it will act through the Bank. And all gilt new issues and regulation of the gilt market are handled by the Bank.

The new primary dealers are an amalgam of the old brokers and jobbers; they employ salesmen who advise institutional customers (in the way that brokers used to)

STRUCTURE OF THE GILT MARKET

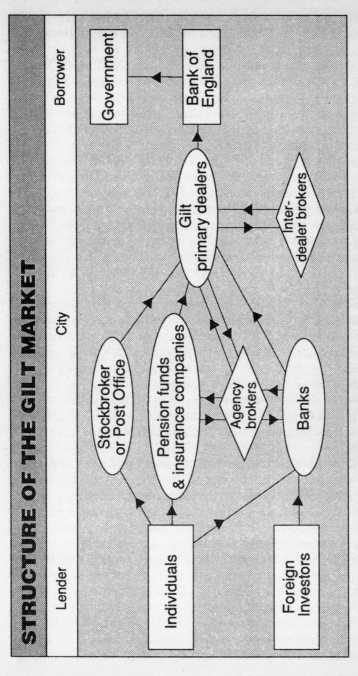

Fig 2.3 One view of the gilt market. Individuals buy gilts directly from the post office, or via brokers and unit trusts. Their pension funds and life insurance companies also invest in the market. Foreigners invest through banks or primary dealers.

and market makers who quote prices where the firm is prepared to buy and sell gilts (like the old jobbers).

Changing the gilt market certainly succeeded in attracting more capital and encouraging competition. At Big Bang 27 firms were licensed by the Bank of England as primary dealers, most being subsidiaries of UK or US banks. Instead of £30m-£40m of capital supporting the jobbers, the new dealers started life with £600m. Competition between them has been fierce and losses heavy – some £200m was lost in the first two years. The government surplus in the late 1980s added to the market's woes as turnover dried up. Indeed, it is no small irony that while the gilt and US Treasury markets constantly call for prudence in government finance, they get fattest when governments borrow most. So fortunately the current borrowing cloud is the gilt market's silver lining. However, that didn't come in time to save 12 of the original crew who retired hurt.

For the institutions, the new structure of the gilt market slashed dealing costs. There is no commission at all – effectively broking is free. And the difference between where market makers are prepared to buy a gilt and where they will sell – the **bid-offer spread** – is roughly half what it was under the jobbing system, making it much cheaper for institutions to trade in and out of the market. In gilts at least the investing institutions have achieved their aim: large investments can change hands at very low cost.

The institutions may have got their way, but that doesn't mean they are entirely happy. Some fear that the structure of the primary dealers means that they have a conflict of interest – salesmen may be tempted to promote gilts owned by their firm, rather than those which are the best investment. Such worries are probably overdone. The gilt market is very competitive – so primary dealers' prices are all very similar. It seems most unlikely that a gilt salesman could hoodwink a fund manager.

Although primary dealers are obliged to quote a buy and sell price to gilt investors, they will not deal with each other. This shyness could cause dislocations in the market – one primary dealer might be sold a large

PRIMARY DEALERS IN GILTS

Still trading	Retired hurt	New boys
Aitken Campbell (Gilts)	Alexanders Laing & Cruickshank Gilts	Daiwa
Barclays de Zoete Wedd Gilts	Cater Allen Gilts	Deutsche
Baring Sterling bonds	Chase Manhattan Gilts	Nikko
Bankers Trust Gilts	Citicorp Scrimgeour Vickers Securities	Nomura
CSFB (Gilts)	Hill Samuel	
Gerrard & National Securities	Hoare Govett	
Goldman Sachs Government Securities	James Capel	
Greenwell Montagu Gilt-Edged	Lloyds Merchant Bank	
J P Morgan	Merrill Lynch Government Securities	
Kleinwort Benson Gilts	Morgan Grenfell Government Securities	
Lehman Brothers Gilts	Prudential-Bache (Gilts)	
NatWest Gilts	RBC Gilts	
Salomon Brothers		
S.G.Warburg		
UBS Phillips & Drew		
Source: Bank of England		

Fig 2.4 Everyone expected the newly competitive gilt market to be a bloodbath, even before Big Bang. That didn't stop the institutions chancing their arm with £600m of capital. Around £200m of that was lost in the first two years.

unwanted block of a particular gilt which another primary dealer was keen to buy. To ease this situation **inter-dealer brokers** (IDBs) were created. These firms operate screens which allow primary dealers to buy and sell gilts amongst themselves cheaply and anonymously. IDBs don't hold gilts, they simply pass them from one primary dealer to another for a small fee.

As well as easing the flow of stock through the market, these brokers keep market makers abreast of price movements. The screens lie at the heart of the new gilt market – and access to the IDB network is limited to primary dealers as another privilege in return for providing a price service to investors.

The other group operating in the wholesale gilt market is the **agency brokers**. They act a bit like old-style brokers, charging investors a fee to buy gilts as cheaply as possible or sell at the highest price they can find.

For individuals buying gilts things have changed less.

Small investors can buy or sell through a stockbroker, and many gilts are available through the Post Office. There is a more detailed explanation of investing in the gilt market in chapter 8.

New issues

In the US, the government has a regular schedule for issues of Treasury bonds which changes only when there is a substantial shift in the need for money. Investors thus know well in advance what kind of bonds the government will issue. The auctions range from weekly three- and six-month Treasury bill sales to quarterly issues of bonds which are not redeemed for 30 years. In the UK, needless to say, things are more haphazard. The government has now adopted a regular monthly auction which is run by the Bank of England, but only because the pressure to raise money is so strong. Investors do not know in advance whether a long-, medium- or short-term gilt will be sold, or even the precise timing of the auction. Though to be fair, the system does progress through a kind of Buggins' turn where maturities which have seen a recent large issue are allowed to lie fallow for a while.

The details of the auction – which can be for up to about £3bn of a particular stock – are announced about a week to ten days before the auction date. Gilt market makers then deal in the stock which is to be auctioned, trying to sell it to investors in advance. Sometimes the stock will be a completely new gilt, but often it is for additional stock in an existing gilt stock. While this can depress the price initially, in the end it normally helps the market by making an issue more widely traded. Frequently market makers will have sold more stock than they own going into an auction so that they can bid more aggressively. The success of the auction is judged by the number of times the auction could have been sold – known as its **cover** – and how closely grouped the bids are – which is called the **tail**. A successful auction might be covered between two and three times and have a very close group of bids.

As an alternative the government can issue gilts to the Bank directly. This is typically a new £200m-£400m slug of an existing gilt issue and is rather charmingly called a **taplet**. Primary dealers can then offer to buy this from the Bank, which means that small investors cannot participate. Taps help the Bank manage the market – by supplying short or long gilts if they are needed or by alleviating a chronic shortage of a particular stock.

What moves gilt prices?

So what moves gilt prices? The simple answer is supply and demand – if investors are selling gilts, prices will fall, and as a result, gilt yields will rise until they attract new buyers. But what causes investors to buy or sell?

Perhaps the most basic factor in the gilt market is the state of government finances. If a government is running a huge deficit it will need to issue a lot of new gilts, and that extra supply will depress prices. Similarly, a government surplus helps boost gilts as investors have fewer bonds available. *Deficits hurt gilts (prices fall, yields rise); surpluses are good (prices rise, yields fall).*

Beyond that, different parts of the gilt market respond to different forces. Short gilts with less than five years to run compete with loans for investors' favour. These gilts are very sensitive to changes in bank interest rates; if interest rates rise gilt yields also rise to keep them competitive. *Rising interest rates mean falling gilt prices*, and vice versa.

Interest rates rise and fall with the state of the economy. If the economy is booming, companies borrow to invest and people borrow to spend, which forces up the cost of capital. Inflation also picks up when the economy is growing strongly, so investors require higher interest rates to protect themselves. By contrast when the economy is in recession there is less demand for capital and inflation falls, so interest rates tend to come down. *Recession is good for gilt prices.*

There are international influences too – if American and German interest rates are rising, they tend to force up rates in Britain. In some ways the gilt market competes with US Treasury bonds as a home for international investors' money. Currency movements also move interest rates. If sterling falls British interest rates tend to rise, both to prop up the currency, and also because a falling currency tends to push up inflation. *Falling sterling means falling gilt prices.*

Long gilts with over fifteen years to redemption are also affected by less tangible factors, such as what investors expect inflation to be in the long run. If investors believe that a government strongly committed to fighting inflation will be in power for a long period, long gilt prices will rise because expectations of inflation are low. On the other hand, uncertainty is bad for long gilts – factors like a government in trouble or international tension tend to force down long gilts.

Speculators – including short-term foreign investors – also influence this part of the market, since long gilt prices are volatile, short-term traders can gamble on bigger price movements. One of the main areas where this happens is long gilt futures – these are discussed in chapter 6. Finally, gilts are also affected by what happens in shares. In 1987 gilts offered very high returns compared to equities. When shares crashed, some investors switched into gilts, and prices rose strongly.

Such rules of thumb can only be a guide. Sometimes factors can work in opposition to each other, and sentiment can be a powerful force – gilts can be bought and sold on fashion alone. Also bear in mind that influences apply for different lengths of time. Sentiment can make the gilt market turn somersaults in the short term, but in the long run economic factors, like gravity, tend to win through.

The Gilt Market

IN A NUTSHELL

1. Governments tend to run deficits because they spend more than they raise through taxes. In Britain the principal way of financing such deficits is by issuing bonds – called gilts.

2. The stock of gilts outstanding tends to rise over time as deficits continue, but their value is eroded by inflation.

3. Gilts are classified according to their repayment date; shorts have less than five years to redemption, mediums between. five and 15 years and longs over 15 years to go. Undated have no repayment date and index-linked have payments tied to inflation.

4. When gilt prices fall the rate of return – or yield – rises and vice versa. Long gilt prices are more volatile than shorts.

5. Short gilts are bought by banks or building societies as an alternative to loans. Long gilts are bought by pension funds and insurance companies, as are index-linked. Small investors buy across the range.

6. Primary dealers both act as jobber (buying and selling gilts) and as broker (offering advice to institutional investors). They must give buying and selling prices to investors and have privileged access to the Bank of England.

7. Inter-dealer brokers ease the market between primary dealers; agency brokers try to find the best buying or selling price for a commission. Individuals deal in gilts through a stockbroker or the Post Office.

8. Most dealings in gilts are in the secondary market. New issues (the primary market) can be via a tender offer, a direct sale to the Bank of England or an auction.

9. Short gilt prices reflect interest rates. When the economy is strong, inflation rises or the pound comes under pressure, interest rates rise, so short gilt prices fall. Recession is good for gilts.

10. Long gilt prices move on more intangible factors, particularly expectations of long term inflation and political uncertainty. They are also more affected by speculators and are loosely connected to the share market.

Chapter 3
Foreign Exchange

The foreign exchange market exists to serve the needs of international trade. Companies exporting to other countries make money in foreign currencies and need to convert these profits into their own currency for use at home. Other groups, like individuals travelling abroad or investors wanting to buy overseas, also need to convert their own money into foreign currency. So, unlike other markets in the City which transfer money from borrower to lender, the foreign exchange market is a bazaar for swapping currencies. And the value – or price – of currencies is driven by the laws of supply and demand. Those in demand go up in value, those which are unwanted fall.

It sounds simple enough, and quite useful. The problem is that the real world of foreign exchange is quite different. In the 1980s forex dealing evolved to become the largest speculative market in the world. Almost everybody involved in finance seems to have started betting on which way currencies will move next; even the old Soviet Union was known to 'play the market' with hundreds of millions of dollars. And the overall amounts involved are staggering – over $900bn changes hands every day in a market which operates around the globe around the clock. Less than one tenth of that turnover relates to international trade; perhaps another 5 per cent is associated with real international investment. The rest is, in varying degrees, speculation.

The good old days

Things were not always like this. After the war a system of fixed exchange rates was established following a wartime conference in Bretton Woods, New Hampshire.

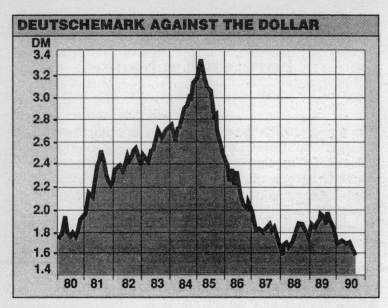

DEUTSCHEMARK AGAINST THE DOLLAR

Fig 3.1 Wild swings in currencies can distort economies. In 1985 the severe overvaluation of the dollar crushed US exporters and made imports into the US very cheap. The central banks only stepped in several months after the dollar had turned.

The major currencies were pegged at a fixed conversion rate against the powerful dollar and to add credibility, the dollar could be converted into gold at a set value.* If one of the major currencies seemed likely to fall or rise from its agreed value, the government concerned was expected to adjust its economic policy to correct for this. (Should this sound horribly familiar, flick on to the section on the European Monetary System.) Fixed exchange rates were useful because they allowed companies to plan their international business with some degree of certainty. However the system was rigid and slow to respond to changes in the balance between different economies.

The Bretton Woods system eventually failed because

---

* This onus on the Americans to supply gold in exchange for dollars didn't fuss them too much, since by the end of the second world war they rather handily held two-thirds of the world's gold reserves in Fort Knox.

the centre could not hold. By the 1970s the American government was spending freely on social programmes and paying for the Vietnam war. Investors lost confidence fearing that inflation and an uncompetitive American economy would eventually force a devaluation of the dollar. First, in August 1971 conversion of dollars into gold was suspended, and then the system was abandoned altogether as huge sums flowed out of dollars and into stronger currencies like the deutschemark.

Since 1972 currencies have been allowed to 'float' against each other – finding their own level according to supply and demand. Even the most important currencies have been very volatile in that time – for example the dollar fell from 3.4 to 1.6 marks between 1985 and 1987. This 'free' market period has been punctuated by several government attempts to control or influence the level of currencies. Most of these efforts have ended in failure, at least partly because the flows of capital through the market have simply grown too large for governments to oppose. The most striking feature of foreign exchange now is the sheer volume of transactions. Even governments working in concert can now only hope to influence events if they are working with the grain of the market.

Who does what?

This vast sea of money swirling through foreign exchange is probably the only true global financial market. Forex dealing happens almost everywhere, but is focused on the three main financial centres – Tokyo, London and New York. The market is busiest or **deepest** in the London afternoon when both Europe and America are open for business and in the right conditions billions can change hands here without moving the values of currencies. If there is ever quiet it comes in the Far Eastern morning, when only a few Asian markets are operating; central banks often intervene then because they face minimum opposition in any attempt to shift the value of a currency.

There is no central marketplace for foreign exchange – it is an **over-the-counter** market which operates like the

STERLING AGAINST DOLLAR SINCE THE WAR

Fig 3.2 Sterling since the war has been a game of two halves. The fixed rate period was punctuated by the famous Atlee and Wilson devaluations. Since floating rates things have been more volatile, but the direction is still firmly down.

gilt market; competing market makers offer to buy and sell currencies from their dealing rooms. Most of these dealers are big international banks like Barclays or America's Citibank, which have dealing teams around the world. These large banks have extensive networks of investors who buy and sell currency, and this provides the dealers with intelligence about the flows of money in the market. The market makers also trade with one another both directly over the phone and through forex brokers. These brokers use screens to display the latest prices, which often only last for a few seconds – and the screens are widely available so investors around the world know exactly the market price of any important currency at any time.

For simplicity currencies are priced against the dollar. And in active currencies like sterling, yen or deutsche-marks, there is so much money being traded that the difference between buying and selling prices is tiny –

making the market very **liquid**; typically a market maker might offer to buy dollars for 1.565 marks or sell them for 1.566 marks. Like many wholesalers, forex dealers depend on making a small profit on large volumes – an average foreign exchange deal might be worth $5m, and a big bank might hope to handle several hundred million dollars a day. Banks can make more money handling orders in less active currencies – an investor moving from Finnish markkas into Thai bhats will find the dealing spreads wider than one swapping pounds for dollars.

No commission is paid by institutional users of the forex market, so the large market makers try to make money from the bid-offer spread – buying currencies more cheaply than they sell them. Because they handle large volumes of foreign exchange every day, these banks can often buy a block of currency from one investor and pass it on to another immediately for a small profit.

Market makers also try to make money by holding on to currencies they think will rise in value and sell short those thought likely to fall, intending to buy them back later on. This is done on a very near-term view – dealers rarely hang on to a currency for more than a few hours – but they will buy and sell a large amount hoping a small currency move will make them some money. A large market making firm might buy $100m-worth of deutsche-marks, hoping to sell them the same day for a profit of a few hundred thousand dollars.

The 'investors' using the forex market are a pretty varied bunch. Companies use the market to unravel the foreign currencies they acquire in the course of inter-national business, and to buy foreign currencies if they intend to invest abroad. Individuals also use the market if they are travelling, though this is normally through a branch of their bank (business on which the banks make large profits). Central banks have also been important in the markets when governments have tried to intervene. Speculators are often banks or funds set up for the purpose.

As always the dividing line between speculators and investors is blurred. Large companies may have very complex flows of different currencies, and their profits can be markedly affected by currency swings. Some companies (like Jaguar in the 1980s) try to mitigate this by hedging themselves – buying or selling currencies for future dates when they know they are due to receive payments. Others try to improve their position by trading currencies. The largest firms – like Shell – have a department within the company which acts like a bank. Whether any (or all) of this counts as speculation is largely a matter of opinion.

Forwards, futures and options

Companies use several methods to hedge themselves against forex movements – the three principal ways are forwards, futures and options. A detailed explanation of these is outside the scope of this book, but put at its simplest a **forward** is a customized agreement between a market maker and a company to buy or sell a specific amount of currency for a fixed date in the future. It takes the current or **spot** price and adjusts for any difference in interest rates between the two currencies in question.

Futures mirror the behaviour of the spot price, but have the advantage that companies do not have to pay out in full for several months. Because they are also standardized, they do not fit individual requirements exactly, but are more liquid because they approximate to the needs of many (see chapter 6). **Options** can either be standardized options on futures or customized options from a market maker. As with any type of hedge, there is a price to be paid for getting someone else to accept your risk. Hedging or taking a risk is a cost companies bear because of the volatility of the foreign exchange market.

What moves currencies?

Because foreign exchange is dominated by speculation – and very short-term speculation at that – it is difficult to come up with convincing explanations of how currencies move. Sterling will rise if it is in demand, but what causes the demand? One common way to look at the factors affecting the market is to divide them up into three groups – the **fundamentals**, **technical factors** and **psychology**.

Fundamental factors are the basic economic forces on a currency. In the long term these are normally the most powerful influence on how a currency moves, but they are often outweighed in the short or medium term by other considerations. Inflation is one of the most important economic factors here. Take the situation where two identical cars, one British, one German, cost the same in Britain as they do in Germany, but Britain has 12 per cent inflation, while Germany has only 2 per cent. After a year the British car priced in pounds costs 10 per cent more than the German car priced in marks, so it is harder to sell the British car in Germany and easier for the German manufacturer to sell more cars in Britain.

One way out of this is to allow sterling to fall against the mark. If the pound fell by 10 per cent, the relative price of the two cars would be restored. This means that *currencies with high inflation tend to depreciate*. However, this depreciation is not without hazard because it means that all imports into the UK will rise in price by 10 per cent – adding to the inflation problem.

Another economic factor affecting currencies is interest rates. Investors will normally choose a currency which offers a high rate of return. But by the same token, they do not want to give the interest earned away through inflationary losses. So investors look at **real interest rates** – the rate of interest after inflation has been deducted. In the early 1980s many investors bought dollars because they expected interest rates to remain high and inflation to be kept under control. As a result the dollar soared to unsustainably high levels.

High interest rates are also attractive because they can be a sign that an economy is growing strongly and many people are competing to borrow money. *High real interest rates tend to push up a currency*. In general, economic indicators which show an economy growing strongly, also mean that interest rates are likely to rise and so boost the currency. But the market is fickle – on occasion high interest rates are interpreted as a sign of high inflation and the currency weakens. In foreign exchange, there is no such thing as a hard and fast rule.

Technical analysts look at supply and demand in the market and use charts of how the value of a currency has moved over time to try to predict future movements. In essence the study of charts is based on the idea that group behaviour follows patterns which repeat themselves over time. So chartists study patterns of price movements, believing that they indicate future trends. They also study how fast a market is moving – any market moving too fast in one direction is likely to snap back soon.

Many people – particularly economists – think that there is little or no justification for charts, but that doesn't stop a lot of other people paying attention to them. Even if the chartists' theories are wrong, their predictions can sometimes become self-fulfilling because so many people act on the strength of them. Charts are a powerful medium-term influence on currency markets.*

Psychology – or sentiment – is usually a short-term influence on the foreign exchange market. Sometimes traders sell a currency because an industrialist was shot or buy one because they respect a government – or even just because they 'like' a currency and think others will buy it too. Although this is usually a short-term phenomenon, it can be very powerful and outweigh other fundamental or technical arguments.

Sentiment is most often seen in the 'flight to quality' – where investors sell what they see as risky investments and try to put money in the safest places – which are considered to be dollars, short term American Treasury debt (known as T-bills) and gold. In 1983 a Korean 747 was shot down by the Soviet Union, and the dollar soared against all major currencies as speculators feared a war and rushed to get their money into the safest and most liquid investments possible. In the rush no one gave a damn about the economy – or the chartists.

* Because the Exchange Rate Mechanism tries to damp down the volatility of European currencies, and imposes artificial restrictions on their movements, charts have become less useful in predicting currency movements inside the EMS.

It is easy enough to describe the range of factors which can affect a currency, but much more difficult to assess which forces are dominant at any particular time. Traders talk to each other constantly, trying to keep up with the latest fads, and at any time a cocktail of conflicting forces will be at work on a currency. The price in the foreign exchange market is only the net of all these – and that makes it hard to predict foreign exchange movements, even if you are on top of the action. For that reason, and because large amounts have to be hazarded to make a profit, foreign exchange is a market dominated by professionals, and private investors play little part.

Snakes and chains

Businesses get pretty fed up with the volatile and sometimes irrational antics of the foreign exchange market. Planning industrial investment is a long-term problem, and companies can find that they spend several years building a factory to serve an export market, only to see the market disappear because the home currency has risen to a level which makes their products too expensive abroad. Similarly, a falling currency can push up a company's costs by inflating the price of imported raw materials.

For these and other economic reasons, governments often try to control the foreign exchange markets. In some cases this takes the form of a specific agreement, for example the Plaza Accord of 1985 which tried to force down the value of the dollar. A group of countries which trade with one another frequently may also try to tie their currencies together more formally into a currency **chain** or **snake**. This restricts each currency in the system to a set band, and helps to make export markets more predictable for members of the club.

Europe is a large trading bloc containing a lot of different currencies and, to help stability and trade within the EC, a currency chain called the **European Monetary System** has been devised; this tries to restrict movements between participating currencies. Founded in

1979, the EMS has several elements – the most important being the **European Currency Unit** or Ecu and the **Exchange Rate Mechanism** or ERM. The Ecu is a basket of set amounts of European Community currencies and is fast becoming a currency in its own right. One Ecu currently contains 8.78 pence, 1.33 francs and 62.4 pfennigs, as well as amounts of other European currencies shown in the table on page 64; the composition of the Ecu roughly reflects the size of members' economies, and is renegotiated every five years.

The Exchange Rate Mechanism

The Ecu acts as a benchmark for that other part of the EMS which has become notorious in the UK in recent years. The Exchange Rate Mechanism is, as every schoolboy may know, the mechanism which is supposed to tie the EC's currencies together. Each currency in the system

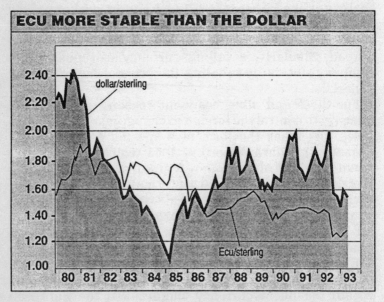

Fig 3.3 By bringing many currencies together in a basket, the Ecu was intended to encourage exchange rate stability.

is assigned a fixed rate against the Ecu, and is not allowed to move more than a set amount either side of that value without government action to try to prevent the drift. When the pound joined the ERM in 1990 it was assigned a rate of 0.693 pounds per Ecu. Similarly political negotiation fixed a rate of 2.044 marks per Ecu. This grid of values allowed each currency to be compared with every other. So, for example, the pound's central ERM rate was 2.95 marks:

$$\text{one pound} = 2.044/0.693 = 2.95 \text{ marks}$$

Before the mechanism all but fell apart in the summer of 1993 most currencies were not allowed to drift more than 2.25 per cent above or below their central rates, though Britain had used wider 6 per cent bands. There was a second constraint to give early warnings of trouble, where any currency which diverged more than three-quarters of the way towards its permitted limit was supposed to stop the drift. Often, though, and perhaps fatally, this second constraint was ignored.

So if, for example, the pound fell against the mark, Britain was supposed to buy pounds and sell marks on the foreign exchanges, while Germany sold marks to buy pounds. If further pressure were felt, the UK might have to raise interest rates and Germany cut to make sterling more attractive to investors and cool enthusiasm for the mark.

All this is history, since the UK was blown out of the ERM in September 1992. Then the theory proved flawed. Germany was in recession with rising inflation as a result of unification with the old East Germany. The Bundesbank – Germany's central bank – kept interest rates up to smother inflation, but that depressed other EC economies and prevented their interest rates from falling. The strain showed in Scandinavia, Italy and Spain, but most attention was focused on Britain. As the UK passed its 75 per cent early-warning point there was little buying of pounds by the Bank of England and no rise in interest rates, which looked politically impossible.

Sterling eventually hit its floor and despite massive

Composition of the ECU

Currency	March 1979	Sept 1984	Sept 1989	Approx. percentage June 5th 1990
West Germany	0.828	0.719	0.624	0.30
France	1.15	1.31	1.33	0.19
United Kingdom	0.0885	0.0878	0.0878	0.12
Netherlands	0.286	0.256	0.220	0.10
Italy	109	140	152	0.10
Belgium	3.66	3.71	3.43	0.08
Denmark	0.217	0.219	0.198	0.03
Eire	0.00759	0.00871	0.00855	0.01
Spain	N/A	N/A	6.89	0.05
Portugal	N/A	N/A	1.39	0.01
Greece	N/A	1.15	1.44	0.01
Ecu	N/A	N/A	N/A	100

Source: S.G.WARBURG

Fig 3.4 The composition of the Ecu is at present fixed by negotiation every five years. Moves to monetary union may change that – the Ecu may get a totally fixed competition or be superseded.

intervention – the Bank of England is thought to have bought over £10bn in exchange for other currencies in a single day – speculators overwhelmed the system and sterling fell out of the ERM. The government did try to raise interest rates right at the death, but they looked literally incredible given the weak state of the UK economy.

The criticism that the ERM forced countries to take action against their best interests proved true. Market speculators had decided that the UK could not take the pain handed out by Germany. Italy and Spain were also forced to devalue or leave, and the ERM was shown to be fragile. The final denoument for the system came in the summer of 1993, when the Bundesbank had still not cut interest rates enough to ease the pressure on other European economies. Most speculation focused on the French franc, since the mark-franc axis was the core of the system, and the French economy badly needed lower interest rates. The French government, committed to its DM link after 10 years of hard work, spent around $50bn of its foreign exchange reserves trying to defend the currency. When the effort failed the Bank of France was left effectively overdrawn by billions of dollars. While the system was notionally relaxed so that the central fixed rates remained the same and the normal 2.25 per cent bands were widened to 15 per cent 'temporarily', most people regarded the ERM as a busted flush.

So it seems that the warnings issued by people like Sir Alan Walters have come true. At times of crisis snakes and chains like the ERM can force governments to take decisions which run counter to the needs of their economies. A currency may be weak because an economy is in recession, yet the ERM requires the government to raise rates to defend the currency at precisely the wrong moment. This is one reason why many economists argue that the Maastricht process of using the ERM to move towards a single currency is fundamentally flawed. Whether economies as disparate as those of Germany and Greece can really be united by a single currency is another and much larger question.

Forward to Union?

The whole Maastricht debate has revolved around how far the EC intends to go towards unity. In economics that has meant a single currency, and some people think that the experience of the ERM crises has killed the idea for good. If there were only one currency then there would be only one interest rate and no possibility of devaluation. If Germany ran into similar problems in future, everyone else would be stuck with them. Besides, the full integration of poorer states like Portugal, Greece and Ireland would in many ways be like the reunification of East and West Germany. Perhaps fortunately, most EC countries look unlikely to meet the criteria for a single currency. Monetary union is a fading vision on the horizon.

Foreign Exchange

IN A NUTSHELL

1. The foreign exchange market is a vast bazaar for swapping currencies; over $900bn changes hands every day in a 24-hour market which operates worldwide.

2. Companies use the market to convert overseas earnings into their own currency, or to buy foreign currencies for investment abroad. Individuals also use currency for travel.

3. Speculators dominate the forex market, accounting for over four-fifths of all turnover. Governments – usually hunting in packs – try to prevent some of the wilder swings in the market.

4. Foreign exchange is an over-the-counter market with no central marketplace. Banks act as market makers and the flow of funds through the market means that it is very liquid.

5. The spot price is today's forex price. To hedge themselves against movements, companies can use forwards (customized forex deals for future dates,or futures (standardized deals based on today's price, but completed later). Options can also be bought in standard or customized forms.

6. Currencies are moved by fundamental, technical and psychological factors. Fundamentals are long term economic forces like inflation and interest rates. High inflation makes currencies fall, high interest rates help them rise.

7. Technical factors are medium-term considerations of supply and demand. They are normally

studied by looking at charts of previous price movements. Psychology (or sentiment) can be the most powerful force in the short term.

8. Governments sometimes link currencies into chains or snakes to limit their movement. The Exchange Rate Mechanism (ERM) of the European Monetary System (EMS) is such a snake.

9. The European Currency Unit (Ecu) is an artificial currency made up of specified amounts of other European currencies. Each European currency is given a negotiated 'correct' value against the Ecu.

10. If a currency in the ERM moves outside tight limits, central banks and governments are expected to intervene in the forex markets, alter interest rates and change economic policy to oppose the movement.

Chapter 4
The Money Markets

A 'market in money' – the very idea seems strange. Perhaps it is necessary to have a market in shares, so that investors can buy and sell, but why do we need a market in money? Even more strangely, if we only need one market for shares – the Stock Exchange – why are there several money markets?

The mystery is fairly simply solved. What people are buying and selling in money markets is the *use* of money for specified periods of time. At a personal level there is often a mismatch between the need for money and its arrival. A salary cheque is due at the end of the month, but the sale bargain is in the window now; or an inheritance arrives in May, but it makes sense to wait until August before buying a new car. The same kind of discrepancies occur at corporate and national levels. What is needed to sort out these knots in cash flow is a mechanism through which surplus cash can be lent to those who need it.

For individuals, banks meet this need. But sorting out the cash flow problems of banks and companies is a larger operation. Some companies, banks and governments have billions in surplus cash, others need it now – as loans for a new machines, or simply to pay the workforce until they sell their goods. The money markets are the mechanism used to even out the flow of wholesale cash.

So the money markets deal with short-term cash flow. Loans are typically for three or six months, and lending for longer than a year is a specialist activity. Long-term capital is bought and sold in the equity or bond markets; the money market is busy dealing in short-term – even overnight – loans.

As the market is one for wholesale money – a typical money market transaction might be for five or ten million pounds – it is a 'professional' market. Those who use it are large banks, institutions and companies, not individuals.* The other odd thing about the money market is that the 'price' of money is the interest rate charged, since what is being exchanged is the use of money for a set time. A lender wants compensation for losing the use of his cash, and a borrower expects to pay a fee for being able to use someone else's money. As with all markets it is the balance of borrowers and lenders which determines the 'price', or interest rate of money in the market.

And why do we need several different money markets? The multiplicity is more apparent than real. All sterling money markets are allied – interest rates in the different markets are closely correlated. But just as in everyday life money is used in different forms (cash, cheques, building society deposits, for example) so big money turns up in a number of guises. For convenience – and by historical accident – these different types of money are traded in different markets.

The inter-bank benchmark

It is perhaps not surprising that the banks are the backbone of the money market – short-term lending is their *fons et origo*. But they are not the only players. There are **money brokers** who shuffle funds between the banks, charging a tiny commission on the billions they handle (which nonetheless adds up to a nice little earner). The **Bank of England** is active as the representative of the government, and there are also the **discount houses**, a peculiar set of institutions which wouldn't be necessary if they didn't already exist, but which act as middlemen between the Bank of England and the banks. In recent years some **large companies** have also started to deal directly in these markets – many setting up what is effectively an internal bank to manage operations. But it is still the 'real' banks which dominate the scene.

* In recent times competition has forced banks to give individual customers with larger balances access to money market rates. Hence the growth of 'money market accounts'.

Although it is not the oldest money market, the **inter-bank deposit market** is the largest and a prototype for smaller money markets. Since banks have no money of their own, any loans they make must be funded from deposits, and any deposits they take (especially since most now pay interest) must be put to work as loans. Sometimes loans and deposits get out of step, so the banks have developed an inter-bank market to lend deposits to one another for fixed periods of time – ranging from one night to five years and at fixed rates for whatever period has been agreed. The inter-bank market thus helps even out the flow of funds between banks.

Whilst the interest rate on any particular deal is fixed for the duration at the time it is struck, just as share prices move, interest rates in the inter-bank market vary minute-to-minute. As with all markets, supply and demand fix the 'price' – in this case the interest rate. However, since interest rates are of central importance to the economy, the government makes great efforts to influence the level of rates.

The Bank of England (as the government's agent) uses one of the smaller money markets subtly to influence the banks' base lending rates (see below), and inter-bank rates vary either side of the 'official' rate, depending on supply and demand. Typically rates in the active three or six month lending periods will move no more than half a point either side of the 'official' rate unless a base rate change seems imminent. However, because they are constantly on the move, inter-bank rates give a better guide to the level and direction of interest rates than the static bank base rate. To give a 'fixed' point in the shifting sands of inter-bank interest rates a benchmark rate for each bank is recorded at 11am every day, and is known as the **London Inter-Bank Offered Rate** or **LIBOR**. Large international loans, syndicated among many banks are often fixed in relation to LIBOR.

As well as smoothing out the flow of funds, banks also use the inter-bank market to bet on the movement of interest rates. For example, a bank which thinks interest rates are likely to fall within a couple of weeks may lend money for six months at a high rate, fund this through

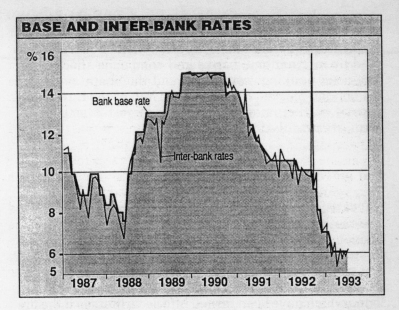

Fig 4.1 Base rates move in neat steps, but in the inter-bank rates vary constantly. Market rates tend to stick near base rates, but often exaggerate official moves. The spike is Black Wednesday.

borrowing the money for two weeks and, when rates have fallen, borrow money at the new lower rate to fund the loan over the remaining five and a half months. Normally this kind of speculation helps banks improve their profits – since they should have a good feel for likely moves in interest rates. But things can go very wrong. Midland Bank badly misread the rise in interest rates in 1989 and 1990 and lost over £100m as a result.

Tagged onto the main inter-bank market are several parallel markets where different institutions lend and borrow. Some companies deal in wholesale money directly – either with each other or with banks – and merchant banks (which have few deposits of their own) often borrow from the money markets. Building societies have started to come to the well too. Historically 'the builders' used personal savings to provide mortgage money, but now up to 40 per cent of their funds can come from wholesale sources. There are also markets in foreign currency deposits (not to be confused with the foreign exchange market). Deposits of dollars held outside the US (known as Eurodollar deposits – see chapter 5) are widely used by international banks and companies. Because of American banking restrictions and the liberal nature of the London market, the City is the hub of the Eurodollar deposit market, and many of the largest international loans are arranged in London.

If it moves, securitize it

Not satisfied with buying and selling deposits of cash to one another, bankers in the money market have yielded to fashion. Over the past twenty years more and more financial products have been **securitized**, that is, turned into some kind of IOU which can be bought and sold any number of times. Just as bonds are effectively long term loans which have been turned into securities, so there are equivalents in the money markets.

Certificates of deposit or **CDs** are one of the most common. As their name implies, they are certificates (or IOUs) which give ownership of a deposit at a bank. Since investors can buy and sell these CDs, they offer significant advantages over conventional bank deposits. Instead of agreeing to deposit money for, say three months, an investor – quite possibly another bank – can buy a three month CD. The investor then has flexibility. He can either keep the CD for the three months, or sell it in the market if he decides that he needs the money before that. This flexibility is worth something to investors and as a result, CDs normally pay a slightly lower rate of interest than conventional bank deposits – just as an instant access building society account pays less than one with a notice period. The CD offers advantages to everybody, a lower rate of interest to the bank issuing the CD and taking the money, and a way out for an investor unsure of when the money will be needed.

Of course, as with bonds, if the CD is sold before its redemption date, then the investor will have to accept whatever the market will pay for it. And as with bonds, if interest rates have risen since the CD was issued, the CD will be worth less because the interest rate it pays will be less competitive. (For a fuller explanation of how prices go down when interest rates go up refer to chapter 8.)

More bills

Certificates of Deposit are not the only security in the money market. The Government also issues short-term IOUs known as **Treasury bills**, which are similar to CDs, except that they are backed by the government, not a bank. They last for three months, and the Bank of England holds a weekly auction on a Friday. However, because the government borrowed less during the 1980s, Treasury bills declined in importance to investors. In part their role as a money market investment has been taken over by **commercial bills** or **bills of exchange**.

Although we have left these until last, they are one of the oldest types of security in the City. Commercial bills were invented to help finance international trade. Companies would make a product for export and had to pay for the material and labour. But by the time the goods had been shipped abroad and the buyer had paid up, several months might have passed.

To cover this cash flow problem (and to guard against default by unknown and untrusted foreign buyers) companies would take the bill of lading (proving that the goods had been loaded aboard a ship for export) to one of the banks which specialized in international trade. On the strength of the bill the bank would pay the company what they expected for the goods, less an amount for interest until the foreign buyer paid up. In the jargon of the time the bank had **discounted** the bill. Because these trade banks accepted bills from international merchants they became known as **accepting houses** or **merchant banks**.

Rather than keep a mountain of such bills, the banks would often pass them on to other investors. To do this the bank stamped the bill with its own seal and sold it on. Stamping the bill meant that the bank accepted responsibility for repaying the bill when it fell due. Since most investors knew and trusted the merchant banks like Rothschilds more than barely-known foreign companies, they were prepared to accept a lower rate of return on the bill than the bank was receiving; for example, if the bank had charged 8 per cent interest to accept the bill, it might sell it to another investor only agreeing to pay 7 per cent. Effectively the bank was using its creditworthy position and knowledge of the overseas companies to make money.

Government influence

These bills are still used in international trade, but they have an importance which goes well beyond that; the Bank of England uses them to influence the level of interest rates. The Bank can do this because it has a role balancing the quantity of money in the banking system – in effect it has a significant role in maintaining supply and demand balance, and so can influence rates. Sometimes the Bank supplies billions of pounds to the market. It does this by offering every day to buy bills from the discount houses (the intermediaries between the Bank and the banks) at interest rates which it advertises. The discount houses also deal in bills with the banks, so if a bank was short of funds, it could sell some bills to a discount house, which in turn might sell them on to the Bank of England.

The wrinkle which gives the Bank of England power is the rate at which it buys the bills. It uses this rate to influence the level of interest rates at which banks lend – any extra money the banks need comes via the Bank of England at a rate the government decides. So if the Bank of England raises the rate at which it supplies money, the banks have a clear incentive to charge the higher rate for any money they lend on. Technically the clearing banks could choose to defy the bank and set their own rate, but under the nod-and-a-wink system which operates in Britain, this is unlikely to happen. In any event, as a final resort, the government controls the Bank of England's printing presses. So it could strong-arm the clearing banks if it chose.

Although the Bank has the final word, there is something of a game of poker played in the money markets between the authorities and the banks.* If the markets believe that interest rates are going to fall, money market rates may move below the rates at which the Bank of England is prepared to buy bills. For example, on a particular day base rates may be 8 per cent, but bills are changing hands in the money market at 7.5 per cent in the expectation of a rate cut. However, the banks are short of money and need assistance from the Bank of England. So what happens next?

The banks and discount houses would be unwilling to sell bills to the Bank of England at a yield of 8 per cent if they had bought them at 7.5 – that would cost them money – but they do need funds. The Bank of England then faces a choice: it can bow to market forces and sanction a cut in the rate at which it buys bills to 7.5 per cent, or it can resist the move, offering to lend money to the discount houses at 8 per cent, rather than buy any bills. This sends a signal to the banks that there will be no official rate cut that day. If the Bank wishes to send a particularly clear signal, it can enforce the 8 per cent rate by lending money for several weeks at the higher rate.

A balance of forces exists between the Bank and the markets, and which party has the upper hand varies from time to time. Even though the government has more control over the money market than it does over foreign exchange, the markets are powerful. Any government relies as much on the skill of the Bank persuading the markets that it is in charge as it does on brute force.

What moves interest rates?

It may seem as though interest rates are set by the government trying to pin the tail on the donkey, but real

---

* As barriers to international capital movement come down, it becomes harder for governments to control their own currency. The foreign exchange markets are already more powerful than most individual governments in determining what an exchange rate will be. Will money markets eventually go the same way?

economic forces are at work. Interest rates tend to rise when the economy is booming, because the demand for money rises. In good times, more companies are prepared to borrow and invest in new plant and equipment and consumers are prepared to borrow and spend more if they expect their standard of living to rise. That demand for money tends to push up rates. Similarly, if the government has a large deficit which it funds through borrowing in the gilt market, that also puts upward pressure on interest rates.

Conversely, if the economy is moving into recession, then interest rates tend to fall as companies cancel investment plans and individuals try to save for the rainy day they suspect is round the corner. Often governments try to balance the see-saw of the private sector by borrowing more in a recession and stimulating the economy, and less in a boom to cool things off. Governments also try to pre-empt market forces of boom and bust, by cutting interest rates if slump seems imminent, or raising rates if the economy is overheating. This process happened in the last few years. After the Crash of 1987, the government feared a 1929-style collapse, and so cut interest rates. As it became clear that the economy was growing too fast in 1988/89, rates were raised to slow things down – both moves were probably overdone. It is certainly true that it is easier to see in retrospect what a government should have done, than it is to get things right at the time.

Inflation is also an important factor. Investors like their money to offer a 'real' return – i.e. more than inflation – and this is particularly so if inflation is endemic. As Britain's inflation problem got worse in the 1970s, real interest rates rose. In the 1960s interest rates were around 2 per cent more than inflation. In the 1980s, that premium increased to around 4 per cent. Overall, when inflation is high, interest rates tend to be high.

There is an international dimension to interest rates. If other countries increase their interest rates to attract international capital, then there will be pressure for the UK to do likewise, otherwise funds might flow out of sterling to more attractive homes overseas. This will then

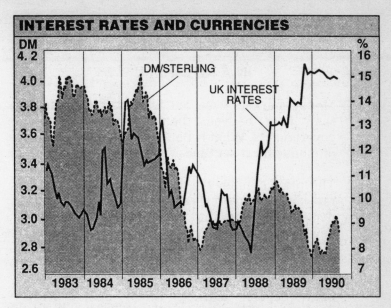

Fig 4.2 Interest rates are often raised to defend a weak currency.

tend to depress the pound. Or if UK rates are comparatively high, sterling will be strong, and that may make UK exporters uncompetitive. One theory of interest and exchange rates says that real interest rates in all countries should be equal.

The flip side of the currency question is that interest rates are sometimes dictated by exchange rates. If sterling is weak, interest rates may have to rise to make the currency attractive, and vice versa. The ERM explicitly uses interest rates to control the level of currencies (see chapter 3). Such strength or weakness may not be entirely caused by economic influences. The advent of a Labour government often causes a flow of funds out of sterling. There are few Labour administrations which have not been faced with a sterling crisis and pressure to raise interest rates in their early days.

The Money Markets

IN A NUTSHELL

1. Money markets even out wholesale short-term cash flow between banks, companies and governments. What is bought and sold is the use of money for a set time.

2. The 'price' of money in this market is the interest rate charged. Interest rates are set by supply and demand of money, but for economic reasons the government tries very hard to influence the level of rates.

3. The linchpin of the money markets is the inter-bank deposit market, where banks swap deposits with one another. Other similar markets are allied to this.

4. Money is also traded as IOUs or securities. A Certificate of Deposit is an IOU for a bank deposit, a Treasury bill is a short-term government IOU and a commercial bill is an IOU for international trade which has been guaranteed by a bank.

5. To supply money to the banking system, the Bank of England buys bills in the money market at rates it advertises. It uses this mechanism to influence the level of interest rates.

6. Interest rates go up when the economy is booming, inflation is high, overseas interest rates are rising or the pound is falling.

7. Rates fall when the economy is in recession, inflation is falling, international rates are coming down or sterling is strong.

Chapter 5
The Euromarkets

The Euromarkets are the home of the yuppie. When the champagne was flowing in the mid-80s, it was Euromarket dealers who were drinking it before staggering home in the company Ferrari. Stockbrokers merely clambered aboard the goods van of this gravy train, and even then only the partners of big City firms made any real money. With the exception of a few 'star' analysts, ordinary brokers had to settle for a couple of years of high salary before being made redundant; it was the Euromarket lads from Essex who really cleaned up.

So what on earth were they doing to earn salaries of £150,000 a year and bonuses to match? What are the Euromarkets and who uses them?

Confusingly, the term 'Euro' does not really mean European. It has become a catch-all word to signify investments in currencies held outside their country of origin – examples might be dollars on deposit in Tokyo, or a Swiss investor who owns a French franc bond. These examples illustrate the two basic types of Euromarket – the Eurodeposit market and the Eurobond market. Although most private investors rarely come across these markets, both are quite easy to understand.

Two types of debt

As currencies have become more internationally traded and the barriers to the transfer of capital have come down, more and more currencies are held outside their own country. Chief among these is the US dollar, which is *de facto* a world currency. Nowadays, for example, it is not remarkable for an individual to hold a dollar account at a British bank. Such an account is a **Eurodeposit** account and would pay interest in dollars and at dollar, not sterling, rates. Increasingly individuals and companies hold such foreign currency deposit accounts, and as the banks developed a market for exchanging ordinary deposits among themselves in the inter-bank market (see chapter 4), so a similar operation has been developed in foreign currency or Euromarkets, chief amongst which is the market in US dollar deposits.

At its simplest the **Eurobond** market is a way for some of the largest companies and banks in the world – such as IBM, the World Bank, Japan Air Lines, and Crédit Lyonnais – to raise money through issuing bonds, much as the UK government issues gilts. Even countries like Sweden and Belgium, which have small domestic capital markets, borrow money in the Eurobond market. What makes the Eurobond market different is that the companies and governments are borrowing dollars from German investors or yen from the Swiss. As a result the Eurobond market is also known as the **international bond market**.

Because these markets involve many currencies in many countries, the Euromarkets are curiously disembodied. They have no central marketplace and are not totally accountable to any particular government. But to the extent that the Euromarkets are based anywhere they are centred on London, largely by historical accident.

How it all happened

In the wake of the second world war Europe was rebuilt with the help of Marshall Aid from America. This brought billions of dollars to the continent, dramatically increasing the number of dollar deposits here, and it was natural that the money should be handled by local banks. As international trade increased and restrictions on the ownership of currencies slackened, all of the major Western currencies – particularly sterling, marks, dollars and yen – began to be held outside their home countries. Both investors and borrowers wanted a way to exchange this currency in Europe.

The second big break for London was the tough tax and

regulatory stand which the American authorities took on investment in the 1960s. Just at the point when Wall Street should have become the focus of world finance because of American industrial might, much of the international business it might have done was driven elsewhere.* London's tradition as a financial centre and the authorities' *laissez-faire* attitude to business made it the obvious choice. Since then the City's geographical position, bridging the time zones between the end of the Tokyo business day and the opening of New York's, have helped reinforce its leadership.

Once London became established as unofficial HQ for the Euromarkets, interested parties gravitated there. The result has been that most Eurodeposits are handled in London and many large loans to companies and governments – including much of the crisis-dogged third world debt – have been arranged by banks in the City. There are Eurodeposit markets in most of the major currencies, although the dollar market is by far the largest, and these are very similar to the sterling inter-bank deposit market discussed in chapter 4.

Eurobonds have also flourished; the vast majority of Eurobond deals are negotiated, arranged and sold to investors by banks and merchant banks based in London, even though the borrower may be a Japanese company and the investor a Swiss gnome. The booming Euromarkets have largely been responsible for maintaining the importance of the City as a world financial centre, despite the relative decline of the UK domestic economy.

Perhaps inevitably, even though the business is based in London, most Euromarkets deals are done by foreign banks based there. American banks naturally play a leading role in the Eurodollar deposit market; leading Eurobond firms include the Swiss-controlled Credit Suisse First Boston and Japanese giant Nomura. Despite

---

* In a curious way the insular nature of the American economy may also have been to blame. Foreign trade forms a much smaller element of the US economy than it does in Britain. This myopia may have made Americans think that international capital markets simply weren't important.

the dominant position of foreign firms, the Euromarkets have become so established in London that they are unlikely to migrate overseas unless the regulators make the British climate too chilly.

A unique freedom

London's liberal nature was crucial in establishing it as the home of the Euromarkets. Unlike most domestic markets, where governments are very keen to make sure they collect the right amount of tax from investments, the UK authorities were happy to allow the international markets to pay interest gross, relying on investors to pay tax in their home countries. Governments also usually like to **register** the owners of securities as a way of checking who owns what, but Eurobonds are normally **bearer** bonds; the holder does not have to disclose his identity and mere possession of the bond is enough to prove ownership. So the Eurobond market developed a reputation as a haven for tax-shy investors; the capital markets' equivalent to paying a workman in cash.

As is usual with such vague suspicions, little firm evidence has ever been presented to justify them. Jokes about Belgian dentists (unfairly picked on as the Europeans most likely to avoid tax) circulate in the market, but there is little to suggest that Eurobond investors are not law-abiding institutions and individuals. However, vague doubts about the legitimacy of the market probably contributed to the rather snooty attitude taken by the Stock Exchange towards the Eurobond market in its early days. This was a great blunder because the infant Eurobond market quickly grew to dwarf the UK equity market. New issues of Eurobonds have approached $200bn in recent years.

Freedom from heavy government control had a far more important impact on the Euromarkets than vague worries about tax avoidance. Because there are so few rules and regulations, financiers are able to produce many innovative ways of raising money. If bankers work out a very cheap way for a company to borrow, or hit on an option

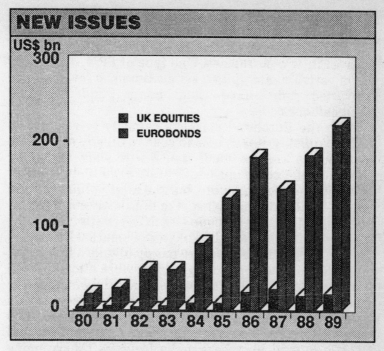

NEW ISSUES

US$ bn

- UK EQUITIES
- EUROBONDS

Fig 5.1 The Stock Exchange's great blunder – the Eurobond market grew from a precocious child to dwarf the much older equity market. In good years it raises $200bn for companies worldwide.

which appeals to investors, they don't have to wait in a queue for official approval. Once the technique has been worked out and a company wants to use it, a deal can be launched the same day. And the market is very efficient; as soon as a bond is issued, rivals from other banks work out how it was done and offer similar deals to their clients. Within days of a banker having a new idea, a dozen bond issues might be launched – raising billions of dollars for companies.

Innovations have come thick and fast. At the birth of the Eurobond market in the early 1970s bonds were similar to gilts; they paid a fixed rate of interest and were redeemed after a set period of time. There were also floating rate bonds – usually called FRNs or floating rate notes – which paid a variable rate of interest refixed every

six months in line with money market interest rates. But
by the early 1980s bonds were issued in dollars, marks,
yen, sterling, francs and then Ecus. Some bonds even paid
interest in two currencies. One type of FRN would only
pay a variable rate up to a set maximum, a few could be
converted into fixed rate bonds under certain
circumstances.

With the Eurobond market's capacity to respond to
fashion quickly, it was able to cash in on any new trend.
An example was the bonds issued with warrants to buy
shares in the company which issued the debt. Similar
ideas had been seen before, but the huge volume of such
bonds issued distinguished the Euromarkets. Particularly significant were bonds with warrants issued by
Japanese companies as the Tokyo stockmarket boomed in
the late 1980s. Investors were happy to take a lower rate
of interest on the bonds they held because they expected
to make a profit from the warrants as the stockmarket
rose. These 'Japanese equity warrant' bonds provided
Japanese companies with very cheap funds, and investors
with a bet on the Tokyo stockmarket. Between 1986 and
1990 Eurobond managers made fortunes by arranging
such deals. But when the Tokyo market fell, Eurobond
dealers had to start looking for a new way to make money.

Flies in the ointment

Unbridled free markets can lead to excess, and there are
fears that this has happened in the Eurobond market.
Often an innovative financing technique is over-exploited
so that investors who initially accept a new type of bond
as a good idea, find the market flooded with similar deals
within a few days, causing a fall in prices. This happened
with the floating rate notes which had an upper limit on
their interest payments — at first investors were keen
because the bonds seemed to pay a good rate of interest.
But as everybody jumped on the bandwagon, supply of
new issues exceeded demand and prices slumped.

Another problem arose when banks issued floating
rate notes with no redemption date in 1985 and 1986. As

with shares, investors relied on an active market where they could sell these 'perpetual' bonds if they needed their money back. Although they were initially popular because of the high rate of interest which they paid, some investors became worried about the reliability of the market in such perpetual bonds – especially because fears were growing about the safety of banks. A wave of panic selling followed and the market collapsed, leaving investors stuck with the issues.* There have also been allegations that some market makers have tried to corner the market in some bond issues – buying so many bonds that they drive the price up to ludicrous levels before flooding the market again.

Such antics have been tolerated because the Eurobond market is dominated by professional investors – very few grannies stray into this area and transactions are usually for several million dollars. Those individuals who do buy Eurobonds (usually continentals) are large and sophisticated investors, who know the risks they run. But latterly even the professionals have tried to introduce order into their lives. Systems have been set up to ease the flow of new issues and the method of market making has changed. Instead of pricing bonds according to the immediate supply and demand, with prices yo-yoing rapidly as unscrupulous operators flood and drain the market, Eurobond dealers now price bonds relative to benchmark issues, which are highly liquid. It is a bit as though the prices of all small engineering company shares were determined relative to the price of Rolls-Royce. Computer checking systems are also now used to prevent any attempts at market manipulation.

So how do they make money?

In the Eurodeposit market money is made in much the same way as conventional banking – banks take deposits

---

* Ever keen to find the silver lining, some Euromarket specialists have spent the last five years looking for ways to re-package and sell these bombed-out perpetual bonds.

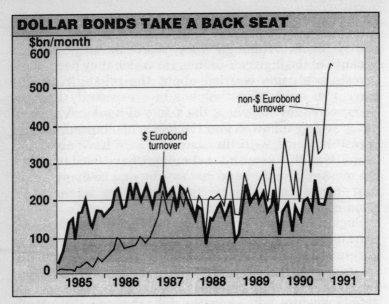

Fig 5.2 The business in dollar Eurobonds has matured, but the Euromarkets have learned new tricks. Attention has switched to raising money in Ecus, DM and other currencies.

at a lower interest rate than they lend the money on. The difference is called the spread and is the profit made by the bank. There are two main areas where money is made in Eurobonds – new issues and trading of existing bonds in the secondary market. The Eurobond market has clocked up almost $200bn in new issues in some years, and so the gross fees on each deal of between 1 and 2 per cent of the amount raised seem to indicate huge profits.

On the face of it the 20-odd firms which handle significant amounts of new Eurobond issues would seem to be sharing out about $3bn in fee income. Unfortunately for them, this market has become very competitive. The main bank arranging the deal (called the **lead manager**) spreads the risk by selling on much of the new issue to co-managers, and handing over most of the fees on these bonds. Even then competition to produce the most finely priced deal means that most of the fees have then to be given away as incentive to investors to buy the bonds. The net result is that the market is very efficient – on a successful deal a lead manager might make a quarter to a half a per cent, which is much less than with many equity issues. However, because of the high volumes and large amounts raised, profits can still be substantial considering the small number of people required to complete deals.

The other way of making money from Eurobonds is by acting as a market maker, quoting prices to investors where you are prepared to buy and sell existing bond issues. The difference between buying and selling prices in this market (the **bid-offer spread**) is typically a quarter to a half per cent of the value of the bond. Again this is much lower than equities, where spreads vary between 1.5 and 10 per cent, but as with new issues, turnover volumes are much higher in Eurobonds so that net profits are still large.

The beauty of this system is that it is quite easy to enter the market. A bank can set up an operation with perhaps ten dealers making markets in several hundred Eurobonds and expect them each to make $1m–$2m a year. In the early to mid-1980s this seemed like money for old rope to many banks, and a frenzy of hiring Eurobond dealers developed. If a dealer could make $2m a year for a bank, (and good specialists could make much more) then how much of that should a bank give away in salary to attract one of the few dealers with expertise? $100,000– $200,000? In the mid-1980s good Euromarkets dealers could almost name their price.

Of course the bubble burst; too many banks with no natural business in the Euromarkets tried to get a piece of the action, leaving too many dealers chasing too little real business. The inevitable shakeout followed. But though their numbers have been thinned, those who survive earn a healthy living, making the most of their continuing inventiveness.

I'll swap you

One of the ideas exploited most successfully by the Euromarkets is the **swap**, which became infamous because of the 1989/90 court case involving UK local authorities – particularly the staggering example of Hammersmith and Fulham. Although the details of swaps can get a little hairy, the basic idea (as with most brilliant suggestions) is quite simple.

There are two basic types of swap – the **interest rate** swap and the **currency** swap. Take the interest rate swap first. Large companies can command very good borrowing terms from banks and investors. Their size means they are a good credit risk and so can borrow money for a long period at a fixed interest rate. Small companies have no such advantage; they are riskier and have to borrow money at an interest rate which floats up and down with the general level of rates – a bit like a domestic mortgage. But small companies are often those which need fixed rate finance the most. If they are going to borrow to expand they need to know how much it will cost them in interest – they cannot afford to take a knock if interest rates rise in the same way that a large company can.

So what happens in a swap is that large and small companies get together to do each other a bit of good. A large company MegaCorp might borrow ten million pounds at a fixed rate of 10 per cent for five years. A smaller company Tiddler plc might borrow a similar sum, but at a floating rate of, say, 2 per cent over bank base rates, again for five years. MegaCorp and Tiddler then agree to swap interest payments – Tiddler pays the 10 per cent and MegaCorp the floating debt. But to make the deal worthwhile for MegaCorp, it only pays 1 per cent over bank base rates and Tiddler chips in the missing 1 per cent. Both sides benefit; Tiddler gets the fixed rate money it needs and MegaCorp gets floating rate finance at a cheaper rate than the banks would lend.*

What makes such deals nice is that the risk to either side is very limited, because they do not actually lend each other money, they only 'lend' each other interest pay-

---

*One of the reasons that the swap market grew so rapidly was the decline of the banks. As one debt problem after another surfaced, their credit ratings slumped, and it became cheaper for companies to deal directly with each other and miss out the ailing middlemen altogether.

ments. The worst thing that can happen to either side is that one company (usually the Tiddler) might go bust. In that case if interest rates had fallen from perhaps 11 to 7 per cent, then MegaCorp would have had to go back to paying the fixed 10 per cent rather than having the benefit of the low floating rate. But even then the difference is only a few per cent, much less than if the whole loan had been lost.

Currency swaps work in a similar way. A Japanese company Dai-Ichi Nippon might be able to borrow yen at a lower interest rate than an American firm FirstAmerica, whilst FirstAmerica can borrow dollars more cheaply than Dai-Ichi Nippon. This happens because each firm is better known in its own country, and banks often offer better rates to customers they know well. But Dai-Ichi might want to borrow dollars to build a factory in the US, whilst FirstAmerica needs yen to finance the purchase of a Japanese company. It makes sense for each firm to borrow in its own currency and then swap the payments.

Hundreds of billions-worth of currency and interest rate swaps have been completed since the early 1980s. In a way, what firms undertaking swaps are doing is exploiting an inefficiency in the way banks and other institutions assess the credit risk of companies. If the banks will not lend the money on the right terms, why not go direct to someone who will? The risks are limited; normally swappers only worry about the likelihood of the small company Tiddler plc going bust. If they are happy with that, everything should be OK. But the fiasco over British local authority swaps cast a shadow over the market, all the more so because the problem was the reverse of the usual worry. Instead of the Tiddler causing the problem, it was the MegaCorp.

Council swapsies

Governments have an even better credit rating than large companies, so naturally enough they too can borrow fixed rate funds at attractive rates. Local authorities have also benefited from this and have traditionally borrowed some fixed rate funds. Sharp-eyed City dealers noticed that local authorities could use this position to swap their fixed rate borrowings for cheap floating rate funds, and this business had been building up since the mid-1980s.

Although there was some disquiet about what local authorities were legally entitled to do, most City firms were happy to act as middlemen in the swaps – finding partners for those who wanted to swap and arranging the paperwork. Some even took on one side of the transaction, either to bet on moves in interest rates or because no partner in the swap was immediately available. All this was a lucrative business for the City firms, and for a while, things went well for the councils. Interest rates fell in 1987 and 1988, and hard-pressed local authorities found themselves making money on their swap dealings – they had exchanged fixed rate borrowing for floating rates, and interest rates were coming down.

As with much else in the economy, council swaps went badly wrong in 1988. Some councils – most notably Hammersmith and Fulham in London – did not limit themselves to swapping their normal borrowings. Hammersmith used the swap market to bet on movements in interest rates; effectively borrowing huge sums at a fixed rate and lending the money out at floating rates in the hope that short-term interest rates would fall and the council could reverse the transactions and make a profit. Such was Hammersmith's enthusiasm that far from just swapping its £100m-odd of debt, it entered into around £7bn worth of swaps. As interest rates rose from a low of 7.5 per cent in 1988 to 15 per cent by the end of 1989, Hammersmith's position worsened. If interest rates had remained high and the swaps had run their course Hammersmith would have stood to lose over £100m.

The district auditors became concerned, legal action followed and the net result was that the courts ruled that local authorities had no powers to make such swaps – effectively ruling them illegal. It was as though one side of the swap had gone bust; the other side had to take up its interest payments. Instead of Hammersmith losing £100m-plus, it was now the banks and other institutions which lost out. In total as a result of all local authority swaps, institutions could lose £500m.

It is a salutary tale, but it is not entirely clear who is to blame. Hammersmith particularly seemed to lose any sense of proportion and prudence, but then the City firms which dealt with the council, knew (or should have done) of the extent of the council's dealings. Moderation would perhaps have benefited both sides. Whatever the merits of the case, it is not really typical of the swaps market; hundreds of billions-worth of interest rate swaps have passed off without incident to the advantage of all concerned.

Rocket Science

As the number of financial techniques has multiplied in the Euromarkets – as well as bonds, deposits and swaps, there are also options, equity warrants, and even options on swaps – so the possibility of producing 'tailor-made' finance packages has increased. Very complex deals can be arranged so that, for example, a smart bank advising a company wishing to borrow Swedish krona might be able to exploit the market to provide very cheap funds. Because these deals may involve a number of transactions with some pretty difficult calculations, banks have hired top-level scientists and mathematicians to work on these schemes. A generation ago these people would have been found at Cape Canaveral, rather than in the City, and perhaps as a result these whizz-kids have become known as **rocket scientists** or **financial engineers**. Fortunately for them, most company chairmen and finance directors only need to understand the conclusions rocket scientists reach, not how they got there!

The Euromarkets

IN A NUTSHELL

1. 'Euromarkets' is a catch-all term to describe investments in currencies held outside their country of origin. There are two main markets; Eurodeposits, for example a dollar deposit in Tokyo, and Eurobonds, perhaps a Swiss franc bond held in Belgium.

2. The dollar is the most important Eurocurrency and the Eurodollar markets are the largest Euromarkets. But because of its *laissez-faire* attitude to business, London has become the HQ for the Euromarkets.

3. The Eurobond market is free from many of the controls which domestic bond markets have. This has led to innovation and rapid development of new ideas, but also allegations of excess.

4. Innovations in the Euromarket include: floating rate bonds, bonds with warrants to buy shares, bonds which pay interest in two currencies and bonds which have a maximum interest rate.

5. Past worries about the market have included allegations of price manipulation and the collapse of a liquid market in some issues.

6. The Euromarkets have been profitable because small teams of professionals can arrange very large deals quickly, exploiting new financing techniques without red tape.

7. Swaps is another important area in the Euromarkets. There are two main types of swap – currency swaps and interest rate swaps. Compa-

nies swap payments because they get better terms than they would from banks directly.

8. In currency swaps companies from different countries swap interest payments in local currencies. In interest rate swaps fixed-rate interest payments are swapped for floating rates. Local authorities got into trouble with interest rate swaps.

9. Very complex tailor-made financial deals are arranged by mathematicians known as rocket scientists or financial engineers.

Chapter 6
The Futures Markets

Visiting the trading floor of a modern futures market is like looking into Dante's vision of hell. Hundreds of demented souls stand, shout and scream in tightly packed circles called pits. All seem tormented – fear, greed and anguish are everywhere. One story from the futures market in Chicago tells of how a trader collapsed with a heart attack in the pits. Predatory traders – some his friends and colleagues – swirled around him, stuffing his pockets with their loss-making trades.

The story must be apocryphal, but standing in a futures market you can almost believe it is true. No one, it seems, would be there by choice. Yet the futures market is no forced labour camp. Many dealers there work for banks or brokers and simply enjoy the tension of this high-octane environment. Others come to buy and sell on their own account; betting their money on the moves in the market. These 'locals' are all drawn by the same vision; the futures market offers a unique chance to get rich overnight.

If all of this seems like a cross between the law of the jungle and a gambling den, then you have some of the flavour of it. But the futures market does have a serious economic purpose. To understand what that is, it is easiest to look back at the foundation of futures markets in nineteenth century Chicago.

Home on the range

When the American Mid-West was opened up by farmers in the last century the food it produced was badly needed. Industrial development meant that the population of Europe was rising rapidly, and the prairie offered a way to feed these extra mouths. Chicago was the ideal port to handle this food: ships could sail from Europe, down the

St Lawrence River, through the Great Lakes to Chicago in the heart of the Mid-West; railways and cattle drives brought grain, pork and beef to the port.

The only snag was the length of time the whole process took. American farmers might have to plant crops a year or more before they were delivered to their destination in Europe, and agricultural prices see-sawed wildly with supply and demand. Shortages might encourage farmers to plant more crops, but who could tell what price they might fetch in a year's time? A good harvest in Europe and America the following year might mean low prices and broke farmers. Such worries were a deterrent to expansion.

European importers also wanted some certainty in the price they would have to pay for food – profits could disappear if raw materials prices suddenly shot up. So both producers and consumers wanted to take some of the risk out of agriculture.

A market solution

To try to alleviate the problem, markets were established in Chicago where people could buy or sell corn, pork bellies and other commodities for future dates. These markets meant that farmers could estimate the size of their crops, go into the markets and sell an equivalent amount of produce for delivery in, say, six months time, but at a price that was fixed today. In effect they were **hedging** their risk. Similarly, importers could go to the markets and buy what they needed, fixing the price well before the goods were due to arrive.

A standard product bought on tick

To make the markets attractive to as many people as possible, the futures markets dealt in standard specified amounts of goods. For example a pork belly deal was for a specified number of pigs of set weight, fat content etc. What was bought and sold on the market was a contract to deliver (or accept) a set amount of goods of a standard quality*. If the goods delivered were not of the specified quality, the price was adjusted according to published tables. The point of this standardization was that although a standard product was not exactly what each farmer had on offer, it was a good approximation for what everyone wanted to buy or sell. That meant as wide a range of people as possible was dealing in the market so that it was **liquid** – i.e. in the market at any given time there was a good chance that there would be both buyers and sellers wanting to deal.

The other important feature about the futures market is that deals were done on **margin**. Anyone buying or selling only had to put up a small proportion of the total price at the time the deal was struck; the rest did not have to be paid until the commodity was delivered. This helped encourage buyers to use the market, since paying for goods months in advance has never been popular, but it also had a more important impact; it brought in the speculators.

Dealing on margin offers speculators the opportunity to make huge gains, and it's not difficult to see how. Say wheat costs $100 a ton, but that someone buying it on the futures market for delivery in six months only has to put up $10 initially. Over the next two months the price of wheat rises to $150 a ton, and rather than wait to take delivery of his wheat the speculator sells his futures contract to close out the deal. The speculator makes a profit of $50, or 500 per cent on his $10 investment, despite the fact that the price of wheat has only risen by 50 per cent. Such speculators help make a futures market more liquid; they might well take a deal on even if there is no natural buyer or seller in the market at any given time. It is the tantalizing prospect of these gains which draws many people into the futures pits.

---

* One nice little jargon curio for aficionados is that a futures contract is often known as a 'car'. This is because in the nineteenth century such contracts were sometimes specified as a railroad car of pigs or cows, of a set quality. The term seems a little odd when applied to gilt or FT-SE 100 futures, but it lives on anyway.

A way to transfer risk...

These then are the essential elements of a futures market. A **standardized commodity** is bought and sold on **margin** for **future delivery**. The key participants are **hedgers** – usually the producers or consumers of a product who want to reduce the risks they run – and **speculators** who are prepared to take on the hedgers' risks in the hope of making a profit. The futures market is thus a way of transferring risk from hedgers to speculators. Bearing in mind the good economic principle that there is no such thing as a free lunch, the hedgers effectively pay the speculators to take on this risk. In aggregate, the sellers of the commodity (who are hedging) receive a slightly lower price than the buyers (also hedgers) pay, and the difference is made by the speculators. These speculators, who are often **locals** – people who are speculating with their own money – also often act as brokers as an additional way to make money: buying and selling on behalf of those wanting to hedge and charging a commission for executing transactions.

...or an unjustified gamble?

The large profits which can be made trading futures on margin give rise to the common misconception that futures are inherently volatile and risky. In fact, futures prices rise and fall in line with movements in cash commodities. What gives rise to the risk is that if a speculator has only to put up a tenth of the cash to buy futures instead of the real commodity, he can buy ten times as much. Futures *are* volatile in proportion to the initial payment which is made, but not in proportion to the total 'real' value of what the investor is buying. But *that doesn't mean that small investors should be gulled by the first futures salesman who comes their way.* If a small investor puts £5,000 into futures he stands at risk of losing the lot – remember he is buying into a basic investment which is really worth £50,000–£100,000.

There is a more subtle argument over whether futures

cause volatility. Proponents of futures markets argue that they reduce price movements because they broaden the number of people participating, so that statistically there is likely to be a good balance between buyers and sellers. And yet, as futures have become more widely used in recent years, markets seem to be more volatile.

One way to square this circle is to realize that although futures markets transfer risk, they may only transfer it between speculators – some of whom want to buy while others wish to sell. If many speculators join in, speculative activity may outweigh 'genuine' hedging and investment. This is particularly so since futures margins allow speculators to buy and sell large amounts of the basic commodity, whereas those wishing to hedge do not use margin to increase the size of their deal; they have a natural amount they wish to buy or sell regardless of the level of margin. Speculators are prone to short-term trading and crowd behaviour, with everyone tending to panic and rush in the same direction at once following fashion or fear; this may well increase short-term volatility in both the futures market *and* in the cash market on which it is based. Just as speculators have come to dominate foreign exchange and make it more volatile (see chapter 3) so speculators in futures markets may make commodities and financial instruments more, not less, volatile.

Back to the future

In recent years the idea of futures as a way to transfer risk has been extended to financial instruments. Starting in Chicago in 1975 various financial futures have been developed and a market – the London International Financial Futures Exchange or LIFFE – was opened in the City in 1982. Although the idea of financial futures may seem a little strange, the idea behind them is exactly the same as with agricultural futures – the transfer of risk from those who want to hedge to those who wish to speculate.

Financial futures are traded in the same way as

agricultural contracts. Dealers – both local traders speculating for themselves and brokers dealing for others – stand in circles called **pits** (there is one pit for each instrument) and shout how much they are prepared to buy or sell and at what price. This is known as the **open outcry** system and in the LIFFE market dealers wear brightly coloured jackets for easy identification. Now that the Stock Exchange floor is no longer used, TV cameras often show hectic dealing on the LIFFE floor if they need dramatic shots of the City.

In London there are several basic types of financial futures contract. In sterling there are futures in short-term interest rates, long-term gilts and the FT-SE 100 equity index. Other important futures include contracts based on US and German interest rates, US, German and Japanese bonds, and some currencies.

Let's take the example of gilts to see how they work. Financial futures, like many agriculture futures, run in quarterly cycles. In January 1993, for example, gilt futures existed which would run out of time in March, June September and December 1993. (In fact, there were contracts running out as far as December 1994.) Investors who wanted to run a futures contract for up to a couple of months would tend to use the March 1993 version; those who wanted to hold the contract for six months would probably use the June 1993 variety. Since a lot of hedging and speculating is short-term, most investors would use the March contract, making it the busiest and most liquid. The contract with the nearest expiry date is known as the **near** contract.

For each of the contracts, investors have to settle up at the end of the relevant month. They could do this either by delivering the physical gilts they had contracted for, or by reversing the futures deal they had done, and completing a corresponding deal in the cash market. In fact, for administrative simplicity, the vast majority of futures contracts are closed out before the futures contract reaches **expiry**.

To see how this works, take the example of an investor in January 1993, who knows he will receive £100,000 in May and wants to invest it in the gilt market. However, in

January he thinks that gilt prices are very low and are likely to rise substantially before his money arrives in May. He could go into the futures market and buy £100,000-worth of June gilt futures in January on margin, get the benefit of any price movements between January and May and, when his cash arrives, close out his futures by selling his contracts and then buy the cash gilts he wanted. By doing this the investor has hedged himself against any price movement between January and May.

Futures are for today

This raises an important point about futures. Futures prices, whether in commodities or financial instruments, do *not* predict what prices will be in the future. The price of futures today is the same as the cash price, with a small technical adjustment made for any interest penalty and transaction costs involved. Take the previous example about gilts to illustrate the point. Say gilts in January yielded 10 per cent, but bank base rates were 8 per cent. If an investor actually had his £100,000 in January, he could do one of two things – either buy the gilts straight away, or buy futures now and then sell the futures and buy gilts in May/June. If he bought the gilts immediately, he would earn 10 per cent on his money, but if he bought futures, he could leave most of his money in the bank where it would earn only 8 per cent. Clearly buying gilts seems the better bet, but sadly, market professionals know that, so that the market price of gilt futures is lower than cash gilts to reflect this interest differential.

The market where this effect is most obvious is the FT-SE equity futures. Since yields on equities are typically 4 to 6 per cent, while bank base rates are frequently over 10 per cent, there is a clear advantage to buying FT-SE futures on margin and leaving cash in the bank, rather than actually buying the shares of the 100 companies which comprise FT-SE. As we said before, the market adjusts for this and the result is that FT-SE futures are normally quoted about 10 points higher than the cash index if base rates are high. So, for example, if FT-SE

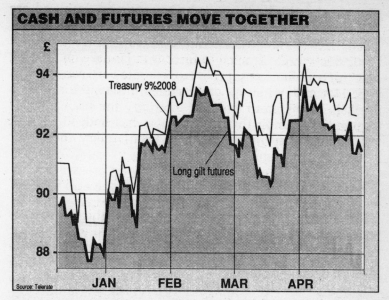

CASH AND FUTURES MOVE TOGETHER

£

94

Treasury 9%2008

92

Long gilt futures

90

88

Source: Telerate

JAN   FEB   MAR   APR

Fig 6.1 Gilt and gilt futures prices tend to move together. Sometimes differing supply and demand between cash and futures markets causes a divergence – arbitrageurs will then tend to pull the markets back together.

stood at 2800, FT-SE futures for delivery in three months might well be quoted as 2810.

The exception to the rule

Having said that the cash and futures prices keep in step with each other, there is, of course, the exception. Sometimes supply and demand vary between the cash and futures markets and so prices get out of step with each other. One example of this might be if American investors buy into the UK equity market. Rather than go through the hassle of buying shares, US investors who think that the UK equity market is likely to rise will often buy futures. UK institutions, who tend to deal in real shares, might be more sceptical. The result would be that the prices of FT-SE futures is driven up, whilst the FT-SE index itself does not move. Under such circumstances the futures premium has sometimes reached 50 points.

However, if the premium is large enough it becomes worthwhile for someone to try to reassert the equilibrium by buying cash stocks (which are cheap relative to futures) and selling futures (which have become relatively dear). When supply and demand between the two markets has settled back to normal, those who have exploited the anomaly can sell their cash and buy back the futures they have sold at a profit. The process is known as **arbitrage** and people who try to equalize prices between equivalent markets in this way are known as **arbitrageurs**. The relationship between cash and futures prices is known as the **basis**. As we have described above, the basis does sometimes vary, and this is exploited by professional arbitrageurs, but cash and futures prices become progressively more closely locked together as the futures contract approaches its expiry date.

A successful LIFFE

Since it was established in 1982, the London financial futures market LIFFE has been very succesful, particularly with its sterling interest rate and gilt futures contracts. But because the size of the contracts is quite large – £50,000-worth of gilts per contract and £500,000-worth of deposits – the market tends to be used by professional investors, banks, gilt market makers and speculators, rather than private investors.

The FT-SE equity contract is also quite large – it is the equivalent of around £50,000-worth of shares – and so might also be expected to be a professional tool. However, it has been less widely used than gilts or interest rate futures. Fund managers claim that this is because they are prevented by trustees from investing in futures – which are seen as speculative – and there have certainly been tax uncertainties in the past about the treatment of futures profits. Nonetheless, the reluctance of equity specialists to use futures probably owes more to the hidebound nature of many fund managers and trustees than to any real problem with futures contracts.

The other option

Although futures are often dominated by professionals, there is a closely allied market where individuals play an important part. Options are often considered alongside futures because they are both based on other quantities – for example, options to buy or sell a commodity or contracts to deal in a financial instrument at a future date – and for that reason futures and options are collectively known as **derivative products**.

Private investors are often keen on options because they offer limited risk. Unlike futures where investors are equally exposed to a rise or fall in the market, options are a one-way bet. This happens because options give the buyer the right *but not the obligation* to buy or sell something at a specified price, before an agreed date. For example an investor might buy an option which gives the right to buy Guinness shares at £11.00 for four months. At the end of the period the option runs out and is said to **expire**. This right without obligation to buy or sell makes options very different to futures.

Sadly, the world of options is swamped in jargon, and it is necessary to understand a little of it. Investors buying an option pay an agreed amount known as a **premium** for the right to buy or sell and the person who sells the option is said to **write** it. Options to buy are known as **calls** and options to sell are called **puts**.

When someone buys an option the maximum loss he can incur is the amount he paid for it (because he does not have to do anything with it). If the value of the option falls to zero, the investor simply writes it off whereas if the price of a futures contract continues to move against an investor, the loss is unlimited. On the other hand if the option moves in favour of the investor, as with futures the potential gain is unlimited.

Take an example

A practical example illustrates the principle. Unfortunately the maths involved in calculating options prices is complex, and is normally done by computer. Here we have taken a real example with computer-calculated option prices to show how things work. Say shares in Guinness are £10.00 and an option to buy the shares at £11.00 for four months costs 20p. If the shares dropped to £9.00 the option might fall in value to 5p, to £8.00 and it would be worthless. However, any fall beyond that would do no further damage to the investor's bank balance – on the other hand should the share price rally again before the option expired, its value would rise again.

Now the good news. Suppose Guinness shares rose to £11.50, the option might then be worth £1.10, if the shares reached £12.50 the option might get to £2.00 and if they soared to £13.50 the option could be worth £3.00. Indeed above that level the value of the option will rise as fast as the share price. So the investor has a limited loss, but the profit is (in theory at least) unlimited. And as with

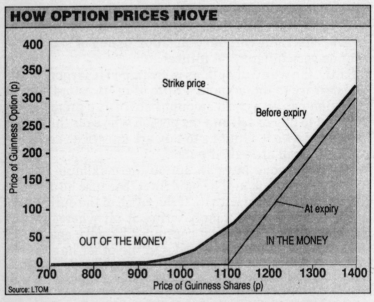

Fig 6.2 This shows how the price of an option to buy Guinness at 1100p moves with the share price. When the option is a long way from being valuable, the option price moves only slowly. At the strike price, the option price rises half as quickly at the shares, and when it is deep in the money the option and share prices rise at the same rate.

futures, the percentage gains in options can be large. In this example if the Guinness share price moves from £10.00 to £13.50 it has increased by about a third, but the value of the option has risen from 20p to £3.00 – a rise of 1,500 per cent! True, if the share price had fallen to £8.00, then the loss would have been 100 per cent, but had the investor chosen to buy futures instead of options, his loss would have been much larger. It is this aspect of options which attracts private investors; the risks are finite, but the percentage gains can be enormous.

Complex issues

As we said before, the maths involved in calculating option prices is complicated, and usually done by a computer. Even an explanation of it is beyond the scope of this book. Suffice it to say that when options are worth little – in this case when Guinness shares are down at £9.00 – then option prices move slowly; perhaps the option price would go up 1p for every 10p rise in the share price. In this state the option is known to be a long way **out of the money**. On the other hand if the Guinness shares are up at £13.50 then the option to buy at £11.00 is a long way **in the money** and then it goes up at about 1p for every 1p rise in the share price. If the Guinness shares were trading at £11.00 (the price at which an option buyer has the right to buy shares, called the **strike** price), the option would be **at the money** and then the option price would move about 1p for every 2p move in the share price.

The value of an option is made up of two elements – called the **intrinsic value** and the **time value**. Intrinsic value is easy. If an investor owns a Guinness £11.00 call and the share price was £11.50 then the option would have intrinsic value of 50p; intrinsic value is the extent to which the option is in the money. (It follows that out of the money options have no intrinsic value.) Time value is more difficult – it measures the probability that the investor will make a profit from the option before it expires. That probability is determined by how close to being in the money the option is (the closer to the money, the more likely a profit), how long the option has to run (the longer you have, the better your chances) and how volatile the price of the underlying commodity is (the more volatile, the higher the probability that the option will jump into the money). At the point when options expire they have no time value left, and so options are only worth whatever intrinsic value they may have. Since out of the money options have no intrinsic value, they expire worthless. In the money options are worth however much the share price exceeds the strike price. For example if Guinness shares are £13.50, a call option at £11.00 is worth £2.50 at expiry.

This dependence on the volatility of prices gives professional investors an opportunity to speculate on both movements in prices and whether a share or commodity will get more or less volatile. For example, during the 1987 crash, the volatility of share prices exploded upwards, and professionals using sophisticated option strategies were able to make money, without taking a decision on whether share prices would actually rise or fall.

Small investors who want to deal in options – especially beginners – should stick to buying conventional puts or calls, rather than trying to get too clever. One particularly dangerous course for the uninitiated is writing options – this is the flip side of buying an option and all the rules are reversed. The writer receives a premium for writing the option, but that is the maximum profit he can make; his hope is that the option will expire worthless. However, if the option moves into the money then the writer's losses can be unlimited. This happened in a couple of celebrated cases during the crash. Because the stockmarket had been rising inexorably throughout 1987, some individuals had been writing put options (i.e. giving others the right to sell them shares) and just pocketing the premium. It seemed like money for old rope until the market collapsed, and at least one was bankrupted for several million pounds. In that sense options act like insurance – individuals are happy to pay a few hundred pounds to insure their car every year, rather than risk potentially huge losses – this is a bit like buying

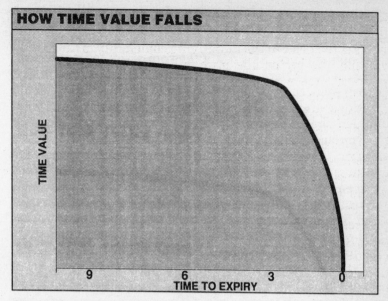

HOW TIME VALUE FALLS

Fig 6.3 The 'time' value of an option falls away at an accelerating rate as it approaches expiry. This is because there is less and less time in which the option can increase in value. At expiry the only value left in an option is the 'intrinsic' value – the amount for which it can be profitably converted.

an option. But would you want to take on an unlimited liability for you neighbour's car in return for £200 a year? That's what you do when you write an option.

Types of option

There are several types of option in common use. Options exist on foreign exchange, commodities and futures (for example there are options on gilt futures) and these are extensively used by professional investors either to hedge themselves or to speculate on market moves.

Options on shares fall into two camps, **traditional options** and **traded options**. Traditional options are (at least theoretically) available on all shares, but they are not very flexible, they last for three months and have to be exercised on set dates. Exercising options is tedious because, for example, if an investor owns a call option on some shares he actually has to buy the shares he has under option and then sell them in the market to realize his option profit. As a result they are of limited popularity.

More important nowadays are traded options, which are traded as part of the futures market, LIFFE. Traded options are available on about 70 of the most widely traded shares for several expiry dates and they have the advantage that an investor does not have to exercise the option, he can sell it again in the market, much as a futures contract does not have to be taken to delivery, but can be closed out. Traded options do offer a way for small investors to participate in the market, particularly as they can be bought and sold in small amounts. However, the bid-offer spread between where a market maker is prepared to buy and sell the option can be quite wide, making it harder for a small investor to make a profit.

The Futures Markets

IN A NUTSHELL

1. Futures markets are a way of transferring risk from those who want to limit it – hedgers – to those prepared to take it on – speculators.

2. Futures deals are contracts to buy or sell a set amount of a standardized product at a specified date in the future.

3. Only a small amount of the total price of the deal is paid when futures deals are struck. This is known as margin. Because of margin, speculators in futures can make large profits – or lose a great deal – relative to their initial stake.

4. Futures do not represent the market's guess of what prices will be at some time in the future. They are today's cash price, adjusted for any effect of interest and transaction costs between when the deal is struck and delivery.

5. Financial futures have been available for about 15 years. They enable risk to be transferred as other futures do, and are available on foreign exchange, interest rates, bonds and equities.

6. Options are a one-way bet on a commodity or financial instrument. Like futures they are based on or derive from something more substantial and so both are known as derivative products.

7. Options prices move in a complex way. The price of an out of the money option moves more slowly than one in the money.

8. Option values are made up of intrinsic value and time value. Intrinsic value is the extent to which an option is in the money.

9. Time value is dependent on when the option expires, how close it is to being in the money, and the volatility of the underlying commodity. Varying volatility adds an extra dimension to options and allows the use of complex strategies.

10. Options are available on commodities and financial instruments like foreign exchange, futures, and shares. The most useful option market in shares is the traded option market.

Section Two:
How to Invest

age   house
marital status   pension
job
risks etc
                            life insurance
                            home insurance
                            health insure

Chapter 7
Financial Planning

So far this book has explained how London's markets work and what they are for, but for most individual investors that is only a background briefing. Having got some idea of what the City does, the important question is then, how does that help me make money from my savings and investments? This section of the book considers how individuals should approach investment, and what kind of investments are on offer.

The first point to remember is fairly obvious – the types of investment you should consider depend upon the type of person you are: your age, whether you have a family, your job, the risks you are prepared to take and a host of other factors. Indeed, people's circumstances vary so much that the best a general guide can do is give pointers to the way individuals should approach financial planning.

This is a pity because there is a bewildering array of choice available to people with money to invest, but good impartial advice is hard to come by. In an ideal world everyone should have a regular financial health-check which takes into account their unique circumstances and gives them the best advice possible. Yet almost everybody providing financial advice has an axe to grind; some are tied agents selling one company's products, others independent advisers who earn commission from your investments; all – from bank manager to broker – are selling something. Even fee-based advisers, who are arguably the most independent, can prove very expensive. It is true that salesmen are under an obligation to provide you with 'best advice' about what to do with your money (see Appendix B) but this is a slippery concept, and except in the case of a gross fraud, it is difficult to establish what constitutes bad advice.

Perhaps concern about bias and suspicion of salesmen

are why so many people turn to the financial press and magazines for guidance on investment. Certainly the postbag at *Investors Chronicle* indicates that people feel that they are on their own when it comes to making investment decisions. But if investment is a do-it-yourself art, there are at least some useful guidelines.

Houses and pensions first

The two most important investments people make are often overlooked because they seem so obvious. For everyone (apart from the very rich) buying a house and contributing to a pension scheme are the two biggest investments they ever make. Both had been a good bet for half a century – though those who bought near the peak of the housing market in 1988 are now suffering.* Over the long term both house prices and the stock market – on which most pension funds rely – have beaten inflation. But there have been substantial shorter-term fluctuations in house and share prices. And whether either will resume their barnstorming run remains a matter of debate.

The downturn in the housing market has directly affected far more people than periodic collapses in the stockmarket. It has also hit individuals harder. Most homeowners pay for the greater part of their houses by borrowing, and the price fall has in many cases left their houses worth less than their debts, and so has cut the value of their own stake in the house by far more than the actual fall in prices.

What actually happens will in part depend on whether UK inflation can be kept at the unusually low levels it had reached by the early 1990s. But the British public's appetite for houses and pensions has also been fostered by successive governments' generous tax breaks. The first £30,000 of a mortgage on the main family home gets

---

* Pensions have been a very tax efficient way to save for retirement, but many have suffered after they retired because their pensions have not been uprated with inflation. Legislation now protects pensioners to some extent.

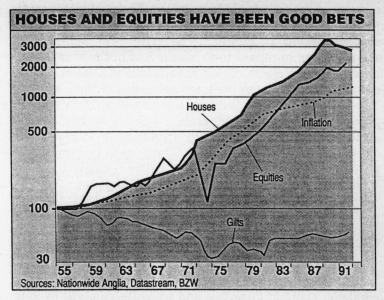

Fig 7.1 Houses and equities have been very good long-term investments despite the recent setback in house prices. Shares would look even better on this chart if we showed income reinvested. By contrast, fixed interest investments like gilts have left investors poor.

income tax relief at 20 per cent (as from April 1994), and there is no capital gains tax on the sale of the main residence. Contributions to pension schemes can also be made gross of tax to quite a high level.

Even nowadays, it is probably sensible to own a property appropriate to your income level, provided you have a decent equity stake. And contributing towards a pension scheme remains a very tax-efficient way to save money for old age.

Mortgaged to the hilt?

Most people know what their housing needs are – the main financial complication with buying a house is getting the right sort of mortgage. The two main choices here are **repayment** or **endowment** mortgages. Repayment

mortgages are much like other loans, where each month
interest and a little of the capital is repaid; at first most of
the repayment is interest, and significant amounts of
capital are only repaid towards the end of the loan. Many
lenders insist on some kind of insurance cover on repayment loans (sometimes unreasonably if the borrower
has no dependants). With endowments, only interest is
paid on the loan, and a separate life policy savings plan is
established, which builds up a lump sum to repay the
capital at the end of the loan. These have become more
popular in recent years, at least partly because advisers
earn good commissions selling the life policies.

Endowment mortgages have the advantage that you can
take the life policies from house to house, just topping
up with an endowment policy to cover any additional
mortgage you take out.* So with an endowment you have
started saving towards paying down any future mortgages from the moment you buy your first house, and
whatever size of house you end up with, you will be able
to pay off at least part of your mortgage early. With
repayment mortgages, you have to start again every time
you move house. However, endowments are not as
flexible as repayment loans; rescheduling the mortgage if
you get into trouble is difficult with an endowment loan.

Recently more complex mortgages have been appearing
– mortgages like endowments but backed by personal
equity plans or pensions are available. So, too, are mortgages which offer interest rates fixed for two or three
years, and even 'capped' mortgages where the interest
rate cannot rise above a certain level. **Fixed rate** mortgages are worthwhile if you think interest rates will rise
substantially, and with base rates low, you can lock in
some attractive fixed repayments. But if interest rates are

---

*It is well worth bearing in mind that you don't need a totally new
endowment when you move. Investors only get the best returns from
endowments if they hold them for the full term, yet the average period
they are held for is only seven years. As this is about the frequency
with which people move house, it suggests they are cashing in their
endowments every time. This is a very bad decision. If you are
borrowing another £40,000 when you move, then only take out an
additional £40,000 endowment to add to your existing one.

very high already, then taking out a fixed rate mortgage may mean locking yourself into high mortgage payments for several years. **Capped** mortgages conceal an option which is probably quite expensive for the protection it actually gives; these mortgages are really a gimmick.

The most exotic home loans are probably **foreign currency mortgages**, where marks, Swiss francs or Ecus are borrowed to buy the house. The attraction of these mortgages is that the interest rates on such loans are usually lower than sterling mortgages, but they are very risky – if sterling falls, the cost of your interest payments *and* the capital loan will rise. Effectively you are betting your home on the currency market.

Two routes to retirement

There are also plenty of options in choosing a pension. Two main routes are available – joining an employers' pension scheme or setting up your own personal pension.* First let's look at company pension schemes; they normally offer the advantage of a solid stable fund where the employer makes contributions as well as the employee. The scandal of the missing Maxwell pension funds has prompted proposals for an official safety net to protect pensioners from fraud or mismanagement. Most company schemes will pay a pension linked to your salary when you retire** and if the scheme has not earned enough through its investments the employer has to take up the strain. They are (relatively) cheap to run, and involve the individual in very little administrative hassle.

However, company schemes have disadvantages for people who change jobs frequently. People who move

* There is also the state scheme SERPS, but as its benefits have been reduced, it is likely to be less important in future.
** Some company pension schemes are money purchase schemes like personal pensions, and so the actual pension paid is less predictable. These are likely to become more common in future years as demographic shifts mean increasing numbers of old people are supported by a declining workforce.

have to choose between taking their money out of the scheme – often on very poor terms – or taking a deferred pension, which is usually equally unattractive. People who are made redundant – particularly in their 50s – can also get a raw deal. Company schemes tend to reward those who stay the course at the expense of early leavers.

In some ways personal pensions are the mirror image of company schemes. The main advantage of a personal pension is that an individual need not feel tied to a single employer. Personal pensions build up a regular fund, regardless of moves between jobs. So there is no need to worry that as a result of planned or unexpected moves you will reach retirement age with a patchwork of pensions. They also offer greater flexibility; many people get to 45 and decide they want to switch job or even career. Moving is reasonably easy for someone with a personal pension.

But there are drawbacks – few employers make a contribution to personal pensions, and personal pensions are **money purchase schemes** which, as the name implies, will only pay out from what has been saved and the investment returns earned on those savings. So if you do not contribute enough or the money is poorly invested, you can get a low income in old age. Charges to administer personal pensions are also higher than those for group schemes, because there is less economy of scale. It is important to shop around for a pension manager with a good investment record who won't eat all of your contributions in charges.

Which pension is right for me?

The first rule of thumb when considering a pension is that everyone should start to make some provision by the time they are 30. If you are going to job-hop a lot, a personal pension may well be best for you – but look around for the best deal considering both likely investment performance, the security of the pension provider (will the firm survive for 30-odd years?) and charges. All of this can be hard, because many firms offering personal pensions seem to be trying to make the whole business as complex as possible. You will also need to choose between **unit linked** schemes which are more risky but may be more lucrative, and **with profits** which are safer, but stolid.

If you are pretty confident when you are 30 that your employer will hand you a gold watch when you get to 65 or that you will only move jobs once or twice, then the company scheme may well be your best bet. It offers a more predictable pension and has the advantage that even if the investment performance of the scheme is poor, the company will have to ensure your pension is the correct proportion of your final salary. Commission-hungry salesmen have tempted some employees out of company pension schemes into inappropriate personal pensions.

At the other end of the spectrum, those in their 50s should almost certainly be in an employer's scheme (and some may also be in SERPS) unless they are self-employed. Those with less than ten years to retirement need to ensure that their pension will be as high as possible. Anyone who has not been in a company scheme long enough to get the maximum pension of two-thirds of final salary (though some employees are subject to a salary limit of £75,000 which is increased for the effects of inflation in the Budget) should consider making extra contributions to boost their pay-out. It's a good way to save for retirement, because total pension contributions (up to 15 per cent of your salary) are made gross of tax. These **additional voluntary contributions** or **AVCs** can either be made to the employer's scheme or, if you are chary about that, to another pension provider. In that case the contributions are known as free-standing AVCs. They have the advantage that they are independent of the current employer's scheme, but are normally more expensive to administer.

People half-way between starting work and retirement may have already made a substantial contribution to an employer's scheme, so should they stick with it or go solo? That decision has to be based on an individual assessment of the future. The longer a personal pension has to accumulate the better retirement income it will pay, and this is particularly so because compound interest on investment returns means that early contributions make a big difference. On the other hand, switching out of a company scheme if you are planning to be there for life is probably a mistake. So think about how likely you are to stay with your current employer, and if you switch to another job, whether your new employer will compensate you for any loss incurred in moving. If you are staying or will be compensated, stick with the company. If you are in an insecure industry, leaving and unlikely to be compensated, made redundant, or likely to switch careers, consider moving to a personal pension.

Whilst these are general principles to bear in mind when considering whether to start a personal pension, the choice is not entirely straightforward. It may well be that even if you intend to job-hop, the company's scheme could prove to be a better bet than a personal pension. Sometimes the value of the employer's contributions can outweigh the penalties of leaving early. We have tried to simplify things as much as possible, but pensions really are one of the most complex areas of personal finance. So the final rule must be that if you are at all uncertain, get professional advice.

As well as housing and pensions, the other basics are making sure you have sufficient life, house and even health insurance. Once all that is done investors can consider other options.

Cash for a crisis

When planning a strategy for your finances there is one golden rule – **everyone should have a spread of invest- ments** to be safe from inflation, fraud, accident, bad luck and poor judgement. However smart you are there is always the unexpected; so unless you are a candidate for gamblers anonymous, you should guard against being wiped out in a single catastrophe by spreading your risk. And because the unexpected quite often happens, the first priority for investors is to build up a safety fund which earns interest but which can be quickly turned into cash.

Banks and building societies are the traditional homes for this type of funds, but not all accounts are the same. Except for small sums, avoid building society ordinary share accounts and bank 7-day deposit accounts – these pay the lowest rate of interest. Fixed notice, variable rate accounts are better – and they offer a higher rate of interest the more you invest and the longer notice period you are prepared to give. For larger sums **high interest cheque accounts** or **HICAs** offer rates closely linked to those of the money market, which is particularly useful when interest rates are rising rapidly. When rates fall, **National Savings** are often quite good, because the government is often a little slow on the uptake about cutting rates. For those who want a guaranteed fixed rate over a period of years, **National Savings Certificates** can be worth a look, but sometimes their rates are less attractive than at others. The principle in these cash investments is to get the highest rate of return, balanced with the least notice to get at your cash. To achieve that, you'll probably need a mix of accounts.

Growth or income?

That done, investors face a choice between two basic types of investments – those designed for **capital growth** and those producing **current income**. Broadly speaking, younger people are saving for the long term and don't necessarily need their investments to produce a current income, because they are still earning. On the other hand, they have to guard against inflation, which could decimate their savings over the long run. Under these circumstances **growth** investments are usually best; these aim to provide a growing capital sum, usually at the expense of a high current income. Most growth investments are ultimately based on shares, and which you should pick depends on how much you have to invest, and how interested you are in actively managing your investments.

The exception to the rule that younger people want growth (and there's always an exception) is **school fees**: if

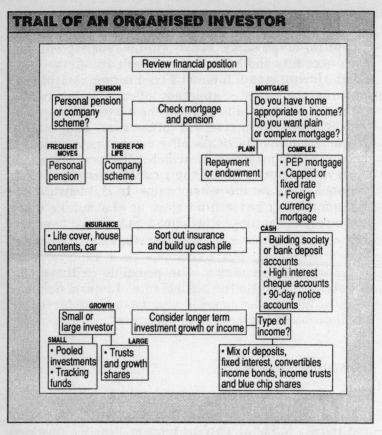

TRAIL OF AN ORGANISED INVESTOR

Review financial position

PENSION
Personal pension or company scheme?

Check mortgage and pension

MORTGAGE
Do you have home appropriate to income? Do you want plain or complex mortgage?

FREQUENT MOVES
Personal pension

THERE FOR LIFE
Company scheme

PLAIN
Repayment or endowment

COMPLEX
• PEP mortgage
• Capped or fixed rate
• Foreign currency mortgage

INSURANCE
• Life cover, house contents, car

Sort out insurance and build up cash pile

CASH
• Building society or bank deposit accounts
• High interest cheque accounts
• 90-day notice accounts

GROWTH
Small or large investor

Consider longer term investment growth or income

Type of income?

SMALL
• Pooled investments
• Tracking funds

LARGE
• Trusts and growth shares

• Mix of deposits, fixed interest, convertibles income bonds, income trusts and blue chip shares

Fig 7.2 The three main stages of investment decisions are houses and pensions, cash reserves and insurance, and then longer term investments.

you intend to educate your children privately, then you'll need a savings plan which will produce sufficient income to pay the fees when your children are of school age. As always, the earlier you start, the better.

When people move into middle age, growth investments are still normally the right thing, but their investments are likely to be larger as a result of higher income and savings accumulated over previous years, so their portfolios are likely to be more complex and diverse than young people's. With a secure capital base behind them, middle aged people may also consider putting part of their savings into some of the more risky investments such as some of the more specialized pooled funds.

As investors approach retirement, their priorities change. Having (hopefully) built up a capital sum, older people need to start switching towards investments which will provide an income once they stop work. Retired people are also less able to take the knocks which can come from growth investments – for although share-based investments tend to do well over the long term, they can yo-yo alarmingly in the short run. So people of that age start looking for **income** investments. But beware, as people are living longer and retiring earlier, they can expect to have to live off their pension and investments for 20 or even 30 years; in that time inflation can do great damage. If you retire at 55, switching everything into income investment from growth could be a mistake; it may well be a good idea to hang on to some of the less chancy growth investments.

Besides deciding between growth and income invest-ments, the other consideration is tax. In recent years the government has provided significant incentives for inves-tors to accumulate tax-free investments particularly through **personal equity plans** or **PEPs** and **Tax Exempt Special Savings Accounts** or **TESSAs**. These are con-sidered in chapter 11. General tax planning is discussed in Appendix A. Now let's look at growth and income investments in more detail.

Going for growth

Assembling a portfolio for capital growth is a real black art. About the most that can be said with certainty is that capital growth funds are based on equities, because, as discussed in the Introduction, equities have risen above inflation over recent decades, whilst fixed income invest-ments like gilts have fallen behind. So shares have been (at least historically) good for growth. Against that background, we can establish two objectives – getting growth in investments which equals the performance of the stockmarket, and then trying to beat it.

In order to match the stockmarket, investors need a decent spread of shares, but this can be impractical for those with a limited amount to invest. A reasonable share portfolio might start with 20 shares, with each holding worth £2,000 and a back-up £10,000 cash reserve. So for those people with less than £50,000 to invest an alternative is needed. A better place for many people to start might be with collective or pooled investments – which are principally **investment trusts** and **unit trusts**. Investment trusts are companies which are established to invest in the shares of other companies, so that an investor could buy one share yet invest in perhaps 100 companies. Unit trusts are in some ways similar: they pool together people's savings to invest in a specified area of shares, gilts or overseas markets. Investors can buy or sell 'units' which each represent a proportion of the fund's investments (the mechanics of how these funds work are given in chapter 9). The other advantage of these funds is that many can be used for regular savings as well as lump sum investments; monthly contributions of as little as £25 can be put into some funds. Investment trusts have similar schemes.

Unit trusts are historically divided into 'income' and 'growth' funds, but nowadays many more classifications are used.* A good place for someone to start trying to match the stockmarket's performance is with a general UK equity fund which will tend to invest in a broad range of UK shares. A more recent innovation is the **tracker** fund (also called an **indexed** fund); these funds have been statistically designed to mimic the performance of some stockmarket index, say the FT-SE index of 100 leading shares or the FT-A All Share index. Such funds should give a similar rate of growth to the stockmarket, although charges and the difference between buying and selling price of units will drag them down somewhat.

*In any event the division into income and growth trusts was something of a misnomer – since many equity income trusts frequently show better capital growth than the growth funds.

Poor investment decisions by fund managers are also a pitfall. Investors can try to minimize this by backing funds (or fund managers) with a good track record of picking winners, but as they say in the ads, past performance is no guarantee of future success. At least by picking a couple of general funds with decent histories, investors are doing what they can to lessen the risks.

If general funds are a way to try to match the market, how do growth investors try to beat it? Not all parts of the stockmarket perform equally well at the same time, so the trick is to pick the next boom area. In pooled investments there are many funds which concentrate on specific types of share – for example smaller companies or technology stocks. If the investor picks the right area, he can beat the market, but at the risk of under-performing if the decision is wrong. One favourite with growth investors is recovery funds. These are funds investing in shares which have fallen on hard times, but which are not expected to go bust; as the companies recover from their difficulties, their shares can do very well.

Another possibility is using funds to invest in overseas markets. Assume that you expect Wall Street or Tokyo to do better than the London market. By buying a general US fund you might beat the UK market, if your premise is correct. The iceberg to watch out for in overseas investment is the impact of currency movements, which can wipe out stockmarket gains.

It is also important not to be too swayed by fashion. Often if a particular area of the stockmarket or an overseas market is doing outstandingly well, a rash of new trusts will be launched to exploit the boom. Plenty of hype goes into these new launches, trying to interest investors in buying units. Yet this may be just the wrong time to go into that area – by the time a market has become fashionable, much of the rise may already have happened, and investors who get in late can find themselves stranded at the high water mark.

Shares can be sexy

Finally, of course, investors can try to beat the market by investing in individual shares. Because they offer investors the most scope for making money, and they are the most interesting aspect of investment, the third section of this book is devoted to various aspects of shares and companies. Safety-first means that any share portfolio should have a fair number of stable 'blue chip' companies like Marks & Spencer, Unilever, Shell or Hanson, which have solid track records, are unlikely to go bust and between them cover a fair number of different types of business.

Beyond that there are over 2,000 companies to choose from. Investors can go for shares in a particular stockmarket sector, say food retailing or engineering, if they think those industries will do well. But bear in mind that you have to pick the particular companies in any sector which are going to prosper. And try to make sure you're not just following a trend. Professional investors spend their lives looking for investment ideas, and by the time you hear in the pub that garden centres are a go-go business, you may well be too late. If the City has already marked prices up there may be little more to shoot for. So keep an eye on the financial press, both for investment ideas, and to find out what's popular with the City professionals.

What is a typical portfolio?

Although there is no such thing as a typical growth portfolio, suggesting a couple of alternatives may help to give some substance to the discussion. Take a 35-year old who is in the happy position of having sorted out his housing, pension, life and other insurance, and children's school fees and still finds himself with £100,000 – what sort of portfolio might he construct?

If he was prepared to take at least a ten year view on the portfolio he might do something like this: put his first £10,000 in an emergency cash deposit fund, and another £10,000 in fixed interest investments like gilts, just in case of disaster. Then he might put £40,000 into unit trusts – perhaps £10,000 each into a UK general fund and an FT-A indexed fund, £5,000 into a UK recovery fund, another £5,000 into a UK smaller companies fund; he might also put £5,000 into a Far East markets fund and the final £5,000 into a European growth fund.* The remaining £40,000 could go to construct a share portfolio, with £2,000 invested into each of 20 shares – ten blue chips, five riskier stocks and five fun punts.

As an alternative, he could put £10,000 each into a cash fund and fixed interest bonds and £10,000 into overseas unit trusts. The remaining £70,000 could then be split between UK index tracking funds and a broadly based share portfolio containing at least 25 shares. The split would be determined by how hard our 35-year old wanted to try to beat the All Share index, and how much effort he wanted to put into the portfolio. If he was interested, had ideas and was prepared to take a little more risk, he could put the whole lot into shares – provided he had at least half his holdings in blue chips. If he wanted a more conservative strategy, then putting £50,000 into a couple of index tracking funds and only £20,000 into trying to spot good growth shares might be for him.

The advantage of the second course – using indexed funds rather than general unit trusts – is that the charges are lower and investors don't have the problem of picking good funds (see chapter 9). Indexed funds give a broad spread of the market at low cost, and investors can then use individual equities to try to increase growth. Fund managers might not like it, but the second type of portfolio may well become more popular than the first, more traditional, suggestion in future.** Depending on individual taste, either type of portfolio could subsequently be managed by our model 35 year-old or his broker. Some people will argue with the strategies we have outlined, and the particular areas invested in will

---

* Some economists think that investors should hold a proportion of their assets overseas in line with their country's tendency to import goods. Since in the case of the UK we import 25 per cent of our goods, the argument says that 25 per cent of investments should be held overseas.

change over time. But such debate and movement is what makes investment an art, not a science.

Portfolio strategies

How you handle a portfolio depends on your personality. If you find the whole business too much sweat, then stick to some large funds, or if your portfolio is large enough get a broker or investment manager to look after things. However, if you're bothering to read this book, the chances are you're at least moderately interested in investment, so what strategies can you follow in a share portfolio?

One of the best ways to tackle portfolio planning is to split your portfolio into equal units with at least ten separate holdings, and preferably 20 different shares. You can vary the theme by giving blue chip shares a double weighting, and only invest a half-unit for some more speculative stocks. But it is important to maintain a diverse selection of shares to spread your risk. Of course, as time goes by these weightings will become wonky. Some shares will rise, others fall. You may want to set loss limits on shares so that if they fall by more than 20 per cent, for example, you sell – deciding that you made a wrong decision. Winners can be a problem too. If you simply hang on to the best performers, your portfolio can become dominated by just a few shares; so if a share doubles in price, consider selling at least half your holding. There will also be rights issues, bids and dividends to take into account, so the portfolio will definitely need some gardening. The system need not be too rigid – if your unit size was £2,000 then holdings

---

**It is surprising that indexed funds have taken so long to catch on in the UK. On Wall Street huge amounts have been invested in this way with the result that charges and bid-offer spreads are extremely low. The relative lack of popularity in Britain might reflect a national belief that the individual can beat the system, or successful marketing by unit trust groups. Indexed funds are a good, cheap way into the market.

might vary between £1,500 and £4,000 without causing a problem. It's also worth valuing your portfolio as a routine – perhaps once a month.

Beyond that the strategy you take for your portfolio will be heavily influenced by your investment aims and your personality. Some people choose to buy and hold shares. They argue that having gone to the effort of selecting stocks, they don't want to ditch them unless things change dramatically. Others like to trade according to the ebb and flow of the market, aiming to sell out when the market is high and buy back shares on any fall. Many ferret around for neglected stocks, combing the *Investors Chronicle* for situations they think the market has ignored. There are also counter-traders who buy shares which the market hates. Others again use charts of share price movements to predict future trends, or analyse the dealings of company directors, who after all ought to know a business best. Which combination you use is really up to you.

One technique which is invalid is buying shares purely on the basis of stockmarket sector. Many sectors are almost arbitrary in their definition, and the shares within them differ by at least as much as they have in common. So buying Widget plc purely because you think engineering companies are going to rise and Rolls-Royce is doing well could be a total disaster.

Investing for income

As we said before, those looking for income from their investments are generally at or near retirement. But such people are as much at risk from long-term inflation as anyone else, so it is important when investing for income to protect your capital as well. If you don't you may find yourself with an inadequate income further down the road. Most of the options for investment which produce high income – like bonds or deposit accounts – only aim to return your starting capital, which can be a problem over the long run. If inflation is running at 7 per cent, £100 of capital will only be worth £50 a decade later.

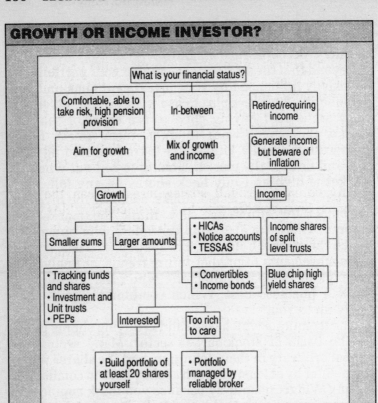

Fig 7.3 The different routes for growth and income investors.

The inflation risk means it's worth trying to keep some kind of equity element in an income portfolio. This can be done by investing part of your capital in a decent spread of blue chip higher yielding shares (such as privatized utilities) which offer a decent income and some capital growth. Unit trusts investing in such shares are also worth considering.

A further possibility is **convertible** bonds, which are fixed interest securities (like gilts) but which can be converted into shares of the company which are issued them at agreed terms between specified dates in the future. These convertibles are a bit like a conventional bond with a share option attached. How much like a bond or share they act depends on whether the bond could be converted into shares on favourable terms. If the price of the company's shares is much lower than the conversion terms – in effect the option is a long way from being useful – then the convertible acts much like a normal bond, and offers a yield similar to that of ordinary bonds. On the other hand, if the convertible can be profitably exchanged for shares, then its yield is lower and it behaves much more like a share.

Many convertibles fall somewhere between the two extremes. So investors who buy these convertibles get a better yield than they would from shares, with the prospect of capital growth if the company's share prices rise over the medium term. (More about convertibles in chapter 8.) Another hedge against inflation is **index linked gilts**, but here the return over inflation is only around 3.5 per cent, so they may not generate enough income unless you have substantial funds. Some investment trusts are also divided up into two parts, one aimed at growth, the other at income; the income part of these **split level investment trusts** can make a useful contribution to an income portfolio (see chapter 9).

Higher yielding equities and convertibles give some protection from inflation, but the average income they offer is a little skinny – perhaps in the range of 4 to 8 per cent. So for higher total returns, income investors will have to mix in some fixed interest securities and deposits such as gilts and corporate bonds.

As well as marketable securities, High Interest Cheque Accounts and National Savings income bonds provide the monthly payments which many income investors seek, and so are likely to figure prominently in any income portfolio. As savings rates fell inexorably in the early nineties, the fund managers came up with several ingenious ways of offering refugees from banks and building societies a high income. Some actually guarantee an above average income, but you may lose some or all of your original capital; some guarantee you your money back (though often only after a set period), but don't make firm promises about income.

These include:

- **lifetime annuities** which give you a very good income, but mop up all your original capital
- **permanent interest-bearing shares from building societies (PIBs)** which offer a high fixed income, and are quoted on the stockmarket, but do not guarantee return of capital and may be hard to sell
- **guaranteed income bonds** from insurance companies, which allow you to lock in a fixed return over a certain number of years and return your capital intact
- **guaranteed stockmarket investment plans** (confusingly also referred to as guaranteed bonds), which offer you a certain percentage of stockmarket growth over a certain period, or – if the market falls – your money back.

However, most of these schemes are gimmicks and investors would usually do better to buy a mixture of gilts and equities or tracking unit trusts.

Income strategies

In any income portfolio the balance between equity-linked income investments to protect against inflation and pure income deposits or bonds will depend on personal circumstances. But there are rules of thumb which will help. Put bluntly, the longer you are likely to have to live off the income from your portfolio, the more thought you need to give to the potential impact of inflation, and the greater element of equity linked investment it is advisable to have. Although the income might be lower than you might like in early years, it may be better than a bad bout of inflation and much lower living standards later on.

Even with an income portfolio there are strategies which can help the investor maximize returns as interest rates vary. When interest rates are low but are expected to start rising significantly (which was the case in 1988) investors should move some of their funds to floating rate accounts like HICAs or money market accounts, which

will reflect the rise in rates. When you think interest rates
have peaked, the best strategy is to lock in the high rates
for as long as possible. Term deposits at banks can lock in
good rates for up to three years, but investors may not be
able to get at their funds easily. Fixed income bonds like
gilts will also lock in good rates, but sometimes long-term
interest rates − on 15-year gilts for example − may not
have risen as far as short-term rates, so if pure income is
the aim, a 3–5 year gilt may be a good bet. If you can take a
lower income on gilts, then long gilts offer the chance of
better capital gains if interest rates are falling.

Mr Bearbull

For those who want to keep a regular eye on developments in income and growth portfolios, the *Investors
Chronicle* runs regular portfolios for growth and for
income. These portfolios, written by Mr Bearbull, alter-
nate and give general views on the market as well as
specific investment recommendations. They are realistic
portfolios which take into account dealing costs and
dividends, and so give a good guide to the options
available. Recently Mr Bearbull has also started speculative and international portfolios for those who like a little
extra spice.

Who am I?

For the most part in this guide to financial planning we
have assumed that you are able to recognize yourself, but
what happens if you don't know where you fit in? Here's a
brief guide to help you decide who you are.

The first step is to act a bit like a company and draw up
a list of your income and expenditure over the past year to
decide where it all went, whether you have organized
yourself efficiently and how much you might be able to
save. It might look like this:

Income	Expenditure
Your salary or pension	Interest payments on mortgages and loans
Any investment income	Insurance and pension payments
Capital gains on any sales of investments or assets	Tax
Lump sums received	Living expenses

You should also draw up a balance sheet of all your assets – like cash, investments, personal possessions and property, and on the other side, your debts such as mortgages, bank loans, credit card and gambling debts.

Hopefully these two statements should point up any glaring anomalies, like having borrowing which might be paid down from cash holdings, or property underinsured. The income and expenditure account should also give you some idea whether you are able to save regularly to build up a lump sum. Having established where you stand you should make sure that you have sorted out the basics of housing, pension, insurance, and a cash fund we discussed at the start of the chapter.

Then ask yourself some serious questions. **What are you investing for?** – growth, income, a new car or your retirement? You must try to pick suitable investments – if you are only saving short-term, banks or building societies are better places than the stockmarket. **How much risk do you want?** Bear in mind that you should spread your investments, but if you have a nest egg that you cannot afford to lose, you shouldn't put it into the options market. **How old are you?** The young tend to aim for growth if they can afford a long-term view. Older people are more concerned with pensions and income. **What about tax?** If you are a taxpayer you should think about some of the tax efficient investments that are around.

Finally, if you're not clear on what you ought to do, get some financial advice before you commit large sums of money, or tie yourself into a long-term savings plan. But shop around, you don't have to buy the first piece of paper a hungry bank manager pushes in your direction!

Financial Planning

IN A NUTSHELL

1. In planning your finances recognize that everyone's needs differ and that there will be more
   than one way to solve investment problems.
   Investment is an art, not a science.

2. First sort out your mortgage. Despite recent
   problems houses have done very well since the
   war, and offer good tax advantages. Do you own
   the right size of property for your income?

3. Then look at your pension provisions. Should
   you have a personal pension or join the company
   scheme? If you are older, should you make tax
   efficient extra contributions to ensure the maximum pension?

4. Also look at your insurance provisions, school
   fees, and health cover. Having done that, build
   up an emergency cash fund in case of crisis. It
   should be balanced between a decent income
   and easy access.

5. Then decide between growth and income investments. Check what kind of investor you are and
   the risks you want to run and always keep a
   spread of investments. Consider your tax
   position.

6. Younger people saving for their old age will tend
   to seek capital growth, which tends to come from
   investments based on shares. Those with a
   smaller amount to invest should used pooled
   investments like unit trusts and investment
   trusts. Shares are for people who are genuinely
   interested and have bigger savings.

7. Retired and older investors normally look for income but should also keep a weather eye on inflation. High yielding safer shares, convertible bonds, split-level investment trusts, bonds, deposit accounts and money market funds can be mixed to increase income and protect against inflation.

8. If you are not certain of your position, try drawing up a balance sheet of assets and debts, and an income and expenditure account for the past year. Can you make your finances more efficient, and save regularly? What are your investment objectives?

9. If you are uncertain, get financial advice before investing large sums of money or taking on a long-term commitment. And shop around; you do not have to buy the first thing you see.

Chapter 8
Fixed Interest

Deposit accounts and fixed interest securities got a fairly rough ride in chapter 7 because they don't offer investors any protection from inflation. Since the war, Britain has had a consistently higher inflation rate than other countries, and those who have relied on building societies and gilts as a home for their savings have seen their purchasing power dwindle. That has led most people in the UK to focus on shares, which offer an indirect link to inflation, and so protects their long-term capital. By contrast, in low-inflation countries like Germany, investors have been happy (and in some cases coerced by government policy) to keep a large part of their money in bonds. If Britain adjusts to the discipline of being a low-inflation economy the UK might yet become a nation of bond-holders. Inflation fell to unusually low levels in the early 1990s, but there is no guarantee that it will stay down as the economy recovers. And for the foreseeable future, British investors are likely to continue relying heavily on equities.

That said, fixed income investments are still important. They offer higher income than shares, and have the benefit that your capital is not at risk unless you hand it over to someone uncreditworthy. So fixed income bonds and deposit accounts are useful for those seeking income, and as a home for everyone's emergency cash funds. They fall fairly naturally into two groups – those based on deposit accounts paying regular (but normally variable) interest, and fixed income securities – essentially gilts and corporate bonds. To relate this to the previous discussion on markets, one type is based on the short-term money market (see chapter 4) and the other on the long-term bond market (see chapter 2). First let's look at deposits.

Your friendly bank manager

Although there is a plethora of bank, building society and other accounts available to investors as a home for cash, they are all really variations on the basic deposit account idea: you deposit your money, and the bank or building society pays you for the use of it at a floating rate. That rate will depend on the general level of interest rates, the institution's need for cash and the perception of the bank or building society's credit: small unknown deposit-takers have to pay a higher rate to attract funds than large prestigious institutions. But investors should beware; a higher rate is not a bargain if the deposit-taker goes bust.

Aside from that, the main variations in interest rate come as a result of the amount you deposit and the length of time you are prepared to leave your money untouched. Broadly, the larger the sum you deposit, the more useful it is to the bank and the less administrative hassle it is – processing one £100,000 lump sum is clearly easier than dealing with 100 customers each depositing £1,000. So the larger the amount deposited, the higher the interest rate the bank or building society will pay. Banks also like to know that they can rely on their deposits; it is every banker's nightmare that all of his customers will come in and demand their money back at once. To avoid that, banks and building societies tend to pay higher rates if you are prepared to give notice before withdrawing your money; the longer the notice, the higher the rate.

Investors then have the job of balancing the highest return they can get with the ease of getting access to their funds. In general, basic building societies' share accounts, bank interest-bearing current accounts or seven-day deposit accounts are not very competitive for anything except very small sums needed at short notice. Most savers should look towards **High Interest Cheque Accounts**, **90-day notice accounts** or **money market funds**; these pay higher rates for larger sums and longer notice. The exact details of minimum investments, notice period and how often interest is paid will vary from account to account, and the institutions quite frequently alter the terms and conditions. Investors should also bear in mind that the frequency of interest payments can affect the rate offered. In general, accounts paying interest monthly will pay a lower rate than those paying quarterly or every six months.*

Currency deposits

As well as accounts in sterling, investors can also hold accounts in foreign currencies such as dollars, marks, or even Ecus! These pay interest rates relevant to the currency in question, which can be higher or lower than the current sterling rates. However, like foreign currency mortgages, you are taking a foreign exchange risk, not only on your interest payments, but also on your capital. Because of that, you should only hold money in foreign currency accounts if it relates to other overseas obligations, or if you can afford to lose it if your speculation goes wrong. There are managed currency funds, but these incur charges, and even professionals in the forex markets have proved badly wrong in the medium term.

How to find the best rates

The variety of accounts on offer makes finding the best interest rate something of a headache for investors – especially because an account which was highly competitive when it was opened might lag behind others six months later. Of course, it doesn't make sense to shift money from one account to another every five minutes, but it is worthwhile checking the rates periodically. The most comprehensive guide is *Blay's MoneyMaster* which gives details of many different types of deposit and is published monthly. Unfortunately it is really designed for professionals and so would be expensive for individuals to buy. But copies are kept at many reference libraries,

---

* This can just be an adjustment for compound interest, but some monthly accounts do offer less attractive rates.

and it's worth checking locally. Three alternatives are the *Investors Chronicle* highest deposit rates table, published weekly in the magazine, which gives current best buys in a number of different categories, and *The Daily Telegraph* or *Financial Times* which also give some details of deposits in their Saturday personal finance coverage.

Deposit insurance

All deposit-takers in the UK who have been authorized by the Bank of England are part of the deposit protection scheme. This guarantees that depositors will get back 75 per cent of the first £20,000 they have on deposit at a bank if it goes bust. Similar regulations cover building societies; here investors can get back 90 per cent of the first £20,000 they have lost. This may sound fine, but it does not mean depositors can relax. As those who dealt with British and Commonwealth Merchant Bank or BCCI found out, even apparently solid institutions can go down, and if they do it can take a long time to get money back. It is a much better idea to pick the institution you leave money with carefully. It is not always possible to spot a bank in difficulties, but unusually high rates of interest are often a sign that an institution has trouble attracting funds. Offshore accounts – like those in Jersey – are not covered by the scheme. Some offshore banking centres have their own schemes, but investors have to take even greater care in picking an offshore bank.

Nailing down a fixed rate

Floating rate accounts are fine, if you think interest rates are going to rise. In that case the bank or building society will increase the rate on your account as base rates go up. But what happens if you think rates are going to fall, or you simply want a predictable income – how do you get a fixed interest rate on your money?

One way of doing this is through a **guaranteed income bond** which guarantees to pay a fixed rate of interest for a

number of years. These are issued by life insurance
companies which want to take fixed rate funds from time
to time, but not all companies offer such bonds all the
time; and the rate and the period for which it is fixed will
also vary. Typically such bonds offer fixed rates for three
to five years and pay interest anything from monthly to
annually. They can be a good bet if you think interest
rates are about to fall. For example, in the summer of 1990
interest rates stood at 15 per cent, but there were
widespread predictions that interest rates would fall. At
that stage investors could have taken out a deposit fixed
for five years at 12 per cent, and doing so would have
been a smart move, since by the summer of 1993, interest
rates had fallen to 6 per cent.

Two words of warning on guaranteed income bonds.
First, it can be quite difficult to get your money out early
if you suddenly find you need it; in general investors
should only lock up funds in term deposits which they
know they will not need. Second, some of the companies
offering the most attractive guaranteed income bonds are
small and (relatively) unknown institutions, with short
track records. For safety's sake it may well be worth
seeking out a well known institution even if it offers a
lower rate.

Another possibility for fixed rate deposits is banks and
building societies. These may offer longer-term fixed
rates for two or three years, particularly through offshore
subsidiaries such as their Jersey operations. However,
these tend to be money market type accounts and so
restricted to larger sums. Again it is difficult to get at your
cash if you need it before the deposit falls due for
repayment.

National Savings

The other traditional home for investors' cash is National
Savings, which – along with the gilt market – is the main
way that the government finances its borrowings.
National Savings thus tend to offer more competitive
rates when government borrowings are high – as in the

early 1990s – and less competitive when the government is repaying debt – as it did in the late 1980s. A variety of products are available such as income bonds which pay interest gross and a capital bond which has a five year fixed rate. The latter rolls up the interest, but investors are taxed as they go – which is a disadvantage for taxpaying savers. Savings certificates offer a fixed rate too, and are tax free – making them attractive to higher rate taxpayers – but they do roll up the interest to the end of the five years, and there are penalties for early withdrawal. The newer one-year First Option Bonds also offer a fixed rate which is sometimes very competitive.

Don't forget the taxman

In any consideration of deposits, investors should bear in mind that they have to pay tax on their income. General guidance can be found in Appendix A, but two changes in recent years have had a particular impact here. First, independent taxation of wives means that each partner in the marriage has a personal allowance and each couple has one married person's allowance. Married couples can choose which partner has the married couple's allowance, or they can each have half of it. This flexibility is useful if one partner earns much less than the other. If there are savings they should be owned, and the income taken, by the person with the unused personal allowance (at least up to the limit of the personal allowance).

The second change is that nowadays if you are a non-taxpayer, you can register to have interest paid gross from banks or building societies. For taxpayers, basic rate tax will be deducted from accounts; higher rate taxpayers then have to pay the extra tax they owe later. If you are a non-taxpayer, it is well worth registering.

Fixed rate bonds

Investors who are looking for a fixed rate of return on their capital are not restricted to guaranteed income bonds or fixed rate deposits, they can also buy corporate bonds and gilts. These bonds are similar to income bonds – they pay a fixed rate of interest and guarantee to repay the capital at an agreed date in the future. But unlike income bonds they are **negotiable**, which means that investors can buy and sell them like shares on the stockmarket. Unfortunately, if an investor sells a bond early, he is not guaranteed to get what he paid for it – in the market the price of bonds is set by supply and demand – but at least there is an escape route in an emergency. The price of bonds is also less volatile than that of shares because investors know that at a fixed date in the future the bond will be repaid at face value – the nearer a bond is to being repaid, the closer its price sticks to face value.

There are two main types of bonds issued: **gilts** (see also chapter 2) which are IOUs issued by the government to fund its borrowings, and **corporate bonds**, which are similar to gilts, but issued by companies. The gilt market is the larger of the two.

Gilts are listed under 'British Funds' at the back of the *Financial Times*, and are classified according to their redemption date. For convenience gilts are divided into groups – **shorts** which have less than five years to repayment (seven years in the Bank of England's reckoning), **mediums** with between five and 15 years to go, and **longs** which have maturities over 15 years. There are also **index-linked** gilts, which have payments linked to the retail prices index, and **undated** gilts which have no final repayment date.

Looking at a table of gilts in the newspaper shows a bewildering variety of bonds, but in fact they are all very similar. The description of a gilt has three parts – its name, the rate of interest it pays and the date it is to be repaid. Let's look at a specific example – Exchequer $10\frac{1}{4}$ pc 1995. The name Exchequer is only there for historical reasons; most gilts are called Treasury or Exchequer but some are called Funding, War Loan or Consols. This does

not matter – all gilts are obligations of the British
Government and equally creditworthy. The only name
with any real significance is Conversion, which offers the
opportunity to switch from one gilt to another. The
second part – $10\frac{1}{4}$ per cent – is more interesting, because it
is the amount of interest the gilt pays each year and is
known as the **coupon** or **dividend**. As with all gilts this
payment is divided in two and paid every six months. The
final part – 1995 – is the year the gilt is due to be redeemed.

So Exchequer $10\frac{1}{4}$ pc 1995 is an ordinary gilt which will
pay interest of $5\frac{1}{8}$ per cent twice a year on the nominal
value until the last interest payment date in 1995 when
the full sum borrowed will be repaid.

Gilt yields

But the yield – or rate of return on a bond – is not the same
as its coupon, because investors don't buy the gilt at its
redemption price, but at the price prevailing in the
market. The coupon on a gilt is fixed, but the yield goes up
and down according to market conditions. So although at
first sight Treasury 12 pc 1995 seems to be a better bet (see
table opposite) because it pays a higher rate of interest
than Exchequer $10\frac{1}{4}$ pc 1995, the secondary market takes
this into account; Treasury 12 pc 1995 changes hand at a
higher price than Exch $10\frac{1}{4}$ pc 1995, so that their yields are
roughly equal.

Because the yield of a bond is more important than its
coupon, it needs closer attention. Yield is calculated in
two main ways. The first method is called the **interest** or
current yield and has the virtue of simplicity, but is
somewhat misleading. Current yield is a measure of the
income an investor receives holding a bond from one day
to the next. It is calculated by dividing the gilt's coupon by
its price, then multiplying by 100 to convert to a
percentage:

$$\text{Current yield} = \text{coupon/price} \times 100$$

So in the particular case set out in the illustration above:

BRITISH FUNDS

Notes	Price £	+ or −	1993 high	low	Yield Int.	Red.
"Shorts" (Lives up to Five Years)						
Funding 6pc 1993‡‡	**100**	......	$100\tfrac{1}{4}$	$99\tfrac{21}{32}$	**6.00**	5.76
Treas $13\tfrac{3}{4}$pc 1993‡‡...	**103**	$-\tfrac{1}{16}$	$106\tfrac{5}{16}$	$101\tfrac{1}{2}$	**13.35**	5.55
$8\tfrac{1}{2}$pc 1994................	**$101\tfrac{11}{16}$xd**	......	$102\tfrac{15}{16}$	$101\tfrac{11}{16}$	**8.36**	5.52
$14\tfrac{1}{2}$pc 1994‡‡	**$105\tfrac{11}{16}$**	$-\tfrac{1}{32}$	$109\tfrac{1}{4}$	$105\tfrac{11}{16}$	**13.72**	5.48
Exch $13\tfrac{1}{2}$pc 1994........	**$106\tfrac{1}{4}$**	......	$109\tfrac{5}{16}$	$106\tfrac{1}{4}$	**12.71**	5.47
Treas. 10pc Ln. 1994‡‡...	**$103\tfrac{31}{32}$**	......	$105\tfrac{21}{32}$	$103\tfrac{31}{32}$	**9.62**	5.52
Exch $12\tfrac{1}{2}$pc 1994........	**$107\tfrac{17}{32}$**	......	$110\tfrac{3}{32}$	$107\tfrac{11}{16}$	**11.62**	5.54
Treas 9pc 1994‡‡	**$104\tfrac{1}{4}$**	......	$105\tfrac{21}{32}$	$103\tfrac{21}{32}$	**8.63**	5.66
12pc 1995	**$109\tfrac{3}{16}$**	......	$111\tfrac{15}{32}$	$108\tfrac{3}{4}$	**10.99**	5.71
Exch 3pc Gas 90–95	**$96\tfrac{1}{4}$**	......	$96\tfrac{3}{4}$	94	**3.12**	5.10
$10\tfrac{1}{4}$pc 1995..............	**$108\tfrac{1}{4}$**	$+\tfrac{1}{16}$	$109\tfrac{7}{8}$	$107\tfrac{5}{8}$	**9.47**	5.88
Treas $12\tfrac{3}{4}$pc 1995‡‡...	**$114\tfrac{9}{16}$**	$+\tfrac{1}{32}$	$116\tfrac{7}{8}$	$113\tfrac{5}{8}$	**11.13**	5.98
14pc 1996	**$118\tfrac{3}{32}$**	$+\tfrac{3}{32}$	$120\tfrac{5}{8}$	$117\tfrac{1}{16}$	**11.85**	6.17
$15\tfrac{1}{4}$pc 1996‡‡	**$122\tfrac{23}{32}$**	$+\tfrac{3}{32}$	$125\tfrac{5}{8}$	$121\tfrac{21}{32}$	**12.43**	6.29
Exch $13\tfrac{1}{4}$pc 1996‡‡	**$117\tfrac{13}{16}$**	$+\tfrac{3}{32}$	$120\tfrac{1}{16}$	$116\tfrac{1}{2}$	**11.25**	6.30
Conversion 10pc 1996 ..	**$110\tfrac{15}{32}$**	$+\tfrac{3}{32}$	$111\tfrac{1}{2}$	$108\tfrac{7}{8}$	**9.05**	6.45
Treas $13\tfrac{1}{4}$pc 1997‡‡...	**$120\tfrac{15}{32}$**	$+\tfrac{1}{8}$	$122\tfrac{9}{16}$	$118\tfrac{27}{32}$	**11.00**	6.65
Exch $10\tfrac{1}{2}$pc 1997.........	**$112\tfrac{3}{16}$**	$+\tfrac{3}{32}$	$113\tfrac{5}{8}$	$110\tfrac{9}{16}$	**9.36**	6.64
Treas $8\tfrac{3}{4}$pc 1997‡‡.....	**$107\tfrac{3}{8}$**	$+\tfrac{3}{32}$	$108\tfrac{11}{16}$	$105\tfrac{1}{2}$	**8.15**	6.65
Exch 15pc 1997	**$129\tfrac{15}{32}$**	$+\tfrac{5}{32}$	$132\tfrac{11}{32}$	$127\tfrac{15}{16}$	**11.59**	6.92
$9\tfrac{3}{4}$pc 1998.................	**$111\tfrac{3}{16}$**	$+\tfrac{5}{32}$	$112\tfrac{5}{8}$	$109\tfrac{1}{16}$	**8.77**	6.82
Treas $7\tfrac{1}{4}$pc 1998‡‡.....	**$102\tfrac{3}{16}$**	$+\tfrac{3}{16}$	$103\tfrac{1}{4}$	$99\tfrac{31}{32}$	**7.09**	6.69
$7\tfrac{1}{4}$pc 1998 A‡	**$102\tfrac{5}{32}$**	$+\tfrac{1}{16}$	$102\tfrac{5}{32}$	$99\tfrac{27}{32}$	**7.10**	6.70
Treas $6\tfrac{3}{4}$pc 1995–98‡‡..	**$100\tfrac{1}{8}$**	$+\tfrac{5}{32}$	101	$97\tfrac{31}{32}$	**6.74**	6.70
14pc '98–1	**$127\tfrac{3}{16}$**	$+\tfrac{1}{4}$	$129\tfrac{1}{2}$	$125\tfrac{1}{16}$	**11.01**	7.26
Five to Fifteen Years						
Treas $15\tfrac{1}{2}$pc '98‡‡......	**$136\tfrac{1}{32}$**	$+\tfrac{1}{4}$	$138\tfrac{17}{32}$	$133\tfrac{23}{32}$	**11.39**	7.10
Exch 12pc 1998	**121**	$+\tfrac{3}{16}$	$122\tfrac{5}{8}$	$118\tfrac{3}{8}$	**9.92**	7.20
Treas $9\tfrac{1}{2}$pc 1999‡‡.....	**$111\tfrac{3}{16}$**	$+\tfrac{1}{4}$	$112\tfrac{1}{2}$	$108\tfrac{5}{16}$	**8.54**	7.01
Exch $12\tfrac{1}{4}$pc 1999.........	**$122\tfrac{3}{4}$**	$+\tfrac{1}{8}$	$124\tfrac{23}{32}$	$120\tfrac{3}{16}$	**9.98**	7.29

Source: Financial Times

Fig 8.1 An extract from the *Financial Times* daily gilt table.

$$\text{Exch } 10\tfrac{1}{4} \text{ pc } 1995$$
$$\text{current yield} = 10.25/108.25 \times 100$$
$$= 9.47 \text{ pc}$$

That is the figure in the column second from the right in the table above. The calculation points up an important point about yields and prices – *as the price of a bond falls, the yield it offers rises.* This happens because the amount of interest a bond pays is fixed, so the less an investor pays for a bond, the greater his rate of return on the money he has had to pay out.

The other method for calculating yield is called the **redemption yield** or **yield-to-maturity** and it takes into account the fact that as well as earning interest, an investor may make a capital gain or loss by owning a bond until its redemption date. Redemption yield is a measure of an investors' total return over the life of a gilt, and so it the most accurate way to compare gilts if you intend to hold them for the full term.

Again taking the example above, on one particular day an investor might buy Exch 10¼ 95 for £108.25; he also knows that the government will only pay £100 to redeem the gilt in 1995 – so our investor makes a capital loss of £8.25 to set against the interest he earns. Divided up over the two years the gilt has to run from late 1993 to 1995, our investor makes an annual capital loss of £4.125 on £108.25, a rate of 3.8 per cent. Deducted from the interest yield of 9.47, this gives a total return of 5.66 per cent.

In practice this is not quite right – the precise details depend on a complex compound interest calculation which requires a high-powered calculator, but the principle is valid. The exact redemption yield of Exch 10¼ 95 works out at 5.88 per cent, the figure in the last column of the *Financial Times* table on page 145.

Redemption yield is the measure used by professionals to compare one gilt with another. All other things being equal, gilts with a similar period to run will have redemption yields which are very close to each other; and as supply and demand for gilts causes prices to rise and fall, yields of similar gilts will tend to move in line. On the day of our example Exch 10¼ pc 95 has a redemption yield of 5.88 per cent, Tsy 12 pc 95 returns 5.71 per cent. The fact that the redemption yield is not easily calculated by the small investor does not really matter – the figures appear every day in the *Financial Times*.

Why yields differ

Two things do cause gilt yields to differ from one another
– the first is the length of time a gilt has to run. As the
introduction pointed out, the longer money is tied up the
greater the return an investor expects – thus gilts with ten
years to maturity should yield more than those due to be
repaid a year from now. A graph of yields given by
different gilts against the time they have to run is called a
yield curve. When this basic investment rule applies the
yield curve is said to be *normal* or **positive sloping**. For
short this is known as a positive yield curve – the longer
to maturity, the higher the yield.

Sometimes the UK gilt market has a much less straightforward shape. Supply and demand for different types of
gilts vary widely. Banks buy short gilts, but will only do
so if the return is competitive with loans they could
make. If interest rates are high (as they often are in
Britain) short gilt yields must also be high.

On the other hand, long gilts are more affected by
expectations of the likely level of long-term inflation.
Pension funds may buy long gilts if they think they can
beat the trend of inflation over ten years – despite the fact
that they might get a better return over a year or two if
they bought a short gilt.

By contrast medium gilts are less popular, not being the
favoured choice of either the banks which like short gilts
or the pension funds which like longs. Such neglect
means that medium gilts often offer higher yields than
longs.

The other factor which causes gilt yields to vary is tax.
No capital gains tax is payable on gilts, but interest
payments are liable for income tax. So it sometimes
benefits investors to buy a gilt which has a lower rate of
interest, but which offers a capital gain. In the table on
page 145, Exch 3 pc Gas 90–95 pays a lowish interest and
will gain 3.9 per cent in value by the time it is redeemed –
its redemption yield is 5.10 per cent. On the other hand
Exch 13½ pc 1994 offers much higher interest, and a
capital loss of almost 6¼ per cent – this is less attractive,
so its yield is slightly higher at 5.47 per cent. This effect is

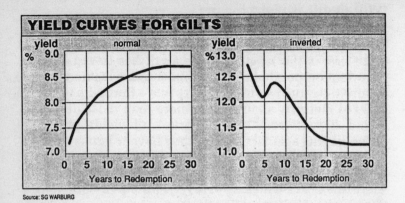

Source: SG WARBURG

Fig 8.2 In a 'normal' situation the yield on long gilts is higher than that on shorts, but in Britain high short-term interest rates have often caused the yield curve to be inverse. A hump also shows the relative unpopularity of medium-term gilts.

most pronounced with very low coupon gilts, which used to be very popular with higher rate taxpayers who could earn a tax free capital gain, and a low taxable income. Because demand for these gilts was high, the yields were correspondingly low. Some gilts will pay interest gross to non-residents of the UK. They are known as the 'A' list, and any broker can tell you which they are.

One final important point about yields: although we have discussed particular examples, selected at random from one day's *Financial Times*, bear in mind that these yields are not set in stone – they vary from minute to minute with the ebb and flow of buyers and sellers in the market. Over the course of a year it is quite possible for the yield on a gilt to rise from 9 to 13 per cent – and fall all the way back again. And as the yield rises, the price falls. Just like shares, investors risk making or losing money if they buy and sell gilts in the market. Only if the gilt is held to redemption is the return guaranteed.

Which gilt is right for me?

Which gilts investors should buy depends on what their objectives are. There are two basic ways to regard gilts, either as long-term investments designed to be held until they mature, or as shorter-term investments which can be bought and sold as interest rates rise and fall. In either event getting the timing right is very important. Long-term holders can lose out badly if they jump into the gilt market when interest rates are about to rise substantially. It would have been quite possible for an investor to buy medium gilts in 1988 which yielded 9 per cent, only to find that the same bond offered a yield of 12 per cent a year later.

First, let's consider investors who intend to hold the gilts to maturity, and get the guaranteed return shown by the redemption yield; they should first decide how long they wish to invest for, and pick a gilt of approximately corresponding maturity. Investors should then look at their tax position and decide whether they wish the gilt to produce an income. Basic rate taxpayers looking for income should go for a medium coupon gilt – ideally one currently priced around £100, the redemption price. This will produce the maximum income without forcing the holder to take a capital loss. Non-taxpayers can consider high coupon gilts, which will pay a good income but will involve a capital loss. Because yields can move quite substantially over the course of a year, timing is very important in deciding to buy gilts – even if you intend to be a long-term holder.

Short-term traders buy gilts when they think interest rates are about to fall. For example, medium gilt yields fell from 11 per cent to 9.5 per cent at the beginning of 1991 as investors expected cuts in bank interest rates. That boosted the price of Tsy 9 per cent 2008 from £84 to £94. Broadly the longer the maturity and the higher the coupon of the gilt, the bigger the price movement. So those who buy are certain interest rates are going to fall soon should buy high coupon long gilts as a speculation. But beware, if you are wrong, high coupon longs are just as volatile when they are going down in price as when they are going up!

The other possibility is to invest in **index-linked** gilts. In theory these sound a very good idea for overcoming inflation problems, but in practice they have not been particularly successful since they were launched. Currently index-linked gilts offer a return over inflation of about 3.5 per cent, whilst ordinary gilts yield around 8 per cent. So to work out whether index-linked or ordinary gilts are the better bet, you'll have to take a stab at what the inflation rate is going to be. In this example, if you think that inflation will average substantially more than 5 per cent for the period, then index-linked will offer a better return than ordinary gilts, since the 3.5 per cent real return plus the inflation at perhaps 7 per cent, exceeds the 8 per cent you could earn on ordinary gilts. If you think inflation will be less than 5 per cent you should choose conventional gilts. But bear in mind that the exact rates of return will vary from time to time. Because they are linked to inflation index-linked gilts are sometimes compared to shares, but have not done particularly well in the decade since they were introduced because the real

Fig 8.3 Long-gilts prices are more volatile than shorts.

returns on equities were higher than those offered by index-linked.

How should I buy gilts?

For most people the way to buy gilts is from Postman Pat. All gilts are on the **National Savings Stock Register**, which means that investors can buy or sell them cheaply through the **Post Office** – interest can be paid out gross of income tax and the PO produces a leaflet which explains how to go about buying and selling. This is fine so long as you have sorted out what you want to do, but if you are really not sure which gilt to buy, consult a stockbroker, although here you will pay a higher commission than you would at the Post Office. It is not worth buying gilts through a unit trust, since the fund's performance is most unlikely to be able to recoup the charges involved.

Other bonds

Apart from gilts there are a number of other types of bonds available to investors which work in much the same way as gilts. **Bulldogs** and **Eurosterling bonds** are larger denomination bonds issued by governments and companies, and for the most part this is a market dominated by professionals. Companies also issue **corporate loan stocks** and **debentures**. Debentures are backed by specific assets of the company issuing the bonds, and so are fairly safe; loan stocks vary – some are secured, others not. What all of these bonds offer is a higher yield than gilts, because the British government is the best credit in the domestic bond market and therefore pays the lowest interest rate. However, some corporate bonds have failed to pay – so investors have to weigh the advantage of higher yield against the risk of default. The market in corporate bonds is also not always as liquid as that for gilts. **Local authorities** also issue bonds which pay a slightly higher rate than comparable gilts; these are normally issued for one or two years and known as yearlings. Sometimes local authorities also issue longer-term fixed rate stocks, but this is something of a specialist market.

Convertibles as a link to equity

As well as straightforward bonds which pay a fixed rate of interest and are eventually redeemed, some companies issue bonds which pay fixed interest but are **convertible** into the company's shares. This conversion happens at set dates in the future and under fixed conditions – a typical convertible might perhaps give the right to buy fifty shares in ABC plc for every £100-worth of bonds on interest payment dates from now until 1998, when the bond is redeemed at £100. The bond pays 9 per cent interest and is currently trading in the market at £90.* From this investors can work out not only what the redemption yield on the convertible bond is, but also the price at which the bonds entitle him to buy shares. Normally, the price at which the convertible entitles investors to buy shares will be higher than the current market price of the equity, and this is normally expressed as a percentage of the share price. Convertibles which have large premiums – i.e. are a long way from being worth converting into shares – trade much like ordinary bonds: their prices are not very volatile and they offer high yields. Those trading close to their conversion terms have much lower yields, and more volatile prices like shares.

Which type investors pick depends on what they are looking for. If income is the objective, but you hope to get some capital gain in the long term, pick a convertible with

---

* Sharp-eyed aficionados may have noticed that the language of convertibles is not dissimilar to options. This is no coincidence. One way to view convertibles is as a fixed rate corporate bond with an option to buy shares attached. In many ways it would be better if convertibles were explicitly constituted in this way, as it would make it simpler for the option to be valued, and the bond and option could be traded separately if desired. In fact this happens in the Eurobond market, but the domestic bond market does like its little traditions . . .

a higher yield, some way from its conversion terms. But make sure you are buying a company which is solid – sometimes high convertible yields are a sign of a company about to go to the wall. On the other hand if you want to buy shares in a company, but are worried that the equity market may be weak, or that the company's shares may be too volatile, then buying a convertible bond near its conversion terms offers the prospect of capital growth without the full risks of a falling share price.

It's also worth noting that there are two basic types of convertible – **convertible loan stocks** are redeemed like other bonds, as are most **convertible preference shares**, though some do have other arrangements. One point about convertible prefs which always causes confusion is that their coupon is quoted net of basic rate tax, while redemption yields are always stated gross. So the yield on convertible prefs always seems impossibly high, simply because the yield and the coupon are stated on different tax bases. The best way to buy convertible bonds is through a stockbroker, who can also advise on what currently looks good value.

Fixed Interest

IN A NUTSHELL

1. Fixed interest securities and deposits offer no protection from inflation, but are useful for income investors and emergency cash funds. Fixed interest investments are related to the bond market and deposits to the money market.

2. There is a constantly shifting plethora of floating rate deposit accounts on offer. Best buys vary, but the larger the sum and the longer you are prepared to leave it the better rate you will get.

3. Fixed interest rates can be had from guaranteed income bonds, some bank deposits and some National Savings products. Fixed rates are a good bet if interest rates are about to fall.

4. Bonds also offer fixed rates if they are held to repayment, and are negotiable – they can be bought and sold in the secondary market. Gilts issued by the government are the most important fixed interest bond market in Britain.

5. Bond yields go down as their prices go up. Total returns are measured by the yield to maturity, which takes in both interest income and capital gain. Long gilt prices are more volatile than short gilts.

6. Investors should consider how long they wish to invest for, their tax position and the state of the interest rate market before deciding on which gilts to buy. The best place to buy them is through the National Savings Stock Register at the Post Office.

7. Index-linked gilts do offer protection from inflation if they are held to maturity. Investors choosing between conventional and index-linked gilts must make a guess at the likely rate of inflation before buying.

8. Those using gilts to speculate that interest rates will fall should use high coupon long dated gilts, as their prices will move fastest. However, as the most volatile gilts, they will go down as fast as they go up.

9. A variety of bonds issued by companies is available to investors. Some, like debentures, are backed by specific company assets, others not. They offer higher yields than gilts, but the market can be less liquid.

10. One type of bond which is useful to both growth and income investors is the convertible bond which is a fixed interest bond with the option to convert into ordinary shares.

Chapter 9
Unit and Investment Trusts

Having sorted out the basics of pensions, mortgages, insurance and cash reserves investors can turn their attention to the stockmarket. This can be lucrative; shares have produced much better long-term returns than bonds or deposits for most of this century. But small investors have a problem because stockbrokers won't construct and manage a portfolio for them unless they have substantial sums to invest. A sensible share portfolio should contain at least ten stocks and preferably 20, but the costs of dealing in shares mean that it's not worth holding a stake in a company of less than about £2,000. Unless share shops catch on and costs come down, direct investment in shares will continue to be for gamblers or those with at least £50,000 to spend.

The way small investors get round this is to pool their investments and achieve economies of scale. Take a hypothetical example – 1,000 people each chipping £5,000 into a fund would have £5m which could happily be spread over a portfolio of 50 shares. That way dealing and administrative costs are kept relatively low, yet everyone has a stake in a wide spread of shares. Both **unit trusts** and **investment trusts** are just such pooled investments.

Units for the small investor

Unit trusts are the simpler to understand. Here the trust owns shares in companies which are then split into units, in strict proportion to the amount invested. So in our hypothetical example if the £5m was split into 1m units each unit would be worth £5, and since in this case everyone chipped in the same starting amount, everyone would have a holding of 1,000 units worth a total of

£5,000. If over time the shares which the trust invested in shot up and the fund became worth £10m, then each unit would be worth £10 and the unit holders' investments would be worth £10,000 each. These funds are collectively managed by professional fund managers.

In reality unit trusts are a little more complex. Normally when a fund is launched, it is offered to the public at a fixed price for about three weeks to get the ball rolling. Investors put in differing amounts of money and so hold differing numbers of units: in our fund, one investor might have put in £10,000 at the start and received 2,000 units, another £500 and received 100 units. Then there are charges (there would be) which are levied by the managers. The initial charge is about 6 per cent of the amount invested, and there is an annual charge of 1–1.5 per cent.

Investors are not locked into the fund – they can sell their investment or buy extra units after the fund has been launched. Suppose in our example an investor missed the opening offer, but decides to put in £1,000 a few weeks later. By chance, the price of the units has not moved, but just like shares, the fund managers quote a price where they will buy units called the **bid** price and another where they will sell known as the **offer**. The difference is normally called the **spread** and it exists because fund managers also have to pay a spread (and commissions) when they buy and sell shares. The spread is normally about 6 per cent, so if the price of the fund has not moved, the units might be quoted as £4.85 bid – £5.15 offered,* so the latecomer can buy units for £5.15.

The fund manager takes the extra funds invested by the late arrival, buys a proportional amount of shares for the fund and issues some new units. Because unit trusts can expand in this way after they have been launched they are known as **open-ended funds**. Ideally, of course,

---

* If you have trouble remembering which way round the bid-offer spread works, just bear in mind that it always works to your disadvantage. If you are selling you are paid the lower price (the bid), if buying charged the higher amount (the offer). Somehow life is always like that.

the fund manager matches up anyone who wants to buy units with sellers within the fund – on one day in an active fund the manager might have buyers of 10,000 units and sellers of 9,000. Then he only has to issue 1,000 new units and can simply transfer the other 9,000. Since he earns the spread on all 10,000 units, crossing within a fund is a nice little earner.

One other wrinkle to unit trusts is the way they pay income. The trust receives dividends from the companies in which it invests and pays it out to unit holders in **distributions** semi-annually or quarterly. As is the case with shares units will tend to rise before a distribution and fall afterwards. As an alternative some trusts reinvest these funds and increase the value of these **accumulation units** at each distribution.

Decus et Tutamen

Unit trusts could develop into quite a racket, since on the face of it there is nothing to stop you, me or anybody else setting ourselves up as fund managers and launching a fund, only to waltz off with investors' money. In fact, under the Financial Services Act, people handling investment funds have to be registered (see Appendix B) and there are other safeguards too. Each unit trust has a trust deed which specifies how it is to be managed, what charges it can pass on to unit holders and what type of investments it can hold. This part of the operation is run by the trustee – often a bank – which is there to ensure that the fund managers run the trust properly. If the fund meets certain criteria, it can be authorized by the Securities and Investments Board, and only authorized funds are allowed to advertise in the UK. Many fund managers also belong to the Unit Trust Association, a trade body which has a code of conduct on the operation of trusts.

There are some unauthorized trusts run by perfectly respectable fund managers established offshore to invest in commodities, currencies and futures. And some unofficial funds are run by stockbrokers on behalf of their clients. If you are uncertain about who you are dealing with, you are most likely to avoid problems by sticking to an authorized fund, operated by a respected fund manager cleared under the Financial Services Act.

Refinements to pricing

These days it is quite easy for trust groups to tot up the value of shares held by a trust, and calculate the value of units every day. But there are aspects of unit trust pricing which have caused concern in recent years. The first is that even in authorized trusts, the guidelines set down by the DTI technically allow most funds to have a bid-offer spread of around 9.5 per cent. This is too wide to attract investors into unit trusts and competition forces fund managers to quote spreads of around 6 per cent.*

However, it is possible for fund managers to shade the spread from one end of the permitted band to the other. If the market is rising strongly, and many investors are buying units, then managers can push the bid and offer towards the top of the band. If some months later funds are out of fashion they can shade the bid down to the bottom of the band and adjust the offer correspondingly. So although the quoted spread is 6 per cent, it floats inside a band almost 10 per cent wide. If an investor buys and sells at the wrong time, he may actually have paid a spread of almost 10 per cent. The practice is known as **bid** or **offer pricing**.

The other problem showed up in the crash of 1987, when many small investors tried to sell in a hurry. Traditionally, dealings in unit trusts are conducted at the previous night's closing valuation. For example the hypothetical trust we constructed might be valued at £4.70 bid – £5.00 offered on a Monday evening, and all of Tuesday's dealings would then be transacted at these prices. Such **historic pricing** normally causes no problems, but in the crash the price established on

---

* Just to complicate matters, there is now pressure to move towards trading units on a single price, as happens in Europe.

Monday night in no way reflected what the fund was worth on Tuesday. In our case the units might only be worth around £4.00 on Tuesday, yet historic pricing meant fund managers should be bidding £4.70! Clearly the managers stood to lose a lot of money, and quickly switched to **forward pricing** where all deals were concluded at the price operating at the close of that day's business – i.e. Tuesday night's closing prices.

Unsurprisingly, this caused a storm of protest. Investors did not know at what price they were selling their units and accused fund managers of moving the goal posts. The real reason for the outburst was that Tuesday night's closing prices were so much lower than Monday's, so investors felt they had lost a lot of money.

Fund managers for their part felt that investors were literally trying to sell at yesterday's prices and were being deeply unrealistic. There was much bad blood all round. To try to alleviate the situation, unit trusts now have to declare whether they are working on historic or forward pricing, and investors can specify that they want their units to be dealt on forward pricing. The one thing investors cannot do is what they would really like to – insist on historic pricing and be guaranteed yesterday's price.

A success, despite all that

Whatever the vagaries of unit trust pricing it hasn't deterred the public from buying them. The amount of money being managed in unit trusts increased well in excess of the rise in the stockmarket during the 1980s, and there are now over 1,500 unit trusts to choose from. Originally, unit trusts were divided into growth and income funds; now there are 22 different categories. The main classifications are:

● **UK growth**. These aim for capital appreciation and tend to have low yields. The type of shares these funds are looking for are bid stocks, shares which have had a hard time but may recover, and shares in growing or fashionable areas.

- **UK balanced**. Here the objective is to give returns similar to the FT-A All Share index, with similar yields and capital growth. In some ways these are a precursor of indexed funds (see below).
- **UK equity income**. This is the kind of fund which an income portfolio ought to consider. Although the return is much lower than that of a deposit account – perhaps only half the immediate income, there will be some capital growth to provide higher income in future years.
- **International**. Unit trusts are one of the main ways for private investors to buy shares in overseas stockmarkets, and there are several sub-divisions in this area. As well as the obvious funds in North America, Europe and Japan, there are unit trusts investing in smaller Asian markets, Scandinavia and South America. Indeed fund managers seem to rush in and start a new fund whenever a foreign market shows any sign of life. One thing to watch out for in these trusts is the effect of currency movements. As in many other investments forex is the danger lurking below the waterline. If sterling is weak or strong against the local currency it can have a dramatic impact on the performance of the fund. Some managers hedge the fund's forex exposure, others do not – but getting that decision right is as hard as picking a fund in the first place!
- **Energy and commodities**. DTI rules prevent trusts investing directly in commodities, so these funds invest in energy and commodity related shares – examples might be mining and oil companies.
- **Property or Financial**. Since these shares have peculiar characteristics, there are trusts which specialize in them.
- **Fixed interest**. There are a number of classifications covering gilt and fixed interest growth and income. As we have said before, it is probably not worth buying a gilt fund – unlike shares they perform very uniformly – but some other fixed interest funds may be worth a look. Investors should still bear in mind that *all* sterling bond prices will ultimately be swayed by the performance of the gilt market. Make sure you are not buying gilts in a rather more expensive wrapping than is available from the Post Office.

● **Investment trusts**. For those who really like to spread their risk, there are even a few unit trusts which invest in investment trust companies. It may well be cheaper to buy a selection of investment trusts instead.

The other group of funds investors can select from are called **managed funds** (sometimes called **funds of funds**). These are run by the fund management groups and switch between different trusts run by the group. For example a managed fund might be invested in the group's Japanese equity unit trust, but having decided this has run its course switches to its UK smaller companies fund, which the managers expect to be the next winner. The fund's performance depends on the quality of such decisions.

Of course, investors can make such switches them-selves. And in order to keep unit holders loyal to one group's stable of funds, the managers often offer the

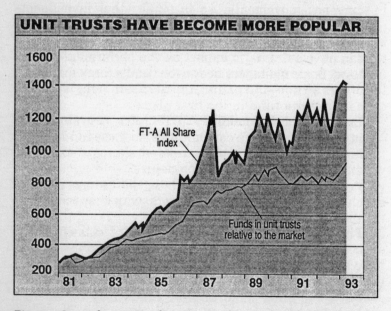

Fig 9.1 Over the 1980s the rise in the stockmarket and heavy marketing have helped unit trusts boom in popularity. Poor market conditions in 1990 made it a bad year. But investment picked up as interest rates tumbled in the early 1990s.

facilities to switch between funds cheaply. This can be useful provided you are in a good group of funds which perform well overall. But remember, if you joined a group because its American funds were good, that is not a reason to think that its Far Eastern trusts are also winners. And bear in mind that because the dealing spreads and costs are high, unit trusts have to be considered a long-term investment. Simply churning from one fund to another in the hope of picking up a small advantage will only make the fund manager rich.

Pick a good manager

Picking the right stockmarket – or the right sector of the stockmarket – is crucial to investing successfully. But in unit trusts it is also important to pick the right fund manager. They make the decisions about which stocks to buy, and so determine the success of the fund. The impact of a fund manager can be so pronounced that some investors make a point of following fund managers when they move from one group to another. So how does an investor choose? The smart answer is – be lucky! Even a fund manager with a good track record may come a cropper in future.

Yet investors want some yardsticks to use, since the choice of fund manager is as important as picking the right market. The best that can be said is that sticking with one of the well-known groups may avoid some of the worst pitfalls. But it is also true that good fund managers sometimes move to head up a small firm or even set up on their own. One trap to avoid is simply picking the best fund of the previous year – the chances are that it will soon run out of steam. Better to look for groups which have been consistently good performers over a period of years.

What is a winner?

Even trying to decide whether a unit trust has done well or badly can be a problem. There is a huge choice of funds and no universally accepted criteria for assessing their performance. Which fund is the best depends on what period is chosen, whether any currency effects are allowed for, whether income is reinvested or not and a lot of other factors. To try to help investors through this maze *Money Management* magazine collates the performance of all authorized funds every month.

The proliferation of funds, and so the difficulty of choosing between them, comes in part from the way that the unit trust industry is dominated by marketing. If, for example, the Malaysian and Thai stockmarkets are booming, unit trust groups often rush to open a new set of funds there even if some perfectly serviceable funds are already operating in the market. They think that the fanfare surrounding a new launch will pull in investors more effectively than re-advertising old funds. So for every stockmarket fashion, a dozen new funds are launched.

One consequence of this is that older funds tend to drop from view – they are not advertised and existing investors may find it hard to keep up to date with prices. It also means that the unit trust business is badly splintered. There are many funds which each only contain a few million pounds all trying to do the same job, making the cost of administration per unit high, and since each small fund has relatively few members trying to buy and sell, bid-offer spreads are wider than they would be if the pools were bigger. Unit trust salesmen argue that this is simply the operation of the free market, but in this case the market seems to be trying to keep salesmen in work, rather than reducing costs to investors.

'I'm not even a bus, I'm a tram'

One way in which the Americans have tried to tackle this problem is by constructing **tracker** or **indexed** funds. These funds are designed to follow some stockmarket index – like the FT-A All Share index – by investing in a statistically selected set of shares, which on past performance have behaved similarly to the index. For example

to mimic the performance of the 800-odd equities in the
FT-A All Share, a tracker fund invests in perhaps 200
carefully selected stocks. The beauty of this system is that
any investors wanting to match the performance of the
All Share index only need to choose between one or two
indexed funds. As a result the funds are larger and costs
lower than conventional trusts. Indexed funds have finally begun to catch on in the UK. You can now buy funds
which track most of the main UK stockmarket indexes
(see pages 177-8); the major foreign indexes; and even
'reverse-trackers', which allow you to make money from
a fall in your chosen market.

How to buy unit trusts

If all this discussion of unit trusts sounds a little
nebulous, that is because it is difficult to give specific
information which is both useful and generally appli-
cable. Whichever way you want to slice the UK stockmarket there are at least a dozen funds to choose from as well
as plenty of options for all major and most minor foreign
markets. Add to that the fact that fund managers move
around – and it's not always possible to find out when
they do – and that their performance will vary, then
finding a winning unit trust from the 1,300-odd around
seems almost impossible. In many ways picking unit
trusts is harder than picking shares; with shares you only
have to select the right company, with unit trusts you
have to find the right investment and the right fund
manager!

One way to put flesh on the bones is to look at a couple
of alternative strategies. Investors tend to buy unit trusts
from a newspaper advertisement or from a financial
adviser. That adviser can either be tied to selling one
group's products, or independent and able to sell from
across the range (see Appendix B for details). If you buy
from a financial adviser he ought to recommend an
investment which is suitable for you – for example a
growth or income fund. However, even if he picks an
appropriate area there is no particular guarantee that he

will be any better than you at picking the best performing
fund. On the other hand, buying a unit trust on the
strength of an advertisement is a pretty chancy business
too.

If guidance is difficult, at least there are some ground
rules. First, your basic stockmarket investment ought to
be in your home country; you do *not* want to put your life
savings on the Taiwanese market. Whatever sort of
investor you are you should have a good proportion of
your money in general UK funds which can be biased for
growth or income, depending on your circumstances.
Then look at what sort of investor you are – active or
looking for a quiet life, high or low risk, interested in
specialist areas like property or looking for a broad
spread. You can add to your core holding of general funds
according to your views and tastes, but *don't* allow the
portfolio to become too unbalanced.

If you feel confident that you know what you're looking
for, then you may decide not to use a financial adviser, but
it is still worth checking the track record of funds in
Money Management before you buy. If you are at sea,
consult a professional, but check the track record of his
recommendations anyway, and watch that you're not
buying that week's fashionable fund – advisers have
advertising pushed at them in the same way that we do,
and if the Mongolian market is being pushed hard by fund
managers, even the soberest adviser may be swayed.

An alternative to holding a spread of UK general funds
is to buy an indexed fund, which will mimic the market
and has lower dealing costs than most other unit trusts.
Investors can then spice up their holding to try to beat the
market by buying a selection of individual shares. In some
ways such a portfolio imitates the way institutional
investors work. They have a core holding of shares which
provides a cross-section of the market, and add to that
their own favourite shares. Such a strategy may be
cheaper for the individual and have a more predictable
performance than a hotch-potch of unit trusts.

One area where pooled funds are particularly useful is
in overseas investment. Unit trusts often give access to
markets which individuals could not otherwise enter.

However, before you or your adviser decide that Korea is the place to be, remember that you should only have

UTA'S SECTOR DEFINITIONS

UK EQUITY GROWTH*	Trusts which invest at least 80% of their assets in equities and which have a primary objective of achieving capital growth.
UK EQUITY GENERAL*	Trusts which invest at least 80% of their assets in equities, have a yield of between 80% to 110% of the yield of the FTA All Share Index and which aim to produce a combination of both income and growth.
UK EQUITY INCOME*	Trusts which invest at least 80% of their assets in equities and which have a yield in excess of 110% of the yield of the FTA All Share Index.
UK GILT AND FIXED INTEREST*	Trusts which invest at least 80% of their assets in UK gilts and fixed interest securities.
UK BALANCED	Trusts which have less than 80% of their portfolio invested in either equities or gilt and fixed interest securities.
FINANCIAL AND PROPERTY	Trusts which have at least 80% of their assets in financial or property securities.
INVESTMENT TRUST UNITS	Trusts which are able only to invest in the shares of investment trust companies.
COMMODITY AND ENERGY	Trusts which invest at least 80% of their assets in commodity or energy securities.
MONEY MARKET	Trusts which invest at least 80% of their assets in money market instruments.
INTERNATIONAL EQUITY GROWTH‡	Trusts which invest at least 80% of their assets in equities and which have a primary objective of achieving capital growth.
INTERNATIONAL EQUITY INCOME‡	Trusts which invest at least 80% of their assets in equities and which have a yield in excess of 110% of the relevant yield figure for the FTA World Index.
INTERNATIONAL FIXED INTEREST‡	Trusts which invest at least 80% of their assets in fixed interest stocks. (All trusts which contain more than 80% fixed interest investments are included under this heading regardless of the fact that they may have more than 80% in a particular geographic sector, unless that geographic area is the UK when the fund would be shown under the relevant UK heading.)
INTERNATIONAL BALANCED‡	Trusts which have less than 80% of their portfolio invested in either equities or fixed interest securities.
FUND OF FUNDS	Trusts which are able to invest only in other authorized unit trust schemes.

NORTH AMERICA	Trusts which invest at least 80% of their assets in North American securities.
EUROPE	Trusts which invest at least 80% of their assets in European securities (including the UK).
JAPAN	Trusts which invest at least 80% of their assets in Japanese securities.
FAR EAST INCLUDING JAPAN	Trusts which invest at least 80% of their assets in Far Eastern securities but which include a Japanese content. (This Japanese content must be less than 80%.)
FAR EAST EXCLUDING JAPAN	Trusts which invest at least 80% of their assets in Far Eastern securities but which exclude any Japanese content.
AUSTRALASIA	Trusts which invest at least 80% of their assets in Australian or New Zealand securities.
CONVERTIBLES	Trusts which invest at least 60% of their assets in convertibles stocks regardless of any geographic specialization they may also have.
UK SMALLER COMPANIES*	Trusts which invest at least 80% of their assets in UK equities of companies which form part of the Hoare Govett UK Smaller Companies Extended Index.

* ALL UK SECTORS INCLUDE: all trusts with at least 80% of their investment in the UK

‡ ALL INTERNATIONAL SECTORS INCLUDE: all trusts with a portfolio which is less than 80% invested in any one geographical area. (But see special definition for the International Fixed Interest Sector.)

Fig 9.2 The official Unit Trust Association classifications of authorized Unit Trusts.

perhaps 25 per cent of your holdings overseas, and check the performance of the specific funds you are considering.

Investment trusts

Unit trusts have been popular in recent years, but there is another much older way for investors to buy a spread of risk on the stockmarket. Investment trusts – first founded in the 1860s – are companies which have been specifically established to invest in the shares of other companies. Many of them are quoted on the stockmarket and investors can buy or sell their shares through a stockbroker.

The fact that investment trusts are companies which have shares and shareholders causes important differences between unit and investment trusts. An investment trust's share price is determined by supply and demand on the stockmarket, whereas unit trust prices are determined entirely by the value of the assets in the trust. If investors choose to sell units in a unit trust, the fund manager simply takes the units back and sells an appropriate number of shares on the stockmarket; conversely if there are buyers, he can issue new units and buy more shares. Investment trusts cannot do this – there are a set number of shares in the company and their price is determined by what people in the market will pay for them. Demand for an investment trust's own shares does not directly influence the size of its investment portfolio. In the jargon, investment trusts are **closed end** funds.

This means that an investment trust's share price does not always accurately reflect the value of its investment portfolio. The net value of an investment trust's portfolio is normally called its **net asset value** or **NAV** and in most cases the NAV per share in the investment trust is higher than the price of the trust's shares. This difference is called the **discount** of the trust. There are several reasons why investment trusts trade at a discount. One is that the trust's shares may well be less marketable than those in which it invests. Investors may be unwilling to buy a less-liquid investment trust than the blue chip shares it contains. Tax is also a problem. Investors who do not normally pay CGT or income tax end up paying tax if they buy an investment trust. Another way of looking at it is to say that the market has little faith that the investment trust's managers will add anything to the companies in which they own shares. Investment trust discounts have varied as the sector rises and falls in popularity. In 1974 discounts reached 45 per cent, but now they have narrowed to nearer 10 per cent as the sector has attracted greater interest.

Discounts are not entirely a bad thing – because they have narrowed so much in the past 20 years anyone buying investment trusts would have seen his capital grow much faster than if he had bought shares in the underlying companies. And, even now, anyone buying shares in an investment trust will typically get almost

£1.10 of assets for every £1 they invest. But the discount does introduce uncertainty – investors might find themselves selling assets worth £1.30 for £1 if the sector were to fall out of favour again.

Wider horizons

Investment trusts have the advantage that they can invest more freely than unit trusts – for example, they can buy into unquoted companies, property or even deal in commodities. They can also borrow money to invest if they choose. Borrowing acts like a lever on investment trusts – if they borrow to buy shares which rise sharply, investment trust shareholders do very well, on the other hand if the shares bought on borrowed money fall – then the trust suffers heavily. Investment trusts with large

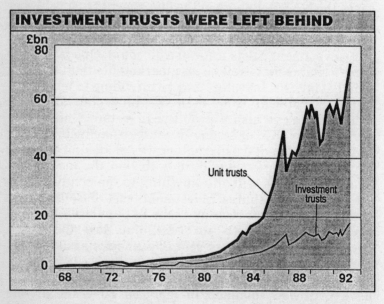

Fig 9.3 The amount of money in unit trusts has outpaced investment trusts despite the longer history and lower charges of investment trusts. The Association of Investment Trust Companies is now trying hard to catch up.

borrowings are said to be **highly geared** – just as when a car is in high gear, the wheels turn many times for each revolution of the engine, so the value of trusts with high gearing goes up or down much faster than the shares which they hold.

Cheap and cheerful

One advantage of investment trusts is that costs tend to be lower than unit trusts. Stockbroker's commission and stamp duty (soon to be abolished) will normally work out cheaper than the 6 per cent initial charge on unit trusts. Bid-offer spreads can be narrower too – large investment trusts may be dealt on a spread of 1-2 per cent; less liquid funds around 5-6 per cent, and running costs are typically 0.5 per cent a year. Lower charges make it easier for investment trusts to do well because more of investor's money goes straight into the market. Unfortunately, investment trusts' new emphasis on marketing has started to push charges up towards unit trust levels.

Dogged by discounts

Despite their advantages, the discount remains a bane for investment trusts. It deters potential investors, and makes it difficult to launch new investment trusts – after all who wants to buy a new issue for £1, only to see the market immediately discount it to 90p?

One way round this is to launch trusts in booming markets – for example many European stockmarkets were booming in 1990 and a number of trusts were launched to invest in them. The hope is that there will be sufficient demand for investment trust shares in these expanding markets for the discount to be kept to a minimum. There are more sophisticated solutions too. Some trusts are launched with warrants attached, giving investors the right to buy more shares at a pre-determined higher price later on. **Split-level** investment trusts are another answer – these trusts have two or three types of share: income shares which take all of the dividends plus a fixed capital sum in the future (usually when the trust is wound up); growth shares which take all of the capital growth; and sometimes zero coupon shares which pay no income but reward investors through a guaranteed capital gain.

Discounts also draw investment trusts to the attention of predators who like the sight of £1-worth of shares trading at 90p. Several investment trusts have been taken over in recent years to unlock this value – the most notable example was when the British Coal Pension Fund took over Globe investment trust in 1990. Globe was the largest investment trust of all, valued at around £1bn. The BCPF decided it wanted to invest more money in the stockmarket, and taking over Globe was cheaper than buying a comparable amount of shares through a broker. There was also a fashion for **unitizing** investment trusts in the 1980s. In this unpleasantly named practice investment trusts were reconstituted as unit trusts to cut the discount.

As newly launched investment trusts have often tried to catch the wave of rising markets in recent years, they have tended to become more specialized than the older general funds. So it's worth checking which areas an investment trust covers before buying. General guidance is available in a booklet available from the Association of Investment Trust Companies.*

Regular savings

In many ways unit trusts and investment trusts are in competition with each other. Unit trusts are normally sold through financial intermediaries who earn a commission on any units they sell. This is usually half the initial 6 per cent charge the investor pays, and can tilt intermediaries towards unit trusts.** Those wanting an investment trust

---

*16 Finsbury Circus, London EC2. Tel (071) 588 5347.
**It is sometimes possibly to buy units cheaply, either from the managers or from brokers pushing particular trusts. Ask, but never pick units just because they are available on the cheap.

would generally go to a stockbroker who would charge normal dealing commissions. But some investment trusts now offer financial advisers the same commission as unit trusts – which cuts into the investor's returns. Both unit and investment trusts are also sold directly to investors through 'off-the-page' newspaper and magazine ads, which invite potential buyers to return a coupon for more information.

To encourage small investors to get the unit or investment trust habit, both sets of groups run **regular savings plans** where investors can buy unit or investment trusts with monthly payments as low as £25 or £50. They are quite a good way to build up a lump sum and get an introduction to the workings of the stockmarket.

Unit and Investment Trusts

IN A NUTSHELL

1. The costs of dealing in shares makes direct investment in the stockmarket impractical for very small investors, so they tend to pool their investments into unit and investment trusts.

2. Unit trusts are run by fund managers with a bank acting as trustee. When they are first launched there is a fixed price offer for about three weeks. Then the offer closes and the price of units are quoted on a bid-offer spread.

3. Because unit trusts can create and destroy units, the price of the trust reflects the price of the shares it owns. If investors wish to buy more units the fund manager can issue them and buy more shares in the stockmarket.

4. Unit trusts authorized by the SIB are restricted in the types of investment they can make. Only authorized trusts can advertise in the UK. Unauthorized trusts are often run from offshore banking centres to invest in commodities, currencies or property.

5. There are over 1,500 unit trusts in the UK covering 22 different sectors. The right choice of fund manager is as important as picking the right market, and investors can only be guided by long-term performance when picking a fund.

6. Investment trusts are companies created to invest in the shares of other companies. They have a wider investment remit than unit trusts and can borrow money. There are around 260 investment trusts divided into 19 categories.

7. Because the price of investment trust shares are dictated by supply and demand on the stockmarket, the price of the trust often differs from the price of the assets it owns. Investment trusts normally trade at a discount to their asset value.

8. This discount often deters investors. It also makes it harder to launch new investment trusts. Some investment trusts have been taken over as a source of cheap assets. Others have been converted into unit trusts.

9. Both unit and investment trusts run regular savings plans which can be a good way to build up a lump sum and get an introduction to the stockmarket.

Chapter 10
Shares

Sometimes people argue that there is no point in holding shares; in their view the stockmarket is a capricious, dangerous place, and costs are so high that investors need a fortune to form a portfolio. Like many views, it has a grain of truth in it, but it does obscure the fact that the arguments for holding shares are just as good as for holding unit or investment trusts. Over the long term shares have earned much better returns than rival investments like bonds or deposits, and total equity returns are well ahead of inflation. Even the traumatic crash of 1987 pales in the longer-term progress of the market.

Investors who are reckless and time their deals badly can lose money, but with a sensible strategy and a long-term view, there is no real reason why investors should not do at least as well out of shares as they do out of pooled investments. Many funds perform badly, and there is no totally reliable way of picking a unit trust which will match the market, let alone beat it. If you buy shares directly you avoid the problem of picking a good fund manager and having to pay his charges. Even small investors may prefer to put the bulk of their funds in an index tracking fund and use individual equities to try to get above average growth.

When it comes to buying shares private investors do have some advantages: they can be far more flexible than professionals, and only have to invest when they are convinced they will really make money. Professionals have very limited discretion to follow their own hunches, and normally have to keep most of their funds in the stockmarket even if they think it is going down. A fund manager reckons he is doing well if the market falls by 10 per cent and his portfolio only falls by 5 per cent! The private investor doesn't have to conform to such Alice in Wonderland logic.

Many small investors also find it more fun to pick their own shares, and enjoy pitting their wits against the professionals. But if you can't imagine getting that kind of a kick from a share portfolio, direct investment is probably not for you.

What's on offer?

There are over 2,000 shares quoted on the London market, and they are pigeon-holed by investors in different ways. Some categories describe the company and its business, others its stockmarket characteristics or what investors expect from its profits or share price in the future. The simplest division is into large and small; big companies are known as **blue chips** and tend to be relatively safe but stodgy – they rarely go bust* and it is easy to trade in their shares. One hundred of the largest are included in an index called the FT-SE 100, which is used as a barometer of the whole stockmarket. These companies cover a whole range of different activities: all that they have in common is that they are large, so their shares do not all move together. In a year when FT-SE rose by a third, one share might double whilst another fell by a fifth.

Another obvious way of grouping companies is by what they do – if you look at a newspaper you will find Sainsbury grouped with other food retailers, some of which are much smaller. The logic of these **sectors** is that companies in the same business share some of the same characteristics and will be affected by some of the same events. This is particularly true of sectors like banks and property (where each company's business is very similar) but less true of a sector like conglomerates (where the only thing companies have in common is that they are made up of different businesses!)

The biggest companies in any sector are grouped into indexes. There are 35 different FT-Actuaries sector

* Polly Peck and British & Commonwealth were 1990's two spectacular exceptions to this rule. For more information see chapter 20.

indexes which are used to measure the relative performance of each group of shares, so investors can check whether retailers are doing better than oil and gas shares, and how both are doing relative to the market. the yardstick for the market as a whole is the FT-A All Share index which covers the 800-odd largest quoted British companies. Relatively new is the FT-SE mid 250 index, which covers the 250 companies immediately below the FT-SE 100. The two together comprise the FT-SE A 350 index. Indexes are also helpful for weighing up the performance of individual companies against the market or the sector to which they belong, and this can be a useful aid to deciding whether a share is worth buying.

Valuing shares

Investors apply two main yardsticks to shares. They measure the income they expect to get by the **dividend yield**. Companies normally pay dividends twice a year and the half-time 'interim' dividend is normally lower than the 'final'. Yields are calculated on the total payout before income tax, and tell you what rate of income the share will produce at its current market price, which then enables investors to compare it with other shares, or even other forms of investment. The second measure used is the **price/earnings ratio** which tells investors how highly a share is priced relative to its earning power. Put crudely, it divides the company's market capitalization by its earnings, and so tells investors how many times they would have to multiply the company's profits to equal the market value of the company. As a result, the PE ratio is sometimes known as the **earnings multiple**. If the earnings ratio is higher than average, it usually suggests that the company is expected to produce above average earnings growth. If the share price of a company falls, the PE ratio will fall, and the dividend yield rise as investors lower their expectations for the company. A third measure used for companies is the **Net Asset Value**, and this is normally applied to some specialist companies like investment trusts, property companies or ordinary com-

panies which are likely to be taken over (see chapter 19)
or in some danger of going bust (see chapter 20).

Investors compare a company's yield and PE ratio with
those of the relevant sector index to see how the company
is rated relative to its peers. If it has a higher PE ratio than
a similar company, there needs to be a good reason. Say
for example Tesco has a yield of 4.4 per cent and a PE
ratio of 9.3, when the food retailing sector as a whole
offers 3.9 per cent and 13 respectively, whilst Sainsbury
yields 2.8 per cent and has a PE ratio of 15.5. This suggests that investors expect Tesco's profits to rise relatively slowly, and Sainsbury's relatively fast, but does not
say whether they are right. This is important because
many new investors think that yields or PE ratios in
themselves are signs that a share is good or bad value –
they aren't. *Shares are good or bad value when their
rating is inappropriate to their prospects.*

Buying shares

Many individual investors first buy shares through new
issues – and in particular millions have caught the share
buying habit through the government's privatization programme (see chapter 17). Buying a new issue is easy
because it involves getting a form and sending off a
cheque, but it is not the way that shares are bought
normally. If you want to buy shares in a company which
is already quoted on the stockmarket, you normally do so
through a stockbroker or a bank (see Appendix C), which
will charge you for the service.

Say you want to buy 1,000 Marks & Spencer shares.
Most daily newspapers divide share prices into sectors,
and you'll find the firm under one of the obvious labels
like retailing. If it shows a price of say 330p, that does not
mean that is precisely what you will pay for the shares.
First the newspaper will have yesterday's closing price;
the shares may be higher or lower today. Second it is the
mid-price, which means it ignores the spread between
buying and selling prices which gives the trader his
profit. This spread is around 1.5 per cent for large

companies and substantially more for smaller ones. The *Investors Chronicle* quotes the 'touch', ie the best buying and selling prices, as well as the mid price. So in this case if M&S shares had not moved overnight, the price might today be quoted as 328p bid – 333p offered by a market maker, and if you wanted to buy you would have to pay 333p. On top of that you will be charged broker's commission and stamp duty. Spreads and dealing costs mean that all told even a large share like M&S will probably have to move by 6-7 per cent for you to show a profit if you sell.

If you deal with your broker – normally done by phone – you should receive a contract note a few days later confirming the details and the charges you will have to pay. Currently the Stock Exchange operates a system of two (and sometimes three) week **accounts**. Any deals

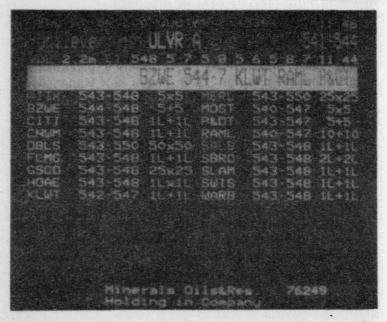

Fig 10.1 An example of a Stock Exchange quotation screen. This shows 18 different market makers quoting bid and offer prices for shares in Unilever at 11.46 one morning. So far that day 2.2m shares had changed hands, and the white strip shows the 'touch' with the best bid 544p and lowest offer 547p. (Source: Stock Exchange.)

done within an account are totalled and set against each other. Six working days after the end of the account, on **settlement day**, you pay up. The share certificate is sent to you separately by the company's registrars – normally one of the clearing banks.

The Stock Exchange's attempt to replace this cumbersome process with an electronic system called **Taurus** was a costly fiasco. The (optional) replacement plan, known as **Crest**, will gradually introduce a rolling settlement system and then an electronic system. Most people will eventually have to settle deals after five days – tough on speculators who trade inside the account period. It would also push private investors into 'nominee accounts', making it difficult to exercise some shareholder rights. Anyone determined to stick to share certificates and an extended account period will probably have to pay through the nose for the privilege.

If you want to deal in the shares of small companies there may be some added difficulties. Your newspaper may not even list the shares and when your broker gets you a price it may be a lot higher or lower than you expect. The spread between the buying and selling price is also likely to be much wider than for a blue chip like M&S; it may even prove almost impossible to deal. And if the reason you're interested is that you've seen a newspaper tip for the shares, you'll undoubtedly find that they will have shot up by the time you get on the phone.

This isn't quite as sinister as it sounds – some small companies shares rarely trade, so a lot of unusual demand can send the system haywire. But a lack of **marketability** sometimes means that the trading in one company's shares is effectively run by one man, which isn't particularly healthy. If you're thinking about buying smaller company shares, it's worth asking your broker about their marketability. In general these shares have to be held for the long-term if you want to get a decent return.

How to choose shares

Before jumping in at the deep end, you should decide what sort of investor you are. Use chapter 7 to analyse whether growth, income or a mix of the two are right for you. You should also decide how actively you want to be involved – are you going to be a regular trader or do you want a portfolio which doesn't require much attention? And bear in mind your personality – are you someone who doesn't want to take many risks, or can't afford to take losses – or are you prepared to accept higher risks for the possibility of higher returns?

Broadly, if you are an income investor, or risk-averse, or want something which doesn't need too much care and maintenance, then a solid portfolio of blue chip shares is probably what you are looking for. The exact constituents will depend on your investment views and the balance you want to strike between income and growth.

But if you are younger and looking for higher growth, or are prepared to take greater risks, or even using shares to beef up a portfolio which contains some solid unit trusts, then you may want to look at riskier smaller shares, or companies which have fallen on hard times, but may yet recover.

Once you have decided whether you want relatively 'safe' shares or are looking for high-growth companies, how do you pick them? Because growth and even blue chip shares move in and out of fashion, you will need to keep in touch with the market through the financial press. An idea for a share purchase can come from many sources – a tip in the press, a good set of company results reported in the news, a personal recommendation from a friend, or even an idea that x or y business is likely to boom under current circumstances – or prove a safe haven in troubled times.

If possible you should try to develop a systematic way of looking for shares. That's easier when you are looking for a stable blue chip than it is in high-growth stocks which come from many different areas. In searching for growth candidates, some people look out for shares on unusually high yields, or ones which stand at a discount to net assets, or even shares which have fallen by 50 per cent in value over the previous year. They then reject those which are pretty obviously going broke, and trawl for a pearl amongst the rest. Other people look at the economy and try to decide which business areas are going to benefit from current trends, and look for companies likely to exploit the opportunity. Many different techniques are used, and the only thing that they have in common is that they don't always work!

Once you have lighted on a possible candidate for your portfolio, evaluating whether it is right for you involves three distinct but related operations:

- You need to check that a share you are thinking of buying has the characteristics you want. How large is the company? How does the share tend to behave compared to the stockmarket as a whole? Is it a business which ought to be doing well at the moment? What is its recent profit record and balance sheet like, and how is it likely to be affected by currency and interest rate movements? (See chapter 14.)
- You also need to use the yield and PE ratio to check whether the share looks cheap or expensive when compared to others. Is the share more or less expensive than its peers, and how does the whole sector stand relative to the market? If the company and the sector have both moved up sharply in recent times, the best of the rise may be past. Once you have done that, you need to decide whether the market's assessment is fair – or whether the share is over-valued or under-valued.
- You must also decide whether this looks like a good time to buy the share. Briefly, this involves considering whether the market as a whole is likely to rise or fall and whether the share you are considering is likely to do well when compared with the market. This **relative performance** will depend quite a bit on current investment fashions. For example, if smaller companies or retailing shares are just coming back into fashion, they are probably going to do a lot better than the market for some months. Conversely, there is no point in buying a share simply because you think it's

VITAL STATISTICS OF THE FT-SE 100 COMPANIES

Company name	Business	Share price (p)	Market value (£m)	PE Ratio	Dividend yield %	Price change % over 1 year	Price change % over 5 years
Abbey National	Bank	414	5,428	16	3.5	+44	n/a
Allied-Lyons	Breweries	537	4,736	14	4.9	−15	+25
Anglian Water	Water	490	1,450	12	5.4	+20	n/a
Argyll	Food	310	3,473	12	4.4	−14	+75
Arjo Wiggins Appleton	Paper	168	1,362	13	4.8	−27	n/a
Asda	Food	62	1,812	16	3.2	+135	−48
Associated British Foods	Food	470	2,107	12	3.7	+11	+60
BAA	Transport	717	3,650	18	2.8	+8	+159
Bank of Scotland	Bank	154½	1,792	32	3.7	+43	+101
Barclays Bank	Bank	481	7,763		3.9	+52	+60
Bass	Breweries	460	3,993	10	5.1	−16	+18
BAT Industries	Tobaccos	416	12,795	24	5.6	+7	+126
Blue Circle Industries	Cement	242	1,672	50	5.8	+15	+10
BOC	Chemicals	654	3,107	13	4.4	+1	+56
Boots	Retailing	422	4,376	16	4.0	0	+88
Bowater	Paper	453	2,256	20	3.6	+21	+146
British Aerospace	Aerospace	427.	1,614	39	2.1	+69	−8
British Petroleum	Oil	299	16,239	21	3.5	+44	+15
British Airways	Airline	304	2,818	21	4.4	+14	+111
British Gas	Gas	291	12,580	15	6.1	+16	+58
British Steel	Steel	96½	1,930		1.3	+64	n/a
British Telecom	Telecoms	410½	25,467	19	4.8	+16	+61
BTR	Conglomerate	361	12,187	18	3.7	+37	+121
Burmah Castrol	Oil	713	1,348	16	4.4	+26	+32
Cable and Wireless	Telecoms	763	8,286	21	2.4	+41	+109
Cadbury Schweppes	Food	448	3,338	17	3.7	−7	+13
Carlton Communications	Broadcasting	762	1,516	24	2.9	+24	+4
Coats Viyella	Textiles	230	1,398	23	3.9	+22	−6
Commercial Union	Insurance	615	3,303	12	5.0	+39	+69
Courtaulds	Chemicals	526	2,109	17	3.3	+6	+87
De La Rue	Printing	642	1,229	18	3.3	+15	+51
Enterprise Oil	Oil	447	2,136	33	4.5	+21	+2
Forte	Hotels	221½	1,876	86	4.2	+32	−14
General Accident	Insurance	622	2,805		5.4	+51	+36
General Electric	Electricals	315½	8,610	14	4.1	+41	+95
Glaxo	Health	556	16,852	15	4.1	−19	+122
Granada	Leisure	410	1,919	19	2.4	+65	+38
Grand Metropolitan	Breweries	415	8,578	15	3.8	−11	+69
Great Universal Stores 'A'	Retailing	1,753	4,330	14	2.9	+25	+72
Guardian Royal Exchange	Insurance	202	1,751		4.3	+50	+8
Guinness	Breweries	467	9,359	15	3.1	−17	+173
Hanson	Conglomerate	237	11,449	15	6.0	+14	+67
HSBC	Bank	659	5,404	13	3.6	+92	n/a
ICI	Chemicals	645	4,650	25	5.3	+15	+21
Inchcape	Distribution	542	2,840	18	3.1	+20	+156
Kingfisher	Retailing	585	3,773	20	2.9	+34	+111
Ladbroke	Leisure	186	2,122	19	7.5	−7	−10
Land Securities	Property	586	2,959	18	4.9	+49	+3
Legal & General	Insurance	500	2,440	27	4.8	+45	+55
Lloyds Bank	Bank	568	7,259	14	4.1	+31	+184

Company name	Business	Share price (p)	Market value (£m)	PE Ratio	Dividend yield %	Price change % over 1 year	Price change % over 5 years
Marks and Spencer	Retailing	334	9,228	19	3.0	+12	+91
MB-Caradon	Conglomerate	280	1,285	18	3.9	+18	+73
National Westminster	Bank	492	8,123	22	4.5	+45	+68
National Power	Electricity	358	4,571	12	3.7	+44	n/a
NFC	Transport	244	1,352	14	3.3	−2	n/a
North West Water	Water	478	1,711	8	5.6	+13	n/a
Northern Foods	Food	255	1,459	14	4.1	−17	+74
Pearson	Publishing	460	2,516	26	3.3	+31	+28
P&O	Transport	620	3,484	26	6.2	+60	+15
PowerGen	Electric	381	2,983	10	3.4	+47	n/a
Prudential	Insurance	339	6,383	23	4.4	+35	+99
Rank Organisation	Leisure	759	2,345	19	5.1	+26	+7
Reckitt & Colman	Household	571	2,136	15	3.6	−7	+51
Redland	Building	469	2,364	21	6.7	−1	+16
Reed International	Publishing	665	3,724	23	3.2	+27	+61
Rentokil	Agencies	198	1,927	25	1.5	+21	+390
Reuters	Publishing	1,400	6,146	23	1.9	+20	+150
RMC	Cement	750	1,470	28	3.3	+40	+57
Rothmans International 'B'	Tobacco	662	4,014	10	2.2	+20	+221
Royal Bank of Scotland	Bank	287	2,273	36	3.9	+56	+101
Royal Insurance	Insurance	319	2,069		2.0	+64	−21
RTZ Corporation	Mining	680	7,024	22	3.6	+24	+61
Sainsbury (J)	Food	436	7,743	16	2.9	−4	+96
Scottish & Newcastle	Breweries	462	1,945	15	4.6	+4	+44
Scottish Hydro-Electric	Electricity	339½	1,301	13	4.2	+27	n/a
Scottish Power	Electricity	317	2,583	13	4.4	+25	n/a
Sears	Retailing	95½	1,440	25	4.6	+16	−27
Severn Trent	Water	478	1,706	9	5.5	+19	n/a
Shell Transport	Oil	616	20,417	17	4.4	+28	+76
Siebe	Engineering	483	1,873	19	2.6	+48	+149
Smith & Nephew	Health	142½	1,468	16	4.1	−1	+9
SmithKline Beecham 'A'	Health	424	5,791	17	2.7	−5	+118
Standard Chartered	Banks	804	1,914	28	3.1	+89	+78
Sun Alliance	Insurance	373	3,003		4.8	+40	+51
Tate & Lyle	Sugar	390	1,396	15	3.9	+7	+84
Tesco	Food	207	4,053	10	4.3	−18	+46
Thames Water	Water	490	1,911	11	5.4	+13	n/a
Thorn EMI	Leisure	906	3,705	16	4.4	+13	+49
TI Group	Engineering	340	1,578	19	3.9	+6	+101
Tomkins	Conglomerate	219	2,442	15	3.6	−5	+108
TSB	Bank	196	2,975	156	4.1	+36	+77
Unilever	Food	977	7,904	14	2.7	+4	+107
United Biscuits	Food	367	1,919	16	5.2	+5	+22
Vodafone	Telephone	439	4,416	20	2.0	+42	n/a
Warburg (SG)	Bank	734	1,578	18	3.2	+60	+129
Wellcome	Health	652	5,620	16	2.7	−26	+24
Whitbread 'A'	Breweries	479	2,165	16	4.6	+8	+61
Williams Holdings	Industrial	318	1,549	19	4.9	+14	+14
Wolseley	Building	612	1,524	21	2.7	+73	+123
Zeneca	Health	618	5,838	14	5.6	n/a	n/a

All information as at 14.7.93

Fig 10.2 The vital statistics of the FT-SE 100 companies in July 1993.

undervalued – it may keep on falling if no one else agrees with you. Some shares are cheap today – and cheaper tomorrow.*

Beating the pros

So how can a private investor hope to find a share that the massed guns of the investing institutions have missed, and how can his judgement be better than theirs? One important point to remember about blue chips is that small investors are most unlikely to ferret out some fact which the professional analysts have overlooked. Where you may score is by using your common sense to arrive at a blindingly obvious conclusion the analysts haven't recognized; sometimes the professionals can't see the wood for the trees. But academic research in America has shown that the better researched a company is, the more efficient the market. That means that small investors have a better chance of finding a winner amongst neglected smaller companies. The risks of small companies are higher, but so are the potential profits. Going against the fashion with your timing is another possibility – if you can spot a trend early you can do well.

Often companies which have a market capitalization of less than £100m are only researched by a few brokers, and fairly infrequently at that. So if you like rummaging around in company balance sheets or going to annual meetings, you may hit on a generally unknown reason for buying the shares. The trouble with this approach is that until the rest of the world finds out the interesting little fact you have discovered, the share price may not budge. So you may need considerable patience, which will only be justified if your discovery is likely to have a dramatic impact on the share price. High costs, wide spreads, poor marketability and a long pay-off period mean that

*Chart purists reckon that timing is the only one of the three priorities which really counts, and argue that the right way to spot the time to buy is to ignore all fundamental information about the company's business and relative value and concentrate on the share price pattern. Whether they are right is pretty hotly debated.

investors need to be really picky about the selection of smaller company shares.

The secret of comedy is timing

Timing is very important when buying shares too. For example, the FT-SE 100 index dropped steadily from 2,700 to 2,300 over the summer of 1992 as sterling struggled to stay inside the ERM. Once it had dropped out, in September, the index moved up equally rapidly to around 2,900 by February 1993. Anyone who sold in May and bought again in the autumn made a useful amount of money, particularly if he had the inspiration then to choose smaller companies – which did much better than blue chips over the period. Of course, hindsight is a wonderful thing, and it simply isn't possible to know exactly when a share or the market has bottomed, but keeping an eye on timing and assessing which shares are likely to do well at different times in the cycle of the market can help improve returns.

Getting the timing right matters more when buying smaller company shares than blue chips. Some sharp price movements in smaller companies' shares – both up and down – occur around the time of their results. If the results are thought likely to be good by the few people who follow the company, the price will probably move up beforehand, and continue to rise, or reverse sharply, depending on how close the results come to expectations. As we said previously, less marketable shares tend to be more volatile, so if you are really interested in a small company it may well make sense to buy their shares in the fallow season.

There are two circumstances when it almost certainly doesn't make sense to buy shares – one is when the price is in free fall, and the other is when a newspaper or tipsheet has recommended them.

- Never catch a falling knife – don't buy shares just because they are cheaper than they were yesterday;

they may well have even further to fall. Spotting the precise turning point, if there is one, is an impossible hope; and sometimes when a share hurtles earthwards, it just keeps going. Remember that if a share is going down it is because somebody is selling it; perhaps he knows something you don't.

- If a newspaper or tipsheet recommends a share in a small company, it's almost certainly too late to buy – even if it was a good idea in the first place, because plenty of others will have got there first, and the market makers read the papers too. What some investors do is hang on to a recommendation and wait for the hullabaloo surrounding the press comment to die down before buying.

How long should you keep shares?

It's a useful discipline to consider how long you intend to hold a share *before* you buy, because that will help you decide whether your investment decision is realistic. If you are intending to invest in a small company for a long period, you should be aiming for substantial capital gains; if you are looking at a blue chip for a shorter time, you can aim to take smaller profits and still make money after expenses. Warren Buffett – a very successful American investor – reckons to hold his shares 'for ever', but he is equally famous for selecting them very carefully and sparingly in the first place.

In general it makes sense to churn your portfolio as little as possible, as this minimizes expenses and stops you changing your mind about an investment every five minutes. But that is *not* an excuse for hanging on to every bad share you ever bought in the hope that it will eventually come right. Admitting you made a wrong decision can be one of the hardest parts of investment, but the sooner you turf out a real dud, the better.

It's also hard to decide when to sell a good share, and whether you ever do so depends on your overall strategy. If you are a genuinely long-term investor, you won't sell a share just because it's a little bit overpriced. But if you bought it purely as a short-term play because it was undervalued and it has reached your target, then you should sell unless you have a new reason for continuing to hold the share. Before you sell a good share from your portfolio you should also have an eye to what might replace it. If there is no obvious alternative, and you want to remain a long-term equity investor, you may not be doing the right thing by selling a winner just because it's had a decent run. The best strategy for shares in the conglomerate Hanson over the past twenty years was to buy the shares and lock them away, though they have marked time in the last two years.

Following the gurus

It is no accident that most good investment books are American. The Americans have never been ashamed to take money-making seriously, and several individual Americans have become very rich by developing idiosyncratic investment strategies.

One of the best books about the great modern American investors* seems to find it easier to summarize their pet hates than their winning formulae. Investment 'dont's' include: avoid popular stocks, fad industries, new ventures, 'official' growth stocks, heavy 'blue chips' and gimmicks. Sensibly pointing out that some winning techniques can be lethal in amateur hands, it ends up recommending a handful of commonsense strategies:

- Only buy a stock or a share in a good business that you know a lot about.
- Buy when stocks have few friends, particularly the stock in question.
- Be patient; don't be rattled by fluctuations.
- Invest, don't guess.
- High yields are often a trap.
- Only buy what's cheap right now, or almost sure to grow so fast that it very soon will have been cheap at today's price.
- If stocks in general don't seem cheap, stand aside.

* 'The Money Masters' by John Train. See bibliography.

- Keep an eye on what the masters are doing.
- Buy investment management if you find investing too difficult.
- Decide on an appropriate investment strategy and concentrate on it.
- Be flexible.

The only thing the book does not tell you is how many lesser Americans have grown rich by reading about the great investors and emulating their strategies. Painting by numbers may curb your wilder excesses – but it's unlikely to produce a Picasso.

Investment aids

Another very successful fund manager, Sir John Templeton, operates from the Bahamas because he doesn't like to get involved in the day to day frenzy of the markets. But most investors are not like that, they want to keep in touch as closely as possible. Professionals have all sorts of analysis and information systems to keep them up to date, so how can the small investor keep up?

Unfortunately, the basic answer is that even to get a second-rate set of investment tools costs a small fortune. Subscription to one of the screen-based systems which offer instantaneous updates runs into thousands of pounds a year, and most private investors simply couldn't justify the cost. But a lot can be done by reading the press intelligently. For enthusiasts, a daily *Financial Times* gives a comprehensive share price service, reports most company news briefly and comments on a small proportion of it. *Investors Chronicle* provides weekly comprehensive advice on larger companies and selected coverage on smaller ones, with useful five year statistical records. It also gives views on the stockmarket and business background. Other newspapers and Ceefax or Oracle on television also provide some City and company news and comment.

If you want more background detail on individual companies Extel and McCarthy services are thorough but pricey. Happily some major public libraries do keep them.

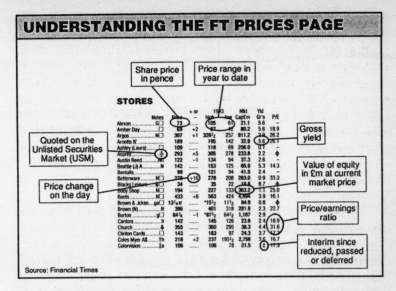

Fig 10.3 A breakdown of the information to be gleaned from the *Financial Times* prices page between Tuesday and Saturday. On Monday the paper publishes slightly different information. A full list of symbols appears at the bottom of the prices page.

Telephone share price services are efficient but expensive. One source which many people turn to for information is of very dubious merit. Many tip sheets have chequered track records and are an expensive way of buying not very good ideas. Most investors would get better value from a wide range of newspapers and ordinary magazines.

Many private investors rely on personal computers to do their backroom chores and draw charts. But that is often because they are enthusiastic about PCs. Most professional investors are not very impressed by even the most sophisticated of the software packages currently available.

Private versus professional

The two biggest handicaps which small investors have to

bear are high costs and a paucity of information. Usually companies tell stockbrokers and the investing institutions far more about their business than any small investor is likely to learn.

In the circumstances it is ironic that the Takeover Panel goes to such lengths to see that all shareholders are treated equally during bid battles (see chapter 19), when in everyday life small shareholders are so disadvantaged. They have virtually no hope of getting a good allocation in a new issue (chapter 17) and the cumbersome charade of rights issues (chapter 18) often involves them in unwanted costs or even tax liabilities.

Yet in some ways the private investor does have the edge. For a start he does *not* have to produce quarterly figures showing his relative performance, as fund managers do. Nor does he have to remain in the market when he would sooner be out. He can buy shares because he genuinely likes their investment prospects, not because he fears being left behind by the market. And he can buy into all but the smallest companies without moving the market price to his disadvantage. Some private investors have been known to sell the lot and go round the world for a year. That freedom may only be the freedom to make mistakes, but it has to be more interesting than joining the fund managers inside the tramlines.

Shares

IN A NUTSHELL

1. Buying individual shares rather than unit or investment trusts may give better performance, if you pick the right shares, and avoids the complication of picking a good fund manager. It is also more interesting.

2. Investors classify shares in different ways. Some describe what a company does or how big it is. Others help evaluate profit growth potential or stockmarket characteristics. Many of the largest shares are grouped into indexes or sub-indexes.

3. Investors use the standard yardsticks of yields and price earnings ratios to compare one share with another. These measures only represent the market's view of a company's value.

4. Unless investors are buying shares in a new issue, such as a privatization, they will probably buy through a stockbroker or bank. Charges and bid-offer spreads mean that even the largest companies have to rise by 6 to 7 per cent for an investor to show a profit and more for smaller, less marketable shares.

5. Selecting shares is an art not a science, but investors can develop methods for identifying which shares to buy. When a potential share is found investors must consider suitability, relative value and timing.

6. Picking the right time to buy and sell shares is important – particularly with small companies. Investors should not churn their portfolios, but should dispose of duds quickly. Think hard before selling a good share.

7. Deciding how long you intend to hold a share before you buy helps clarify your investment objectives. Small companies have to be bought with a longer-term view and higher profit objectives than blue chips.

8. Private investors do not have as much information as professionals, but the press and television are useful. Some further information is available in libraries. Tipsheets and telephone share services are expensive.

9. The individual shareholder's great advantage is his flexibility. He does not have to follow fashion like a fund manager. That offers opportunity and makes investing interesting.

Chapter 11
PEPs and TESSAs

The government has been trying hard in recent years to encourage individuals to save and invest. Another of its objectives has been to reverse the steady fall in individual share ownership. No wonder, then, that many of its schemes, enabling people to invest without paying tax, were designed both to stimulate savings and to push them towards the company sector.

The **Business Expansion Scheme** or **BES**, expiring at the end of 1993, was used to promote investment in young companies.* **Personal Equity Plans** or **PEPs** are designed to tempt people into shares and pooled investments. **Tax Exempt Special Savings Accounts** or **TESSAs** are there to boost ordinary savings. Depending on your tax position and the type of investment you are looking for, it could make sense to invest in either of PEPs or TESSAs.

But keep a few points firmly in mind. First, it never makes sense to invest purely in order to save tax; you need to check out the attractions of the underlying investment too. Secondly, most tax savings schemes are of most use to people who would otherwise pay high taxes; if you don't pay much tax, and charges are high, you may not benefit. Thirdly, most tax savings schemes involve locking your money up for a relatively long period; don't go into a scheme which penalizes early withdrawal, if you are likely to have to pull out.

*****RIP BES.** The life of the Business Expansion Scheme was nasty, brutish and long. Intended to encourage investment in fledgling companies, it was regarded as a prime tax-dodge scheme for the rich throughout its existence. Every time the revenue blocked one loophole, ingenious financial experts found another. It will be greatly mourned by many of the financial advisers who survive it.

Personal Equity Plans

PEPs got off to a slow start when they were introduced by
Nigel Lawson in his 1986 Budget. But they have subsequently become much more popular. Their belated success stems from two interconnected changes. First, the
government has steadily altered the rules to make PEPs a
more useful tool for the investor. Secondly, the mass
savings media have started marketing PEPs aggressively,
because unit and investment trusts can now play a full
part on the PEP scene. So what are the rules on PEPs now,
and how do they work?

Investors can now put up to £6,000 each tax year into a
general PEP and a further £3,000 a year into a PEP investing in a single company. The general PEPs can be
invested in shares, unit trusts or investment trusts, or any
mixture of the three. The main rules are fairly straightforward, though there are additional rules for both
general and single company PEPs.

The basic ground rules are:

- PEPs are available to anyone aged 18 or over.
- Each individual can invest up to £9,000 a year in PEPs,
  £6,000 in a general PEP and £3,000 in a single company PEP. So married couples can invest up to £18,000
  a year.
- Investors can take out only one general PEP and one
  single company PEP each year. But once you have put
  money into a PEP you can keep it there free of tax for as
  long as you like – and take out new PEPs the next year.
- PEPs are not liable for income tax on dividends or
  capital gains tax on capital gains. Income can either be
  paid out or reinvested.
- You cannot normally transfer shares you already own
  directly into a PEP. You have to sell them and buy
  them back for the PEP, which may result in a tax liability (if the sale produces a capital gain). You can,
  however, transfer new issues (including privatization
  issues) into either type of PEP within 42 days of the
  launch.
- If you withdraw some or all of your money from any

PEP, you can't put it back later.

- PEPs have to be run by an approved manager.

Additional rules for general PEPs are:

- A general PEP can be invested in UK and European Community shares, or authorized unit and investment trusts. It can be in just one of these varieties of investment or in a mixture. But you need to be careful which trusts you pick or the PEP may lose its tax exemption.
- If you want to put more than £1,500 in an individual trust, it needs to be what the Inland Revenue considers to be a 'qualifying trust'. This means that the trust has at least 50 per cent of its portfolio in UK or EC shares.
- If you opt for a 'non-qualifying' trust, you cannot invest more than £1,500 and the whole of the rest of the PEP has then to go directly into UK and EC shares. But even a non-qualifying trust has to satisfy certain criteria to win any place in a PEP: it has to have at least 50 per cent of its portfolio in shares – though they don't need to be UK or EC shares. So trusts with a heavy weighting in gilt-edged stocks, for instance, won't pass muster.
- You can keep cash in your general PEP for as long as you choose, provided you intend eventually to put it into qualifying investments. So if you sell one of the shares or trusts in your PEP, you can keep the proceeds in cash within the plan until you actually want to buy another one.

Additional rules for single company PEPs* are:

- A single company PEP has to be wholly invested in the

---

*Corporate PEPs, frequently and understandably confused with single company PEPs, are not a distinct breed in the eyes of the Revenue. They are general or single company PEPs, sponsored by an individual company, normally with the aim of encouraging investment in its own shares by employees and other investors. They usually have very low charges, but can be abnormally restrictive in that the money may often only be invested in the shares of the sponsoring company. Not usually a good idea, unless you positively want a major investment in the sponsor.

shares of one particular company at any one time. It
can be switched from one company to another as often
as you choose, but any cash has to be invested within
42 days.
- You can transfer shares from an approved company
profit-sharing or savings-related scheme directly into a
single company PEP – provided you do so within 90
days.

Pros and cons

All of this sounds quite good – after all, why pay tax
when you don't have to? The problem is that PEPs have to
run by a manager, so that charges can eat up a fair amount
of tax-free benefit, particularly if you are a low taxpayer.
PEPs make most sense for those who have substantial
investments and have to pay CGT, because they will
benefit most from the tax breaks. And since £9,000 can be
invested every year, those with large investments have
the added advantage of being able progressively to build
up their portfolios in a tax-free home.

But even if you don't currently pay CGT it may be
worth considering a PEP if you think you are likely to
have larger investments in future years. Because if you
don't take out a PEP in a particular year, you lose that
allowance for ever. So even those with modest investments, who anticipate saving and investing more in subsequent years, may want to shelter their investments to
avoid future problems with CGT. If you invest £9,000 a
year in shares, it will not be too long before you have to
start worrying about capital gains tax! For such investors
the immediate benefits of investing through PEPs may be
small, but the longer-term gains may be worthwhile.

Another plus for PEPs is that they are quite flexible
ways to invest. Some PEP schemes allow people to make
monthly contributions, others allow cheap switching between investments. Investors can also get at the money in
their PEP quite easily if they need to. However, if you
withdraw money from your PEP you will both lose the tax
advantage and have paid charges on the investment. Add

to that the fact that the money is in UK or EC shares or pooled investments mostly in the UK, and that these can be quite volatile, and it is clear that investors should regard PEPs as long-term investments.

One other difficulty with PEPs is comparing performance between different schemes. In many ways this is similar to the problem of deciding between different unit trusts (see Chapter 9) but is even more of a headache, because there is no common benchmark against which to measure all PEPs. Plans differ so much that it is almost impossible to compare the majority of them in any meaningful way.

How to choose a PEP

Multiplicity is the curse of the saving classes. There are now over 700 different types of PEP on the market, and forests of newsprint devoted to the subject. To avoid getting lost in the undergrowth, keep a few fundamental points in mind.

The first distinction to make between PEPs is to separate **general PEPs** from **single company PEPs**. Most people are best suited by a general PEP. When selecting one investors should look at much the same criteria as in other financial planning. PEPs are part of an equity portfolio, not cash or fixed interest holdings and as such they are long-term investments. As with other investments you must decide whether you are aiming for income or growth, and take account of how the PEP fits into the other equity investments you hold. You must also consider whether you want to choose the investments in the PEP yourself, or have them chosen by the plan manager, and whether you are interested in individual shares, pooled investments or both. The level of charges levied by the plan manager is also worth bearing in mind, though the plan with the lowest charge is not automatically the best. Charges vary quite a bit between different PEPs, so it is important not to pay for features of a PEP which you are not going to use. It is also worth keeping an eye out for penalty clauses.

If you have a large portfolio of shares and unit trusts, it probably makes most sense to use a PEP to invest in individual equities, because you already have a decent spread of risk. In that case (and if you are also interested in managing your investments yourself) you may well want to choose your own shares for the PEP to complement the shares you already own. If, however, you only hold a small amount of pooled investments, you may well prefer to use the PEP to buy some more unit or investment trusts or a mixture of unit trusts, investment trusts and blue chip shares. Novices and very small investors, or those who are not very interested in managing a portfolio, may also prefer to use a plan where the manager selects the investments, or one based on a good general unit or investment trust or indexed fund.

Some self-select plans still have restrictions on the number of shares or units that can be held in a PEP, and some do not allow investors freedom to switch between shares – others charge for doing so. On the other hand the performance of PEPs selected by the managers is very difficult to assess; many have only short track records and have very little in common, making comparisons difficult.

The 1992 Budget, allowing general PEPs to be fully invested in unit or investment trusts, has allowed fund measurement services, such as Micropal or Finstat, to compare the performance of PEPs based on these trusts with each other. But it remains impossible to make comparisons across the full range of managed PEPs.

The other major distinction is between growth and income. For income investors shares still offer relatively low yields, but do offer the income investor some long-term protection against inflation, and PEPs help boost the yield because the payout is tax free. Several PEP managers have produced plans designed to produce an unusually high income – though capital growth may suffer.

PEPs are available which pay income quarterly or even monthly and self-select PEPs can be constructed which pay out at the appropriate intervals. However, investors should not be entirely swayed by the initial yield of a managed plan, nor should they select shares or unit trusts simply because they pay out at the right time. It is important to get an investment which is likely to grow, and then consider when it pays dividends rather than the other way round. Also bear in mind that the investment offering the highest yield today may not be the one which is worth most next year.

Growth investors face the usual imponderable about selecting those investments which are likely to rise in value. Those going it alone can at least determine their own destiny. It is not yet clear that plan managers have been any more successful than unit trust managers at picking growth winners.

Once you have decided whether you are interested in growth or income, a self-select or a managed plan, shares, trusts or a mixture, you will have a pretty good idea of the type of PEP you want. You can then choose between those which meet your criteria, bearing in mind the pedigree, past performance and charges of the plan manager. A useful aid at this stage for selecting the right PEP is the **Chase de Vere PEP Guide**, which tabulates the main features of plans currently available, both alphabetically and by PEP type.

Single company PEPs

Like other types of PEP, single company PEPs seem to have become successful only when put to a use other than the one for which they were first intended. The original idea was to increase enthusiasm for employee share schemes by providing an additional tax haven for the shares once they left their original one. But single company PEPs have in practice been more popular among ordinary investors who have already filled up their £6,000 general PEP and want to put another £3,000 into a single company PEP.

A single company PEP enjoys exactly the same tax advantages as a general PEP but has slightly different operating restrictions (see page 197). Most obviously, they can only be invested in one share at a time. But you can switch shares as often as you choose, and, like general PEPs, can be either managed or self-select. Some plan managers limit your choice of shares.

These PEPs have one advantage over general PEPs and one disadvantage. The advantage is that if you want to transfer shares from an approved company profit-sharing scheme or savings-related scheme directly into a PEP, you have to put them into a single company PEP. If you put them into a general PEP, you have to sell them and put the proceeds into your PEP – and then buy them back. This will inevitably involve dealing charges.

The disadvantage is that any cash in a single company PEP has to be invested within 42 days – whereas general PEPs have no such time limit. This can be inhibiting if you don't like the market or are uncertain which share to buy. One way of coping with this restriction is to avoid opening a single company PEP until you have decided to buy a particular share. But that still doesn't address the problem of what to do if you've sold your original share and don't want to buy another within the stipulated grace period. So it's probably sensible to put shares you may need to sell in your general PEP and select the safest long-term holdings for your single company PEP.

You can take out a single company PEP with a different plan manager from the one running your general PEP. Some managers encourage client loyalty by offering reduced charges on single company PEPs to customers who already have a general PEP with them. But some will only open a single company PEP for you if your general PEP is already full – ie has got £6,000 in it.

The fact that single company PEPs are more popular with investors who already have extensive portfolios may go against their creators' intentions, but it makes good investment sense. One of the basic rules of financial planning is to spread your risks. Owning only one share is the antithesis of risk-spreading.

Choices and charges

The big fund managers' battle for the hearts and wallets of PEP investors has both increased choice and produced a

more complicated but generally cheaper charging structure. The discriminating investor can benefit from both
changes. PEPs have become as much the object of 'flavour
of the month' marketing as pooled funds have always
been. For example, the fall in interest rates during 1992–3
drove savers out of bank and building society deposits. It
also gave stockmarket-based investments in general and
income PEPs in particular obvious appeal. Several PEPs
were launched with a specific high yield either targeted
or guaranteed. Some ingeniously wrapped a PEP round
some other savings product, such as an annuity or the
income shares of split-level investment trusts, or dabbled
in options. The snag is that unusually high income inevitably comes at the expense of capital growth and security.

Also aimed at the building society refugee are PEPs
which guarantee return of capital – though the guarantees
normally only apply to investors who have hung on to
their PEPs for a set period.

Less ingenious but more appealing to many middle of
the road investors are PEPs based on **tracker** or **indexed**
funds (see page 164) which are designed to follow some
particular stockmarket index, such as the FT-SE 100
share index. These PEPs are self-evidently incapable of
'beating the market' as defined by whatever index they
track. But since the majority of unit trusts do worse than
the market, settling for a PEP based on an indexed fund
could be more profitable than trying to choose a winning
fund management group. And they have lower charges
than most other PEPs.

There are only two types of PEP which it is sensible to
select mainly on the basis of costs: a self-select PEP and
one based on an indexed fund. If you are buying a managing fund, its investment performance matters more. But
that's not to say that any investor should ignore charges.
If you are investing mainly to enhance your income, a
high-charging fund may cancel out all the income tax you
save, particularly if you are a low taxpayer. But even if
you are investing mainly for capital growth, unusually
high charges will at the least handicap your fund
managers, particularly if they are levied early on in the
life of your PEP.

Generally, the increase in competition has cut charges. For example, many PEPs, particularly self-select PEPs, do not make any initial charge. But there are plenty of other fees and charges to watch out for: an annual PEP charge, a dividend collection fee, exit and withdrawal charges, a dealing fee for share purchases and sales, a charge if you want to attend annual general meetings. And if the PEP is invested in unit trusts, there are the trust's bid/offer spread and its own initial charge and management charge to consider.

Sorting out which schemes operate which charges sounds mind-boggling. But here again the PEP Guide does the hard work for you. You can trawl through its comprehensive lists searching for a PEP offering your chosen mix of investments, with a good performance record and charges appropriate to your expected investment strategy.

PEP mortgages and pension planning

Endowments have long been used to help repay mortgages. With an endowment loan, the borrower pays interest on the mortgage to the bank or building society and takes out an endowment policy (normally for a period of 25 years). This acts as a savings plan and life cover, so that at the end of the 25 years, the endowment has built up a large enough sum to pay off the mortgage. Recently people have started using PEPs to replace the endowment policy. As with endowments, the PEP is intended to build up a capital sum which will repay the mortgage. However, not all lenders will accept PEPs as a way to repay mortgages, since they have a much shorter track record than endowments, and the value of PEPs is likely to be more volatile than that of endowments. In some ways this is like the difference between 'with profits' and 'unit-linked' savings schemes. With profits and endowments are safe and steady, but PEPs and unit-linked schemes may perform better if the stockmarket continues to do very well in the 1990s.

Some more adventurous plan managers are also looking at PEPs for school fee or retirement planning.

Tax Exempt Special Savings Accounts

John Major's innovation in his only Budget as a chancellor was to introduce the Tax Exempt Special Savings Account which came into operation at the beginning of 1991. This title is a bit of a mouthful, and it is pretty obvious that he only came up with the name so that he could shorten it to TESSA. The carrot to attract people into TESSAs is that the interest on the account is free of income tax, and the chancellor hoped that this tax break would encourage people to save more. Naturally enough there are rules to limit the operation of TESSAs: and the fall in interest rates in the early 1990s considerably reduced their appeal. Nonetheless for those who can afford to save for the medium term, the TESSA is worth considering.

If you are the kind of saver who would never consider a stockmarket-based product, a TESSA will almost certainly give you a better return than an ordinary bank or building society deposit. If you are rich enough to have a very well-spread portfolio, a TESSA is a good way of sheltering some of your deposit income. If, however, you are a middle of the road investor, happy to keep most of your savings on deposit when interest rates were high, you should probably shift your emphasis towards stockmarket-based investments if interest rates continue low.

The basic principle behind TESSAs is that everybody can save up to £9,000 tax free, provided they leave their money in the special account for five years. Savers cannot pile all their money in at once; the maximum TESSA deposit in the first year is £3,000, then in the second, third and fourth years up to £1,800 can go in, leaving only £600 in the fifth year. Of course, savers don't have to follow that pattern – if they have only put £7,000 into their TESSA in the first four years, they could put in a further £2,000 in year 5.

Interest on the account can either be rolled up or paid out, but if savers choose to take the income as they go it is paid *net* of basic rate tax, and the tax-free extra is only paid out at the end of the five-year period. Investors can also take their money out of the TESSA if they need it, but they lose the tax break on money which is withdrawn. Savers can only have one TESSA, but can move from one TESSA provider to another if something better turns up (for restrictions, see below). As far as the basic rules are concerned, that's just about it. TESSAs are pretty straightforward, and the tax savings can be worthwhile.

How to choose a TESSA

TESSAs are one of the few financial products which have no major drawbacks. Even those people who are not sure they can afford to part with their money for five years should consider opening an account, because they can always back out later. The only *caveats* to that are that investors should satisfy themselves that they are with a solid savings institution, and that they should shop around to get the TESSA that suits their needs. The other thing to watch is that you cannot make partial withdrawals from a TESSA. So if you may want some of your savings, only put a smaller amount into the TESSA and keep a cash reserve. Otherwise you risk losing your tax advantage on the whole amount.

There are two main factors to consider when picking a TESSA: getting the highest interest rate you can, and avoiding onerous conditions from withdrawing early or moving to a different TESSA. How you balance these considerations will depend on your own circumstances. For example, if you think you may need to get your money out early, you will need to pay close attention to the terms for withdrawal. Even if you are certain you won't need the money, it's still worth considering penalties for moving into another account, because a different TESSA provider may come up with a substantially better offer in the future, and you should try to retain the flexibility to move where the grass is greenest.

Picking the highest interest rate isn't as simple as it might seem either. Because interest rates are variable, the bank or building society offering the best TESSA rates today may not be the market leader tomorrow. TESSA rates will depend on the general level of interest rates and other factors like an institution's need for funds, or even its management's attitude to attracting retail investors. Sometimes banks or building societies offer special deals for limited periods because they particularly want to attract funds, or they wish to raise their profile with the public.

The other thing that savers can do to try to ensure they get a good rate on their TESSA is to pick one of the schemes which offers a rate linked to some fixed point. Such schemes are less likely to be affected by the whims of managers than ones which merely offer a good head-line rate now. Many TESSAs also offer loyalty bonuses if you stay the course, or incentives to join the scheme, but most of these are relatively small beer when compared to the impact of interest rates. Bonuses are frequently £100 or £200, but getting an extra 1 per cent interest is worth almost £400 if you invest the maximum amount over five years.

One way to ensure you get a known return is to opt for a fixed rate TESSA. But this is only a good idea if you think interest rates are going to fall, because you can lock in a high rate. If interest rates are low and likely to rise, you will be better off with a floating rate account. Investors should satisfy themselves that their money is in safe hands before going with a small institution, regardless of the interest rate being offered.

Some of the best TESSA deals are offered to those who will commit themselves to invest the full £9,000 over the course of a scheme. They can get up to 1 per cent more in interest, and bonuses, but it is still worth checking that you are not irrevocably tied to one TESSA. What seems highly competitive today may not do so next year. Other TESSAs are best suited to lump sum or regular saving, and the list of best buys is constantly changing. the *Investors Chronicle* and the personal finance pages of the national press provide regular updates of the best offers.

Tax Efficient Investments

IN A NUTSHELL

1. The government has been keen to promote wider share ownership and saving, and is using the tax system to promote these aims. This offers opportunity for investors.

2. Personal Equity Plans allow investors to hold shares without paying income tax or capital gains tax on their holdings. The PEP is run by a plan manager who levies charges which use up some of the tax benefit.

3. Everyone can take out one general PEP each year up to a value of £6,000. This may be invested directly in shares or in approved unit or investment trusts. If you do not take out a PEP in any given year, you lose the entitlement.

4. Investors may also take out a single company PEP up to a limit of £3,000. These are most useful to employees who own shares from savings schemes. They can put in shares they already hold without tax liability.

5. New issues may be put into a PEP within 42 days of launch, but no other existing holdings can be sheltered. Cash can be held in a general PEP for as long as you like, but in a single company PEP it has to be invested within 42 days.

6. PEPs are equity investments and must be regarded as long-term holdings. Investors can choose between PEPs where the managers select the investments, or self select schemes. They can also choose plans which invest in shares, pooled investments or a mix, and between growth and equity schemes.

7. Tax Exempt Special Savings Accounts allow investors to save up to £9,000 over five years, without paying income tax on the interest they earn. Only one TESSA may be held, but investors can move between accounts.

8. Interest in a TESSA can be rolled up or paid out as income. If the interest is paid out, basic rate tax is deducted, but is paid out at the end of five years.

9. In choosing a TESSA investors must balance ease of access to their money with the interest rate or bonuses offered. Because savers can withdraw from TESSAs and only lose their tax relief, almost everyone should consider starting one.

Chapter 12
Futures and options

When we discussed futures and options in chapter 6 it was from the perspective of the professional investor. To the institutions, futures markets are a way to transfer risk from those who want to hedge to those who want to speculate. A gilt market maker who owns £10m worth of stock will sell £10m worth of futures to hedge himself, and is not overly concerned with the costs of doing so.

But the private investor views futures through the other end of the telescope. What is important to him is that the way futures and options markets work allows him to make – or lose – a fortune. The way this happens is simply explained; futures markets work on **margin** which means that an investor doesn't have to pay the full cost of his investment immediately. The importance of this becomes clear if we take our agricultural example from chapter 6. Say wheat is trading at £100 a tonne and a speculator decides to buy 100 tonnes (total value £10,000) on the futures market because he thinks the price will rise. In the futures market he only has to put up 10 per cent of the amount – £1,000 – as a sign of good faith when he takes out the contract for delivery in three months. Over the next month wheat rises from £100 a tonne to £150 a tonne. Our investor decides to take his profit and sell before delivery. He nets a profit of £5,000 or 500 per cent on his original investment, despite the fact that wheat has only gone up by 50 per cent. Even by the standards of stockmarket stags, 500 per cent profit in a month is pretty phenomenal.

The problem comes because things can go just as badly wrong. If wheat had fallen to £50 the loss would also have been 500 per cent, and if our fearless speculator had bet £50,000 instead of £1,000 he would have lost £250,000. Dealing on margin is an example of **gearing** or **leverage** and it shows why the futures and options markets are so seductive – and so deadly. With gearing you can take out a much bigger investment than you could afford otherwise, so your profits and losses are correspondingly magnified. That may be acceptable to professional 'local' speculators (see chapter 6) who stand in the futures pits all day and make use of futures gearing to bet large sums for a living, but it is no place for widows, orphans or private investors.

That goes for financial futures too. Amongst other things investors can trade in UK interest rates, gilts, the FT-SE index, currencies and foreign bonds on The London International Financial Futures Exchange – LIFFE.* Most financial futures are outside the range of private investors. Even one gilt contract is the equivalent of £50,000-worth of cash gilts. To buy ten an investor would only have to put up £5,000 in margin, but if long-term interest rates then moved up by one per cent he would lose around £18,000. Equity futures are even more explosive. With footsie at 2,000 one contract to buy the FT-SE index is the equivalent of buying around £50,000-worth of shares. If you owned ten – for a margin of around £15,000 – and the FT-SE index then fell from 2,400 to 2,000 – as it did after the Iraqi invasion of Kuwait – you would lose £100,000. On the flip side you stand to make equally large gains if the market moves in your favour. But if you use margin to increase the size of your deals you are taking substantial risks.

The rules of the financial futures market won't let you blow your brains out in quite such spectacular style unless you can really afford it. Every day investors' profits and losses are totted up on the futures exchange and have to be settled immediately. So if things started to go wrong, you would soon get a **margin call** – a demand to put up more money to support a loss-making trade. But even given the constraints, financial futures are too rich for the blood of all but the wealthiest and bravest private investor.

*LIFFE and the options market LTOM have merged to form a single London Financial Futures and Options Exchange, and not before time.

Commodity futures

If dealing in financial futures is risky for small investors, trading in commodity futures is pure Russian roulette. In London commodities are split up amongst several exchanges. Metals – aluminium, copper, lead, nickel, tin, and zinc – are traded on the London Metal Exchange (LME); soft commodities – sugar, soya, cocoa, coffee, potatoes, wheat, barley and pigs – on the London Commodity Exchange (LCE) and oil on the International Petroleum Exchange (IPE). As well as futures dealings other commodities are dealt for immediate delivery, in spot markets.

The problem with commodities from a small investor's point of view is that in these markets individuals really do stand at a tremendous disadvantage. Those companies which use such commodities as their raw materials go to great lengths to determine the likely trends in supply and demand and thus what prices will be. For example chocolate companies send representatives into the Ghanaian bush to count the cocoa crop on the trees before it is even harvested. And naturally enough chocolate companies have a pretty good idea of what demand for cocoa will be. Armed with information like that, the professional is in a much better position to make an informed decision in the futures market than the individual sitting at home who thinks 'I wonder if cocoa is going up?'

All investment involves a measure of subjective judgement, and often individuals vie with professionals. But in commodities the private investor is betting against the house, even with the help of a friendly 'expert'. Despite his protestations, your broker probably has no better idea than you where crude oil is going next. Commodities are both more volatile and less predictable than shares, and trading commodity futures on margin is a mug's game.

Another option

So is there any way for individuals to use the attractive aspects of gearing, without going bust in the process?

Partly-paid new issues (see chapter 17) and nil-paid rights (chapter 18) are both geared – investors do not have to put up the full value of their investment in either case – but they are only available rarely. Options are the most flexible way for private investors to use gearing while limiting their risk. For investors who are interested in shares, two main types of option are available – **traditional options** and **traded options**.

As we said in chapter 6 an option is the *right but not the obligation* to buy or sell a share. That distinction is important because if the option goes wrong, you can just walk away from it and all you have lost is the amount you originally invested, whereas if the share moves in your favour, you get the benefits of a geared investment. Traditional options are available on most shares and come in three forms: the right to buy a share – a **call** – the right to sell a share – a **put** – and the right to do either – a **double**. They last for three months and are the right to deal at whatever the market price is at the time the option is granted.

The amount that an investor has to pay for the option is called the **premium**, and the size of the premium will depend on how volatile the share is expected to be, which in turn depends both on the type of share and the state of the market. In normal, fairly 'quiet' conditions stable blue chips might have premiums of about 7–10 per cent of the share price, so if M&S shares were 330p, a three-month call might cost 25p. That means that M&S shares would have to rise above 355p before you showed a profit. But if they did really well and reached 400p before the three months was up, your option would be worth 70p – a profit of 180 per cent on your 25p premium. On the other hand, if M&S fell below 330p, your option would expire worthless, and so you would have lost 100 per cent of your investment.

Premium rates will shoot up if the market becomes particularly volatile – for example option premiums rocketed during the 1987 crash – and they are normally higher for shares which are likely to be volatile. Blue chips like Bass rarely moves as dramatically as in the example we quoted, so premiums are reasonably low, but smaller company shares often move rapidly, and therefore premiums are correspondingly higher – small company premiums can be in excess of 20 per cent. It's a bit like car insurance: young tearaway drivers are more likely to have an accident, so their insurance premiums are higher than those of sedate middle-aged managers. Blue chips have more stable prices than small companies, so the options premiums are lower.

Put option rates are sometimes lower than calls, but again that depends on the state of the market. Doubles are a little less than twice the price of a call, but a share has to be pretty volatile for it to be possible to make money from them. The chances of an investor coming to the conclusion that a share is going to be pretty volatile, but having no idea which way it will move, seem remote.

Oddly enough there are a few circumstances when this might happen – for example if a large order was about to be placed, and would materially affect a small company. Getting the order would mean a rosy future, losing it could mean catastrophe. Another possibility is in a bid, where the target might get a counter bid, forcing the shares higher, or the deal might be referred to the Monopolies Commission and turned down, causing the target's share price to fall. In either case using a double might be a good tactic – but (you guessed it) market makers take just such factors into account when pricing options, so a double in either of these examples would be a lot more expensive than normal.

The problem with traditional options are that they are not very flexible. Neither are they negotiable – so investors cannot sell them if they rise in value. To take a profit on a traditional option, investors have to **exercise** the option – which means buy or sell the shares they have under option. Brokers have the facility to re-sell the shares immediately, closing out the position, so that investors don't have to find the full value of any shares they have under option, but the whole process is rather cumbersome. It doesn't help that options can only be exercised on set dates, limiting room for manoeuvre.

A flexible alternative

Traded options overcome some of the rigidities involved in traditional options because they are **negotiable securities** which can be bought and sold throughout their lives. They also offer investors greater flexibility in the type of option they take – calls and puts can be bought giving the right to buy or sell a share at a number of different prices, and for a variety of periods. The drawback is that they are only available on 70-odd of the largest shares, the FT-SE 100 index and the FT-SE Eurotrack 100 index.

In most cases traded options are deal in contracts to buy or sell 1,000 shares in a company, which makes options sound a little frightening. If a typical share price is £5, then the minimum underlying investment in an option is £5,000-worth of shares. But this is where gearing comes in. A three month traded option at the current market price would cost about the same as a traditional option – in a blue chip say 7 per cent of the share price. So the right to buy a share at £5 for three months would cost about 35p, making the minimum investment in options only £350. Of course many people deal in larger amounts, but the market is well within the reach of small investors.

The traded options market divides the year up into three quarterly sequences:

- January, April, July, October
- February, May, August, November
- March, June, September, December

Each share is allocated to one of these sequences, and options are available in it for up to nine months ahead. So for example Hanson shares are allocated to the second sequence, and in June, options investors could buy options which expired in August, November or the following February. Say Hanson shares were 230p, options would be available at a variety of prices, and the most popular might be 200p, 220p, 240p and 260p. Investors could buy either calls or puts at any of those prices.

Option pricing

Options range from those which can be exercised profitably – an example might be a Hanson 200p call if the shares were 230p – which are known as **in the money**, to those which have a long way to go before the investor can exercise them profitably – perhaps Hanson 260p calls in the same example, which are known as **out of the money**. As we mentioned in chapter 6, the way option prices are calculated is complex, and these days is normally done by computer. Options prices are composed of two elements: **intrinsic value** and **time value**. Intrinsic value is fairly simple – it is the extent to which an option is in the money, so in the Hanson 200p call example, the option contains 30p of intrinsic value if the shares are 230p. Time value is more difficult, but is based on the length of time an option has to run – clearly an option which has longer to run has more chance of getting into the money and so is more valuable. In the money options have both time and intrinsic value, out of the money options have only time value.

The way option prices move is also complicated, but as a broad rule of thumb, the price of options which are a long way in the money move in line with any movements in the share price, whereas the price of options which are a long way out of the money move a lot more slowly. With the shares at 230p a Hanson 140p call would probably go up 1p for every 1p rise in the share price; a 360p call might only go up 1p for a 10p move in the shares. Time value varies in a complex way too. It declines slowly when the option has a long time to run, then much more rapidly as its expiry date nears. For more details refer back to chapter 6.

Option strategies

Investors can take a variety of approaches to trading in options. The simplest strategy is to buy straightforward puts and calls. Perhaps you think Boots shares are going to rise. Say in January the shares are 360p but you think there is a good chance they will reach over 400p in the next few months. You could buy April 390p calls for about 12p, which means that if Boots shares rose above 402p, you would make a profit. If the shares got to 420p just as they were about to expire you would have made 18p – which is 150 per cent profit. Contrast that with buying the shares at 360p, and seeing them rise to 420p; here your profit is only 17 per cent. Of course, if you are wrong and Boots shares fall to 330p by April, the options will expire worthless – but if you see things going that way in February or March, with traded options you at least have the flexibility to sell and recoup part of your stake.

An alternative might be to buy the July 390p calls, if you thought the rise might take longer. Because you are buying more time value, the July options will be more expensive – perhaps 21p, and your break-even point is

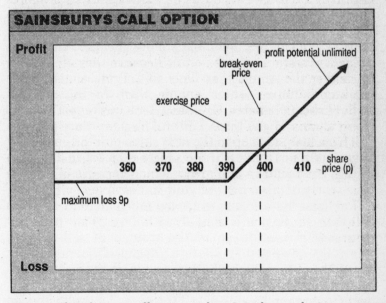

Fig 12.1 This shows a call option to buy Sainsburys shares at 390p when the shares are 364p. The option costs 9p, which represents the maximum loss if the option expires worthless. If an investor bought the option he would break even at 399p (390p plus 9p premium) and the potential profit is unlimited.

411p because you have paid more for the option. If the
shares again rose to 420p, you would have made a 9p
profit, or 43 per cent. Your profit is lower, but you have
longer to be right. Another possibility is to buy an option
at a different exercise price. Buying options with a lower
exercise price – say 360p calls – will cost more but they
are more likely to expire at a profit. In the money options
are less geared and less speculative investments. That
means the profits will be more limited than with an out of
the money option, but you are taking less of a risk. Buying
in the money options is the equivalent of backing the
short-odds horses in a race. Options which are a long way
out of the money are definitely outsiders.

Puts work in much the same way as calls, but are less
popular, possibly because most people are optimistic, or
because they find it easier to think about share prices
rising rather than falling. In any event, puts are quite
useful because they are a way of **shorting** shares, which is
normally difficult for private investors. Shorting is selling
shares you don't own in the hope that their price will fall
so that you can buy them back more cheaply later. Most
private investors cannot do this because they are unable
to deliver the shares they have sold. Professionals have
lending facilities which enable them to borrow and
deliver shorted shares. Options offer a convenient way to
short shares. If you think Ladbroke's shares are going to
fall from 300p to 250p in the next three months you might
buy a 300p put for 20p. if the shares then fell to 250p you
would have made a 30p profit, which because of gearing
was worth 150 per cent of your initial investment.

Puts also offer a way to hedge your portfolio. Say you
felt that the market was likely to fall by 20 per cent, but
you didn't want to go to the trouble of selling your
carefully constructed share portfolio. One possibility
would be to buy some FT-SE puts, which represented the
same underlying value as your portfolio. If the market fell,
you would then be able to sell the puts at a profit, and set
this against any falls in the value of your portfolio.
Unfortunately this is not a perfect hedge unless your
portfolio is a reconstruction of the FT-SE index. If you
own a lot of shares which are not in FT-SE, or your blue

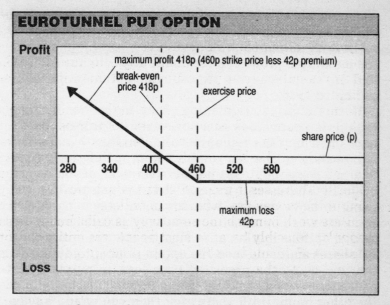

Fig 12.2 In this case the put option gives an investor the right to sell Eurotunnel shares at 460p, when the shares are 465p. The maximum loss is the 42p premium, whilst the break-even point is 418p (460p minus the 42p premium). The maximum profit is also 418p, which would only happen if the shares became worthless.

chip shares are heavily weighted towards a few business sectors, then the portfolio will not necessarily move in line with the FT-SE index. But it does at least offer some protection.

Bolder strategies

It is possible to get very sophisticated in options and tailor-make the risks you want to take. Many of the most involved strategies are outside the scope of this book. But there are some reasonably straightforward strategies the beginner can pursue – and some he should avoid at all costs. As well as buying options, it is possible to grant them to other people – and this is known in the options jargon (and there's an awful lot of it) as **writing** options.

This reverses the risks of buying options. Instead of paying a premium and having a limited risk in the hope of making an unlimited profit, you take a premium which is the maximum profit you can make from the transaction and in exchange you expose yourself to a possibly unlimited loss.

If this sounds frightening, it is meant to. Writing options is a dangerous business – even for professionals – and small investors should only consider it in limited circumstances. One reasonably safe way to write options is to sell someone a call on shares you own. If you owned 5,000 BP shares and thought that the market was not going to move over the next few months, you could sell someone 5 call options (representing 5,000 shares) on the traded options market at or slightly out of the money. If BP shares suddenly rose, the option price would take off, but you would be protected from loss, because the BP shares you owned would be rising to match the option. On the other hand, if BP shares fell then you would have a loss on your shareholding, but would be partially compensated by the option premium you had received. The ideal circumstance is for BP shares to stay exactly where they are – then you receive the premium income and have a shareholding which is worth just what it was.

This technique is known as **covered call writing** and is used by some fund managers to increase the income they get on their share portfolios. Small investors can use it safely, provided they match their shareholdings and option positions properly. If you want to write covered calls on options which do not have traded options, your broker may be able to arrange a traditional option for you, but these are less flexible because you cannot easily change your mind part of the way through. Covered calls sound like manna from heaven – extra income and no risk! But there is a hidden cost involved. What you are effectively doing is giving someone else the right to buy from you any of your shares which do well. The person buying the call will be the one who makes money if a share in your portfolio rises. So be careful that in enthusiasm for taking premiums, you are not giving away the rights to all of your best shares.

Much more dangerous is **naked call writing**. This is where you write call options for shares which you don't own to take a premium. Here your loss really is unlimited, and this technique should be avoided by everyone but maniacs. The same goes for writing **all** puts. There is no such thing as covered puts (there would be if you were short of the shares, but this is somewhat unlikely) so your loss on writing puts is always unlimited. Writing puts gives other people the right to sell you shares if the market falls in return for paying you a premium. This is what some 'clever' investors were doing throughout 1987, banking a premium cheque every month and watching the market rise. They thought they were on the gravy train until the crash in October, when they found out what unlimited losses really mean. At least one went bust to the tune of several million pounds.

Other option strategies include **straddles** which are a bit like doubles in traditional options. If you buy a straddle you expect the share to move dramatically one way or the other. You could also sell the straddle, which means that you expect the share to stay exactly where it is, but this is another form of naked writing where you receive twice the premium for taking twice the risk. Avoid. Professionals also go in for calendar spreads, where they buy puts and calls for different dates, or combine straddles with positions in the underlying shares, and plenty of other games.

Costs

One final point about options: sadly the commissions charged are related to the underlying investment you have made, and so are quite high. If you have a marginal trade, that can quite easily make the difference between a profit and a loss. So check before you deal.

Futures and Options

IN A NUTSHELL

1. Private investors view futures and options as geared investments, where they only have to put up a small fraction of the total value of their investment.

2. As a result of gearing, the total profits or losses investors can make from dealing are much larger than if they were dealing in the underlying security. Geared investments are very risky.

3. Futures are available in agricultural or other commodities and in financial instruments like bonds, interest rates and FT-SE, but private investors should avoid them because their losses as well as their profits are unlimited.

4. Commodity futures are particularly dangerous, because they are volatile, unpredictable and professionals always know more about the state of supply and demand than private investors.

5. Options are a better way for investors to use gearing. Buying options involves limited risk but potentially unlimited profit. Options to buy are known as calls, and options to sell, puts.

6. In shares investors can deal in traditional or traded options. Traditional options are available on a wide range of shares, but are not very flexible. There are traded options on 70-odd blue chip shares at a variety of prices for a number of dates.

7. Traded options are negotiable, meaning that they can be bought or sold throughout their life.

8. As well as buying calls or puts, investors can use options to hedge themselves, either by buying a put in a share, or hedging their portfolio with FT-SE puts.

9. Investors can increase income by writing covered calls on shares they own. Writing naked calls or any puts is very dangerous, and can lead to unlimited losses.

Chapter 13
Investing Abroad

In the good old days customs officials used to stop travellers at airports and ask them how much sterling they were taking out of the country. This rather quaint practice was designed to stop people exporting from Britain capital which, in the view of the government, was badly needed for industry. The theory ran that, unless they were barred by customs, unscrupulous capitalists would cart suitcases full of cash to overseas markets, leaving Britain as an industrial wasteland. Officials also feared that large amounts of sterling held overseas might help speculators start a run on the pound. Companies were constrained too – a huge department of the Bank of England was charged with controlling international financial transactions.

If this seems like a tale from a bygone age, it's worth remembering that these foreign exchange controls were only abolished in 1979. And far from lagging the pack, Britain was one of the first countries to allow free movement of capital. In 1983 the French government was so scared that the franc would collapse that it stopped French tourists taking more than 4,000 francs out of the country, and many other governments still maintain strict capital controls.

The British government now views capital flows as part of the free market. Exchange controls did not prevent Britain's industrial decline, nor did they stop pressure on the pound. On the other hand, today's conventional wisdom is that if capital is allowed to flow freely in or out of Britain, the discipline of the market will force British industry to offer competitive returns if it wants to attract investors.

As a result of the abolition of exchange controls, the 1980s saw a boom in overseas investment. Britain now holds more overseas assets than any other country except

Japan. Foreign investment has attracted individuals as well as institutions. Overseas markets offer an opportunity to spread investment risk, and frequently provide higher returns than are available in Britain. The great attractions lie in having a portfolio which is not wholly dependent on the UK economy, and the tantalizing prospect of being in a go-go market which doubles or trebles in a matter of months. But there are risks – some foreign markets are volatile and illiquid and investors also have to take into account currency fluctuations. A British investor is no better off if he puts money into the Thai stockmarket which then doubles in value, if at the same time the Thai bhat halves against the pound.

Going abroad

As with domestic investments, investors looking overseas have a choice between bonds, deposits and equities, and have the additional possibility of speculating with currencies. However, because of the extra risks involved, investors should regard all overseas holdings as part of their riskier investments, and consider them all alongside their portfolio of UK shares. As a rule of thumb, no one should have more than a quarter of his risk investments overseas without being very clear why he is doing so. Even if his investments are spread between several foreign markets, a sudden rise in sterling would seriously damage his portfolio.

Those thinking of investing in bonds or deposits abroad are often looking for higher interest rates than are available in the UK. However, it is a sad fact that you usually have to go quite a long way to find a country which has higher interest rates than Britain for any length of time. Countries which do – Australia is an example – tend to have very poor inflation records and as a result, weak currencies. That means that the extra interest earned on a foreign currency deposit can be quickly wiped out by a fall in local currency.

Some investors prefer to take the opposite course and accept a lower interest rate than is available in Britain and invest in a low-inflation currency like the Swiss franc or the mark. Investors hope that these currencies will rise against the pound to compensate them for loss of interest. In either case the movement of currencies is central to investment performance, because foreign exchange fluctuations tend to be at least as large as the differences in interest rates. As a result, foreign bond and currency deposits can be viewed as a way to speculate on the currency markets. This is not wholly a good thing. Forex movements can be quite large and unpredictable, and even the 'experts' frequently get them wrong (see chapter 3). Currency speculation is a luxurious way of losing money, which really should be left to professionals or very wealthy private investors.

Similarly, pooled schemes which invest in overseas deposits or bonds should be regarded with suspicion. This includes unit trusts investing in fixed interest securities or offshore deposit or currency funds. To make these work the investment managers need to get the currency moves right, and it is not clear that anyone consistently does so. The one factor working in their favour is that sterling has been a weak currency over many years, and so holdings in many foreign currencies have outperformed sterling. The government intends this decline to be a thing of the past. If the discipline works, foreign currency deposits will no longer be bailed out by a falling pound.

It is a pity that currency fluctuations can have such a dramatic impact on overseas bond investments, because many countries – particularly in Europe – invest in bonds more heavily than equities. But to invest there, British investors have to take risks which are much higher than the returns offered by the pure bond investment.

Foreign shares

One area which can justify the risks of crossing the water is investment in overseas equities. Here the prospects of capital gains on foreign bourses can be sufficiently good to brave the currency risks. However, investors must still

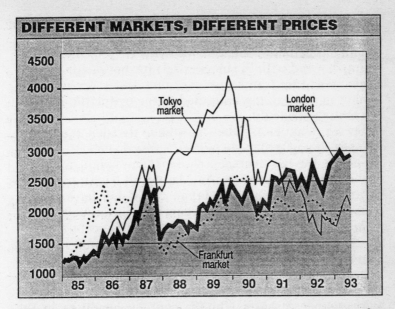

DIFFERENT MARKETS, DIFFERENT PRICES

Tokyo market

London market

Frankfurt market

Fig 13.1 Investing overseas can help spread risk in the same way that a diversified portfolio avoids keeping all the eggs in one basket. Since 1985 the Tokyo market has first outperformed and then under-performed Britain whilst Frankfurt has fared less well.

be cautious – currency movements will affect their total returns, and foreign markets are frequently moved by factors which are not obvious in the UK. It can be difficult to tell the difference between a speculative bubble and a go-go stockmarket until after the event, and many investors have lost fortunes rushing into a small but booming foreign market, only to find they bought at the top. Even the Japanese stockmarket has burnt many fingers in recent years. A sure sign of impending doom is the publication of 'expert' opinions which explain why this or that market is different and will go on rising for ever. When that sort of special pleading appears, investors should consider taking profits.

That said, a sensible approach to overseas investment can help spread risk and increase total returns. The world economy does not work completely in synch, so that some countries are in recession while others are making hay.

And by the same token stockmarkets have bull and bear runs at different times. On occasion, markets move broadly together – the rise and fall of 1987 is a good example – and with the increasing internationalization of investment this trend may continue. But there is still a benefit in not being wholly tied to the ups and downs of the British economy.

So what happens when you have decided that Hong Kong is the right place to be now? How do small investors go about buying overseas shares? The simplest way is through pooled investments. Many unit trusts specialize in one overseas market – Japan or the US for example, others in a group of smaller markets like the emerging tigers of South East Asia. Indeed, pooled investments can be the only way small shareholders can invest in many markets. Some investment trusts also specialize in particular countries, and even many of the general funds have a substantial holding in overseas shares. Unit trust performance is shown under country headings in the *Financial Times* or the Saturday editions of papers like *The Independent* or *The Daily Telegraph*. A full run down of performance is given monthly in *Money Management*, showing how the fund has done both in local currency terms and in sterling. Details of the holdings of investment trusts can be obtained from the **Association of Investment Trust Companies**.

Although investors buy these pooled investments in sterling, the funds themselves are no more immune to currency movements than any other kind of foreign holding. Fund managers take different approaches to this problem: some hedge all of their foreign exchange exposure, others none, and some hedge all or part as the mood takes them. So overseas fund managers face two challenges – buying the right shares in the market and predicting the currency movements correctly. In practice, many fund management groups split this responsibility – the fund manager picks the shares and specialist currency dealers handle the foreign exchange.

If you don't even want to take responsibility for deciding which foreign market to back, you can let the fund managers do it for you by investing in a **fund of**

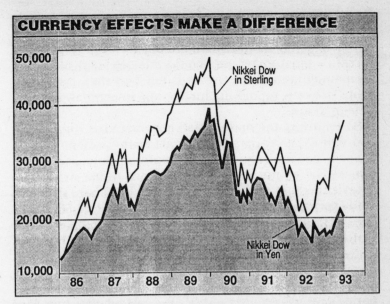

CURRENCY EFFECTS MAKE A DIFFERENCE

Fig 13.2 Currency effects are the great iceberg in international investment. The divergence between returns in the local currency and returns translated back into sterling can be quite marked. Since 1986 returns from the Japanese market have been better in sterling, reflecting the weakness of the pound in 1985/6.

funds. Most fund management groups run one of these, and they select units from the stable of trusts they run. That will probably include some UK holdings, but a fair mix of overseas units too, and are in some respects similar to general investment trusts. Although they do not offer a balanced portfolio, they do give investors some stake in overseas shares. **Indexed funds** are also available for the American, European and Japanese markets for those investors who want to mimic the market.

Direct investment

Nowadays investors are not restricted to collective investments if they want to go overseas. It is quite easy to buy many European or American blue-chip shares directly from a stockbroker. There are some extra points to look out for, but in principle it is almost as easy to buy shares in BMW as in British Aerospace. Again there are caveats – most investors should stick to large blue-chip companies, and there are still the currency risks, but many brokers report an increasing interest in holding foreign shares.

So what are the main differences between buying UK and overseas shares? For a start many foreign shares have a 'heavier' share price than those in Britain. A typical UK equity might have a price of £3, whilst an American share could cost $100, and one share in Swiss food company Nestlé would set you back SFr 8,500! That doesn't mean that American or continental companies are worth more than British ones, only that there are fewer shares issued. But a heavy share price can prevent investors from buying small amounts.

A second point to bear in mind is that settlement periods for shares vary – deals are settled after two days in Germany, but once a month – or for cash – in the main French market. And nearly all shares on the continent are **bearer** securities – which means that whoever holds the shares is considered to own them. This makes them very much like cash, and so most shares are held permanently in vaults. Any change in ownership is recorded by book transfers. With the growth of international investment, the need for these secure warehouses has increased, and banks such as Barclays or Citibank act as **global custodians**, holding shares and bonds and charging annual administration fees.

The minimum practical investment is also higher than in the UK – brokers regard £5,000 as a sensible starting point, and minimum commissions are higher too – ranging from £50 to £75. Above that some brokers stick to the standard UK commission rate, others charge a little more. As well as commission you will have to consider any currency dealing charges, custodian costs and possibly the commission of an overseas broker if one is needed. Bear in mind that these vary quite a lot between different countries. Dealing in small amounts in overseas shares can also mean poor marketability. For deals below around £10,000, bid-offer spreads often widen quite dramatically, which means that the shares need to move further for you to show a profit.

As for dealing, there are currently two main ways your broker can buy the shares. Many large foreign companies – including a lot of American firms and over 230 European blue chips – are now quoted directly in London on the Stock Exchange's SEAQ International system. These have the advantage that the foreign exchange transaction is included in the deal, and prices are quoted in sterling (but the shares you buy are still denominated in foreign currencies). Deals may also be completed more quickly and easily in London than abroad. On the other hand, bid-offer spreads are often a little wider than they would be in the share's home market. The other option is to go direct to the foreign bourse where the share is quoted. Here the price will be slightly better, but you will probably have to pay a local broker a commission. Your UK broker is compelled by the **best advice** rule to advise you which is likely to prove the best way to deal.

The other main consideration for UK investors buying foreign shares is dividends. Most brokers will arrange to collect these for you from the custodian, and will sort out the administration on tax. With European or American shares **double taxation** agreements apply, where UK investors end up getting a dividend net of basic rate UK income tax. In some other markets investors may be stung for both local and UK income tax on dividends, so check with your broker before you buy.

Investors can find out about the performance of large European companies in the *Financial Times* or the *Investors Chronicle*, which both report business developments and the annual results of Europe's blue chips. The *Financial Times* also has coverage of many American companies.

One final point here. British companies earn almost half their profits from overseas trade and operations. Which means investors can get some exposure to other economies simply by buying the right shares on the London market!

Investing Abroad

IN A NUTSHELL

1. Britain relaxed restrictions on overseas investments in 1979, and the UK is now the second largest holder of foreign assets. Many other countries have since followed suit.

2. When investing abroad investors have a choice between deposits, bonds and equities, but must always bear in mind that they face the risk that currency movements may affect the returns they earn on their investments.

3. For small investors the risks of an adverse currency movement outweigh the returns available from most bonds or deposits.

4. Shares offer the prospect of capital gains which can make the currency risks worthwhile, but foreign markets are often volatile and illiquid. Speculative bubbles may not be obvious from Britain.

5. One way for small investors to get into foreign stockmarkets is through pooled investments. There are unit and investment trusts which specialize in particular bourses, others in regions.

6. Funds of funds and general investment trusts also often contain an overseas element, and tracking funds are available on the Japanese and American markets.

7. Direct investment in overseas equities is now quite easy. Stockbrokers can either deal directly

on a foreign bourse, or in London, where many European and American blue chip companies are quoted.

8. Dealing costs tend to be higher than with UK shares, and the minimum investment is also larger. Most European shares are bearer securities and are held by bank custodians.

9. For American and most European stocks, dividends are covered by double taxation agreements which mean that British investors pay UK income tax.

Section Three
Companies

Chapter 14
Types of Share

How do the ways the stockmarket classifies company shares help investors find the type they want? Some methods of classification are merely descriptive: they tell you whether a share has equal rights to vote or receive dividends, for instance; the size of the company; or what its main line of business is. Other classifications help you to evaluate the business's profit potential or the shares' stockmarket characteristics. For example, how good is the management? Is the company unusually influenced by economic cycles, or changes in foreign exchange or interest rates? Does it operate in an expanding market?

These groupings move independently of each other. And any share will fall into a number of different categories. Investors consider the overall mix of its attributes in predicting whether its profits will grow faster or slower than the market average over various periods of time. If they think its profits will grow faster than average for several years, they are prepared to pay more for the share in relation to its current earnings than they would for stodgier companies' shares. Such a share is **highly rated**.

Investors are constantly trying to spot changes in companies' profit potential or inappropriate share ratings. If they buy before other investors, and the relative rating improves, they benefit as the share price moves up.

Some of the standard investment yardsticks are discussed in the next chapter. This one looks at the main ways in which investors group shares, explains how the big investing institutions use these classifications, and how they affect share prices. First, though, make sure you don't buy the wrong type of share by mistake.

Ordinary and Extraordinary

Most shares in a company rank equally, with similar legal rights and financial entitlements. They are called **Ordinary** shares. But some companies have other **classes** of share. Most of these classes are much smaller, with different and often inferior legal rights and financial entitlements. The prices of shares in these classes are determined by different factors from those of the Ordinary shares and they are often much harder to buy and sell. Some shares like convertible issues may be of particular interest to income investors, but when most people consider investing in equities, they are thinking of Ordinary shares.

A holder of 1,000 **Ordinary** shares in a company gets the same dividends as any other holder of 1,000 shares, and half as much as the holder of 2,000 shares. The same goes for his vote on matters affecting the company. But as part owner of the company, he cannot complain if his income expectations are disappointed, and Ordinary shareholders are last in line after all the other creditors if a company has to be wound up.

Preference shares are by far the most common alternative to Ordinary shares. They come ahead of the Ordinary in liquidations and in dividend payments. Precise dividend and capital repayment rights vary, and should always be checked if you are thinking of buying. In many cases the dividend is fixed, and the shares are valued like similar fixed interest securities. However in good times **participating preference shares** may get a second bite at the cherry, because as well as a fixed payment, the dividend may be increased if the company does well. Holders of **cumulative** shares may also be able to claim unpaid dividends later on. **Redeemable** preference shares have a fixed repayment date, like debt issues, and may be entitled to more than their nominal capital value. Probably the most interesting are **Convertible** preference shares, which can be converted into Ordinary shares at pre-set dates on pre-set terms. These hybrids usually yield less than a normal fixed rate security, since there is some hope of capital gain. They can be profitable if the underlying shares do well.

A few companies still have some Ordinary shares, often described as **'A' Shares**, with **limited** or **no voting rights**. They get the same dividends and the same share of assets as the Ordinary in the event of liquidation. But their reduced franchise means that they often sell for less on the stockmarket, particularly if there is a bid in the offing.

The government's privatization programme has also left it with a **Golden share** in some companies. This gives it a casting vote if it decides to use it, say to block a takeover. But in most cases the Golden share only lasts for a limited time and its rights can be waived.

Deferred shares usually do not qualify for a dividend until a company's profits have reached a prescribed level, or until a particular date. They may have normal voting rights, and usually have some claim on the company in the event of liquidation.

Partly-paid shares have become a common element in privatization issues. The shares are paid for in instalments, and the market price adjusts upwards just before the payment falls due. Paying the additional instalments is a legal liability, not an option. When the shares are only partly-paid, they often move up and down unusually sharply, but they cease to do this once the additional instalments are paid up.

Bearer shares are far more common on the continent of Europe than they are in the UK. The certificate itself is the proof of ownership, with no register of owners, and dividends are collected by sending off coupons. Good for secretive, careful investors.

Hereafter any mention of shares means Ordinary shares, unless stated otherwise.

Big and small

The modern stockmarket is dominated by large investing institutions. Most of them prefer to invest only in large companies whose shares can be bought and sold easily and cheaply in large quantities. And the increasing internationalization of the major stockmarkets has exacerbated the emphasis on size. **Blue chips** such as Shell or Unilever tend to be rated more highly than smaller companies, but a minority of smaller companies' shares do much better than blue chips.

Many of the 2,000-odd UK companies quoted in London are much too small to interest big investors. International investors don't look much below the 100 or so stocks which can also be traded on Wall Street or other major exchanges. Large British investors are prepared to invest freely in the top 700 or so. But only funds which specialize in smaller companies tend to pay much attention to those further down the list; to most fund managers any company with a market value of below £100m counts as small.

This discrimination in favour of large companies tends to be self-reinforcing. The main result is that in normal or stagnant markets shares in large companies are more highly rated than those in smaller companies. But the reverse is often true at the tail end of a bull market, when small growth stocks come into their own, and private investors frequently chase the shares of smaller companies up indiscriminately.

Over the long term shares of smaller companies have been shown to do better than those of large companies in most periods, but this is only because a small number of star growth stocks raises the smaller companies' average. Many small companies' shares do extremely badly, and are often particularly vulnerable to recession. In 1990 shares in smaller companies performed atrociously, and investors began to boycott them, but they made up some lost ground when the market recovered early in 1991.

The tiered market system has several side-effects which the investor should watch:

- Shares in the largest companies are normally more highly rated than those of smaller companies.
- Foreign buying interest can make favoured large companies' shares soar, but they can fall just as dramatically when foreigners lose interest.
- Shares in smaller companies often look relatively cheap, but that does not necessarily mean that they are going to be re-rated upwards.
- Investors who want to buy smaller company shares

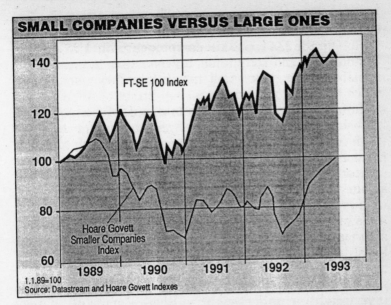

Fig 14.1 Sometimes companies of different sizes perform differently. As the recession struck small businesses were hit hard, and their shares fell badly relative to blue chips in 1990.

should recognize that they may not find it easy to deal and that their costs will be high. Problems will be particularly acute if the original owner of the company or other long-term shareholders own a large proportion of the equity.

● Small companies are less likely to move in line with their business sectors than large ones, partly because they are usually specialists, partly because the quality of management and financial controls is so variable.

● Small company shares are often assessed in their own right whereas large ones tend to be looked at against the sector to which they belong.

Sector classifications

Sector classifications matter partly because companies in the same line of business do have a lot in common, partly because large investors act as if sectors mattered. The most popular classification is the FT-Actuaries indexes which divide the top 800-odd companies into 35 specific sectors. For the individual investor they are a bit like social rules: once you understand how they work, it's up to you how far you conform.

Different sectors move in and out of fashion with investors. But most investing institutions aim to make their funds replicate the market as a whole fairly closely – because that limits the extent to which they can **underperform** the market. So they allocate the majority of their money according to fairly standard **sector weightings**. They know that, say, oil shares account for roughly 13 per cent of the London market. If they like oil shares they will have slightly more than 13 per cent of their UK portfolio in oils; dislike them and they'll have slightly less. Since there are just two big oil companies, BP and Shell, their only real bit of share assessment is to decide whether to go **overweight** or **underweight** in Shell – or in BP. If they think the oil price is going up, they will probably increase their weighting in BP, because a greater proportion of BP's profits come from crude oil extraction.

Any company which is in one of the FT-Actuaries sector indexes automatically gets a certain amount of support from investing institutions. For a big fund to have no shares at all in an FT-A company is equivalent to giving it the black spot. And a company that is newly elected to an index usually rises in price.

After a sector first comes into fashion, the **re-rating** normally takes some time, as a large number of fund managers ponderously increase their sector weightings. So a sector showing **relative strength** often continues vigorous for quite a long period. The same applies to individual large companies which are re-rated within their sector.

If private investors want to have a portfolio which matches the stockmarket, they should buy an **indexed** or **tracking** unit trust. Otherwise few individuals are rich enough to construct a portfolio which even begins to mimic the market as a whole. So they can afford to regard the fund managers' sector weighting urges merely as an

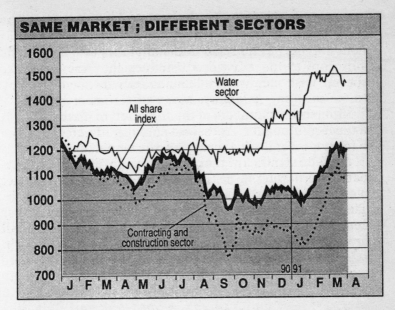

SAME MARKET ; DIFFERENT SECTORS

Fig 14.2 Similar businesses are classified into sectors, which quite often diverge from the market. During the recession in 1990 the advantages of stable profit growth from water companies meant that they outperformed the market, whilst the badly-hit construction sector lagged behind.

interesting tribal habit. Like many such habits, there is some common sense and a lot of self-interest behind the practice. But note that:

- Many sectors are dominated by just one or two companies. For example, the *Telephone networks* sector was only created to provide a home for BT.
- Some sectors, such as *Mechanical* engineering, cover an excessively wide area: everything from garden trowels to cigarette-making equipment. Others, such as *Contracting and construction* include groups whose fortunes can diverge substantially: roads sometimes get built when houses don't.
- Many companies have interests which spread across a number of sectors.
- Even in large companies, really good or bad management can make sector classifications meaningless.

Management matters

It does indeed, but it's hard to say anything very sensible about how to identify good management. Anyone can come up with examples of managers who have transformed an ailing company. Many of the most brilliant entrepreneurial managers of the 1980s fell to pieces when the times got tougher. And some managers fail to pull off the trick a second time if they move companies.

It must be significant that Hanson and BTR, two of the greatest corporate success stories of the past 25 years, have succeeded partly because there were so many badly-run companies around to take over. Investors certainly value the shares of companies with good management more highly. But by the time you read the manager's profile in your favourite Sunday paper, it's probably time to sell.

Cyclical stocks, growth stocks and recovery shares

Both long-term changes in the economy and short-term fluctuations in the pace of economic growth significantly affect the profitability of individual companies. A **cyclical** share is one whose profits tend to ebb and flow with economic cycles: growing while the economy is expanding, declining during recession.

The most sought-after type of **growth** company is one which operates in an industry whose overall importance to the economy is increasing sharply: electronics rather than shipbuilding, for instance. But changes within mature industries can also allow particular types of company to enjoy above-average growth until the industry has settled into a new pattern. And a minority of companies grow by imposing their management philosophy on to a wide spectrum of different businesses. Identifying which companies fall into exactly which category is an essential part of weighing up shares.

Not all companies are equally affected by business cycles, and some are affected earlier than others. Thus if consumer spending starts to flag, the first to notice will be

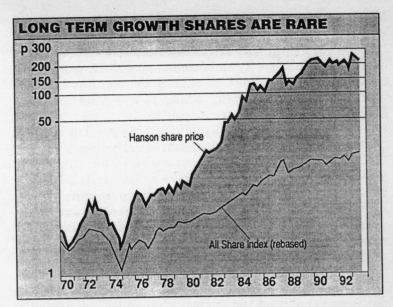

LONG TERM GROWTH SHARES ARE RARE

Hanson share price

All Share Index (rebased)

Fig 14.3 You have to go a long way to find a share which has consistently beaten the market over decades. Hanson is one of the few that has managed it, and even it has run out of steam lately.

the housebuilders, retailers, motor distributors, and other companies which deal directly with consumers. But weakening demand in the high street soon passes back to the companies which supply it with goods and services, who in turn will cut back on both on their capital investment and their raw material intake. The Stock Exchange's classification of companies into **Consumer** and **Capital** recognizes the distinction between frontline troops and the others.

Both company managers and fund managers try to lessen the adverse effects of downturns. Neither succeed completely. Cyclical companies in mature industries may, like ICI, increase their emphasis on the part of their business which is less vulnerable: demand for specialized chemicals fluctuates less than that for bulk chemicals, and pharmaceuticals is a fast-growing market. Other managements deliberately try to construct a 'portfolio' of businesses which react differently at different stages of the economic cycle. The trouble with the former approach is that it provides only a partial cushion against recession. The drawback to the latter is that **portfolio** companies almost by definition never do exceptionally well. And some fund managers dislike them on the grounds that the company managers are trying to do their job for them.

The fund manager's way to fight back against cycles is to go underweight on cyclical shares before recession sets in and overweight before it bottoms out. But this will at best mean that his share portfolio performs slightly better than the market as a whole. And since everybody is playing the same game, the market tends to anticipate economic changes long before they actually occur. Fund managers also try to buy **defensive** shares, such as food companies and possibly brewers, ahead of recessions, in the hope that their businesses and shares will suffer less.

Technological change is the most important generator of new expanding industries. Electronics, for instance, has spawned a large number of new growth companies. But there are usually several casualties in any new boom, too. And part of the interest in weighing up a growth sector is trying to sort out which is which. Often the beneficiaries of a technological development operate in apparently unrelated industries. One example is that of distribution companies which store and move goods for big retailers: these expanded greatly in the 1980s to cater for electronic stocktaking and ordering.

It is also true that trends like the surge in waste disposal businesses and in the leisure industry result from changes in the social environment, not technological development. Eventually, though, whatever the reason for expansion, all growth industries run out of steam. Hence the insistence of some go-go company managers that either clever acquisitions or abnormally efficient management will allow their company to continue growing regardless.

Investors need to be alert to the possibility that a growth company or industry is slowing down; past growth rates do not guarantee future growth. And since the stockmarket always overdoes its enthusiasms, growth stocks often have a long way to fall once disillusion sets in. Even if a growth trend remains intact, growth shares often do less well than cyclicals when an economy starts to emerge from recession; short-term the better-managed of the cyclical shares probably have more scope.

Recovery shares are a dangerous bunch. The label includes well-managed cyclical companies which are ready to expand profitably the moment the economy picks up, good companies which have hit a particular problem or failed to meet investors' expectations, and companies teetering on the brink of failure. One mechanical way of investing in such companies is to buy a broad selection towards the end of the recession and hope that on average they do well. An alternative method is to examine each company in considerable detail to assess how realistic its recovery hopes are.

An even more dangerous type of share, popular with private investors during mature bull markets, is the **penny share**. True penny shares are those in small companies which literally sell for a few pennies each. The share price is so low because at some stage in the company's history its problems have caused the price to fall very sharply. Sometimes new management moves into these tiny companies to take advantage of the fact that the company has a stockmarket quote and injects other business interests into the company, completely revitalizing a moribund firm. These companies are aptly described as **shells** and a classic example of the type was WPP, which had been a supermarket trolley manufacturer, but was taken over by ad-man Martin Sorrell, who turned it into a huge international advertising business. These shells frequently have a series of rights issues in the early stage of their development, and investors have to decide whether to back the manager. Those shells which work can produce fantastic returns for investors, but the majority fail.

In the latter stages of a bull market all penny shares tend to be sought avidly and indiscriminately by private investors, often relying on **tipsheets**. Strong demand and a limited number of shares can produce some amazing price rises. But since only a minority of penny shares are real growth stocks or even recovery stocks, there is usually a very nasty day of reckoning.

Currency and interest rate sensitive shares

Many businessmen say they mind less about the absolute level of foreign exchange and interest rates than about their volatility. Both affect a wide range of companies in different ways.

The level of the pound determines the sterling value of profits earned in foreign currencies by a company's foreign subsidiaries. It also influences both the competitiveness of British exports in foreign markets and that of imports into Britain. And it affects the prices of imported raw materials.

Say a company has an American subsidiary which earns $100m. When the pound was at $1.05 in 1985 those profits were worth £95m when converted back into sterling. In late 1990 the pound was worth $1.97. Assume that the company was still making $100m worth of profits. The sterling value of those profits would have dropped to £51m – the company's profits have dropped by £44m just because of a currency change. True, the company can hedge (see chapter 3) either its expected sales or its expected profits for several years ahead. But that can be costly, and is merely deferring its profits setback if the change in the currency rates proves lasting.

Still more damaging is the effect on exporters. If a company is exporting something costing £10 to America with the dollar at $1.05, its $10.50 US price may make it very attractive against a locally produced item selling for, say, $12.50. Assume a sterling rate of $1.97 and the £10 price leaps to $19.70, making it quite uncompetitive with the local product. Any reduction in the UK manufacturer's imported raw material costs is unlikely to compensate fully.

The effects of any given change in sterling on particular companies varies enormously. It is not just a question of working out where their exports go. In many cases British exporters are competing with companies in, say, Germany for customers in other countries. And in many cases customers cannot switch overnight. So the effects of a currency movement may be felt for a long time.

Interest rates have two different effects on businesses: there is a direct effect on companies which have very large borrowings. But interest rates also have an indirect effect through their influence on the economy. A prolonged period of high interest rates, as in 1989–90, will stop consumers spending and help tip the economy into recession.

Companies with very high borrowings suffer a direct hit on their profitability. Take a company with shareholders' funds of £100m and relatively modest borrowings of £50m. A 15 per cent return on capital employed (shareholders' funds plus borrowings) gives it profits of £22.5m before interest charges. With interest rates of 10 per cent, its interest bill is £5m, leaving it with profits of £17.5m before tax. But if interest rates doubled to 20 per cent, its interest charges of £10m would cut profits before tax to £12.5m, nearly 29 per cent down. If its sales drop because consumers are being squeezed by high interest rates, it may have to borrow even more money to finance surplus stock, and if the market for its goods is slack it will have trouble keeping its prices up, so profit margins may also be falling. Property developers and highly borrowed retailers were two types of company suffering from exactly this type of pincer in 1990.

The final blow is when the bankers start getting nervous and won't continue lending money. Then, even if companies are **solvent** (have more assets than liabilities) they will have **liquidity problems** (lack of ready cash to pay bills) since only certain types of asset can be sold at short notice.*

Rumours about borrowing and liquidity problems tend to get round the market, even if no official announcements have been made. But the first the private investor usually knows about it is when the share price of the troubled company collapses.

* Solvent is a slippery word. It is used both in this sense and as a near synonym for liquid. An illiquid company, which cannot pay its bills as they fall due, is technically insolvent (see chapter 20).

Types of Share

IN A NUTSHELL

1. Company shares are classified in a number of different ways. Some ways merely describe the business or the shares. Others aim to evaluate the business' profit potential or the shares' stockmarket characteristics.

2. These groupings operate independently of each other. Investors have to decide how a particular share's mix of attributes is likely to make its price move compared with those of others.

3. Some shares have more rights than others. A full description of the share will usually make these clear. These attributes can affect its price and performance very significantly. Most investors usually buy Ordinary shares.

4. The stockmarket divides shares according to the size of the company. Large companies, known as blue chips, are easier to buy and sell and are generally considered safer. But the fastest growth stocks start as small companies. Big companies are normally valued more highly than small ones — except at the tail end of a bull market.

5. Over 2,000 different UK shares are quoted on the London stockmarket. The FT-Actuaries indexes divide the 800-odd biggest companies into 35 different business sectors. Investors assume that companies in the same sector will tend to behave similarly.

6. Good or bad management can be a major determinant of company growth and profitabi-

lity. Investors value the shares of companies with good management more highly.

7. The relative growth and profitability of different types of business is affected both by economic cycles and by constant industrial evolution. Investors value shares in businesses which will benefit from either trend more highly than others.

8. Company profits are influenced by changes in foreign exchange rates or interest rates to differing degrees. When either type of rate moves or is expected to move, investors revise their valuation of the shares of the companies most affected.

Chapter 15
Valuing Shares

Valuing shares is not an exact science. In this respect, ordinary shares differ from debt issues. With a bond the income and redemption yield are known and the only imponderable is the risk of default. But the income paid on shares is variable and they have no redemption date, so it is not possible to know for certain either what an investment will yield whilst you have it, or what you will get for it when you sell it, or even what risks you are taking in holding it for the returns you might earn. In short, it is not possible to know for certain any of the things an investor would really like to know to make an informed judgement.

However, investors do use a number of yardsticks to measure shares which give an idea of whether shares are cheap or expensive relative to one another. Translating these measurements into valuations of what the shares are worth involves a considerable amount of subjective judgement and even guesswork, and these assumptions are often wrong – because, at heart, what investors are trying to measure is the **future** profitability of companies.

As we mentioned in chapter 10, the three standard yardsticks for measuring ordinary shares are the **dividend yield**, the **price earnings ratio** and the **net asset value**. The degree of importance which investors attribute to each of them depends partly on the type of company being assessed, and partly on the general business and stockmarket climate at the time. Yields and PE ratios are used mainly to compare the relative attractions of different investments. Net asset value, or NAV, is sometimes used as an absolute measure of value.

The dividend yield

The dividend yield measures the income you should get on a share, and is used to compare the income of different shares, different stockmarket sectors – or even to compare shares with other types of investment. It tells you how much income you can expect to receive on a share if you buy it at the current market price. An **historic** yield shows how much you would get if the company's future dividends were paid out at the same level as in the recent past. A **prospective** yield attempts to work out what future dividends are likely to be, and bases the calculation on this forecast. But neither kind of yield is certain – a company's dividends broadly reflect its profitability, so if a company is doing badly, it may omit or reduce its dividend. Large companies are not immune from this rule – as Midland Bank proved when it halved its dividend in 1991.

Dividend yield calculates are complicated by the fact that investors receive company dividends net of basic rate tax, but dividend yields are worked out on the gross dividend. For example, assume that a company pays annual dividends of 20p a share – the interim payment at half time is 5p, and the final dividend at the year end is 15p – but that 20p is assumed to be after basic rate tax has been paid at, the current rate which is now 20 per cent.

To work out the yield, first add back the tax which has been paid: this is known as **grossing up** the dividend. So if the relevent rate of tax is 20 per cent:

$$\frac{20}{80} \times 100 = 25p$$

That's your gross dividend per share. The yield depends on the share price: the higher the share price the lower the yield, so if the share price were 500p, the yield would be:

$$\frac{25}{500} \times 100 = 5.00 \text{ per cent}$$

Should the share price halve to 250p, the dividend yield doubles:

$$\frac{25}{250} \times 100 = 10.00 \text{ per cent}$$

and if the share price doubles to £10, the yield halves:

$$\frac{25}{1000} \times 100 = 2.50 \text{ per cent}$$

All of these yields are historic, based on the last payments the company actually made.

Now assume that the company forecasts it will increase its interim dividend to 10p a share (net). If it does not tell you anything about its intentions as far as the final dividend is concerned, you can conservatively assume that it will stick at the same level as the previous year, to give a total of 25p net, or 31.25p gross. If you feel more gung-ho about the company's prospects, you might assume that the final dividend concerned will also double to 30p, making a total pay-out of 40p net or 50p gross. Your guess will be governed by your estimate of the likely growth in profits and earnings. On the share price of 500p, the **prospective** yield on the conservative assumption is then 6.25 per cent; and on the adventurous estimate 10.00 per cent (The example is exaggerated to show the effect of both share price and dividend payment on the yield.)

There are three main ways to use dividend yields:

- **To measure future income**. Investors and funds interested primarily in income will include some high yielding shares (normally blue chips) in their portfolios. But they will still probably balance the size of the yield against the chances of capital growth. Even shares which yield well above the market average will tend to yield much less than a bank deposit or bond, so it only makes sense to include them if they offer some measure of capital growth.

- **To pin-point potential recovery shares**. Very high yielding shares are often dangerous as individual investments: the yield may be a signal that investors expect the dividend to be cut, or that it may not be paid at all, or even that investors think the company is going bust. But some investors think that buying a collection of high yielding shares is worthwhile, since a good capital performance from the survivors will make up for the few casualties. Portfolios selected for high income thus also sometimes produce above average capital growth.
- **To compare shares or groups of shares with each other**. Looking at comparative yields is normally only the start of the investigation. Take for example the situation where a textile share yields 8 per cent, a pharmaceutical share 3 per cent and the stockmarket as a whole 5 per cent. The relative yields suggest that investors are expecting an above-average capital performance from the pharmaceutical company and a below-average one from the textile firm. Investors then do further tests to see whether the market is making the right broad judgements about these types of business, or may look for companies which seem unfairly rated within these groups.

   The same approach is used to measure the attractions of shares against other investments such as gilts. Over the past 20 years equity yields have been consistently below that of gilts. Usually gilts have yielded between two and three times as much as equities, though this ratio has been lower at the bottom of bear markets – as in 1973/4 – and higher at the top of bull markets – as in 1987. Some investors use this **gilt/equity yield ratio** to try to spot stockmarket turning points. They argue that when the ratio falls below two the equity market will rise and/or the gilt market fall, and when it rises above three, equities will fall and/or gilts rise. This is probably valid, although investors sometimes have to wait a long time for this kind of gravity to assert itself.

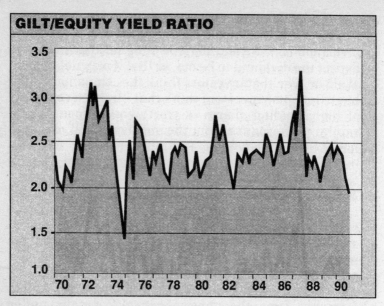

Fig 15.1 The gilt/equity yield ratio gives a measure of relative value between shares and bonds. A low number means that shares are cheap relative to gilts, a high number means they are expensive. The two notable points on the chart are the spike down in 1974 (the start of the 13 year bull market) and the high in 1987 (just before the crash).

Dividends as a sign of corporate health

A few types of business, such as insurance, have such erratic earnings that investors place an unusually great emphasis on dividend yields, because there is no easy alternative. Fund managers also like companies which increase their dividends steadily, but the yardstick here tends to be the average growth in dividends, rather than the dividend yield itself. Some professional investors go one stage further and treat a dividend cut as a betrayal of shareholders by a company's management.

This attitude was particularly noticeable at the start of the 1990s, after a long period of above-average dividend growth in the 1980s. Many companies had been increasing their dividends faster than their profits or earnings had grown so that their **dividend cover** – the earnings divided by the dividend payments – had fallen sharply. This is important because dividend cover is a measure of how easily a company can continue to pay its dividend. When the recession of 1990/91 hit, dividends were very vulnerable to cuts because companies were only just earning enough to pay the dividends in the good times, let alone the bad. This led to pressure from some institutions – most notably M&G – to make sure companies maintained their dividend payments.

How useful are dividend measurements?

They can be useful as part of an overall valuation exercise, but it is never safe to rely on dividend yield alone when deciding whether shares are good value. Those managements which choose to maintain a dividend in a bad year may be giving a signal of future prospects and long-term health, but those that maintain dividends purely in order to keep shareholders sweet may be hastening disaster.

The price earnings ratio

The price earnings ratio (PE ratio) relates the current share price of a company to the amount per share earned or expected to be earned by that company. It is calculated by dividing the current share price by the earnings for each share, and is used to measure the **relative** attractions of different shares. Broadly, the higher the PE ratio, the greater investors' expectations of profit growth for that company. Analysts try to decide whether the varying outlook for different companies is correctly reflected in their different ratings.

As with yields, an **historic** PE ratio is based on the earnings for a company's latest completed financial year, and a **prospective** PE ratio is based on an estimate of profits and earnings over the coming year. Most investors concentrate on forward-looking ratios, but the figures reported in the newspapers are historic. (Where possible they are updated after the profits for the first six months of a company's year are announced.) Comparisons of PE ratios are only useful if the ratios relate to the same financial period and are worked out on the same accounting basis.

A simplified example explains the basic calculation. Assume a company has share capital of £100,000 divided into 100,000 shares. Say its profits are £46,000 before corporation tax, and the tax rate is 35 per cent. Tax takes roughly £16,000 leaving total earnings, all of which belong to shareholders, of £30,000.

Divide the total earnings by the number of shares in issue and the earnings per share come out at 30p.

$$\frac{£30,000}{100,000} = 30p$$

This is the total amount earned for each share in a particular year, and many companies include this figure in their annual accounts. In theory all of this money is available to be paid out in dividends; in practice, most companies keep some of it back to plough into future investment.

If the share price of the company in our example is 500p, then the ratio of the price to the earnings per share – the PE ratio – is 16.6:

$$\frac{500}{30} = 16.6$$

The PE ratio can be described as the number of years' earnings required to equal the company's market value.

If the share price halves to 250p, the PE ratio also halves to 8.3:

$$\frac{250}{30} = 8.33$$

and if the share price doubles to £10, the PE ratio doubles, to 33.3:

$$\frac{1000}{30} = 33.3$$

Note that the higher the share price moves, the higher the PE ratio rises, and vice versa. The PE ratio moves in the opposite direction to the dividend yield.

At this point we can also make a rough calculation of the dividend cover. Assume that total dividends per share for the year are 20p net of tax. Dividend cover is then net earnings per share divided by net dividends per share*:

$$\frac{30}{20} = 1.5$$

In other words, the company could pay out half as much again without having to dip into profits from previous years. It is possible for companies to pay out more in dividends than they have earned in a particular year, provided they have enough reserves saved from previous years. Such a dividend is sometimes called **short earned** or **uncovered**.

Looking forward

Working out prospective PE ratios is something of a black art because analysts are having to make an estimate of a company's future earnings. These estimates can either be done on the back of an envelope or by sophisticated analysis, but essentially the analyst is trying to second-guess what future profitability is going to be. Sometimes a company will give guidance, saying perhaps that 'profits are currently running 20 per cent above last year's levels, and we look forward to another year of increased

---

* The net dividend is used because the company has usually already allowed for basic rate tax when paying corporation tax. It does not have to pay tax on these earnings twice. Statistical purists do a far more complicated sum to work out cover. But this is really only necessary if a company has either an unusually low tax charge, or gets the majority of its profits from abroad.

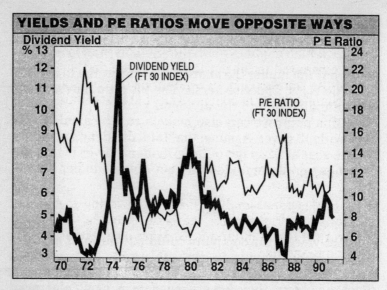

Fig 15.2 For a company earning a fixed level of profits, a fall in its share price will mean its PE ratio falls, whilst its yield rises. Both yields and PEs showed shares were cheap in 1974 and expensive in 1987, but beware of commentators bearing hindsight!

earnings.' But such forecasts are not guarantees, just informed guesses.

Using PE ratios

In itself a PE ratio tells you nothing about whether a share is good or bad value, and even when looking at a group of PE ratios, the only thing they tell you is what sort of profits growth investors are expecting from each company. The investment analyst's skill lies first in deciding whether those expectations are realistic, and then in comparing these share ratings and expectations with other similar company's. He is looking for anomalies, but even if he finds one, he has to decide which way the market is going to adjust.

Take a couple of food retailers: A has a PE of 12, B one of 17. If their prospects are **identical** and there is no other obvious reason for the discrepancy, either A's shares are too low, or B's too high. Analysts first weigh up the prospects in detail; then search for any other fact or statistic which might explain the anomaly, and look at the sector compared to the market. Only then do they form a view of the shares. That view might be that both are good value compared to the market, but that one is much more attractive than the other.

How useful are PE ratios?

Many professional analysts have been trying to find an alternative to PE ratios for years. But provided investors are aware of their limitations, they are useful tools. These limitations include:

- The rating exercise is very approximate. It is not even clear how far investors are looking into the future when making their comparisons.
- Using prospective PE ratios involves forecasting future profitability. That forecasting is often wrong.
- The accounts on which historic PE ratios are based are surprisingly subjective (see chapter 16). For instance, stated profits and earnings can be considerably affected by factors such as stock valuation which, in turn, depends upon estimates of future trading patterns. Even professional analysts are uncertain how to treat some non-standard items; for example, some companies are in the habit of selling off buildings and booking this as a trading profit; others treat interest charges on new developments as a capital cost.
- It is rare to find companies which are totally comparable. Most big firms have a mix of businesses and many small ones are idiosyncratic, so it is not surprising that PE ratios vary.
- PE ratios are no use for companies with erratic earnings – like insurance companies or commodity traders – or other specialist companies like investment trusts or property companies where investors are mainly concerned with the value of assets.
- International comparisons are dangerous. First,

because accounting conventions vary and second, because global investment is in its infancy. Shares influenced by domestic and international factors can move in different ways. But even similar businesses like British Airways and Japan Air Lines trade on wildly different PE ratios, because of the different expectations of Japanese and European investors.

Net asset value

The net asset value per share tells you what you might expect to get as a shareholder if the company stopped trading, all its assets were sold off and the proceeds handed back to shareholders. It is calculated by aggregating all of the company's assets, deducting its liabilities, and dividing the result by the number of ordinary shares in issue. Most companies' shares are worth far more than their net asset value, because investors expect them to continue earning profits in the years ahead. In a case where a company's shares get badly hit because investors expect it to go bust, yet it is likely to recover, then trading at a discount to net assets is not justified. By implication this suggests the shares are a buy. Some companies where the key indication of the company's worth is the value of their assets, such as property or investment trusts, are assessed according to their net asset value.

To see how it works for ordinary companies, take the Marks & Spencer balance sheet shown on page 276, and focus on the net assets figures of £2,966.9m. Knock off the minority interests of £17m and the £1.4m of preference capital (shown in the footnote, not on our table), and you get the Net Assets for Ordinary shares which rounds to £2,948.5m. Another part of the accounts tells you that there are 2,757m ordinary shares in issue, so the net asset value is:

$$\frac{£2,948.5m}{2,757m} \times £1.07$$

To make it easy on the layman, most companies give the NAV figure somewhere in the accounts. Many novice

FT-SE Actuaries Share Indices UK SERIES

		Day's Jul 6 change %	Year ago	Dividend yield %	Earnings yield %	P/E Ratio	Total Return
	FT-SE 100	2848.1 +0.3	2493.7	4.02	5.91	21.07	1023.77
	FT-A ALL-SHARE	1413.02 +0.3	1199.87	3.92	5.85	21.34	1059.58
1	**CAPITAL GOODS(214)**	997.80 +0.3	805.60	3.99	4.25	31.27	1170.74
2	Building Materials(28)	1057.92 +0.4	890.51	4.42	3.72	37.55	1221.99
3	Contracting, Construction(29)	937.18 −0.3	782.27	3.51	1.45	80.00†	1292.55
4	Electricals(15)	2972.81 +1.1	2449.53	4.54	4.89	26.08	1197.30
5	Electronics(38)	2707.57 −0.5	2000.42	3.18	6.13	20.19	1183.51
6	Engineering-Aerospace(7)	412.29 +1.0	325.90	3.58	‡	‡	1423.57
7	Engineering-General(48)	578.04 +0.1	481.69	3.75	6.37	19.49	1154.07
8	Metals & Metal Forming(10)	392.10 −0.6	313.97	2.79	‡	‡	1237.24
9	Motors(20)	415.77 +0.8	335.35	5.23	4.49	31.19	1138.22
10	Other Industrials(19)	2111.31 +0.6	1731.13	4.27	5.40	22.11	1088.03
21	**CONSUMER GROUP(235)**	1615.55 +0.1	1585.61	3.56	6.98	17.45	935 34
22	Brewers and Distillers(30)	1871.40 −0.5	2039.12	3.93	8.34	14.49	911.12
25	Food Manufacturing(22)	1298.11 +0.3	1244.05	3.92	7.58	15.88	998.91
26	Food Retailing(17)	2802.54 −0.1	2799.66	3.33	9.22	13.47	877.07
27	Health & Household(30)	3312.43 +1.2	3760.87	3.71	6.62	17.66	787.04
29	Hotels and Leisure(20)	1350.84 −0.5	1202.89	4.40	6.23	20.11	1070.76
30	Media(33)	2027.05 +0.2	1523.05	2.56	5.01	24.20	1124.43
31	Packaging and Paper(24)	839.19	767.01	3.51	5.82	21.13	1091.45
34	Stores(39)	1151.20 −0.3	1012.53	3.09	6.16	20.75	1006.29
35	Textiles(20)	794.02 +0.2	649.70	3.85	6.00	20.90	1081.22
40	**OTHER GROUPS(142)**	1495.70 +0.6	1249.11	4.29	7.31	16.59	1055.76
41	Business Services(28)	1640.54 +0.4	1374.58	2.79	7.16	16.02	1091.61
42	Chemicals(23)	1507.60 +0.1	1379.38	4.36	0.28	‡	1083.10
43	Conglomerates(11)	1410.31 −0.1	1251.01	5.40	7.57	14.85	1039.10
44	Transport(15)	2921.88 +0.4	2449.36	3.94	5.14	24.66	1076.78
45	Electricity(16)	1802.53 +0.7	1371.71	4.37	12.49	9.92	1169.28
46	Telephone Networks(4)	1791.37 +1.4	1394.78	3.78	5.85	21.05	1062.99
47	Water(13)	3205.47 +0.2	2837.02	5.50	13.66	8.05	1012.63
48	Miscellaneous(32)	2250.56 +0.1	1982.72	4.55	7.50	15.95	927.52
49	**INDUSTRIAL GROUP(591)**	1433.80 +0.3	1284.97	3.89	6.53	18.81	1016.43
51	Oil & Gas(18)	2457.19 +0.5	1980.48	4.45	5.69	22.26	1118.41
59	**"500" SHARE INDEX(609)**	1524.66 +0.3	1351.25	3.95	6.44	19.13	1026.76
61	**FINANCIAL GROUP(90)**	1063.90 +0.4	719.57	4.00	3.56	41.75	1244.60
62	Banks(9)	1462.61 +0.4	933.85	3.69	4.23	32.55	1253.86
65	Insurance (Life)(6)	2043.78 −0.1	1470.58	4.37	4.70	26.76	1188.78
66	Insurance (Composite)(7)	679.95 +0.1	499.27	4.58	‡	‡	1110.19
67	Insurance Brokers(10)	913.46 −0.3	813.29	3.96	6.11	22.03	1204.10
68	Merchant Banks(6)	675.89 +0.1	454.73	3.32	7.18	17.20	1372.42
69	Property(29)	875.58 +1.4	622.56	4.63	4.65	28.72	1399.61
70	Other Financial(23)	387.95 +0.6	241.95	4.30	5.72	23.59	1309.88
71	Investment Trusts(110)	1522.73 +0.1	1142.62	2.69	2.13	46.89	1155.66
99	**FT-A ALL-SHARE(809)**	1413.02 +0.3	1199.87	3.92	5.85	21.34	1059.58

Source: Financial Times

Fig 15.3 A table in the *Financial Times* gives the performance of each of the FT-A sectors, as well as their yield and PE ratio.

investors are surprised that net asset value is not given greater weight by professionals, because they feel it is somehow more 'real' than the other two measures. The fact that share prices are much higher than asset value is also a shock. M&S shares are worth around £3.30, but its net assets are only £1.07.

But in good times, investors are interested in how much money a company can make as a going concern, and there is no standard relationship between a company's assets and its profitability. Indeed, that will vary dramatically from business to business. Car manufacturers need many more fixed assets to make a profit than advertising agencies do.

Asset values are important, however, in some circumstances:

- When a company is in trouble, and shareholders are worried that it may go bust. Asset values (if they are reliable) may then put a floor under the share price.
- When a bid is made for the shares. A bid below asset value is unlikely to be accepted by shareholders.
- If a company's asset value is above its market price it may indicate that the assets are being badly used, or that the market is undervaluing assets in that company.

Relying on asset values can be dangerous, because in many cases they do not reflect the tax which would have to be paid if the company was wound up, and if the company is in trouble its assets might not fetch as much as expected in a **fire sale**. In any event these NAVs will be based on accounts which may be out of date and contain subjective valuations.

Other yardsticks

Other ways of monitoring companies come in and out of fashion. The **borrowing ratio** – borrowings as a percentage of shareholders funds – is one that becomes popular in recession. So do **liquidity ratios**, designed to show how easily companies could pay off their short-term creditors if they got impatient (see chapter 20).

Cash flow measurements and **shareholder value analysis** are both becoming more popular with sophisticated investors. They try to look behind the accounts and to minimize the impact of varying accounting practices. The former checks that more cash flowed into than out of the business during the year, and the latter checks whether the year actually left shareholders better off. One measure which some City observers find useful is a **turnover/ market capitalization ratio**. This shows how well sales are doing relative to the value of the company and indicates how well companies are using their assets. For example, when turnover collapsed in the retailing trade in 1988/89, the turnover/market cap. ratio slumped. Later, earnings and share prices followed.

Valuing Shares

IN A NUTSHELL

1. Valuing shares is not an exact science because shares do not pay a fixed rate of return and have no redemption date. Most ways of measuring shares are relative.

2. Investors use three main measures to assess share values: dividend yield, price earnings ratio and net asset value. The first two are relative, the third an absolute measure.

3. The dividend yield tells investors what kind of income they can expect from a share, and can be used to compare shares with each other or different types of investment. As share prices rise, yields fall.

4. Yields can be historic and based on the previous year's profits, or prospective and based on estimates of future earnings. Most investors look at future earnings.

5. Price earnings ratios give a measure of how high a company's share price is relative to its earnings. A high PE ratio means that investors expect earnings to rise sharply. As share prices rise, PE ratios rise.

6. PE ratios can be useful in evaluating how companies compare but can be suspect because businesses frequently differ, and earnings valuations are sometimes unreliable. International comparisons are often invalid.

7. Net asset value measures what shares in a company would be worth if it was wound up. It

is used in situations where a company seems in danger of going bust, or where assets are very important to the firm – particularly investment trusts and property shares.

8. Net asset values are normally far below share prices because investors are concerned with a company's ongoing business. They may not give a true representation of what a company would actually fetch if wound up.

9. Other measures of company performance include cash flow analysis, liquidity ratios, borrowing ratios and shareholder value analysis. These tools move in and out of fashion.

Chapter 16
Company Accounts

Some investors never look at company accounts because they are put off by the jargon and the numbers. Yet annual reports are important documents and can be very useful in investment analysis. Of course they do have their shortcomings. If a company is determined to be secretive or misleading, the accounts may tell you nothing more than a Mills and Boon novel. And since all reports look alike, it is difficult to tell the sheep from the goats. To some extent you will need to rely on instinct, a healthy sense of scepticism and dark hints in the newspapers to avoid the crooks. The starting point must be to decide whether a management is trustworthy – if it is there is some chance you can believe in the figures which the board provides. By the way, do not be taken in by the fact that accounts are audited by reputable firms of accountants. Auditors are paid by companies and have a strong incentive to do what the company wants in order to keep the audit for next year. The spectacular failures of recent times show that companies which looked solid at the year end can go bust within months.

That said, for reputable companies annual reports provide a lot of information, and companies or their **registrars** are normally happy to send out accounts on request. The key parts of the financial information are the **profit and loss account**, the **balance sheet** and the **cash flow statement**. The P&L tells you what happened during the last year and how much money was made or lost. The balance sheet is a snapshot of what the company owned and owed at the year end, and the cash flow statement shows how much money flowed into or out of the business during the year.

Following on from the excesses of the 1980s there have been substantial changes in company accounts in the last few years, so this chapter has been completely changed from the first edition of this book. As an example of how accounts should be done we have used the 1993 Marks & Spencer accounts which make clear the changes so far.

Legal standing

Companies are obliged by law to produce a set of accounts annually. They are automatically sent to shareholders a few weeks before the **Annual General Meeting**. Also included are a notice of the meeting and motions shareholders are invited to vote on. The essential elements of the accounts are the **directors' report to shareholders**; the profit and loss account, balance sheet and cash flow statement and an **auditor's report** on the financial items from the independent accountants which tells shareholders whether the accounts give a **true and fair view** of the company's financial state. The elasticity of that phrase is a long-standing part of UK accounting which has also allowed a lot of abuse.

Stockmarket standing

The Stock Exchange insists that quoted companies publish two other slugs of information.

- Interim results, reporting on profitability in the first six months of the year. Companies may also declare an interim dividend and include an interim balance sheet and cash flow statement.
- Preliminary annual results for the year. This contains much of the headline information in the accounts and, as it comes out first, is the report most widely written up in the newspapers. However, the preliminary announcement does not have to be audited. Nor does it contain the notes to the accounts which have much of the detail. Investors can thus be misled, and it is still very important to look at the full accounts.

Any other serious development, such as a bid or warning that profits will be much lower than expected, also has to be reported to the Stock Exchange and announced on the SE's news service.

The profit and loss account

The P&L tells you whether a company's annual income exceeded its expenditure, and how large the resulting profit or loss is. It allows you to check that profit against the previous year so that you can judge its progress. And it tells you what happened to the profit – how much went in tax, how much was paid in dividends, and how much was retained to use in the business. The P&L is the document most people look at but it can be misleading. There are plenty of ways that companies can try to inflate their profits, and just because something shows as a profit doesn't mean the company has the money in the bank.

At the top of the P&L is the gross amount which the company earned in a year, then line by line are taken away the different areas of spending, ending up with the amount of profit – or loss – which is left to add into the business. The two main changes to the P&L which have been made recently are the separation of continuing business from operations which have been sold or closed, and the effective banning of **extraordinary** items. These were usually large losses and used to appear as a kind of footnote almost as though they didn't count. Such items now appear in the main P&L. The references to notes in the P&L guide the reader to detailed breakdowns of the figures which we have not included. So, here is how Marks & Spencer's 1993 P&L panned out.

● **Turnover.** Another word for sales, and pretty self-explanatory for a retailer like M&S. Note how the continuing operations have been separated from the discontinued part – which is mostly the closed Peoples department store chain. It is the continuing business which matters, and you would normally hope that sales would be up on the previous year. In this case M&S's sales are only up 3.4 per cent on 1992, which shows how the recession has slowed M&S down. Analysts will look at the half-year figures to get a feel for how sales are trending in the second half against the first, and the divisional and geographical breakdown to identify successes or failures.

MARKS AND SPENCER PLC				
CONSOLIDATED PROFIT AND LOSS ACCOUNT				
for the year ended 31 March 1993				
	1993		1992 restated	
	£m	£m	£m	£m
Turnover				
Continuing operations	**5,925.2**		5,728.0	
Discontinued operations	**25.6**		99.5	
		5,950.8		5,827.5
Cost of sales		**3,879.6**		3,857.3
Gross profit		**2,071.2**		1,970.2
Other expenses		**1,334.5**		1,292.5
Operating profit				
Continuing operations	**739.9**		681.7	
Discontinued operations	**(3.2)**		(4.0)	
		736.7		677.7
Discontinued operations provision used		**3.2**		1.5
		739.9		679.2
UK profit sharing		**18.1**		16.2
Loss on sale of fixed assets in continuing operations		**7.8**		8.2
UK head office restructure		**—**		16.9
Provision for discontinued Canadian operations				
Provision set up	**—**		59.8	
Cost incurred	**43.6**		2.3	
Provision used	**(43.6)**		(2.3)	
		—		59.8
Profit before interest and taxation		**714.0**		578.1
Net interest receivable		**22.5**		10.8
Profit on ordinary activities before taxation		**736.5**		588.9
Tax on ordinary activities		**239.5**		218.3
Profit on ordinary activities after taxation		**497.0**		370.6
Minority interests		**1.5**		2.6
Profit for the financial year		**495.5**		368.0
Dividends		**223.6**		194.5
Undistributed surplus		**271.9**		173.5
Earnings per share		**18.0p**		13.5p

Fig 16.1 Marks & Spencer's P&L for 1993.

- **Cost of sales.** What M&S paid its suppliers for clothes, food services and so on, plus the difference between stock levels at the start and end of the year. This figure is only up by 0.5 per cent, showing that Marks' knows that times are tough and if sales are growing slowly it must keep cost growth lower if it is to increase profits. Stocks (shown in the balance sheet) are barely up on a year earlier.

- **Other expenses.** Mostly staff costs, but it also includes an allowance for wear and tear on the shops – known as **depreciation**. This total increased by slightly less than sales, but analysts noted that staff costs would rise in the next year because of a new pay award.

- **Operating profit.** This is the profit the company would make if it didn't have to pay interest on its debt, and so gives a feel for the underlying business. Again this is split into continuing and closed operations. Continuing operating profit is up by 8.5 per cent, showing the benefit of cost control. Analysts check the relationship between profits and sales – Marks' profits are about 12.5 per cent of sales – and compare it to the previous year (higher) as well as competitors' performance to check how the company is doing. Very nicely, thank you.

- **Discontinued operations provision used.** Money had previously been set aside in previous P&Ls to cover the cost of closing a business. It cost £3.2m in 1993, so £3.2m of the war chest is added back as the loss has effectively already been taken.

- **UK profit sharing.** Even the staff get a cut.

- **Loss on sale of fixed assets.** Previously if a company sold property for more than it cost, then it could take the difference as profit. That might seem reasonable enough, except that companies also revalued their properties in the balance sheet from time to time (see page 276). Doing both meant that they showed themselves having a lot of assets, and making big profits when they sold too. Some stores groups and brewers made a lot of their 'profits' that way in the late 1980s – showing how slippery the P&L can be. This is really having your cake and eating it, so now companies have to compare the amount they get when they sell a property with its value in the balance sheet. M&S's directors last revalued properties in 1988, near the peak of the market, so it tends to show losses on disposal.

- **UK head office restructure.** This is an **exceptional** item – ie one which is unusual. In 1992 there was a £16.9m one-off charge for cutting back staff at head office, but nothing in 1993.
- **Provision for discontinued Canadian operations.** In 1992 the company decided to close its Peoples department stores and scale back its M&S shops in Canada. The notes to the accounts show that £30m was an exceptional item for cutting back M&S Canada, just like the head office costs. However, £29.8m was an **extraordinary** item – ie one which is so mind-bogglingly rare that it goes at the bottom of the P&L and so does not get noticed – for closing Peoples. These extraordinary items have now been banned because companies were using them too frequently. That means that all profits or losses now appear 'above the line' – ie before the final profits and earnings figures are calculated. M&S has done the right thing and re-stated the Peoples extraordinary item as exceptional. £2.3m of the cost of closure was incurred in 1992 and £43.6m in 1993, and the money set aside in 1992 has been released accordingly. That means that of the £59.8m set aside, £13.9m is still available to set against future Canadian costs.
- **Profit before tax.** The headline figure, and reasonably so in most cases. M&S is up by 25 per cent – but that is partly because it set aside the £59.8m for Canada in 1992. So the improvement in the underlying business is not so marked. It is also worth glancing down to the **earnings per share** line, which is up 33 per cent at 18p. Again this is distorted by Canada. Any divergence between earnings and profits is worth examining. If, say, a company has bought another for shares the profits may be up, but the return on each share may be down. That's an alarm bell. Earnings are calculated on profits after tax, so tax can have an impact. M&S's tax charge fell from an unusually high level in 1992, helping earnings increase faster than profits.
- **Tax.** Depressingly familiar. One point which is worth making about tax is that basic rate at 20 per cent is deducted from dividends and counts towards the

company's corporation tax payment. This is so that
investors are not taxed twice on profits and to make
sure that tax does not distort how much money is kept
in companies rather than paid as dividends. However,
if companies have large overseas earnings – on which
they pay foreign taxes – but little in the UK, they may
not have enough UK corporation tax to offset the
amount they have paid through dividends. Unfortunately they cannot claim this back but can save up the
payment against future UK taxes. The corporation tax
rate is currently 33 per cent of profits. Companies with
lower tax rates have allowances to offset against tax,
companies with higher rates often have this overseas
earnings and dividend problem. M&S's tax rate is 32.5
per cent – ie normal.

- **Minority interests.** If one of a company's subsidiaries
  is partly owned by someone else, this is where their
  slice of the profits is deducted. It only matters if
  it's big.
- **Profit for the year.** The bottom line. If you knock off
  any preference share dividends – according to the
  notes that's only £0.1m in the case of M&S – then you
  have the **earnings** figure, which is used to calculate the
  earnings per share. To save calculator power, that's
  shown below.
- **Dividends.** Although the cash total is shown it is rather
  ridiculously hard to tell from the P&L what the dividend per share is. In the directors' report, however, it
  says that dividends per share were 8.1p (next of basic
  rate tax) in 1993, up 14 per cent on 1992. In a mature
  business like M&S, that's some guide to the directors'
  view of longer-term growth. What the P&L does, however, is help you calculate the safety of the dividend.
  Total earnings are 2.2 times the total cost of dividends
  on ordinary shares, so there is no real worry that M&S
  can afford to keep paying. This ratio is called **dividend
  cover**. Some companies with insufficient earnings in
  one year can pay an **uncovered** or **short-earned** dividend if they have enough earnings saved from previous
  years and think the dip will be temporary. On the other
  hand, companies spending very hard on growing the

business may keep back more of the earnings than
average.

- **Undistributed surplus.** This goes into the company's
coffers and is used to expand the business or reduce
debt. It is added to the accumulated **profit and loss
account** in the balance sheet.

The balance sheet

The balance sheet provides a snapshot of everything the
company owes and owns at the end of the financial year.
Because big firms like M&S have subsidiary companies
they have set up or acquired, the M&S company balance
sheet does not tell the full story. So the accounts also
show **group accounts** which **consolidate** all the subsidiaries into one big balance sheet as though they were a
single company. This group balance sheet is the one to
focus on. It tells you how much the shareholders have got
invested in the company, allows you to work out whether
it is making an adequate return on capital and whether it
is **solvent** (assets exceed liabilities) and **liquid** (cash exceeds short-term debts). It gives you a view of the financial strength of the company, warns you of some potential
problems and shows why a bidder might be interested in
the company, yet few investors bother to look at it!

This time, start at the bottom. This shows you how
much the company is worth to shareholders, then tells
you how the money is being used.

- **Shareholders' funds.** This is what shareholders would
theoretically get if M&S shut up shop, sold off its
assets, repaid its creditors and distributed the rest to
shareholders.
There are four elements to shareholders' funds. The
share capital is shown at nominal face value even if the
shares were sold for more when they were first issued.
Thus each M&S share is treated as worth 25p even though
its market value is many times higher. The **share premium account** recognizes part of that anomaly. If shares
are issued above their nominal face value, the excess goes
into the share premium account. The **revaluation reserve**

MARKS AND SPENCER PLC
BALANCE SHEET at 31 March 1993

	The Group 1993 £m	1992 restated £m
Fixed assets		
Tangible assets:		
Land and buildings	2,453.4	2,359.0
Fixtures, fittings and equipment	417.1	385.6
Assets in the course of construction	38.1	32.1
	2,908.6	2,776.7
Investments	19.4	4.7
	2,928.0	2,781.4
Current assets		
Stocks	344.2	338.3
Debtors – receivable within one year	406.1	358.0
– receivable after more than one year	323.4	290.2
Investments	53.9	50.6
Cash at bank and in hand	634.1	487.7
	1,761.7	1,524.8
Current liabilities		
Creditors: amounts falling due within one year	1,230.7	1,168.8
Net current assets	531.0	356.0
Total assets less current liabilities	3,459.0	3,137.4
Creditors: amounts falling due after more than one year	446.4	401.5
Provisions for liabilities and charges	45.7	75.8
Net assets	2,966.9	2,660.1
Capital and reserves		
Called up share capital	690.6	686.4
Share premium account	129.7	103.0
Revaluation reserve	445.9	454.8
Profit and loss account	1,680.7	1,402.8
Shareholder's funds	2,949.9	2,647.0
Minority interests	17.0	13.1
Total capital employed	2,966.9	2,660.1

Fig 16.2 Marks & Spencer's balance sheet for 1993.

is the amount by which assets – basically property – have been revalued by the company's directors and periodically checked by independent chartered surveyors since they were bought. It is an attempt to keep the value of the company's assets up to date, since long-standing companies like M&S would look silly if all their property were shown at pre-war values. However, property revaluation was used by some 1980s cowboys to make their companies appear as though they had lots of assets and were financially strong. Lots of jiggery-pokery with revaluations or sale and leaseback of property is often a

warning sign. No problem with M&S, though, its policies
are very conservative. The last part of shareholders'
funds is the **profit and loss account**. This is the profits
accumulated over the years which have not been paid out
as dividends. The P&L account in the balance sheet
increased by £6m more than the undistributed surplus in
the 1993 main P&L. The relevant note 25 explains how
exchange rate movements and shareholders taking dividends as shares are responsible for the difference.

The top half of the balance sheet is devoted to how
shareholders' funds are deployed, and what other (borrowed) funds are being used in the business.

- **Fixed assets.** For M&S this is mainly shops and fittings;
  for other companies it might be factories or machinery.
  Since most assets wear out, fixed assets tend to have
  their balance sheet values steadily reduced over their
  working lives. This reduction is the counterpart of the
  depreciation charge discussed in the P&L account. It is
  worth checking in the blurb of the accounts what the
  company's policy on depreciation and the revaluation
  of property is. Companies may have been over-
  cautious or over-optimistic in their views. For
  example, a very low depreciation charge will tend to
  increase profits – since it is not deducted from the P&L,
  and it may also show fixed assets as being worth more
  now than they actually are. On the other hand, writing
  everything off immediately may be an attempt to blame
  the last guy and make things look better later. This is a
  favourite trick of newly arrived chief executives or
  predators which have just taken over a company.
- **Investments.** Now split between long-term investments under fixed assets and shorter-term holding
  under current assets. In longer-term holdings companies sometimes have substantial amounts invested
  in other businesses – for example the shares of another
  company. Not very significant in M&S's case. The
  notes show just a few shares, gilts and pre-paid tax,
  plus a joint venture in property development with
  J. Sainsbury called Hedge End Park.
- **Current assets.** Here is the remarkably small increase
  in stocks we noted earlier. If you see a company whose

stock shoots up, watch out. It may be having trouble selling its goods and might have to discount them later. Other current assets are the company's debtors – ie the people who owe it money. If the company is having trouble collecting money these can rise sharply, which squeezes the company's cash flow. Also included are short-term investments and M&S's cash pile.

- **Current liabilities.** These are short-term borrowings, trade creditors and unpaid tax. Current liabilities have risen much less than current assets – mainly because M&S is piling up cash. Its net current assets have thus increased substantially. When these assets (or liabilities) are added to the fixed assets, the **total assets less current liabilities** figure gives a measure of the short-run strength of the group.

Once longer-term borrowings and other liabilities are deducted, the **net assets** figure shows the sum of what the group owns. It is equal to the shareholders' funds. The top half of the balance sheet is thus the net figure for what the company owns, and the bottom half is how the capital has been raised to buy it.

Two other points about balance sheets. M&S has cash in the bank, but many other companies have borrowings. If these become too large they threaten the survival of the business, since it may not even make enough money to pay its interest bill. Analysts thus looking at the ratio of net borrowings to shareholders' funds known as the **gearing ratio**. In general, if a company has gearing much higher than 50 per cent, it had better have a very good reason.

It is also worth noting that many companies write off a portion of the price they paid for a company after they have acquired it. If the bidder has paid more than the assets are worth, the excess is known as **goodwill** and is cut directly from the balance sheet, not shown as a loss in the P&L. This weakens the company – especially if borrowed money has been used for the bid. Many bidders also use **fair value provisions** to write off stock and such from acquired companies. Currently this is also directly written off from the balance sheet, but if the stock were

MARKS AND SPENCER PLC		
CONSOLIDATED CASH FLOW STATEMENT		
for the year ended 31 March 1993		
	1993	1992 restated
	£m	£m
Operating activities		
Net cash received from customers	**5,893.3**	5,775.3
Cash payments to suppliers	**(3,878.7)**	(3,868.0)
Cash paid to and on behalf of employers	**(711.2)**	(709.0)
Other cash payments	**(524.6)**	(476.8)
Net cash inflow from operating activities	**778.8**	721.5
Expenditure against exceptional provisions	**(15.7)**	(33.3)
Returns on investments and servicing of finance		
Interest received	**51.3**	46.4
Interest paid	**(33.7)**	(31.1)
Dividends paid	**(188.3)**	(175.8)
Net cash outflow from returns on investments and servicing of finance	**(170.7)**	(160.5)
Taxation		
UK corporation tax paid	**(201.4)**	(205.5)
Overseas tax paid	**(14.1)**	(10.7)
Tax paid	**(215.5)**	(216.2)
Investing activities		
Purchase of tangible fixed assets	**(254.9)**	(291.9)
Sale of tangible fixed assets	**17.3**	10.2
Purchase of fixed asset investments	**(27.9)**	(4.7)
Sale of fixed asset investments	**13.2**	—
Sale of subsidiary	**4.3**	—
Net cash outflow from investing activities	**(248.0)**	(286.4)
Net cash inflow before financing and treasury activities	**128.9**	25.1
Financing and treasury activities		
Shares issued under employees' share schemes	**30.9**	40.0
Other borrowing	**115.2**	10.9
Repayment of amounts borrowed	**(150.0)**	—
(Purchase)/redemption of non-cash equivalent deposits and short term investments	**(139.9)**	(119.5)
Net cash outflow from financing and treasury activities	**(143.8)**	(68.6)
Decrease in cash and cash equivalents	**(14.9)**	(43.5)
Decrease in net borrowings	**135.9**	65.7

Fig 16.3 Marks & Spencer's 1993 cash flow statement.

subsequently sold for more, it would show up as a profit!
Many fake fortunes were made by manipulating such
tricks in the 1980s, and this **acquisition accounting** is
now being looked at. Anyone who makes extensive use of
it deserves suspicion.

Cash flow statement

Because of tricks like acquisition accounting, investors have started to focus on cash flow as a more tangible measure of how a company is doing. The new statement is divided up into five areas:

- **Operating activities.** This shows how much cash flowed in from customers through the tills, and then deducts cheques written out to suppliers and salaries paid to staff to give a net cash inflow from the operating business. Healthy in M&S's case and 7 per cent up on last year. Any exceptional cash expenditure is then deducted.
- **Returns on investment and finance.** Shows the amount of interest earned and paid and deducts shareholders' dividends.
- **Tax.** Pretty obvious, though note that the cash tax paid is not the same as the tax incurred in the P&L account.
- **Investing activities.** If the company buys or sells fixed assets like stores, it shows up here, as do other investments, like shares. M&S's capital expenditure programme was clearly running at a lower level in 1993 than the previous year.

These first four areas show how much cash the business brought in, how much was paid in tax and dividends and how much re-invested in the future of the business. The net figure or **net cash inflow (or outflow) before financing activities** shows whether the company is throwing off cash like M&S or absorbing it rapidly. This is the key line in the cash flow statement and shows the net position of the company. If there are large cash outflows from the business, start asking very difficult questions and be mistrustful of the answers.

- **Finance.** This is what the company did with the cash inflow – in M&S's case – or how the company finance a cash outflow in the case of some others. M&S raised some new capital from employees' shares, took out some new bank loans but repaid more of other borrowings. Note one quirk of the new statement: if M&S buys short-term securities like six-month CDs, these do not count as cash and shows up as a decrease in cash equivalents. So while borrowing fell by £135.9m, some £14.9m of cash is shown to have flowed out of the group.

Other financial information

There is plenty of useful information in the notes to the main accounts which is worth trawling through. Other important areas are the **report of the auditors** which is supposed to check that the company is not being misleading. Occasionally auditors **qualify** accounts, meaning they disagree with the management. This is normally a bad sign. If the auditors say the accounts are prepared on the assumption that the company is a **going concern**, it is almost certainly going bust.

Chairman's statement and report of directors

The chairman's statement is the soft sell of the cheer leader; the directors' report the hard facts they are required to give such as details of acquisitions, future developments, etc. Of the glossy bits at the front of the annual report, that at least is worth a read.

Company Accounts

IN A NUTSHELL

1. A company's annual report and accounts tell you more about its business and financial affairs than any other document it produces after it gets a stockmarket quote.

2. However, the accounts are only as honest as the directors who prepared them. Many recent cases have shown that auditors have let bad guys through the net. So decide about the management before you put faith in the numbers.

3. The profit and loss account is the first thing to turn to. It tells you how much money was made in the year. Recent changes have split out results of continuing operations from closed businesses and banned extraordinary items.

4. The balance sheet provides a snapshot of everything a company owns and owes at the end of the year. It allows you to check on the business's financial health.

5. Because of accounting abuses there is a new cash flow statement. It shows how much cash came into the company, how much was spent on dividends, tax or investment, and how the remainder was used or financed.

6. It is also worth trawling through the notes, auditors' report and directors' report. Look at the glossy pictures if you like, but don't be swayed by them.

7. It is dangerous to put too much faith in accounts. Plenty of companies have gone bust shortly after producing 'satisfactory' reports.

Chapter 17
New Issues

Most companies first join the stockmarket in order to raise money, either to expand the business, or to allow their owners to realize some of the rewards of their hard work. Any company joining the market does so through what is called a **new issue**. There are various types of issue, but in essence investors are offered the chance to buy shares which will then be quoted on the stockmarket. The company gets not just money, but a wider spread of shareholders and a much more active market for its shares. Usually the founders of a small business keep the majority of the shares and continue to run the company; many find this preferable to selling their company to another company in its entirety, and having to work for someone else. Privatization issues are unusual in that the whole of the equity may be sold – since there is no family wanting to keep control.

New issues are a popular way for private investors to buy shares, partly because of the government's privatization programme, partly because they can be a way of making overnight profits. There are three main types of issue:

- An **offer for sale** in which some shares are offered to the public at large, though a certain number may be reserved for special categories of buyer.
- A **placing** in which some shares are sold privately to a group of friendly investing institutions.
- An **introduction** in which no new shares are on offer, since they are already widely held, but trading is put onto an official footing. No new money is raised.

There are several variations on the standard offer for sale. And sometimes new issues are a mixture of different issue methods: some shares will be offered for sale and some placed, for instance. The company chooses whichever method it reckons will raise any money it wants as cheaply as possible, and ensure a good secondary market in its shares.

The offer for sale is the most expensive method. All the big privatizations have used it. But only large issues have to use this mechanism, and an increasing number of smaller companies are coming to the market through placings.

Preparations for an issue

Before any company makes an issue, it has to ensure that its business, financial structure and reporting systems are acceptable to the Stock Exchange. It hires financial advisers: a stockbroker and sometimes a merchant bank, a lawyer, an accountant and perhaps later on a public relations firm. Many financial advisers reckon that it can take two years to get a company ready for its stockmarket launch, with a minimum of three to six months.

The company has to decide whether it wants to raise money through the issue. If so, is the money needed for the business or is it going to existing shareholders? Does it want its new shareholders to be institutions or private investors? How can it both establish a high price for its shares, and ensure that it sells all it wants?

A typical offer for sale

The offer for sale is the method readers are most likely to encounter. A standard offer involves the sale to the public of a fixed number of shares at a fixed price. A real example is the easiest way of explaining the timetable.

Specialist retailer Tie Rack came to the market in 1987. It raised £12.4m by selling 8.6m shares (a quarter of its equity) at 145p each. All the shares being sold were new ones, and the money was going into the company – to fund expansion – not to existing shareholders. The expenses of the issue totalled around £1m, and the net amount the company expected to receive was £11.4m.

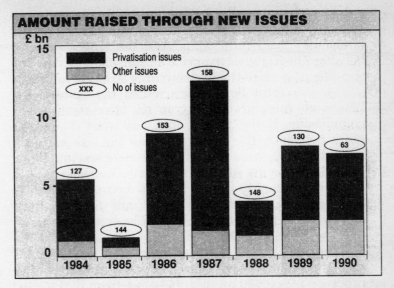

AMOUNT RAISED THROUGH NEW ISSUES

£ bn

- Privatisation issues
- Other issues
- xxx No of issues

1984 · 1985 · 1986 · 1987 · 1988 · 1989 · 1990

Fig 17.1 New issues tend to be more frequent when the stockmarket is booming and share valuations are high. Although relatively few in number, privatizations raised most of the money in the second half of the 1980s.

- **Pre-launch publicity**. Stories about the Tie Rack issue started appearing in the press at least a year before the launch, and intensified following the successful issue of Sock Shop, another niche retailer, in Spring 1987.
- **Pricing and underwriting**. The bank and broker would have discussed the probable terms weeks before the issue took place. Normally advisers make sure that the investment measurements determined by the sale price – PE ratio, dividend yield – offer slightly better value than those of comparable companies which already have a stockmarket quote. If the equity market background is stormy, they will be very cautious in fixing the price. On the other hand if the market is buoyant, and the company has a good name, they may price the shares more ambitiously. Tie Rack was well known by the personal investors likely to buy its shares, and similar companies were very fashionable, so its advisers aimed high. But the actual price would

not have been finally settled until the last possible
moment. If the stockmarket background changes, the
terms may need rethinking. And the longer the gap
between the fixing of the price and the closing date for
the offer, the more the **underwriting** is likely to cost.

The merchant bank **underwrites** the issue – i.e.
agrees to buy all the shares on offer itself for a
commission, if the public does not want them, and
(with help from the broker) lays off the risk across a
spread of fund managers (**sub-underwriters**) just like a
bookmaker laying off bets. Normally underwriting is
more of a formality than it sounds, because it usually
involves a good fee and little risk for the fund
managers. But occasionally it is difficult to get an issue
underwritten, and sometimes the issue flops and the
underwriters have to **take up** the shares. In Tie Rack's
case the underwriters shared 2 per cent of the offer
proceeds (£250,000 all told) between them.

● **2 June 1987. Impact day.** The **prospectus** was released
to the press. It included details of the offer; information
about the company's business and financial history;
reasons for the offer; an explanation of what the
company was doing with the money; a review of
current trading and future prospects; an accountants'
report; and an application form. The section entitled
key information showed the basic investment sums: the
offer price valued Tie Rack shares at 31.5 times historic
earnings and the historic dividend yield was 1.0 per
cent. This was very expensive by the standards of the
market as a whole, but not when compared with shares
such as Sock Shop and Body Shop. The prospectus was
available from the company, its financial advisers, 30
clearing bank branches and most Tie Rack shops.

Investors had a week in which to decide whether to
apply for shares. The novel risk was that this issue
straddled a general election.

● **3 June 1987. Advertising.** The prospectus (including the
application form) was published in the *Financial
Times*, and a separate application form was published
in *The Daily Telegraph*.

● **10am 9 June 1987. Oversubscription.** When the offer

closed the company had received 315,000 applications
for a total of 728m shares with a value of £1.06bn. In
other words investors had applied for nearly 85 times
as many shares as were actually up for sale. (If the issue
had been unpopular, and **undersubscribed**, it would
have been reported that a certain number of shares had
been **left with the underwriters**.)

● **10 June 1987. Basis of allotment**. Tie Rack's bankers
announced the complicated method it had chosen to
decide which applicants got how many shares. It was a
combination of a ballot and a scaling down of
applications. Many applicants got none, and even
successful ones got far fewer than they had applied for.

● **15 June, 1987. Letters of acceptance** (which act as
temporary share certificates and can be sold through a
stockbroker) were posted.

● **16 June 1987. First dealings**. Dealings in the shares
began on the Stock Exchange. The opening price was
around 195p, and they rose to 202p (nearly 40 per cent
above the offer price) before closing the day at 168p.*

Tender offers

Tender offers work much like normal offers for sale, but
investors have to bid for the shares, and the price at
which they are sold is determined by the prices tendered.
There are different types of tender:

● Tender to determine a **strike price**. This may well be an
offer for sale to the public. The company's advisers will
suggest a minimum price and leave it up to the
individual investors to name their own. Once all the
bids are in, the advisers work out what price will
ensure that they sell all the shares but still keep an
active market afterwards. Everybody bidding at or
above that price gets at least some shares at the strike
price. Those bidding below get none.

* Tie Rack is an exaggerated example of what can happen with a very
popular new issue in a bull market. The timetable is typical; the
massive oversubscription was exceptional.

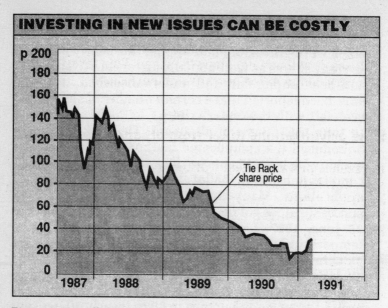

Fig 17.2 Not all new issues go on to great things. Tie Rack was launched near the top of the market in 1987, and has since been hit by the downturn in the economy.

- **Pay what you bid** tenders. Successful applications are normally accepted in full and at the price tendered. They are often part of a large issue which uses more than one sale method. Sometimes they are open to the public, but often they are limited to institutions.

  For example, part of BAA's issue in 1988 was by tender. The tenders had to be above 245p (the price, payable in two instalments, for the fixed part of the offer). In the event tenders ranging from 282p to a rumoured 310p were accepted. The average price bid was 290p, but all the bidders paid what they themselves had offered. When dealings started the shares began trading at around 144p, the equivalent of 289p fully paid – much in line with the average tender price.

- **Offers for subscription**. These resemble standard offers for sale, but they are usually only partially underwritten. Often what are being sold are new shares in a new company – and the venture may only go ahead if the issue is a success. The company will normally set a minimum subscription level, and if it does not find enough prospective purchasers by the time the offer closes, it will usually abort the issue. This form of offer is very common for new investment trusts.

How privatizations differ from other offers for sale

In essence privatizations work much like other offers for sale, but their size, and the government's desire to attract as many private investors as possible, means that the timetable is longer and that they have some special characteristics.

- **Priority applications** and **incentives**. Most privatizations have given priority to customers, and **registration** with the share office has usually entitled customers to **loyalty bonuses** (free shares or discounts on routine bills). Thus BAA offered a one for ten scrip issue to shareholders who held on to their shares for three years.
- **Instalment payments** and **partly paid shares**. Privatizations have normally sold shares on the instalment basis, e.g. the BAA offer for sale was at 245p, with a first instalment of 100p, and a second one ten months later.

  This system means that the immediate dividend yield usually looks very tempting when worked out on the partly paid price, and that shareholders have to remember that they are legally liable for the further payment(s). Moreover, when only the first instalment has been paid, the partly paid shares are **geared**, which exaggerates price movements.
- **Prospectuses**. Most privatizations have published both a **pathfinder** prospectus (an early one with everything but the price) and a **mini-prospectus** (a simplified version of a full prospectus intended for laymen).
- **Timing**. Investors usually have a longer time to decide whether to apply for the shares. There is also usually a longer gap between the closing of the offer and the start

of dealings. But even so shareholders often do not receive their allotment letters until *after* dealings have started. It also often takes some time for applicants to get the balance of their money back, if they get fewer shares than they ask for.

- **Multiple applications**. The government tries to stop investors from putting in several different applications to try to get more shares by declaring this illegal and making rigorous checks. A few people have been prosecuted.
- **Cheap dealing**. In most privatizations there are arrangements allowing shareholders who wish to sell their shares rapidly to do so easily and comparatively cheaply – for a limited period of time.
- **First dealings**. Most privatization issues have traded at well above the offer price when the stockmarket has started dealing in the shares. The notable exception was when the government sold a large holding in BP at the time of the 1987 stockmarket crash.

Placings

Companies and institutions both like placings. They are easy, cheap, fast and free from stress. The company still goes through the same business and financial checks with the Stock Exchange. But the sale mechanism is far simpler. Its financial advisers work out a price, and sell the shares to the investing institutions. It's like an underwriting exercise – except that it's permanent.

Take an example: Proteus International, a computer software company specializing in modelling and designing biomolecular structures. In May 1990 it placed a quarter of its capital to raise £4.5m gross, though expenses whittled the issue proceeds down to £4.2m.

The placing document showed losses, did not forecast any dividends, but contained technical and scientific background which might whet the appetite of the adventurous fund manager. The placing document was circulated on 18 May 1990, and dealings started on 29 May. Within two months the shares had nearly doubled from their 84p placing price to 140p. Even though the shares were not available to the public initially, they had received some favourable comment in the press.

Any company wanting to raise less than £15m can do so through a placing with the broker's own clients. Issues in the £15m to £30m bracket need to involve at least one other outlet for the shares. But only when an issue tops the £30m mark does the issuer need to offer at least part of it direct to the public.

Introductions

Introductions are unlike other new issues in that they do not raise any new money for the company. This mechanism can only be used by companies whose shares are already widely held by UK investors. All that happens is that the company submits itself to the scrutiny of the Stock Exchange, and that trading in the shares is put onto an official footing. Major foreign companies, which are already quoted in their own country but want a London quote as well, will often join the London market through an introduction.

One recent domestic example was Wiggins Teape Appleton, the paper company which was floated off by BAT in June 1990, as part of its plan to **unbundle** itself once it had fought off the takeover bid from Sir James Goldsmith's Hoylake. The WTA shares were given* to existing shareholders of BAT, more than 100,000 of them, and once dealings started, WTA had a market value of slightly over £1bn. Since some BAT shareholders wanted to sell their WTA shares, there was a very active market in them once dealings started.

New issue premiums

Shares in most new issues go to a premium over the sale price when dealings first start, particularly during a bull

*The market price of BAT shares dropped to reflect the fall in the worth of the parent company. So the 'gift' was not as generous as it sounds. WTA is now Arjo Wiggins after a merger.

market. There are plenty of exceptions to this generalization, but why are premiums the norm?

Financial advisers say it is almost impossible to price an issue 'correctly'. And since a company whose shares fall to a discount after the issue gets a bad reputation with investors, the advisers usually aim for a premium of around 10 per cent. But they still find it difficult to hit this target. When the electricity generators came to the market in March 1991, for instance, the premium in early dealings was around 40 per cent.

Even shares which come to the market through a placing often rise to a substantial premium when dealings start.

Stagging

Stags are short-term speculators who apply for shares in an issue in the hope of being able to sell them at a profit when stockmarket dealings start. They often apply for far more shares than they could afford to hold as a long-term investment. It sounds the ideal way to make a quick buck. Unfortunately successful stagging depends on the issue being an offer for sale, the stag getting a large allocation of shares, and the shares going to a substantial premium over the issue price when dealings start. This combination of circumstances is increasingly rare.

As mentioned above, the number of companies which choose the 'offer for sale' method of coming to the market is shrinking. And the companies' sponsors usually do their best to stop the stags getting too big an allotment, and are increasingly vigilant in guarding against multiple applications. In many privatization issues, dealings start before investors get their letters of allotment, so stags have to sell 'blind'.

But the biggest single deterrent to stagging is that investors tend to get puny allotments in very popular issues, which are the ones most likely to go to a big premium. When brokerage and the cost of borrowing money to stag the issue are taken into account, stagging profits can all but disappear.

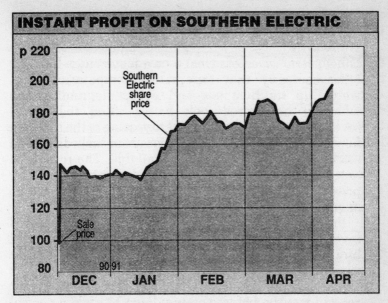

Fig 17.3 The traditional privatization give-away saw Southern Electric shoot to a 40 per cent premium on the first day of dealings. After that the solid earnings prospects of the shares helped them move higher still.

How to profit from new issues

Investors and stags have different objectives:

- Stagging is unlikely to make you a fortune nowadays, but it is fun. Even if you decide *not* to stag a particular issue, it's still worth registering (if relevant) and getting prospectuses. Make sure your bank will make finance available, and check the probable cost against your potential profit. The two points to consider are the estimated size of your allotment, and the likely size of the premium. In some privatizations, such as water, it has been fairly obvious that you stand a better chance of getting a worthwhile allotment in some companies than others. 'Consumer' issues, such as Tie Rack and Laura Ashley, tend to be too heavily oversubscribed for you to stand much chance of making money.

It is usually unwise to buy investment trust shares in a new issue. They almost always fall to a discount soon afterwards.

- Longer term investors treat a new issue much like any other company: they look at the company's record, weigh up its business and prospects and decide whether the shares look better value than rival investments. The advantage of investing at the time of a new issue is that an unusually large amount of detailed information and comment is available. The trouble is that the growing prevalence of placings means that private investors have no chance to get in on the majority of issues nowadays.

  Probably the most sensible thing for thwarted investors to do is to keep the prospectus to hand, and buy when the market price falls back to what you consider a sensible level. If the new issue market is bubbling, popular issues often stay at frothy levels for several months before coming down to a more normal rating. That's the time to pick them up if you are interested. New issue flops can also be rewarding to discriminating investors.

- The general message is that you are more likely to make money buying a good share in the secondary market than chasing new issues.

New Issues

IN A NUTSHELL

1. New issues are the way in which companies raise money by selling some of their shares to investors before getting them quoted on the stockmarket. Sometimes the money goes into the business, sometimes it goes to the existing shareholders.

2. The three main types of issue are offers for sale, placings and introductions. Most privatization issues are offers for sale, and these are the issues of most interest to private investors.

3. An offer for sale to the public offers a fixed number of shares at a fixed price. Most offers follow a fairly standard timetable.

4. Tender offers differ from others in that the price is not fixed in advance but depends on what investors offer to pay. In some tenders all successful investors pay the same price; in others they pay what they bid.

5. Privatization issues follow a similar but longer timetable to other offers for sale. But there are some areas, such as registration, bonuses and rules against multiple applications where they differ.

6. Placings are an increasingly popular way for smaller companies to come to the market. Introductions are unusual in that they do not raise new money. Neither gives private investors the chance to participate.

7. Shares in most new issues rise well above the sale price when stockmarket dealings start. These premiums encourage speculators called stags, who hope to make a fast profit.

Chapter 18
Rights and Scrip Issues

A new issue when a company first joins the stockmarket is not the only time a firm can raise money from shareholders. Once they are listed on the stockmarket companies can raise further equity capital through a **rights issue**. Rights issues involve a company offering its existing shareholders the chance to buy new shares, and are the main way British quoted companies raise additional equity. The reason most companies need new equity is to finance the growth of their business: perhaps a specific acquisition or investment in new buildings or plant. But sometimes a company which has been going through a bad patch, and has high borrowings, will have a rights issue just to reduce its debt. Both companies and their bankers get worried if debt becomes too high in relation to the Ordinary share capital. The company is scared that the bankers may stop lending; the bankers want a substantial equity 'cushion', so that if the company goes bust they have a better chance of getting their loans back.

It's always harder to borrow an umbrella when it's raining. And the stockmarket usually gives a warmer welcome to rights issues from companies which want money for expansion than to those from companies trying to repair their balance sheets. But sometimes a company's share price will go up on a **rescue rights**, because investors are relieved that the company is not going bust or being forced to sell its best subsidiaries to stay alive.

It is also easier for any company to make a rights issue when the stockmarket as a whole is rising. The investing institutions are trying to get cash into the market and like rights issues in good companies because they can increase their shareholdings substantially without forcing the price up against themselves. Rights issues also provide them with a chance to earn underwriting fees.

Most issues are **underwritten**, i.e. the company's broker gets prior agreement from a group of institutions that they will buy the new shares if existing shareholders do not want them. This ensures that the company gets its money. The underwriting commission is normally 2 per cent of the money being raised.

Cynics claim that it is fear of losing their underwriting commissions that has made British investing institutions such devoted champions of the principle of shareholders' **pre-emption rights** i.e. that the new shares *have* to be offered to existing shareholders first. In America when a company wants to raise new equity finance, it sells the shares to anyone who wants to buy them. Often it will get competing bids from securities houses for the whole block, and the house which offers the best price then has the job of selling all the shares on to investors at a profit. Alternatively, the company may sell the shares directly to a group of large investing institutions. Both methods are quicker, cheaper and more efficient than a cumbersome British-style rights issue. Many British companies would like to be able to use similar methods, but are stymied by the British investing institutions.

The upshot of this company/shareholder tussle so far has been that companies are normally only allowed to by-pass the rights issue procedure – and sell shares directly to institutions in a **placing** – if the issue is a small one. One rather messy compromise is a variation on the placing, whereby existing shareholders have a right to claim their shares back from the institutions if they wish. Rights issues may be an endangered species, but as yet they live on in Britain.

How rights issues work

The idea that existing shareholders lose value if new shares are sold to someone else is contentious. But it helps explain the mechanism of a traditional rights issue. Here new shares are offered to existing shareholders at, say, 20 per cent below the market price. The company makes sure that the new shares look 'cheap' compared with the

Fig 18.1 Rights issues are more common when the stockmarket is riding high. A high valuation means that companies raise money cheaply, hence the rush in 1987. 1991 saw a lot of rights issues because companies needed the money to pay off debts. In 1993 companies have also been rushing to take advantage of high share prices.

market price – for fear shareholders may turn the offer down, particularly if the market falls during the three weeks or so for which the offer remains open. Shareholders have the choice of accepting the offer, and sending off a cheque for their new shares, or selling their rights to the new 'cheap' shares.

But shareholders who accept the offer are not really getting cheap shares. For once the offer has closed, both new and old shares normally trade at a level somewhere between the 'cheap' offer price and the level at which the old shares were trading before the rights issue was announced. What has happened is that some of the value of the old shares has been transferred to the new ones.

The market value of all the shares after this price adjustment will theoretically be equal to the combined sum of the old shares' market value before the issue plus the new money paid for the rights shares. And if the same investor still owns both, no one has gained or lost. If he sells his rights for a sum equal to the fall in value of his old shares, he has not lost either.

A practical example is the easiest way of explaining how it works. In late January 1991 grocery group Tesco surprised the market when it announced a £572m rights issue to fund part of its continuing £1.4bn store development programme. The company had started planning the issue the previous November. It had been fully underwritten at a cost of £12m.

- **29 January 1991**. Tesco announced that it was offering shareholders two new shares at 197p for every eleven shares they already held (known as a **two-for-eleven** in the jargon). It had 1,633m shares in issue and was selling another 297m. The share price was near its all-time peak at 247p in the market, and the existing shares had a total market value of just over £4bn. A **rights**

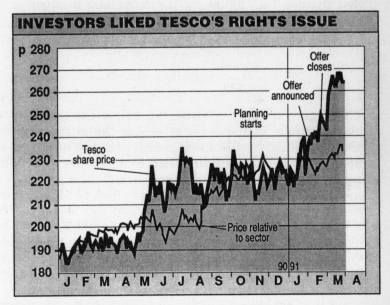

Fig 18.2 Because rights issues mean an extra supply of shares, they often depress a company's share price. But sometimes (as with Tesco) investors' enthusiasm for the company's plans can cause the shares to rise.

offer document, explaining why the directors wanted the money, and giving up-to-date trading, profit and dividend forecasts was sent to all shareholders.

At this stage any shareholder could calculate what should *in theory* happen to the Tesco shares. Take a shareholder with 1,000 shares. With a market price of 247p, these are worth £2,470. As he is entitled to 2 new shares for every 11 he holds he can now buy 182 shares at 197p each.

$$\frac{1,000 \times 2}{11} = 181.8$$

At the rights price of 197p, buying the new shares will cost him £358. He can work out what the market price is likely to be after the issue by adding what he will have to pay for the new shares to the market value of his old shares: £2,470 + £358 = £2,828. And then he just divides this figure by the combined number of shares: 1,000 old and 182 new, gives a total of 1,182. So the sum is:

$$\frac{£2,828}{1,182} = £2.39 \text{ a share}$$

That figure of 239p a share, 8p below the previous market price, is the level at which the share price should in theory settle down after the issue. The jargon name for it is the **ex-rights price**. Since he can buy his rights shares at 197p, and expect to sell them at 239p, the rights are worth around 42p a share. And his rights to 182 shares should be worth around £76 all told.

- **1 February 1991**. Provisional allotment letters to the new shares were sent to all shareholders, and they were told that they had three weeks (until 22 February) in which to decide whether to accept the offer. If they want to accept, they have to send back the allotment letter with a cheque.

The shareholder's problem is that his existing shares look set to fall by around 8p a share. So he is going to miss out unless he buys his quota of new shares, or sells his rights. There are two ways of doing this: selling his rights **nil paid** on the stockmarket, or waiting for the company to sell them for him, and send him a cheque. They will do this automatically if he takes no action.

- **4 February 1991**. The Stock Exchange starts trading in the rights and the old shares separately. Old Tesco shares open at 237p **ex-rights**, 7p below the previous day's closing level. (The ex-rights tag warns the buyer that the seller keeps the rights.) Dealing also starts in the new Tesco shares **nil paid** at 39p, slightly below the theoretical price calculated above. For a couple of weeks the Stock Exchange allows investors to sell their rights to buy the new shares without actually putting up the money. The allotment letters to the rights count as quasi share certificates, and can be sold. The actual opening price was slightly disappointing, but over the next couple of weeks Tesco's nil paid shares traded within a range of 37p to 45p, remarkably close to the theoretical calculation.

In Tesco's case, as with other rights issues, the shareholder has three options. He can send off his cheque for the new shares. He can either sell his rights in the market or wait for the company to sell them for him. Or he can sell enough of his rights to finance his purchase of the remainder of the shares he is being offered. Investors will be influenced both by whether they have the spare cash available to top up their investment, and by whether doing so will unbalance their portfolio.

If our Tesco shareholder wants to sell in the market he will have to pick his time. The price of nil-paid rights fluctuates a great deal because the price is determined by subtracting the subscription price from the (theoretical) ex-rights price. Selling through a stockbroker will also involve commission.

Selling enough of your rights to pay for taking up the remainder involves another calculation. But there's a formula for working out roughly how many rights you have to sell to pay for taking up the other shares. Multiply

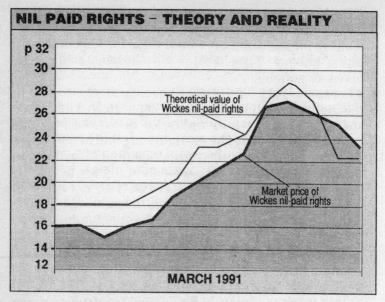

Fig 18.3 Inefficiencies in markets can mean that nil-paid rights do not always trade at the theoretical value, but they usually stay fairly close — as the rights issue for Wickes demonstrates*.

the nil paid rights price by the number of new shares you are being offered, and divide by the ex-rights price. In our example of someone with rights to buy 182 Tesco shares at 197p, it works like this:

$$\frac{42 \times 182}{239} = 32$$

* Risk-loving investors sometimes speculate by buying nil-paid rights shares. Like all highly-geared investments (such as futures and options, see chapters 6 and 12) these can be very profitable – or disastrous. Our chart shows what happened to the nil-paid rights of a loss-making building materials group called Wickes, which made a 1 for 1 rights issue at 32p in February 1991, when its shares were 48p. At that time the theoretical value of the nil-paid rights would have been 8p. By the time dealing started the theoretical price was 18p and the market price subsequently rose to 27p, partly because investors hoped the issue would help Wickes to get out of trouble, partly because the market as a whole was rising. Gambling in nil-paid rights is not for beginners.

Buying 32 new shares will cost him (197p × 32) £63. He finances this by selling the remainder of his rights (182–32 = 150) at 42p each for (42p × 150), which is again £63. Sadly broking commission will distort this neat sum.

The investor may take up his rights fully if he has the money to do so and accepts the arguments why the company is raising extra money. In this event, his financial commitment to Tesco will go up because he has put more money into the company – but the proportion of Tesco's shares which he owns remains the same.

- **22 February 1991**. The rights offer closes.
- **25 February 1991**. Tesco announces that 94 per cent of the rights shares have been taken up, and that it has sold the remainder in the market for the benefit of shareholders entitled to them. These passive shareholders get the equivalent of 47p per new share. This is usefully more than most private shareholders would have netted by selling in the market. But Tesco's is a slightly unfair test, since the stockmarket was rising strongly as the Gulf war finished.

Tesco's rights issue was big in absolute terms, but in other respects it was not unusual for a solid company. The sum of money being raised amounted to around 15 per cent of the previous market value of the equity, and the rights shares were offered at a discount of around 20 per cent to the previous market price.

Variations on the theme

Why did Tesco make its offer two for eleven at 197p? Several other ratios could have raised the same amount of money if it had chosen a different rights price. For example, a 'one for six at 215p' or a 'two for seven at 125p'.

A one for six at 215p would have represented a 13 per cent discount to the previous market price of 247p. If the market as a whole had fallen or investors had disliked the Tesco issue, its market price might have fallen back near the rights offer price. Logically this would seem to be irrelevant, since the issue was underwritten anyway. In practice an issue flop counts as a black eye for the company. The overhang of shares takes some time to clear, and the share price remains sluggish.

A two for seven at 125p sounds a lot more appealing. It's what's known as a **deep discount** issue.* If Tesco had chosen to issue shares at half its current market price, there would have been no chance of a flop. So it could have done without underwriters and saved its shareholders £12m in costs. Many investors argue that deep discount rights issues are the best answer for shareholders. And several big financial groups, such as Barclays and the Prudential, have followed this route. The snag is that deep discount rights issues can involve capital gains tax complications for investors.

If you sell rights, it counts as a disposal for tax purposes – even if you sell some of your rights purely in order to finance your take-up of the others. The Inland Revenue has conceded that if you sell rights worth no more than 5 per cent of the market value of your total shareholding, no gains tax liability will occur. And normally there isn't a problem. But because a deep discount issue transfers an unusually large proportion of the old shares' value into the new shares, you may well find yourself disposing of more than 5 per cent of your total holding, to finance the purchase of your remaining rights shares.

Companies sometimes offer Ordinary shareholders a different security by way of rights. For instance, in the mid-1980s there was a fashion for offering convertible preference shares. The principle is much the same, but individual shareholders may find themselves holding a small amount of a security they don't want.

Placings with clawbacks are another alternative to an ordinary rights issue which can work against the individual investor. As we said above, many companies don't like rights issues. And when they need to sell new shares to finance the purchase of another company, they sometimes place the new shares directly with a group of

---

* These are popular with companies in difficulties as the only way to get a rights issue off the ground in difficult market conditions.

friendly institutions. But shareholder pressure has meant that these placings are subject to a **clawback**. This means that existing shareholders have the right to reclaim the shares they would have been entitled to under a rights issue. The trouble is that if they do not wish to do so they receive no compensation for any loss of value of their existing shares, since there are no nil paid rights to sell. The companies argue that these placings are usually only slightly below the market price – and that if investors like the underlying deal the share price may actually go up.

Why scrip issues are different

Scrip and rights issues both give investors more shares in the company they own, but they are very different. A rights issue is designed to raise additional capital for a company; a scrip issue raises no new money. A scrip issue simply gives existing shareholders more shares but the value of their holding does not rise because no new money has gone in to the company. Scrip issues are just book-keeping exercises.

Scrip issues increase the number of shares a company has in issue, and simultaneously lower the market price of each share. They are also known as **bonus issues** or **capitalization issues**. Their purpose is to bring the company's capital into line with the size of its current business by making the shares more **marketable**.

A simplified example explains the point. Many companies start life with a share capital as low as £100, divided into 100 shares. Assume such a company trades successfully for ten years, and ends up with annual pre-tax profits of around £3,000 and total shareholders' funds of perhaps £7,500. Its earnings might be around £1,950, or £19.50 a share. And even a modest PE ratio of 10 would make the shares worth £195 each. They would be rare and costly, qualities which work against an active market in shares.

If the company had a 'nine for one' scrip issue, meaning that it gave shareholders nine additional shares for each one held, the number of shares in issue would increase to

1,000. Since no extra money had gone into the company, the market price should fall to a tenth of its former level, £19.50.

There is also a technical adjustment to the company's balance sheet. When the issued share capital was still £100, all the remainder of its shareholders funds – £7,400 in our example – counted as **reserves**. The scrip issue entails moving £900 of the reserves into **capital** – hence the alternative name **capitalization issue**.

In most real cases the proportion of the scrip issue to the existing share capital will be far lower: one for five or one for ten are common ratios. Many companies make a habit of having such issues once a year, and will often maintain the old rate of dividend on the new capital, thus effectively increasing the level of payout. For example, if a company pays out 10p a share on five shares but maintains the payment after a one for five scrip, it is actually increasing its dividend rate by 20 per cent. (It would have paid out 50p on five shares; now it pays out 60p.)

Companies need to get shareholder approval for scrip issues, but this is usually just a formality. The nuisance for shareholders is keeping records up to date. A scrip does, for instance, alter the effective price at which you bought your shares, so you need to take account of it in your tax returns.

One additional complication is that some companies pay what is called **scrip dividends**. This usually means that shareholders are offered a choice between a conventional dividend, and receiving additional shares *in lieu*. In some ways scrip dividends are more like a rights issue than a scrip issue. In 1993 some companies which wanted to hang on to cash or had high overseas taxes issued **enhanced scrip dividends**. These offered shareholders a dividend in shares perhaps 50 per cent higher than the cash alternative. They are controversial and certainly should be regarded as mini-rights issues.

Rights and Scrip Issues

IN A NUTSHELL

1. Rights issues are the way in which British companies raise additional equity finance – either for expansion or to refinance an overborrowed balance sheet.The new shares are offered first to existing shareholders.

2. Some British companies would prefer to sell their shares directly to investing institutions, or in a single block to securities firms, as they do in America, but investing institutions won't let them.

3. Shares offered to investors by way of rights are sold at a discount to the market price. But the new shares are not really 'cheap' because some value is transferred to them from the old shares, whose price drops once the issue is over.

4. The new shares are offered to shareholders in proportion to their existing holdings. If they do not wish to buy them, they can sell their rights.

5. A standard rights issue might raise from 15 to 30 per cent more equity capital, and the new shares would be sold at a discount of around 20 per cent to the market price. Companies are wary of making issues at a very small discount, even though they are underwritten.

6. Deep discount rights issues offer shares at a price very much lower than the existing market level, and save costs because they do not need to be underwritten. But they can cause gains tax complications.

7. Variations on the rights issue theme include offering shareholders a different type of security by way of rights and placings with clawbacks. Private shareholders can lose out under placings with clawbacks.

8. Rights issues should not be confused with scrip issues. The latter do not raise any new money for the company, but are a book-keeping exercise designed to keep the number of shares in issue in line with the growth in the business.

Chapter 19
Takeovers

Bid battles provide great excitement for the stockmarket. The tactics – frontal assaults, sneak attacks, dawn raids, secret intelligence, disinformation and councils of war – are straight out of military textbooks, and the managers involved fight as though their lives depend on the outcome. For shareholders, bids are a great opportunity to make quick profits. They are also one of the few occasions when small investors wield real power; proud managers beg for the support of people they normally ignore.

There can be good economic reasons for takeovers; for example, companies may want to expand their share of a market by buying up competitors, or think they will strengthen their hand by moving into allied businesses; some firms even want to diversify because their existing markets are shrinking. Buying another company can be a much quicker way to achieve these aims than starting a new business from scratch. But the sub-plot is that managers often bid because they want to run a bigger company, and those on the receiving end fight to defend their jobs. It is this struggle for power, not the economic rationale, which captures the public imagination. No wonder the newspapers love bids.*

Bare knuckle fights

The basic objective of any company attempting to take over another is to get control of the majority of the voting

---

*Racy press coverage gives a very distorted picture of company mergers. The reality is that nine out of ten takeovers are amicable deals involving unquoted companies and involve the sale of an old family business, or a founder taking his profit.

power in its target; in most cases that means buying at least half of its ordinary shares. But a bidding company cannot do whatever it pleases to win control, it has to abide by the City rules of fair play, and may have to satisfy the government that its bid is acceptable.

To make sure that all shareholders are treated equally and to ensure company managements don't have to live in a state of permanent siege, there are strict rules drawn up by the **Takeover Panel** which govern how one firm can try to take over another. The government uses the **Office of Fair Trading** and the **Monopolies and Mergers Commission** – both responsible to the Secretary of State for Trade and Industry – to make sure that companies are not acting against the public interest in bids. If the government is happy that a merger is not going to form a monopoly or a cartel, and that it will not destroy vital national interests, then it leaves the decision up to the shareholders involved. But a reference to the MMC holds a bid up for at least three months and can stop it dead in its tracks. A new player on the scene is the **European Commission** which has responsibility for the largest takeover battles across Europe and is threatening to take a more active role in EC mergers and may well try to alter takeover rules in Britain.

The Takeover Panel is an unofficial City watchdog which exercises influence through the rather old-fashioned technique of threatening to cold-shoulder anyone who doesn't observe its rules. Its code is designed to make sure there is a level playing field where all shareholders can act on the basis of the same information. For example, the Panel will not allow a bidder to go back on something he has said, except in exceptional circumstances. So if a predator bids for a company at a certain price he cannot withdraw unless he finds out there is something seriously amiss with the target. And once a bid has been declared final, the predator cannot increase it, even if a rival bidder emerges and bids more. There have been several attempts to breach these rules in recent years, and in some cases the Panel has had to bend to *realpolitik*, but most firms still stick to the rules. At the heart of the code is a timetable and a series of hurdles which a bidder has to clear if he is to succeed.

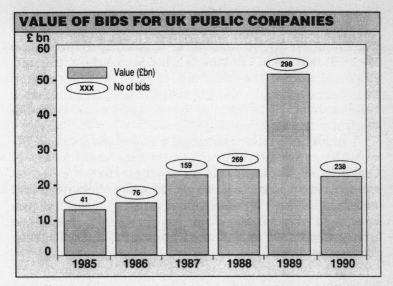

VALUE OF BIDS FOR UK PUBLIC COMPANIES

£ bn

Value (£bn)

xxx   No of bids

| 1985 | 1986 | 1987 | 1988 | 1989 | 1990 |

41 — 76 — 159 — 269 — 298 — 238

Fig 19.1 1989 was a bumper year for takeovers in Britain, but experience since then suggests that many companies overpaid for their targets, and their balance sheets are now showing the strain.

More stakes than a Berni Inn

An early indication that there may be a bid on the way can come from the accumulation of a small share stake. To keep companies informed of who owns their shares, all shareholdings above 3 per cent have to be declared to the Stock Exchange. Of course, the majority of these are perfectly innocent holdings by friendly institutions, but companies keep a careful eye on their share registers, just in case. A predator can buy up to 15 per cent of a company's shares on the stockmarket before he has to pause – sometimes this is done in one early-morning spree called a **dawn raid**. Once the 15 per cent level has been reached, the predator has to wait a week before buying more; there is a similar fire-break at 25 per cent.

If a predator buys more than 30 per cent of a company's shares he must then offer to buy all the rest. And once a full bid has been formally launched the clock starts ticking – the bidder has just 60 days to win control of the company.* If he fails, he must then wait a year before he can try again. Of course, a predator does not have to flag his intention by accumulating a steadily rising share stake. It is possible to mount a bid without owning any shares at all. But the advantage of owning 30 per cent of the shares before bidding is that the predator then only needs another 20 per cent of the company's shares to win control.

A bidder can offer the target's shareholders cash, its own shares, or a mixture of both. But whatever the form of the offer, it is important to realize that the bid is conditional on success. If the bid fails, the offer lapses and so accepting the offer does not necessarily mean that you have sold your shares. Even if you accept a predator's offer you can normally change your mind and withdraw your acceptance.

A war of words

Both sides bombard shareholders in the target company with information designed to further their case. The two principal documents are the **offer document** and the **defence document** and these contain important financial information, as well as statements about the strategy which both sides will adopt if they have control of the company after the bid. Whilst neither side can lie in these documents, there is no compulsion on the participants to provide unbiased assessments of the situation. Indeed many bid battles are marked by vituperative attacks on the motives of the bidder or the record of the defending management. Shareholders are wise to treat with caution anything said by those involved; even the financial statistics chosen by either side are carefully chosen to flatter its case.

Defensive strategies

In some ways the predator has the easier ride in a bid. He has only to attack the record of the existing management

* If another bidder enters the fray, the clock is reset to zero.

and offer his money; promising to improve the future is always easier than defending the past. Even if the bidder is offering shares in his own company so that shareholders are being invited to choose between two managements, it is hard for the defence to argue that the predator would make a worse fist of the target company. And the chances are that the bidder is offering well above the market price of the shares before the bid to get control, so shareholders are sorely tempted.

Under these conditions the defence is hard pressed, but it does have some cards to play.* It can leak out information through the course of the bid in an attempt to wrong-foot the predator and offer the prospect of better times ahead for shareholders. The two classic tactics are a profits forecast and an asset revaluation and both are designed to show that the company is worth more than the bidder is prepared to pay. Exactly when these aces come out of the hole depends on the conditions of the bid. Ideally, the defence likes to hold on to them for as long as possible. Shareholders have to be given at least two weeks to consider any offer, which effectively means that the bidder cannot increase his bid after day 46. And to ensure 'fair play', the defence is no longer allowed to unveil important new financial information after day 39. On the other hand, if the predator looks like achieving an early knockout, the defence may have to declare earlier. One classic example of a profit forecast killing a bid was when Pilkington confounded expectations in 1986 by producing a glowing profit forecast which stymied the bidding conglomerate BTR.

Two other tactics are for the defence to take up some of the bidder's ideas or appeal to the regulators to step in and prevent the bid. BAT did both of these when it was threatened by Sir James Goldsmith's Hoylake consortium. Hoylake wanted to buy the tobacco and insurance giant and sell off the retailing, paper making and insurance subsidiaries. BAT responded by tying Hoylake up in American court hearings and producing its own

* To the great distress of defences in the UK, the American poison pill defences (where a company can trigger all sorts of spoiling provisions if it is subjected to a bid) are not available over here.

plans to sell off its retailing and paper making arms. It survived.

The final refuge of a company about to fall into the jaws of a big bad wolf is to seek a more acceptable bidder, who will be friendly to the defence management. By calling in such a **white knight** the defence loses control of its company, but the managers hope to keep their jobs. Occasionally, a defence management even tries to become its own white knight by launching a counter bid or management buy-out of the company.

When this lousy war is over

Once a bidder has 50 per cent of the votes in a company he will usually declare victory by announcing the bid **unconditional as to acceptances**. The offer has then to remain open for at least another two weeks to allow other shareholders to accept. Many do so at this stage because remaining as a minority shareholder has a number of disadvantages. If the bidder eventually gets over 90 per cent of the shares bid for, then he can compulsorily purchase the remainder.

Should the bid fail then those people who have accepted the offer will not have sold their shares, but the predator may well be left with a substantial stake either from his initial shareholding or from any shares he may have bought in the market during the course of the bid.* This rump shareholding is an irritant to the defence management and can form a decisive bridgehead for a renewed bid in a year's time.

One aspect of bids is often overlooked in all the attention paid to the target company. Bids also have an impact on the predator, yet shareholders in the bidding company are rarely consulted. If the bidder wins but fails to earn enough from the acquired company to justify the

---

* A bidder can buy shares in the market during the course of a bid if the share price falls below what he is offering. The target's share price may fall below the offer price if the bid is expected to fail or if an MMC reference is expected.

price he paid, he can be in serious financial trouble. Many of the go-go companies of the 1980s went 'a bid too far'. One of the most recent examples was probably WPP's purchase of Ogilvy & Mather. WPP's chief executive Martin Sorrell had been regarded as the advertising man who could avoid the pitfalls of ambition, but high debts and an advertising industry in recession brought his company into serious trouble. Other agreed deals like the Asda/MFI and FKI/Babcock mergers went so badly that they had to be unstitched later. Being a predator is no guarantee of financial success.

How to make money from bids

As we said earlier, bids can be profitable for share-holders. The price which a predator has to pay for control of a company is often much higher than the market price to buy or sell a few hundred shares. One good example of this was the bid for carmaker Jaguar. Before the bidding started, Jaguar shares were trading at around £4.30. By the time the struggle between Ford and General Motors had been resolved in Ford's favour, Jaguar shares had reached £10, and anyone who held shares from before the bid had done very well.

But how do you make the most of a bid? There are many pitfalls for the unwary. For example in the Jaguar bid, shareholders might have been tempted to sell in the market when the shares reached £7, on the grounds that the government would block the bid, and so would have missed the best of the rise. By contrast, when Severn Trent Water bid for waste group Caird, the target's shares moved up from 70p to just over £1.00. Some shareholders sold whilst Severn Trent was buying and were wise to do so because the deal eventually collapsed and Caird's shares fell back to 45p. As usual there is no cast-iron way to ensure success, but there are some pointers. What you should do depends on whether you are a shareholder in the target, the predator or a bystander looking to get involved.

Shareholders in the target company

You have two basic decisions to take. First, a long-term investment question: do you think that keeping your money in the target's shares is the best way of getting the long-term returns you are looking for? Second, the short-term tactics: if you are thinking of selling, how and when should you act to get the best price?

The first question gives you three options: staying with your existing shares; accepting any package offered by the predator and taking your money out and putting it into something entirely different. The best general advice is to keep your eye on the stockmarket prices and delay your decision as long as possible, since a lot of the relevant information will be published during the bid battle.*

There are several points to check out when you get the formal offer document. Turn to the paragraph headed **financial effects of accepting the offer**. Weigh up the package (or cash) that you are being offered against the shares in the target you hold. Which would you expect to produce the better return in the foreseeable future?

Loyalty is not the question; your own company's recent performance is more relevant. If it has been a really poor performer, and the board had shown no signs of life until the bid, you may feel the bid-inspired price rise has taken the shares as high as they are likely to go for several years – in which case it is foolish to stick with your board. And an asset revaluation which shows that the company is worth more than originally thought is not necessarily a good sign – it may only show what a poor return the incumbent management has been making on the company's assets. If they forecast an unexpectedly good set of profits or a dividend jump, think hard: are they going to be able to repeat this performance in future or is this a one off? Are they even being helped out by some clever accounting?

Then look at the bidder's credentials. Remember that if

---

* It's worth bearing in mind that accepting a cash offer counts as a disposal for gains tax purposes; accepting a share package does not.

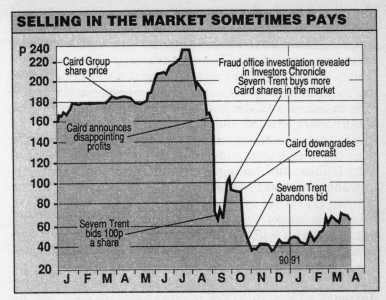

SELLING IN THE MARKET SOMETIMES PAYS

Caird Group share price

Fraud office investigation revealed in Investors Chronicle
Severn Trent buys more Caird shares in the market

Caird announces disappointing profits

Caird downgrades forecast

Severn Trent abandons bid

Severn Trent bids 100p a share

Fig 19.2 Severn Trent thought it was getting a bargain when it pounced on waste group Caird. But when the *Investors Chronicle* revealed a fraud office investigation, investors who sold in the market did well. Severn eventually abandoned the bid and the share price collapsed.

you are thinking of accepting a cash offer, the bidder's prospects, share price and personality are irrelevant. In cash bids *pecunia non olet!* If you are considering taking shares in the predator, weigh up the bidder's shares just as though you were buying them in the market. The offer document, sniping from the defence, and press comment should tell you everything you need to know.

If you opt for a cash alternative, because you are not worried by gains tax or don't want to remain as a holder of either share, make sure it will remain open after the first closing date of the bid – 21 days after the offer document was posted. It's also worth considering a loan note alternative, which can be offered by a bidder to those who don't want shares, but don't want a gains tax bill either. But before you accept a loan note, make sure you're happy a bidder's credit is good.

And remember that if you're thinking of taking cash, or

don't want to accept a share offer, you don't have to wait until the end of the bid. You can sell in the market at any point. Although you risk missing out on a higher offer you will get your money earlier and you may also ensure that you don't lose out if the offer fails or is withdrawn. When considering selling early, weigh the prospects of a higher offer, a counter-bidder, a white knight entering the fray on the one side, and the offer failing or being withdrawn due to exceptional circumstances on the other. If the market price goes well above the value of the bid in anticipation of a higher offer, consider selling if you don't think the increased bid will materialize.

Also watch out for a possible reference to the Monopolies Commission – at the very least that will hold things up, at worst it will kill the bid. Since no one is quite sure what the government's policy on takeovers really is, no investment strategy over a Monopolies reference is really safe. But ignoring common sense can be expensive. For instance, when the OFT referred Kingfisher's bid for Dixons to the MMC in 1990, many investors were taken by surprise, yet the possibility had been mooted in the press as soon as the bid was made. Shareholders could have made a good profit by selling to the speculators who pushed Dixons' shares above the bid level.

Shareholders in the predator

Shareholders in companies making bids too often assume that the bids are nothing to do with them; it's rare for there to be any organized shareholder opposition. When institutions holding 11 per cent of Boots' shares voted against its plan to acquire Ward White in 1989 some other institutions were shocked. Other fund managers took the view that if you don't like your company making a bid, you should sell the shares.

Private investors should realize that the more generous the bid, the harder it will be for the predator to squeeze a good return out of the target. As a predator shareholder, make sure you get hold of all of the documents sent to target shareholders, read the press carefully, watch the share price and if you think your company is going to bid too much, sell your shares. The key phrase to look out for in the papers will often be that the acquisition will **dilute** the predator's earnings. Another possible worry can be a surplus of the predator's shares **overhanging** the market after a successful bid.

Outsiders

Even if you're not involved on either side at the start of a bid, you can still hope to get involved. If you think that a higher bid is coming you can buy shares in the target, hoping to profit from the second leg of the rise. But if you think the bid will fail or be referred to the Monopolies Commission, you have a harder job. **Selling short** – selling shares you don't own in the hope of buying them cheaper later – is not for novices, and most brokers will only allow long-standing clients to do it. Whether you are buying or selling you must bear in mind that you are taking a much higher risk strategy than normal. If you buy in after a bid has been launched you may be burned badly if it fails. And shorting Jaguar shares at £7 would have proved very expensive.

Another possibility is dealing in **traded options** in the bid target (see chapter 12). These are available on around 70 of the largest companies, but bear in mind that option prices will have risen on the bid announcement. Option market makers expect bid shares to be more volatile, so they will have marked up the price of both calls and puts to compensate.

If you don't want to deal in the bid company itself, you can profit from any knock-on effect on similar companies. Thus when the French bought shares in some of the British water companies after their launch, all of the others shot up. The rise in price can come either from the expectation that similar companies will soon be bid targets, or from a revaluation by the market of what such companies are worth. Either way it can take some time for the market to respond, but make sure that you're leading not following the professionals. If the price of the shares you're thinking of buying has risen, or its PE ratio is already as high as the bid target's, it might be wise to give it a miss.

A real life example

The story of a £140m bid battle for a British fastener company illustrates many of the thrills and spills which can occur. Over roughly 12 months, the share price of Avdel (previously known as Newman Industries) doubled as it moved from being a long-standing recovery situation, to being the target of two American suitors.

At the start of 1988 Newman Industries shares were trading at around 40p. Then a well-known predator called Suter – which had previously held a share stake in Newman and sold out – bought a 20 per cent stake in Newman from a troubled Australian investment house. Suter then held 28 per cent of Newman, which rechristened itself Avdel after its strongest operating company. Now read on.

- **August 1988**. American conglomerate Banner Industries buys an option to acquire 28.5 per cent of Avdel's equity from Suter at 70p a share. Avdel shares jump 6p to 64p.
- **October 1988**. Banner, which owns 2 per cent of Avdel outright, bids 80p a share, cash, for Avdel. Avdel's shares move up to around 84p.
- **November 1988**. An obscure Panamanian company buys a small stake; Avdel attacks Banner's balance sheet; the first closing date passes.
- **December 1988**. Avdel gets a couple of small share blocks disenfranchised. The OFT decides not to refer the bid to the MMC. Banner revises its bid up to 88p a share and buys another 13 per cent in the market. It now claims 47 per cent of Avdel and confident of victory, declares its bid final.
  Avdel then says it has found a white knight who will outbid Banner, provided that Banner agrees irrevocably to accept. British institutions with 34.8 per cent of

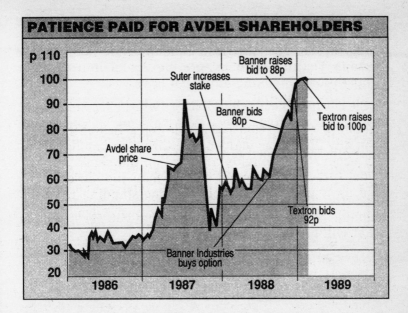

PATIENCE PAID FOR AVDEL SHAREHOLDERS

Fig 19.3 Avdel (a long standing recovery stock) was always under threat from a share stake held by Suter. This eventually went to predator Banner, and Avdel produced white knight Textron just in time. In this case, investors who hung on to the death did best.

Avdel's shares say they will accept the white knight's offer.

White knight revealed as Textron, another American conglomerate. It bids 92p a share just 10 days before Banner's bid is due to expire. Banner says it won't accept, and it looks like a stalemate with neither suitor likely to get 50 per cent. Shortly before Banner's 88p offer expires, Textron claims 44 per cent.

- **January 1989**. Banner's bid has expired, though it is still buying Avdel shares in the market at 95p. (Under an obscure part of the takeover rules, a bidder can acquire a further 2 per cent of its target even though its bid has failed. Banner cannot reach the magic 50 per cent, but may get a higher offer from Textron.)

Textron raises its bid to 100p a share, and has acceptances for over 92 per cent including Banner's shares. Everybody agrees an exit PE ratio of 17 is generous, and it's all over bar the shouting, but . . .

- **April 1989**. The American Federal Trade Commission stops Textron from integrating Avdel into its own operations, invoking anti-trust laws.

Clearly in this case shareholders who held on to the end did the right thing. Those who sold out at 88p in the market thinking it was all over – and that included some institutions – missed out on the final act. Banner's over confidence in trying to force a decision by declaring its offer final cost it the bid, but it almost worked. Avdel produced the white knight only just in time. If this example proves anything it shows that you never can tell what will happen next in a bid.

Takeovers

IN A NUTSHELL

1. Bid battles are exciting fights for corporate power and provide shareholders with good opportunities to make money.

2. The UK authorities' attitude to takeovers is benign, provided all shareholders have an equal opportunity to benefit, and the merger does not create a monopoly.

3. The Monopolies and Mergers Commission defends consumers and the national interest, while the Takeover Panel ensures a level playing field for companies and shareholders. The Takeover code specifies share hurdles and time limits in bids.

4. Both sides issue documents to shareholders advancing their case. They cannot lie, but the documents are not impartial. Bids can be in cash, shares or a mixture, depending partly on the state of the market and fashion.

5. The predator has an easier job because he can attack existing practices. Defences include profit forecasts, asset revaluations, appeals to regulators, adopting some of the predator's ideas and white knights.

6. In considering a bid, shareholders should decide whether sticking with the board will produce the best long-term returns for them. If not, then try to sell at the best price.

7. If the bid is for cash, the prospects and nature of the bidder are irrelevant. If he is offering shares,

weigh up the predator as though you were buying his shares in the market. If you don't like the look of him, consider selling in the market.

8. Timing is important. Weigh up the chance of a higher offer or a counter bid against the chance that the bid will be referred to the MMC, fail or be withdrawn. Also check your tax position.

9. Shareholders in the predator should also check that their management are not endangering their own company's prospects by bidding too much. Organized shareholder rebellions are rare, but unhappy holders can always sell in the market.

10. Outsiders who want to get in on the action can always buy shares (and may be able to short them) but these are high risk strategies. Options or buying lookalike stocks are alternatives, but are also risky.

Chapter 20
Liquidations

Why do companies go bust? And how can investors avoid getting caught in one that does? Very few of the thousand or so UK companies which go bust in a normal year are quoted on the stockmarket. Even in bad years, such as 1990 or 1991 when recession more than doubled the 'normal' casualty count, the number of quoted companies that go under is counted in tens, not hundreds. But the collapse of two major FT-SE companies (Polly Peck and British & Commonwealth) highlighted the danger. And any investor caught up in the failure of a quoted company will get little comfort from the reflection that it is a statistical rarity.

A company goes bust when it is unable to pay its bills or its debts, and one of its creditors puts its solvency to the test, finds it wanting and puts in the corporate equivalent of the bailiffs. But this is like saying that the patient died because his heart stopped beating. The underlying reasons why companies fail are far more complex.

Some businesses go bust because they would not be viable under any circumstances, or because they were in the wrong place at the wrong time. But companies which get as far as the stockmarket usually have both a plausible business concept and a reasonable business plan. The broad reasons that companies founder are either that the business is badly managed or that the finances are badly organized: often the killer is a mixture of both.

Bad management is a catch-all phrase. A good business may grow complacent and fail to keep up with the competition; management may be reluctant to admit that a good idea has ceased to work; a good idea may be implemented inefficiently; an enthusiastic management may overtrade. None of these failings necessarily lead a

company to collapse. A sleepy company with solid
finances may be taken over instead.

But if inadequate management is coupled with inadequate financial organization or exposed to unexpected
outside shocks, the company is probably heading for
trouble. If, say, it has a net cash outflow year after year, it
will eventually run out of money, no matter how solid its
original financial structure.

A company's finances need to be both reasonably solid
in their own right and suitable to the underlying
business. Thus any company which gets most of its
capital from borrowing is potentially less stable than one
with a majority of equity finance. But if the business itself
is particularly stable, high borrowings may not be as
dangerous as they look. And any company which is
expanding rapidly – or trading unprofitably – may run
into trouble faster than a stagnant company: financial
resources which looked perfectly adequate at the end of
one year may appear dangerously meagre after a year of
rapid growth.

External influences, such as a recession, or a sharp rise
in interest rates, can exacerbate the effect of internal
weaknesses. A rising number of company failures, often
concentrated in particular geographic or business areas,
is one of the symptoms of recession.

Spotting companies headed for financial trouble is
much easier with hindsight. But financial analysts do
have a checklist of points to look for in annual accounts.

The two main ratios analysts look at are **gearing ratios**
and **liquidity ratios**. The former relate a company's debt to
its equity capital; the latter measure its cash position.

Borrowings as a percentage of shareholders' funds

A very crude rule of thumb is that anything under 50 per
cent is reasonable; 50 to 100 deserves a second look; over
100 per cent and there needs to be a good reason. But such
rules are dangerously simplistic.

There are two reasons why a company whose borrowings are high in relation to its equity capital may be

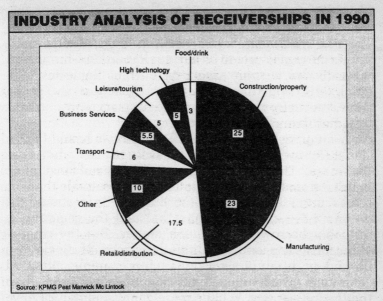

INDUSTRY ANALYSIS OF RECEIVERSHIPS IN 1990

Food/drink

High technology

Leisure/tourism

Construction/property

Business Services

5   3

5

5.5

25

Transport

6

Other

10

23

17.5

Retail/distribution

Manufacturing

Source: KPMG Peat Marwick Mc Lintock

Fig 20.1 Not surprisingly, construction, property and retailing companies figured prominently in 1990's corporate casualties.

vulnerable. First, its earnings will be more sensitive to rises and falls in operating profits, because, for example, if interest on borrowings absorbs 50 per cent of profits, a 50 per cent fall in profits produces a 100 per cent fall in earnings. Second, equity acts as a 'cushion' for creditors: the smaller that cushion, the likelier they are to panic and try to get their money back if the company runs into difficulties.

If a **highly geared** company also has high fixed **operating costs**, it requires even closer scrutiny. Profits of companies such as airlines fluctuate widely because the fixed cost of running the aircraft does not rise and fall in line with sales: a certain volume of sales is necessary to cover the fixed cost; above that level every passenger is nearly pure profit; under that level every lost passenger is nearly pure loss. Unfortunately airlines tend also to have high borrowings, because of the large amount of capital tied up in their business.

Liquidity ratios

The two traditional liquidity ratios both relate a company's current assets to its current liabilities. The **current ratio** divides current assets by current liabilities. The **quick ratio** (sometimes known as the **acid test**) makes the same comparison, but deducts stocks from current assets first. Both are effectively checking what would happen if every creditor held a gun to the company's head at once. Could it pay them all off? The quick ratio acknowledges that in such circumstances the company would be unable to sell its stock rapidly at its balance sheet value.

The norm here is that the current ratio should be around 1.5 – any lower than that and the company is probably borrowing too much money. But the composition of assets and liabilities is crucial. If stocks are illiquid or of dubious value – for example outdated computers – the realistic figure may be much lower than the theoretical one. What's more, many companies have wildly fluctuating capital requirements. A Christmas cracker company with a 31 December balance sheet and a comfortable looking current ratio may be overstretched in the autumn. Another point to note is whether large loans are due for repayment soon.

The quick ratio assumes that the gun-toting creditors demand instant satisfaction, and that there is no point in the company holding an emergency sale of its stock. If the ratio is less than one, the company gets the bullet. But it's still dangerous to generalize. Many large businesses operate with a ratio below one, because they know they can get credit from their suppliers while demanding cash from their customers. This is fine, as long as they retain the confidence of their suppliers. Any unexpected change in a long-standing supply agreement can be a danger sign.

Other points worth keeping an eye out for are **cash flow** and **contingent liabilities**. If newspapers report a significant deterioration in the flow of cash through a company, or that it is likely to need more working capital, these can be danger signs. Contingent liabilities are costs which the company may have to bear if the worst happens. Lawsuits often fall into this category. The residual value of leases is another. The contingent liabilities of Atlantic Computer's leases was a major factor in the failure of British & Commonwealth.

Accountants have an additional list of unusual accounting practices which may be warning signals. Most of them reflect excessive optimism on the part of the directors: valuing assets too highly or expecting them to retain their value for an unusually long time; capitalizing expenditure or interest charges (i.e. inflating profits by taking a revenue cost and treating it as an asset). But sometimes excessive pessimism can be equally suspect. If a company writes down the goodwill of an acquisition (see chapter 16) or makes a big charge for reorganizing its operations, it may be able to inflate the following year's profits by releasing some of the unnecessary provisions. Changes in accounting policies can also be suspect if the change flatters the results.

First Aid

Many sick companies recover. If the company's management or shareholders diagnose the problem in time there are usually several possible cures. The trouble is that sickness is regarded as culpable in a company – its shareholders and creditors desert it, its enemies close in. And many companies go to their graves with their managers denying that the company has ever had a day's illness in its life.

Some managements manage to transform sclerotic companies by buying and selling subsidiaries. For example, TI had a frenetic period of selling off large numbers of existing businesses and buying new ones: the group at the end of the 1980s would have been almost unrecognizable to someone who hadn't looked at it since the start of the decade.

That counts as preventive medicine. If the company is seriously ill, and displaying any of the cash crisis symptoms outlined above, existing management may opt for surgery and/or a blood transfusion. Surgery can include selling off subsidiaries or assets; doing a sale and leaseback of properties; cutting back on capital commitments; or reducing its level of trading. The problem about the last two options is that they may solve the immediate problem but weaken the chances of longer-term survival. A more sensible remedy is to cut the dividends to shareholders. But the investing institutions tend to panic if this happens and the ensuing fuss may provoke the very problems the cut was intended to avert. So companies often opt for a blood transfusion instead, raising fresh capital through borrowing or equity finance. Borrowing may not be possible unless the company has room left before it hits its borrowing ceiling. But getting shareholders to stump up more money can also be tricky in these circumstances.

Occasionally a company in real trouble will opt for a total **capital reconstruction**. This often means that a major new shareholder or a group of investing institutions put up a mixture of debt and equity finance – and existing shareholders' stake in the company is reduced. Such drastic surgery is sometimes undertaken by professional **company doctors**, usually accountants by training. One notorious capital reconstruction was the rescue of helicopter manufacturer Westland in 1986. Here two rival reconstruction plans were on offer and the tussle between them almost brought down Mrs Thatcher's administration. But this is unusual.

Suspensions

If a company is reorganized, the directors will normally ask the Stock Exchange to suspend dealings in its shares. This means that to all intents and purposes dealing in the shares dries up. The suspension procedure is intended to protect shareholders and prevent the shares being traded whilst investors are ignorant of important information which might affect the price. It is a procedure used in a wide range of circumstances, not all bad – when a takeover bid is believed to be pending, for example.

But if a company's shares are suspended because it is

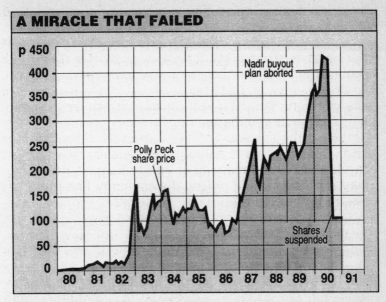

A MIRACLE THAT FAILED

Polly Peck share price

Nadir buyout plan aborted

Shares suspended

Fig 20.2 Polly Peck was so long held up as the ultimate growth share, despite the fact that few people knew how the company worked. In the end, chairman Asil Nadir proved to have feet of clay.

in trouble, the suspension may last for months or even years. This penalizes investors who are then locked into a holding of dubious value. And even if they suspect the worst, they may be unable to claim a capital loss on their shareholding for gains tax purposes until the Revenue is satisfied that it is finally dead.

Insolvency

Once it becomes obvious that a company cannot pay its bills or raise additional finance, it starts to go bust. There are now two main routes to final collapse, but the end is the same, the assets are sold for the benefit of creditors and the company ceases to exist. Creditors may get some or all of their money back, shareholders rarely get anything. Stronger companies may voluntarily enter a process called **administration**, in which their affairs are

sorted out during a period lasting at least three months.
Whole businesses may be sold from the administration as
going concerns before a **liquidator** is called in to dispose
of what is left. Weaker companies normally find that their
chief secured creditor puts in a **receiver** (corporate debt
collector) to take charge of the company's affairs, and he
normally calls in a liquidator very rapidly. The main
processes work as follows:

● **Administration**. If a company is insolvent, but has at
  least some healthy businesses, it may apply for a court
  order putting it into administration. This provides the
  company with protection from its creditors. An
  accountant will move in to run the company with at
  least three months' grace before he can be called to
  account by creditors. The viable businesses will be
  kept going for as long as possible, and may well be sold
  off or even refloated on the stockmarket. The sale
  proceeds are used to repay as much as possible of what
  is owed to creditors. What will almost certainly not
  survive is the original company, which is usually
  wound up by a liquidator (see below) once the
  administrator has got what he can out of it.
  There is seldom enough money to repay creditors in
  full and ordinary shareholders are most unlikely to get
  anything back. A company is only allowed to go into
  administration if it can persuade the court that there is
  a reasonable prospect of at least some of its businesses
  surviving, and that administration will produce more
  money for creditors than selling all the assets in short
  order. A supportive attitude from its creditors, notably
  the bankers, is essential.
● **Receivership**. If a company is in dire straits its bankers
  and other creditors are likely to oppose any attempt to
  put in an administrator, for fear that more of their
  money will be wasted trying to keep an unviable
  business going. Normally one creditor (usually a
  clearing bank whose loans were secured against the
  company's assets) will appoint a **receiver** (an accountant) in order to recover the debt. In theory the receiver
  could sell enough assets to cover the relevant debt and

depart. In practice, he usually calls in a **liquidator** (another accountant) to hold a fire sale for the benefit of all creditors.

- **Liquidation**. (Also known as winding up.) There are several varieties of liquidation. Creditors' voluntary liquidation and compulsory liquidation are similar. In the first case, the company's management agrees to go quietly, in the second, a court order is necessary, but the procedure is the same: the creditors appoint a liquidator who sells off all the assets and distributes the proceeds to creditors according to a strict pecking order. A members' voluntary liquidation is the odd man out in that it is the orderly disposal of the assets of a solvent company, whose shareholders simply wish to stop trading.

- **Payment of creditors**. There is seldom enough to pay all creditors in full, but the order in which creditors get paid depends on what type of claim they have against the company. Secured creditors and the liquidator are first in the queue. The secured creditors are those (such as a mortgage lender) who hold a **fixed charge** against a specific asset, or those (such as a bank) who have a **floating charge** against almost all of the company's assets. Such debts have to be satisfied in full before unsecured creditors (such as suppliers) get a look in.

Theoretically second, but in practice sometimes first, come the **preferential creditors**: the government under various guises, such as PAYE, VAT, National Insurance and betting taxes; and employees in respect of salaries and holiday pay up to certain (very modest) limits.

Then comes the mass of unsecured creditors, all of whom are paid pro rata – if there is any money with which to pay them. As the liquidator sells off the assets, he will periodically declare dividends to the unsecured creditors. This process can last for years.

In the unlikely event that anything else remains in the kitty, it is returned to shareholders. But it is extremely rare for ordinary shareholders to get any money back. Indeed, some liquidators don't even bother to tell shareholders what is going on.

Keeping Track

Shareholders who see the price of their company plunging for no obvious reason may be witnessing the first unofficial sign that it is heading for liquidation. Similarly, if the shares are suspended with a fuzzy statement that the directors are trying to clarify the financial situation or reorganize the company's affairs, it is often an ominous pointer. But neither signal is reliable. The first official news a shareholder can expect about the company going bust is a newspaper report that a receiver or administrator has been appointed. If he misses that, he is unlikely to get any individual notification, though his broker should be able to tell him what has happened.

Thereafter very little information trickles down to shareholders, unless they happen also to be creditors (who are kept informed) or unless the liquidation is newsworthy. Then reports will appear periodically in the press. Sometimes the liquidator will save money by cancelling the share's stockmarket listing. And the Stock Exchange authorities do not keep any official record of what happens to companies which have lost their listing. It's worth keeping a note of the receiver/liquidator's firm and telephone number: he will usually answer a personal query, even if he does not bother to write to shareholders. The *Investors Chronicle* sometimes publishes information about companies which have gone bust.

A Real Example

Sock Shop, the specialist retailer, came to the stockmarket in May 1987 on a tide of popular enthusiasm. Its founder, Sophie Mirman, won awards as Business Woman and Entrepreneur of the Year, as profits and the share price soared, valuing the company at £73m at one point. In early 1990 the company went bust, and by mid-summer it was clear that there was no money for shareholders. What actually happened? And could investors have spotted the warning signs early enough to get out with at least some of their money ?

- **May 1987**. Sock Shop International issues 18 per cent of its equity at 125p a share, raising £4.9m. Some £1.8m went to the company for expansion. It had 43 small shops, and Lord Sieff of Marks & Spencer fame was a non-executive director. The issue was 53 times subscribed attracting £250m. When dealing started, the shares traded between 205p and 270p, settling down around 250p.
- **October 1987**. The directors explained plans to open the first US store in the new year. One investment tipsheet argued that there was scope for 1,000 Sock Shops worldwide.
- **February 1988**. The annual accounts for the year to 30 September 1987 confirmed that profits had topped the May prospectus forecast and showed net debt equivalent to 43 per cent of shareholders funds. The board said that it planned to add 30 more outlets to the existing 60. American retailing shares were very weak, but Sock Shop's board continued to be enthusiastic about US expansion.
- **March/April 1988**. Sophie Mirman was voted 1987 Business Woman of the Year, an award sponsored by the Institute of Directors.
- **May 1988**. UK interest rates started their long climb from 7.5 per cent to reach 15 per cent in late 1989.
- **July 1988**. The interim results for the six months to March 1988 showed a 75 per cent increase in profits to £2.2m before tax. There were now 80 shops including six in New York. Although the company made a £150,000 provision for the US operation, it was expected to break even by year end.

  The year end was changed from September to February which meant a 17-month accounting period to February 1989. Shareholders would not see any audited accounts until well into 1989. It was a very hot summer in Britain, with several transport strikes. Many of the UK shops were in railway stations and some women went bare-legged. The share price started to slide and was down to 150p by the end of 1988.
- **January 1989**. Profits figures for the 12 months to September 1988 showed pre-tax profits had risen over

50 per cent to £2.6m. The figures included the £150,000 provision for US start-up costs, with another £150,000 expected. The number of US stores was planned to rise to 19. The share price continued falling.

- **August 1989**. Profits for the 17 months to February 1989 were a disappointing £4.3m before tax. The company had made less profit over the 1988/89 winter than in the previous one, despite the rapid expansion. Ms Mirman said that the company had not made any money so far in 1989. Trading in the UK was suffering from sluggish high street spending and competition from non-specialist retailers. In the US, city centre robberies meant heavy costs in armed guards. Borrowing was now double the total of shareholders' funds and capital expenditure was being reined back.

  The accounts for the 17 months to February contained a number of worrying items: a net cash outflow of £8.8m over the 17 months, a £10m reduction in liquidity and bank overdrafts of nearly £12m. Development costs had been capitalized and net debt was over 240 per cent of shareholders' funds. The company planned to ask shareholders at the September AGM for permission to increase its borrowing powers to 3.5 times shareholders' funds to cover 'short-term capital requirements'. The vast majority of the company's assets represented premiums paid for short-term property leases. Interest payable on loans over the period amounted to £700,000, but over £400,000 of this had been **capitalized**, i.e. not charged against profits but treated as an asset. With interest rates at 14 per cent, interest charges on the February level of borrowings could have reached £2m in a full year. With interest rates still rising and borrowings increasing the actual charge seemed likely to be much higher.

- **Autumn/Winter 1989**. Rumours circulated in the stockmarket and Lord Sieff retired as a director. The company closed its 17 American shops and the share price was down to 60p.

- **January 1990**. Talks about refinancing and a possible restructuring of the US operation were announced.

- **1 February 1990**. Sock Shop warned of 'material' losses for the 12 months to end February. Refinancing talks continued. The share price slumped to 50p.

- **9 February 1990**. Interim losses of £4m for the six months to August 1989 including £1.1m relating to the US. US write-offs of £4.8m expected for the full year. A special shareholders' meeting was scheduled for mid-March, since net assets were now worth less than half the called-up share capital of £1.1m. Borrowings had risen to £16m.
- **20 February 1990**. Trading in the shares suspended at the company's request 'pending an announcement'. Share price at suspension 34p.
- **21 February 1990**. The board asked the Companies Court to appoint administrators. Two Binder Hamlyn accountants appointed.
- **March 1990**. Year end changed from 28 February to 31 May. Borrowing powers increased to £20m.
- **May 1990**. Rationalization involved closure of 58 shops. Administrators got a three-month extension to continue negotiations and formulate proposals for creditors.
- **June 1990**. Year end deferred again to 31 August.
- **August 1990**. Business of company plus 85 shops sold to clients of venture capitalists Murray Johnstone for £3.5m. New company is to be called Sock Shop Holdings and gets £3.75m of working capital. No money for unsecured creditors of Sock Shop International. Listing cancelled, and the company goes into liquidation.
- **October 1990**. New Sock Shop starts expanding; Sophie Mirman opens Trotters in Kings Road, Chelsea.

Lessons from Sock Shop

Experience hasn't stopped a lot of professional investors getting caught in collapsing companies. But to try and help the novice spot the next one, here are some of the lessons of Sock Shop.

- **Inadequate capital**. Sock Shop raised a paltry £1.8m for the company's business when it went public; rival

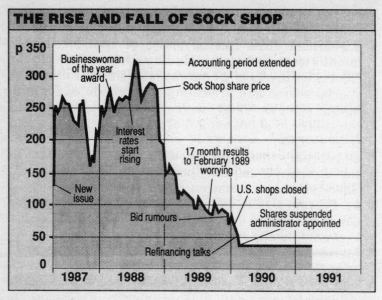

Fig 20.3 Sophie Mirman was a star in 1987, three years later Sock Shop was in ruins. There were plenty of hints of possible trouble along the way.

Tie Rack pulled in £11.5m a few months later. Given its grandiose expansion plans, the company was bound to be strapped for cash.

- **Excessive borrowings**. An inevitable consequence of the first problem. Allowing borrowings to get over double shareholders' funds was rash. The fact that interest rates doubled rapidly compounded the problem. When a company wants to increase its borrowing powers, shareholders should look carefully.
- **Expensive purchase of illiquid assets**. (Also known as Gunn's disease.) It would have been bad enough if the company's assets had been surplus stock. But the bulk of the spending was on short-term leases on City centre cubbyholes. There was unlikely to be a market for these as recession bit.
- **Capitalized interest charges**. Any attempt to turn expenditure into an asset requires scrutiny. To turn the cost of financing an illiquid asset of dubious value into an additional asset is very optimistic.

- **The American graveyard**. Any number of much larger British companies have come a cropper in the US. Sock Shop charged in when US analysts were worried about retailing shares.
- **The great and the good are not infallible**. The fact that Lord Sieff was a non-executive director showed that the company was run by nice people, not that the business was bound to succeed.
- **Pioneering is dangerous**. Sock Shop was a good idea, but established stores soon moved to compete. Mammon is on the side of the companies with the deepest pockets.
- **Believing their own publicity**. Those whom Mammon wishes to destroy he first makes Business Man or Woman of the Year.
- **Changing a year end**. It's often a bad sign when a company changes its year end: in this case shareholders saw no accounts for 17 months even though the company was expanding frenetically.
- **Brave talk about refinancing**. Occasionally a company does just that, but it's normally a sign of desperation, and bankers try not to lend to anyone who really needs the money.
- **Sagging share price**. It is normally safer to believe the share price than the chairman when the crunch approaches.

Liquidations

IN A NUTSHELL

1. Companies can become unhealthy and sometimes even die. The immediate cause of a
   company going bust is that it runs out of money
   and becomes insolvent. But the underlying
   causes are more varied and complex.

2. Few businesses are intrinsically unviable, but
   companies run into trouble because the business
   is badly managed or the company's finances are
   badly organized or inappropriate.

3. External factors, such as a recession, or a sharp
   rise in interest rates, can exacerbate internal
   weaknesses.

4. Potential problems can sometimes be spotted in
   a company's annual accounts.

5. If problems are spotted in time asset sales,
   management changes, exchanges of debt for
   equity or financial reconstructions can head off
   crisis.

6. A company's shares are sometimes suspended
   by the Stock Exchange whilst solutions to its
   problems are being sought.

7. If a company fails it may be put into administration or receivership to get creditors' money
   back. Most companies then pass on to liquidation.

8. If a company is put into administration its
   businesses will be kept going and may well be

sold off, though the company itself dies. If the company is liquidated the assets will be sold, but the businesses may die as well as the company.

9. Creditors are paid off according to a prescribed order. There is hardly ever any money left over for ordinary shareholders.

Chapter 21
What moves share prices?

Some outsiders find the behaviour of the equity market puzzling. They cannot understand how the market can reach a record high when unemployment is rising strongly, as in 1991, or why investors keep on buying when everyone agrees that the market is ridiculously overvalued, as in mid-1987. The answer is that the market both anticipates and exaggerates.

Investors are always looking forward. So when share prices rose strongly in early 1991, this was partly because of relief at the end of the Gulf war, but also because investors were looking beyond the recession to the recovery they knew would follow. People who ignore that point find it difficult to understand why share prices often treat an important event as an anticlimax. The market's response to a Conservative election victory, something the City would usually welcome, is often either a very brief rally followed by a rout, or else no rally at all. The answer to this is that 'it's all in the price'; the market had anticipated the win, and risen before it happened. In the jargon traders will 'buy on the rumour, and sell on the news'.

This anticipation can be matched by alarming naivety. Many pundits spent 1987 saying that equity prices were too high. But when shares continued upwards, investors started finding reasons why this boom was different and would continue. Needless to say, they were wrong. It was the same with the Japanese market in 1990. That, too, finally burst in the way that all speculative bubbles eventually do. The combination of these two characteristics, anticipation and excess, can make market movements appear totally random. They are not.

The long view

Long-term bull and bear markets are what a lot of people spend their time looking for. It makes it much easier to decide if an investment is right if you think the whole market will continue rising for some time. These trends are determined by **fundamental** factors: the state of the economy, the political background, the relative attractions of other markets and alternative investments. How far ahead investors are prepared to look will vary, but it is commonly said that the equity market is looking at conditions about eighteen months hence. That does not, however, mean that the market gets it right, and new factors can always come into the assessment. So something which might be well catered for in the long-term view like the recession of 1990/91, can deliver a short-term shock to the market if reported company profits turn out to be much worse than had been expected.

Part of the reason for these jolts is simply the unpredictable nature of some events, but differences sometimes occur because two disparate groups are trying to assess the stockmarket: economists and analysts. Economists work 'from the top down' trying to work out from a picture of the whole economy what the implications are for particular companies or sectors. Analysts work from the 'bottom up' aggregating a series of facts about different companies into an overall view. Often these two approaches produce startlingly different results; on occasion both are completely wrong. And it doesn't help that the two groups are not very good at talking to each other.

The long-term influences on the stockmarket don't always begin at home. Over a long period London shares have shown a marked reluctance to break free of the influence of Wall Street. There is some logic to this: the behaviour of the US economy has a profound influence on the rest of the world, and especially so in Britain, which depends more heavily than most other industrial countries on international trade for its prosperity. If Wall Street rises London shares may start to look relatively cheap. And there is always the more banal explanation

that if traders in London are looking for a lead, why not
hang on to Wall Street's coat-tails? Britain's longer-term
slavery is harder to rationalize, and it will be interesting
to see whether London continues to follow Wall Street
doggedly as Britain moves closer to the Continent and the
effects of the ERM bite. If Britain becomes more intimately
tied to European economic conditions, and the EC takes
an even larger share of British trade, then Britain ought to
become more firmly allied to continental markets.

Reading the medium-term runes

No market moves in a straight line, and medium-term
stockmarket movements often contradict the long-term
bull or bear market trend. Medium-term moves can last
several months and are often determined by **technical
factors**. In essence this comes back to supply and demand
in the market. If the investing institutions have more cash
coming in than going out, they need to put it somewhere.
Ideally they would like to add to their long-term holding
of equities, but they may choose to put substantial sums
on deposit for long periods if they don't like equity market
conditions, which is what happened after 1987. The idea
that institutions have cash to add to the equity market is
known as the **weight of money** theory, but it seldom
works on its own. If, however, there are other reasons
why shares might rise, institutional liquidity will help
them do so, and may make them rise faster as all of the
fund managers charge into the market at once.

Besides investors putting more savings into institutions, other factors can also affect liquidity. A series of
successful cash bids will increase the funds available to
institutions, while a wave of rights issues or new
companies coming to the market will slow down the rise
of shares. Bids made in shares have little impact either
way.

Demand for shares can sometimes come from the
futures market and feed through to conventional shares.
Overseas investors and some institutions may for convenience decide to buy FT-SE 100 index futures rather than

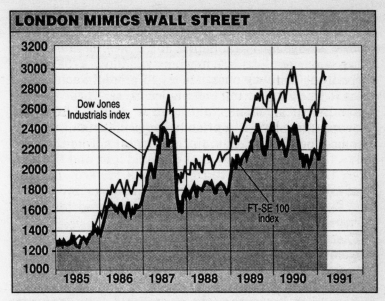

Fig 21.1 Sometimes London's slavish mimicry of Wall Street makes you wonder why the UK doesn't just become the 51st State of the Union.

shares, and this will subsequently drag up share prices (see chapter 6). Watching the relationship between futures and the underlying share markets can give a short-term indication of institutional attitudes.

One school of investors, **chartists** or **technical analysts**, believes that purely by studying patterns of share price behaviour they can make money. Many of their jargon phrases and voodoo techniques seem to hold some measure of common sense when they are translated into English. For example, **resistance levels** means that a lot of investors bought shares at this level some time ago, before the share price fell, and they will unload them the moment the price reaches that level again. So prices are unlikely to get much higher than this until the last of these unhappy holders has sold. Charting is a way of using historical prices to assess supply and demand.

Another type of technical factor makes use of the fact that investors tend to behave like a crowd, and that such mass psychology is predictable. What this comes down to is that investors act like a stampeding herd and always overdo things through panic, so sooner or later every sharp movement in the market will have a balancing **correction**. One way chartists try to predict such corrections is by constructing **moving averages**. These average share prices or index values on a rolling basis, and demonstrate how far a price is deviating from its trend. The faster and further the price deviates from its trend value, the more overbought or oversold it is, and the more likely that it will start to correct back towards its long-term average. Typically such trends are measured over 40 or 200 working days, giving a medium- and long-term perspective on the price.

There are other mathematical tools which measure the **momentum** with which a price is moving away from the long-term trend. But investors should beware of relying too heavily on overbought or oversold signals. A market or share can be overbought or oversold for a long time before it corrects, and when it is heavily overbought, a price can be very volatile.

Fear and greed

Very short-term market movements are in the nature of knee-jerks; they are powerful and uncontrollable forces which can cut across other considerations. This is where the two dominant market emotions **fear and greed** come into their own. An unexpected event can have a very powerful short-term influence on a market. If the President of the United States were shot, the market would forget all about the economy, recession or even petty party politics; the uncertainty caused would drive the market down sharply.

Occasionally such knee-jerks occur in slow motion. Thus it took investors several days to decide that the Iraqi invasion of Kuwait was very bad news. Initially market participants were uncertain what the political reaction would be, or how to measure its impact, and so ignored it.

But once the consequences of the invasion had sunk in, investors panicked, and share prices fell a long way.

It is possible to make money out of all of these trends – the chartists sometimes say that 'the trend is your friend'. Go with the long-term trend and bet against an excessive short-term movement. But if you mistake one for the other it can be very expensive.

Sector relatives

Individual stockmarket sectors tend to follow the overall trend of the market. But just as the market vibrates either side of the long-term trend so sectors move up and down against the market. Sometimes a sector will **outperform** or **underperform** for months or even years. As with the market as a whole, it is crucial to try to identify which type of divergence it is before backing the move. The more fundamental the reason for the divergence, the longer it is likely to last.

For example, retailing shares started to underperform the market in 1985, mainly because stockmarket enthusiasm for 1980s retailing methods had driven them to very high levels, but also because excessive competition was starting to cut profit margins even while consumer spending was still going strong. By 1990, when the bulk of the bankruptcies and profits collapses happened, the sector had turned and was beginning to show a **relative** improvement. But anyone who decided that retailing shares had fallen far enough by 1988, would have lost a lot of money by 1990. The length of this relative decline was unusual, and it happened because a setback which started with fundamental problems in the retail industry was exacerbated by a downturn in the whole economy.

There is a standard list of the types of business which suffer earliest and most in recessions. In the front line are those which deal directly with the consumer, particularly in high value items, or those which depend heavily on borrowed funds, such as motor dealers, housebuilders, advertising companies and retailers. Their shares nor-

mally start to fall well before a recession bites, and pick
up well before it has passed its worst. Again, this is the
kind of trend which can be spotted on relative strength
charts – or by anyone following the FT-Actuaries indexes
closely.

The fact that investing institutions have 'sector weightings' in their portfolios tends to reinforce the movements.
For example, if food retailing shares picked up and an
unfortunate fund manager had too few in his portfolio, he
would rapidly try to buy more to remedy the deficiency. If
he didn't then he would underperform the market – the
worst sin in the fund management book. The only shares
he could usefully buy are some of the 16 members of the
FT-Actuaries food retailing group, a sub-index of the FT-
A All Share. That will tend to reinforce the rally in the
shares, adding a twist to the rising circle. Because of this,
shares often rise when they have been promoted into an
index – fund managers often feel they have to buy them,
even if they don't much like the company.

Of course, it's dangerous to put too much reliance on
sector movements, particularly if you are trying to ride the
trend in a sector by holding a single share. For although
shares in a sector do move together sometimes, the
average movement disguises big variations, and the
differences between shares in a sector can be as large as
the difference between the sector and the market as a
whole.

Following sectors is particularly hazardous for small
company fans, since small companies are not part of the
actuaries' indexes. And like all fashions, sector movements are usually exaggerated, and this excess is
followed by correction.

Sectors are not the only groups

Sometimes it's a share's other attributes which determine
its performance. For example, in 1990/91 small companies
and those with very high borrowings were unpopular,
because the market's worry at that time was that high
interest rates were pushing companies into recession,

and those two groups were considered the most
vulnerable.

Similarly if there is a sharp currency movement – for
example a fall in the dollar – which has a bad impact on
companies which export to the US, all of their shares are
likely to suffer. The market usually has a group of
companies which it thinks are under threat from a
takeover bid – if one of them is actually attacked, the price
of the others may well rise too.

Sizing up individual shares

Some shares are more volatile than others. Shares which
normally exaggerate any move in the market are described as having a high **beta** factor. A share which moves
in line with the market has a beta of one; another which is
unusually inert has a beta of less than one. Investors
theoretically demand a higher total return from shares
with higher betas, because they are riskier. But fund
managers may buy more high-beta shares if they think the
market is about to rise, and vice versa. Private investors
do not normally have enough shares in their portfolios for
this kind of **risk analysis** to be useful.

Individual shares respond partly to market and 'peer
group' influences, and partly to investors' assessment of
their individual merits. As with markets, an individual
share's movement **relative** to the market or its sector can
be explained by long, medium and short-term factors.

Take Tesco, the supermarket group founded by Sir Jack
Cohen on the 'pile 'em high, sell 'em cheap' philosophy,
which has moved steadily upmarket under its current
management. During the 1980s the shares outperformed
the food retailing sector substantially, for the **fundamental** reason that its move upmarket to compete with
Sainsbury paid off. But the share price actually rose even
faster than profits, because investors' perception of Tesco
changed. Instead of being rated less highly than other
grocers, it became more highly rated because its management had proved it could deliver the goods.

That was the long-term trend. But if you look at a chart

of Tesco's relative performance, it doesn't move in a straight line. Sometimes there is a **correction** as investors decide they have been too enthusiastic, and the share price relative to the sector moves down for a while. How long such a correction lasts depends on whether investors think the share price has just got a little ahead of itself, or whether they view Tesco's long period of above-average growth as coming to an end. If the latter, the correction could be large and spell the end of the trend.

Medium-term movements inside a share price trend are often caused by supply and demand variations. If every investing institution which wanted to buy Tesco shares already owned them then the price might stop rising simply because there was no new demand. Similarly, if an issue flops, or a company issues too many shares in the course of acquisitions, the share price may get bogged down because the increase in supply has not been matched by extra demand. If the supply glut is temporary, it may cause no particular damage, but if the new shares concentrate investors' minds on the company's prospects, there may be trouble ahead. For example, shares in another thrusting supermarket group Dee (later to become Gateway) performed relatively well in the mid-1980s, because investors were impressed by its takeovers. But it had issued shares like confetti, and when investors began to wonder whether the management was any good at running grocers' shops the share price stalled and never recovered. Eventually the company fell to a bid.

Short sharp shocks

Short-term movements in company shares tend to happen when the unexpected turns up. This can be something outside the company's control, as for example when the Gulf war hit airline traffic and airline shares, or it can be something directly relating to the company, like a bid, a profits warning or a change in investors' perceptions. Often there is more than one element at work. In early 1991 brewer Bass issued a guarded profits warning and its shares tumbled: the company's caution had forced investors to revise their image of the brewer as a classic **defensive** share, which was unlikely to suffer despite a downturn in the economy.

The most influential outsiders are probably stockbrokers' analysts. They have a symbiotic relationship with the companies they study: the companies hint information to the analysts because if trading circumstances have changed they would rather have a gradual adjustment than a sharp shock. Often analysts have meetings with the companies, and the very fact that such a meeting is scheduled can affect the share price.

When an influential analyst publishes an unexpected buy or sell recommendation, it can have dramatic results. In one spectacular case building analyst Angus Phaure visited Magnet, the fitted kitchen group. For months he had been their greatest fan, but at the railway station on the way home from his visit, his worries about the group crystallized and he phoned his office with a sell recommendation. The share price collapsed.

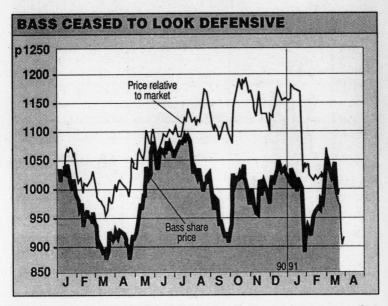

Fig 21.2 Brewers are traditionally seen as defensive investments, but a profit warning from Bass changed market perceptions, and the shares slumped.

In some ways the press is in a similar position to analysts. The companies will try hard to get favourable comment which will support their share price, but if an influential and respected newspaper or magazine – particularly the *Financial Times* – publishes a story which contains price-sensitive information or a strong view on the company's prospects, the share price can move rapidly.

Insider dealing

Even more difficult to anticipate is insider dealing or share price ramping. The technical definition of insider dealing is trading shares on the basis of unpublished price-sensitive information obtained by virtue of your job. It is a criminal offence. If you pick up a takeover story because you overhear a conversation between people not

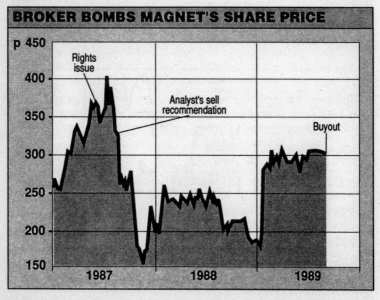

Fig 21.3 The power of a respected analyst can be enormous. Angus Phaure's cold feet about the prospects for kitchen group Magnet hit the share price hard.

connected with you, you may be hearing insider information, but you are not an insider yourself, so if you trade on what you have heard, it isn't a crime. If you pick up the same information as a company employee or an adviser, and deal on it, you are a culpable insider.

A few convictions have been secured, but outsiders often suspect that there is a lot more of it around than has ever been proved. The way so many share prices move before a bid is announced cannot all be explained away as good luck or psychic power. The Stock Exchange has an insider dealing group dedicated to tracking down suspicious price movements and it has the power to force disclosure of dealings. But there are still many more suspicious price movements than insider convictions.

Sometimes the opposite happens. Speculators take a position in some shares, put round an untrue story which will move share prices their way, and wait for the market's fear and greed to move the shares. To be really successful these stories have to catch the mood of the market. So if there has been a spate of bankruptcies, speculators may sell short (sell shares they don't own) and put round rumours saying that the company is in trouble or going bust. If the **bear raid** is successful, down go the shares and the speculators buy them back at a lower price.

Forcing shares up in a similar way is known as **ramping** and at their crudest ramping and bear raids are done by anonymous letters or phone calls to brokers and financial journalists. Sometimes there is a grain of truth in them: letters were sent to the press about computer group Amstrad shortly before founder Alan Sugar announced he was selling part of his very large holding in the group. The anonymous letters were inaccurate and didn't move the share price, but there was something going on at the company.

Account closing is a phenomenon which may be on the way out as institutions move to a rolling settlement system. In the last day or so of an account, share prices often reverse direction, because market makers know that people dealing inside the account period are about to start closing out earlier deals. The professionals adjust

their prices because they can see the trades coming.
There are some causes of price movements investors can
allow for – and there are some they can't.

What moves share prices?

IN A NUTSHELL

1. Investors are more interested in what is going to happen than in what has happened; share prices are trying to discount future events. Markets also tend to exaggerate price movements.

2. Long-term market moves are affected by fundamental factors like economics; in the medium term technical supply and demand factors can be decisive, and investor psychology can be the most powerful short-term influence.

3. Investors can profit from backing a long-term market trend, or by opposing a shorter-term over reaction. But it is expensive to mistake one for the other.

4. Sectors broadly follow the overall market trend, but do diverge from it. Spotting which sectors are going to show relative strength can be profitable, but relying on sectors too much is dangerous.

5. Individual shares are also affected by long-term trends or economic factors. Oversupply of shares can blight the outlook, but inclusion in an index can help boost a price. Unexpected shocks can move prices dramatically.

6. Brokers' analysts can have an important influence on share prices. They are often fed information by companies to shade expectations, but when influential analysts change their views price changes can be rapid.

7. In some ways the financial press performs a similar role to analysts; companies try to influence comment, but when a respected journal reveals important information or a strong view, prices can move.

8. Insider dealing, bear raids and ramps affect share prices. There is little an investor can do about these.

Appendix A
Tax

BY ANDREW RADICE*

According to Ben Franklin, nothing is certain in this world except death and taxes. Two hundred years later, governments still seem pretty keen to part people from their money. That's as true of money made from investment as any other kind – the government always wants its share. But although the costs of taxation can be quite high, it is not the prime consideration when considering investment. The suitability, safety and prospects for an investment have to be clear before tax needs to be considered. A further caveat is that if you become a serious investor, you probably ought to seek professional tax advice, because it can become complicated.

Having said that, it is worth becoming familiar with the general principles of UK tax to see how the land lies. So this appendix gives a brief – and hopefully painless – introduction.

Of the many different UK taxes, only two are of much concern to private investors.

Income Tax

Sadly this is pretty familiar to most of us. With few exceptions, income is taxable. The rates and thresholds for income tax are announced annually in the Budget. The picture changes every year with adjustments for inflation and other refinements. (Governments do like to tinker!)

---

*Andrew Radice is an independent tax consultant. He can be contacted on (0722) 790 350.

In 1993/94 there are three rates of income tax: 20 per cent (lower rate) on the first £2,500 of taxable income, 25 per cent (basic rate) on the next £21,200 and 40 per cent (higher rate) on income over £23,700. To lighten the load a little everyone gets a tax-free allowance (in 1993/94 £3,445) and a married couple gets an additional allowance, worth £1,720 in 1993/94. This is given to the husband in the first instance but couples can elect to transfer the whole or half of the allowance to the wife. Salaries and pension income are taxed automatically under the PAYE system, but what happens to income from investments?

Investments

A few UK investments – such as National Savings and British Government Stocks (gilts) bought on the National Savings Stock Register – pay income gross, without deducting tax (unfortunately this does not necessarily mean that they are tax-free). However, all dividends on UK shares and unit trusts have tax deducted before you receive them. The company pays you a dividend net of 20 per cent tax, and pays the tax to the Inland Revenue on your behalf.

So for example, if you receive a net dividend of £80, the dividend voucher will state that you have a 'tax credit' of £20. For tax purposes you are treated as having received a gross dividend of £100, on which tax of £20 has already been paid. If you have little or no other income so that your allowances have not been used, you can claim the tax credit back. If you only pay tax at 20 or 25 per cent, there is no more tax to pay. If you pay tax at 40 per cent, you will have to pay £20 to the Inland Revenue later (the difference between the £40 which is due on income of £100 and the £20 already paid). The higher rate tax has to be paid by 1 December following the end of the tax year.

Cash investments

The method for taxing interest paid to personal depositors at banks and building societies works in a similar way to the system for dividends, except that the tax credit is at the basic rate of 25 per cent. So if you only pay tax at the lower rate of 20 per cent, you can recover the 5 per cent difference from the Inland Revenue, and if you do not pay any tax at all, you can recover the full 25 per cent deducted by the bank or building society. The different rates of tax credit affect the net returns on cash and equity investments for taxpayers on low incomes.

Non-taxpayers can sign a declaration that their income is expected to be less than their personal allowance. They can then receive their interest gross. To prevent abuse, the Inland Revenue has been given vastly extended powers to obtain information about depositors' accounts from banks and building societies. The TESSA (Tax Exempt Special Savings Account) is another way of receiving interest gross. Every individual aged 18 or more can have one TESSA with a bank or building society which will earn tax-free interest on a maximum investment of £9,000 spread over five years. Withdrawals of capital within that period trigger an income tax charge on all the interest earned in the account, as will depositing more than the £9,000 ceiling in the TESSA. The TESSA must not be assigned to anyone or used as security for a loan, as this will also result in the tax privileges being withdrawn.

Here's a simple example of how income tax works:

A single woman aged 32 earns £31,645 in 1993/94 from which PAYE of £7,525 has been deducted. She also receives National Savings Bank interest of £500 and UK dividends of £320. Her tax position is as follows:

		Income	Tax deducted
Earnings		31,645	7,525
National Savings		500	—
Dividends	320		
Tax credits	80		80
		400	
		32,545	7,605

Less:
Personal allowance   3,445

Taxable income   <u>29,100</u>

Tax 2,500 @ 20%   500
     21,700 @ 25%   5,425
     4,900 @ 40%   <u>1,960</u>

Total tax   7,885

Less tax paid: <u>7,605</u>

Tax due   280

The woman has paid the correct amount through PAYE, but has an additional tax bill of £280 (payable in December 1994) because of her investment income. It is made up of tax at 40 per cent on the National Savings Bank interest of £500 (£200) and an extra 20 per cent on the gross dividends of £400 (£80).

Working out your tax bill can get complicated if your dividend income is partly in the basic rate and partly in the higher rate bracket. Here's a simple example.

Basil is a widower aged 46. His income for 1993/94 is:

Business profits   £22,000
Building society interest   3,445
Dividends (cash amount)   4,200

The dividends gross up to £5,250, and Basil's taxable income, after deducting his personal allowance of £3,445, is £27,250. The gross dividends of £5,250 are treated as the top slice of his income. The first £1,700 of these dividends fall within the basic rate band and there is no further tax to pay. The remaining £3,550, however, is liable to higher rate tax. Basil will have to pay £710 (20% of £3,550).

It's worth bearing in mind that even modest investments can cause a tax problem. We've considered dividends and interest; other forms of investment such as life assurance bonds and friendly societies have their own tax regimes, but they are really beyond the scope of this appendix.

Reducing your tax bill by investment

There are still legal ways of limiting the tax you pay. Many people get income tax relief on contributions to personal or company pension schemes (a subject which could easily fill a book).

Capital Gains Tax

The other main type of tax which affects investors is Capital Gains Tax (CGT). Unlike income tax, CGT seeks to tax the increase in the capital value of investments. In 1993/94, the first £5,800 of an individual's capital gains is exempt from CGT; after the tax is charged at the highest rate of income tax paid.

To work our your liability for CGT, you first calculate your capital gains for the tax year (see below) and then treat the gains as if they were your top slice of income. Under the independent taxation régime, husbands and wives living together are treated as separate people (as for income tax).

To see the point clearly, let's take an example:

The single woman in the income tax example also makes *taxable* capital gains (i.e. gains in excess of the exempt amount) of £8,000 in 1993/94. Her tax position will be:

	Income /Gains		Tax
Total taxable income (as above)	29,100		7,885
Capital gains	8,000	8,000 @ 40%	3,200
	37,100		11,085

Like the higher rate income tax, the CGT is payable on 1st December 1994.

CGT is generally less painful than income tax for the following reasons:

- The first £5,800 of net gains for 1993/94 are tax-free. The £8,000 gains in the example are *after* using the exemption; i.e. the taxpayer has made £13,500 of gains. In fact because of the exemption, the vast majority of taxpayers never pay CGT. But bear in mind that CGT is not only payable on shares; if, for example, you make a capital gain on the sale of a second home, CGT is payable on this even if you have not realized any gains on share dealings.
- CGT is only payable when a gain is *realized*, i.e. when you sell an investment. If you hold an investment which goes up in value, no tax is payable until you decide to turn your profit into cash.
- You only pay tax on your *net* capital gains after deducting capital losses as well as the £5,800 exemption. If you realize capital losses in the same year as you realize capital gains, the two must be set off against each other to produce a net gain or loss for the tax year. But if you are unfortunate enough to make a net loss on your investments in a tax year, you can carry forward the loss against gains of future years. These brought forward losses have the added advantage that they can be saved up against gains. They do not have to be used in full if that would cause you to waste the annual exemption limit.
- There is no CGT payable on gilts on most fixed-interest stocks.

Here are some examples:

a) Andrew makes capital gains of £8,000 in 1993/94 and losses of £5,000. His CGT position is:

	£
Gains	8,000
Less: losses	5,000

Net gain   3,000

Andrew's net gain is below the exemption, so no CGT is payable, but £2,800 of the exemption is effectively wasted because it cannot be carried forward.

b) Basil's share dealings for 1992/93 and 1993/94 produce the following results:

		£
1992/93	Gains	5,000
	Losses	−11,000
1993/94	Gains	13,000
	Losses	−3,500

his CGT position is:

1992/93	Gains	5,000
	Less losses	−11,000
	Net loss	−6,000
1993/94	Gains	13,000
	less 1993/94 losses	−3,500
	Net	9,500
	Less 1992/93 loss brought forward	−4,000
	Net gain	5,500

It is only necessary to bring forward £3,700 of the £6,000 loss for 1992/93 to eliminate any tax payment (because the tax-free allowance is £5,800), leaving a loss of £2,300 to set against future years' gains. So although in 1992/93 Basil has had to waste his exemption, he pays no tax in 1993/94.

There is a further wrinkle which makes CGT less of a burden. Sometimes investments rise in value simply because of inflation. The taxman makes an allowance for this and investors only pay CGT on the amount by which an investment has risen in value, over and above inflation.

This 'indexation' works by increasing the value of an investment in line with the Retail Prices Index. So, put crudely, if inflation doubled prices in a year, the taxman would assume that the value of your investment had also doubled and CGT would only be paid on any increase in excess of inflation. Tables of factors are available to show how inflation has moved between any two months since the system started in April 1982. Any capital gains before that date have effectively been written off. For unknown reasons, the Inland Revenue is a bit mean about handing out these tables to individuals, but they are published periodically in the *Investors Chronicle*. Any increase in the value of an investment is then multiplied by the relevant indexation factor.

How to calculate CGT gains and losses

The basic rule is that you deduct the base cost, i.e. the price paid for the shares (including the expenses shown on the broker's contract note such as stamp duty and commission) from the net sale proceeds received from the broker (i.e. after deducting selling expenses). The effect of the indexation allowance is that the base cost is adjusted in accordance with the Retail Prices Index, so that only capital profits which beat inflation should fall into the CGT net.

The easiest way to look at this is through an example: You buy 5,000 shares in XYZ PLC for £10,000 (including expenses) in January 1987. You sell them for £8,000 (after expenses) in January 1988. The rise in the RPI between those dates is 3.3 per cent, so the indexation factor is 0.033. Your CGT computation is:

	£	£
Sale proceeds		8,000
Less costs	10,000	
Indexation (0.033 × 10,000)	330	

	10,330
Loss	2,330

Thus although you have lost £2,000 cash, you have £2,330 of tax losses available to carry forward.

The intention of the 1988 Budget, which introduced the present indexation rules, was to exempt from CGT any gains arising before 31 March 1982 (when indexation was introduced in its original form). So for investments made before 1982, this is achieved by substituting the value of your investment at 31 March 1982 for its actual cost in your CGT calculations.

This basic principle applies if your investment has risen steadily in value since the time you bought it. If, however, it was worth less in 1982 than when you bought it, or if you are now selling it at a loss, things are a little more hairy. In these circumstances, you need to compare the actual profit or loss you make with the profit or loss you would have made if you substituted the March 1982 valuation for real cost.

The rules in outline are:

- If you make a gain on your shares both by reference to cost and the March 1982 valuation after taking into account indexation, then you are taxed on the smaller gain.
- If you make a loss (after indexation) using cost and the March 1982 value, you only get relief on the smaller of the losses.
- If you make a gain on your shares by reference to cost, but a loss if you use the 1982 valuation (both after indexation) then you are treated as having made neither a gain nor a loss.
- If you make a loss by reference to the actual cost (allowing for indexation) but a gain if you use the indexed 1982 valuation, you will also be treated as making neither a gain nor a loss.

The object of these complex rules is to prevent people obtaining relief for inflation before March 1982. You can elect to over-ride these provisions and to use 31 March 1982 values for all subsequent disposals of assets you held at that date. But this is a big step and investors should take professional advice before making such a decision since it will remain in force for the rest of your life and applies to *all* capital assets – including houses.

If you did not begin to invest until after 31 March 1982, the CGT calculations are relatively straightforward. If you held shares on that date which do not fall within the complex rules outlined above, the capital gain (or loss) on their disposal is calculated by treating their value at 31 March 1982 as the base cost, and applying the indexation factor to the value at 31 March 1982.

For example:

You bought 5,000 shares in PQR Ltd. (now PQR PLC) in December 1973 for 20p a share. At March 1982 they were quoted at 50p a share. In April 1993 you sold your entire holding for £10,000. The table shows that the indexation factor between April 1982 and April 1993 is 0.770. Your CGT computation is:

	£	£
Sale proceeds		10,000
Value at 31.3.82 (50p × 5,000)	2,500	
Indexation (2,500 × 0.770)	1,925	
Total		4,425
Net gain		5,575

Pooling and indexation

Of course investors don't always buy or sell a complete holding of shares. An investor might well buy some shares, sell part of the holding, then later buy some more. To calculate the CGT liability in such a situation, the value of shares is calculated by an averaging process known as 'pooling'.

The basis of 'pooling' is that a holding of shares is treated as a single 'asset' which grows as more shares are bought and diminishes as shares are sold. The pool of shares is indexed every time there is a transaction in the shares, so that CGT is paid on the change in average value of the shares, after allowing for inflation.

Attempts to massage the value of a pool of shares by short-term trading are banned – the taxman has rules to prevent people from obtaining 'excessive' indexation allowance on purchases and sales of shares within a short period (up to ten days).

Let's see how pooling works in practice:

You buy 10,000 shares in ABC PLC for £10,000 in March 1985. You sell 5,000 shares for 10,000 in March 1988. You sell the remaining 5,000 shares for £25,000 in February 1993.

Pooled costs

Date	Number	CGT cost £	Actual cost £
March 1985 bought	10,000	10,000	10,000
Index (0.122)		1,220	
		11,220	
March 1988 sold	5,000	5,610	5,000
Pool after sale	5,000	5,610	5,000
Index (0.333)		1,868	
February 1993 sold	5,000	7,478	5,000

The CGT computations for the two sales are:

March 1988	£
Sale proceeds (5,000 shares)	10,000
Indexed cost	5,610
Gain	4,390

January 1990	£
Sale proceeds (5,000 shares)	25,000
Indexed cost	7,478
Gain	17,522

In this example the taxpayer has had a total allowance for indexation of £3,088, i.e. 30.9 per cent of his original cash investment.

If you hold any particular stock for any length of time you will probably receive scrip issues and rights issues (see chapter 18). A scrip issue does not involve any payment by you and thus your base cost is not affected. A rights issue is, in effect, a purchase by you of further shares in the company and the cost of those shares needs to be added to your indexed pool of expenditure at the time of issue.

Takeovers

You may find that you hold shares in a company which is taken over by another company. If you receive only cash, the CGT position is simple: you have sold shares for cash and the normal rules apply. Quite often, you will receive a mixture of cash and shares in exchange for your shares. In this case you will effectively only pay tax by reference to the cash element. The CGT liability attributable to the new shares you have taken will only become payable when you decide to sell them.

Stock dividends

Many quoted companies offer additional shares instead of a dividend. For tax purposes you are treated as having received the cash dividend and reinvested the proceeds. The cash alternative thus becomes your CGT base cost.

Planning

There are two entirely legitimate ways in which you can make maximum use of your allowances. First, if you own shares that have appreciated in value since you bought them, and you have not used up your annual CGT exemption, you can sell the shares and then repurchase them soon afterwards. This is known as 'bed-and-breakfasting'. In this way you realise a capital gain which is covered by the £5,800 exemption and establish a higher base cost for the re-purchased shares. You may also want to realize a loss in order to reduce other gains you have made in the tax year. The second method (married people only) is to gift shares to your husband or wife (which is free of tax) before they are sold. The spouse can then use his/her annual exemption of £5,800.

A word of warning

CGT is now payable on gifts of quoted securities to members of your family other than your husband/wife.

Other Taxes

VAT and Stamp Duty are unavoidable for most people, although Stamp Duty on shares is due to be abolished when paperless trading is introduced.

Inheritance Tax (IHT) does affect most investors but it

is not generally a tax that should influence your investment decisions, although it is likely to become more
relevant as you grow older. In 1993/94 IHT is levied at a
flat rate of 40 per cent on estates at death over £150,000. If
you own a house in Southern England and some shares it
is extremely likely that your estate will exceed this figure
when you die.

The effects of this tax can be mitigated, but, as always,
tax is not the only consideration, and you should take
professional advice before entering into any arrangements. Generally, however, gifts from one person to
another more than seven years before the owner's death
are free of IHT (although there may well be CGT to pay on
gifts of portfolio investments to anyone other than your
husband or wife).

Tax

IN A NUTSHELL

1. There are two main taxes which affect investors, income tax and capital gains tax. Income tax is payable on share dividends and interest on bank or building society accounts as well as salaries or pensions.

2. Gilts on the National Savings Register and National Savings pay interest gross, but dividends and bank/building society interest is paid net with a tax credit. Insurance and friendly societies have different rules.

3. A few investments avoid income tax, notably TESSAs, PEPs and pension contributions.

4. Capital gains tax is payable on the increase in value of any investment, from shares to property (but excluding the main residence).

5. CGT is only payable when a gain is realized, i.e. an investment is sold, and capital losses can be set against capital gains. Capital losses can be carried forward to future years.

6. Capital gains are also adjusted to take account of inflation. This 'indexing' began in April 1982 and tables of index factors are published regularly in the *Investors Chronicle*.

7. When an investment is sold in part of a holding increased, the value of the investment is averaged or 'pooled' and indexed every time a transaction occurs.

8. Investors should also look out for VAT, Stamp Duty and Inheritance Tax (IHT), which are also out to get them.

Appendix B
How to Complain

BY RUTH SUNDERLAND

There are two sides to investment regulation: the first is trying to stop people being given defective advice; the second is compensating those damaged by such advice. The British system for dealing with both aspects is based on the **Securities and Investments Board (SIB)**. But the system itself is up in the air at the moment, with major changes expected.

First, though, what counts as 'defective advice'? It does not, alas, include all advice which fails to make you money. It does include fraud, advice from people not qualified to give it and advice which is patently unsuited to the recipient's specific financial requirements.

The original system, with a host of different regulatory bodies for different types of financial firm, was confusing, expensive and didn't seem to work very well. The blueprint for the new system is based on a new body called the **Personal Investment Authority**, which will look after all financial firms dealing mainly with individual customers buying packaged products. So it will take in financial advisers, life assurance companies and unit trust groups. Stockbrokers, concentrating on individual shares but also offering more general financial advice, will stay outside under their own regulator. And banks and building societies will also be regulated separately – at least as far as their deposit-taking activities are concerned. The current compensation arrangements are also under review.

One other major change on the drawing board concerns life assurance commissions. One of the biggest criticisms of many financial salesmen is that they recommend the products which bring them a large commission. This is particularly invidious when the investors cannot find out what the commission is. Independent financial advisers already have to tell you what their commission will be – if you ask. But life assurance companies have hitherto managed to wriggle out of any such obligations. Now the Chancellor of the Exchequer has demanded that they come clean. They will have to say how much commission is payable – in cash terms – on any packaged product whoever sells it to you. They will also have to give buyers a far better idea of the likely returns on their investments, in terms that ordinary people can understand.

But this Brave New World had not come to pass as this book went to press. So here's a brief explanation of the old regulatory framework.

An investor's bill of rights

The Financial Services Act 1986 (FSA) introduced a bill of rights for investors. An enormous piece of legislation, the FSA was designed to consolidate existing investor protection rules, and plug some gaping holes. Before the FSA, for example, anybody could set up shop as an 'investment adviser', without any form of vetting or authorization. And there were no across-the-board compensation arrangements for investors.

The FSA system for protecting investors is based on self-regulation. In other words, the industry itself, rather than a government department, is responsible for policing investment business. The government delegates regulatory powers to a group of watchdogs in the financial services industry. The key regulator is the **Securities and Investments Board** (SIB), which in turn delegates regulatory powers to four SIB-lings or **Self Regulating Organizations** (SROs), and nine **Recognized Professional Bodies** (RPBs). Each SRO currently covers a separate sector of the industry: for example, independent financial advisers are regulated by FIMBRA, and stockbrokers are governed by the SFA. The RPBs are professional institutes such as the Law Society or the Institute of Actuaries, which regulate practitioners who give investment advice in the course of other business. For a full explana-

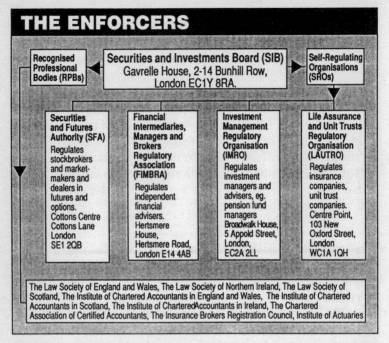

THE ENFORCERS

Recognised Professional Bodies (RPBs)	Securities and Investments Board (SIB) Gavrelle House, 2-14 Bunhill Row, London EC1Y 8RA.	Self-Regulating Organisations (SROs)

Securities and Futures Authority (SFA)	Financial Intermediaries, Managers and Brokers Regulatory Association (FIMBRA)	Investment Management Regulatory Organisation (IMRO)	Life Assurance and Unit Trusts Regulatory Organisation (LAUTRO)
Regulates stockbrokers and market-makers and dealers in futures and options. Cottons Centre Cottons Lane London SE1 2QB	Regulates independent financial advisers. Hertsmere House, Hertsmere Road, London E14 4AB	Regulates investment managers and advisers, eg. pension fund managers Broadwalk House, 5 Appold Street, London, EC2A 2LL	Regulates insurance companies, unit trust companies. Centre Point, 103 New Oxford Street, London WC1A 1QH

The Law Society of England and Wales, The Law Society of Northern Ireland, The Law Society of Scotland, The Institute of Chartered Accountants in England and Wales, The Institute of Chartered Accountants in Scotland, The Institute of CharteredAccountants in Ireland, The Chartered Association of Certified Accountants, The Insurance Brokers Registration Council, Institute of Actuaries

Fig B.1 The Securities and Investments Board oversees the financial services industry through self-regulating organizations and recognized industry bodies. But LAUTRO and FIMBRA are likely to be engulfed by the Personal Investment Authority.

tion of the regulatory structure, refer to 'The enforcers' flow diagram which is shown above.

Not all investments come within the scope of the FSA. Deposit-type investments, such as bank and building society savings accounts, are covered by the Banking Act 1987, and the Building Societies Act 1986 respectively. Investment-type life assurance (endowment policies or insurance bonds) is covered by the FSA, but general household and motor policies are not.

What's on offer?

What protection does the FSA offer? The four main planks of the investor protection regime are as follows:

Authorization. It is now a criminal offence to carry on investment business without proper authorization from the SIB, an SRO or an RPB. In order to gain authorization, a firm must show that it is properly run and has adequate financial resources.

Polarisation. Investment advisers must now be either completely independent, recommending products from across the whole range on the market, or tied agents, selling the wares of one company only. The polarization rules were introduced so that investors should not unwittingly receive biased advice. In the past, advisers might nominally be independent, whilst maintaining an informal arrangement with a 'pet' insurance company or unit trust group. Independent financial advisers are usually members of FIMBRA.

Warning. Tied agents are not directly regulated under the FSA – they are supervised, often inadequately, by the company to which they are tied. Nor are they covered by the Investors Compensation Scheme. Companies are liable for the misdemeanours of their tied agents, but the extent of this liability is unclear.

Best advice. All financial advisers are duty bound to guide you towards a generic type of investment which is suitable for you; if they don't have a suitable product in their range, or are not experts in that area, they should tell you so. Having suggested the right type of product, an independent adviser should then give 'best advice' in recommending a particular investment from the full range available. He should base his advice on your requirements (growth or income, say), the past performance of individual trusts, and his views on the outlook for the market. Tied agents must recommend the best product for you in their company's range, and if nothing is suitable, they must say so.

Warning. Most advisers are paid by commission on the products they sell. The best advice rules were introduced to deter advisers from recommending high commission products, whether or not they were most suitable for investors. But some advisers may still be loath to recommend products which do not pay commission, for example, National Savings.

Compensation. The Investors Compensation Scheme was established to help people who invest money through a firm which subsequently goes bust. The scheme will pay out 100 per cent of the first £30,000 invested, and 90 per cent of the next £20,000, i.e. a maximum of £48,000. Banks and building societies have separate schemes. Should a building society go under, savers are eligible for compensation up to 90 per cent of the first £20,000. The Banking Act currently limits compensation to 75 per cent of the first £20,000, though this is likely to be increased. The Policyholders Protection Act covers investment type life insurance, up to 90 per cent of your investment, with no overall limit.

Warning. Some businesses (see above) are not covered by the compensation scheme. In any case, the scheme has an overall limit on payouts of £100 million in any one year – less than was lost through Barlow Clowes alone. So there is no guarantee of getting your money back.

A short course in self-defence

It's no insult to the regulators, in spite of all their efforts, to say that the best form of investor protection is still self-defence. No amount of regulation is enough to let you off the basic responsibility of looking out for yourself. There are a few basic questions you should ask in order to find a good investment adviser.

Is the adviser authorized? Check by ringing the SIB central register on 071 929 3652. Also ascertain what an adviser is authorized to do – is he allowed to handle clients' money, for example?

Is the adviser independent or tied? It may not be immediately obvious that an adviser is acting as a tied agent, so always ask.

How is the adviser paid? There's nothing to stop you asking how much commission an adviser will receive from the products he recommends. And if you want to be sure that there is no conflict of interest between good investment advice and filthy lucre, you may want to choose a fee-charging adviser. If an adviser is paid by fees alone, there is no potential for bias towards high-commission investments such as endowments.

What questions does the adviser ask? Nosiness is not a character defect in a financial adviser. In order to recommend suitable products, an adviser will have to apprise himself of your age, health, family circumstances, present financial circumstances, tax position and future personal and investment aims. So be wary of the incurious.

What qualifications and experience does the adviser have? Some investment advisers have had several decades of experience in the industry, and boast a clutch of qualifications. On the other hand, you may come across a sharp young salesman, hoping the commission he earns from you will buy his first Porsche. (And if finance doesn't work out, he'll try double glazing.) Do a bit of probing to reassure yourself you can have confidence in an adviser's recommendations.

Are the promised investment returns suspiciously high? Always a danger signal, this one. That was how Barlow Clowes drew in its customers – likewise Dunsdale Securities, which ran aground in 1990 after promising returns of over 20 per cent on gilt-edged investments. Be suspicious also of investment opportunities which must be taken 'immediately'.

Are you getting the hard sell? Cold-calling, or contacting potential clients without an invitation is still allowed for unit and investment trusts, pensions and life assurance.

Warning. Cold-callers are likely to have been trained in various psychological techniques – how to overcome your objections, how to make you agree with their pitch, and how to make it difficult for you to refuse to buy. The best way to deal with this is to point out firmly that you are not interested; don't get drawn into conversation. If the caller becomes a nuisance, complain to his company.

Just a couple more tips. Don't make cheques out to the adviser, but to the company you are investing in. And don't sign on any dotted lines until you have found out what cancellation rights you have.

How to complain

Along with all the other measures it has introduced, the FSA has beefed up the investor's right to complain. All authorized businesses are now obliged to set up proper complaints procedures.

So if you have a grievance, your first port of call should be the firm itself. Make your complaint in writing, and provide documentary evidence if possible. The firm must then call in an experienced employee to investigate.

Should this prove unsatisfactory, investors can then turn to the firm's regulatory body. All SROs have arrangements for the independent investigation of complaints, which are designed to be accessible to investors, and to provide an alternative to the costly process of settling a dispute through the courts.

Complaints to **LAUTRO** may be passed on either to the Insurance Ombudsman, or the Investment Ombudsman for independent arbitration. the Insurance Ombudsman, currently Dr Julian Farrand, can award investors sums of up to £100,000 – this is binding on the company concerned. Richard Youard, the present Investment Ombudsman, is also used by **IMRO**. He can also make awards of up to £100,000 in favour of investors.

FIMBRA has replaced the Investment Ombudsman scheme with an adjudication scheme run by the Chartered Institute of Arbitrators. Awards of up to £50,000 can be made to investors. FIMBRA also has an independent Complaints Commissioner, with a watching brief over its handling of complaints against FIMBRA members.

SFA runs a Complaints Bureau, which will try to arrive at a mutually agreeable settlement of disputes. If this does not work, complaints involving sums under £50,000 may be taken to the SFA Consumer Arbitration Scheme. There is a separate scheme for larger claims. An independent Complaints Commissioner oversees the work of the Complaints Bureau.

Readers will have realized by now that the present complaints system is fragmented and confusing. Many people have been lobbying SIB to set up one Ombudsman as a clearing house for complaints about the whole investment industry. *Investors Chronicle* would certainly welcome such a move. In the meantime, investors should not worry too much about complaining to the wrong place – the various bodies will direct grievances to their proper destinations.

USEFUL ADDRESSES

The Insurance Ombudsman Citygate 1, 135 Park St, London SE1 9EA. 071 928 4488.
The Investment Ombudsman 6 Frederick Place, London EC2R 8BT. 071 796 3065.
The Complaints Bureau (SFA) Cottons Centre, Cottons Lane, London SE1 2QB. 071 378 9000.

There are also Ombudsmen schemes for banks and building societies, if your complain has reached deadlock.
The Office of the Building Societies Ombudsmen 35-37 Grosvenor Gardens, London SW1X 7AW. 071 931 0044.
The Office of the Banking Ombudsman Citadel House, 5-11 Fetter Lane, London EC4A 1BR. 071 583 1395.
FIMBRA Hertsmere House, Hertsmere Rd, London E14 4AB. 071 538 8860.
The Investors Compensation Scheme c/o SIB, Gaverelle House, 2-4 Bunhill Row, London EC1Y 8RA. 071 638 1240.
The PIA 071 929 0072.

How to Complain

IN A NUTSHELL

1. The City is regulated by a system of self-regulation, established under the Financial Services Act (1986). The key regulatory body is the Securities and Investment Board (SIB) which exercises power on behalf of the government. It delegates this power downwards.

2. The SIB wants to reorganize the current system of retail regulation. It wants a new body, called the Personal Investment Authority (PIA) to regulate all firms selling packaged products to the public. Stockbrokers would continue to be regulated separately by the Securities and Futures Authority. The deposit-taking activities of banks and building societies would also continue to be regulated separately. Many financial firms object strongly to this proposal.

3. The SIB then delegates its authority to four self regulatory organizations (SROs), covering different areas of investment and nine recognized professional bodies, in allied areas like law or accountancy.

4. The four SROs are FIMBRA, covering independent intermediaries, IMRO dealing with investment managers, SFA handling securities and futures, and LAUTRO representing life assurance and unit trusts. FIMBRA and LAUTRO would disappear inside the PIA if it were approved.

5. The four main tenets of the Financial Services Act are: that investment advisers must be

authorised as competent and solvent, polarized
into independent or tied agents, must give best
advice and investors should be protected by a
compensation scheme.

6. Investors should ensure their adviser is authorized, and check whether he is tied or independent, and how he is paid – commission, fee,
   salary.

7. You should also look out for the type of
   questions the adviser asks and try to determine
   his qualifications and experience. If you are
   getting the hard sell, that is probably a bad sign.

8. One glaringly obvious point to look out for is
   investment returns which seem too high – if it
   looks too good to be true, it probably is. Fraud-
   sters play on greed.

9. The complaints procedure varies from one SRO
   to another, and not all investments are necessarily covered by compensation schemes. If in
   doubt, check.

10. Banks and building societies are covered by
    separate legislation and have their own com-
    plaints procedure and compensation arrange-
    ments.

Appendix C
Finding a broker

BY RUTH SUNDERLAND

Choosing a stockbroker is one of the most important investment decisions you will ever make. It is also one of the most difficult. Country-wide, there are around 200 firms ready and willing to take on individual investors. Here, we supply a list of private client brokers who participated in a survey we published in *Investors Chronicle* in August 1993.

Before scouring through the tables, readers should first decide on the level of service they need. The most basic service is **dealing only** or **execution only**. Orders are normally placed over the telephone or by post, and the broker simply carries out your instructions. Dealing only services are suitable for investors who have the time and inclination to make all their own decisions. Equally, an execution only deal might be attractive in specific one-off situations – stagging privatization shares, for example.

Dealing with advice is the traditional province of the stockbroker. Clients can call the broker for advice, and, to varying degrees, brokers will take the initiative, and contact clients with recommendations. The amount of love and attention you get will vary according to the size of the firm, and the value of your business.

Portfolio management provides a more comprehensive service, for investors who wish to delegate most of the decision-making and paperwork to their broker. Most portfolio managers will carry out periodic portfolio valuations, produce year-end gains tax statements, and perhaps send out investment newsletters. There are two levels of service: **advisory** and **discretionary**.

In the former case, your portfolio manager cannot carry out investment decisions without consulting you. With discretionary management, on the other hand, your broker is free to deal without referring to you first. Many brokers claim that they can serve clients' interests best with the discretionary service. Given full discretion, a broker can act on an investment hunch more quickly. And advisory services entail a great deal of costly and time-consuming contact with clients.

We can't pick out best buys for dealing with advice or portfolio management services. The quality of a broker's investment recommendations is just as important as charges and services, but we have no means of evaluating that. Use our tables to help you narrow down the field, by identifying brokers who are willing to handle your size of portfolio, and then shop around for yourself.

Almost all the brokers in our 'Portfolio management' table offer discretionary and advisory services. Several brokers stick to advisory management only – they are listed separately in our 'Advisory services' table. Virtually all the brokers included in the portfolio management and advisory services tables offer dealing with advice. A handful of brokers **only** offer dealing with advice.

This information was compiled for the *Investors Chronicle* in mid 1993, and was correct then. Since that time brokerage rates, telephone numbers etc may have altered – so check before you deal.

Choosing a broker

When you're shopping around for a stockbroker, there are a number of points you should be aware of:

Minimum portfolio size. Some private client brokers are very fussy, and won't take you on unless you have a portfolio worth £100,000 or more. But smaller investors need not feel left out in the cold. Several brokers mentioned minimum portfolio sizes of £10,000 or under, whilst a goodly proportion do not specify any formal minimum at all. Readers should note, though, that just because a broker sets no formal minimum does not mean that all clients, however small, will be welcomed with open arms.

Commission. Stockbrokers earn their crust in the form of a percentage commission on every deal they do for clients. Most brokers charge commission on a scale, for example: 1.65 per cent on the first £7,000 of consideration, 0.55 per cent on the next £8,000, and 0.5 per cent after that. A higher rate of commission will be charged by many brokers if your business comes to them through a financial intermediary. 'Divisible' rates, as they are known in the trade, because the intermediary shares in the commission, can be up to 30 per cent higher than the standard scale. Commission paid to an intermediary is shown on contract notes, but even so, too few investors realize that they are paying more than if they were to go directly to the broker.

Advisory and discretionary commissions are the same in most cases, though some brokers charge slightly higher rates for advisory.

Fees. Many brokers now charge annual management fees on top of commissions; the typical fee scale will start at 0.5 per cent of the first tranche of funds under management, and reduce progressively after that. Annual fees are subject to VAT. Some brokers give clients the option of a management fee and discounted commissions, or no fee and full commission rates. The fee might be a better bet if your portfolio is actively managed, but you should consider the options carefully with your broker.

There is a lobby within the industry which sees a move towards fee-based management as healthy for clients and brokers. Brokers who are remunerated wholly or partly by fees have less incentive to 'churn' portfolios – that is, to deal purely in order to generate commission income. Percentage fees also encourage the broker to make the portfolio grow, so his fee will grow with it.

Other charges. Watch out for any additional charges. There may be contract charges or compliance charges of, say £5 on each deal, and perhaps an extra charge for clients using a nominee service.

Overseas shares. Virtually all the brokers we surveyed are willing to deal in overseas shares. Clients should keep a close eye on charges here. Brokers normally stick to their standard commission scales, but there may be a handling charge of up to £50, and perhaps other add-ons as well.

Non-stockbroking services. Many brokers nowadays are keen to provide clients with an all-round financial service. They may offer in-house unit trusts or PEPs, and a range of other investments. Personal financial planning is often available, either through the broker itself, or through a related company.

Digging deeper

Potential clients should also make a point of finding out how staff are paid. Large firms generally pay staff a salary, but there are still bands of 'half commission men' around. Half commission men use a firm's offices in return for giving up – you've guessed it – half the commission they earn. These chaps clearly have more incentive to switch clients' investments about than salaried staff. If you do link up with a half commission man, be prepared to field lots of phone calls, and to discuss every investment recommendation in detail.

It is also sensible to find out how much experience the broker has, and what research materials are available. The basic tools of a broker's trade are the Topic screen and Extel cards. Some smaller brokers may not have much more in the way of research materials than this – in consequence, the number of shares they follow is likely to be quite limited. Bigger firms, by contrast, may have sophisticated, well-staffed research departments, but charges are likely to reflect this.

Once you've signed up with a broker for an advisory or discretionary service, you should still stay alert to potential pitfalls. Be wary of handing over pet shares at the start. Larger brokers normally have an in-house 'buy list'; if your shares are not on it, they may well be sold, landing you with an unexpected gains tax bill. It is becoming increasingly common for brokers to suggest or even insist that clients go into a **nominee account**. Here the broker handles all the admin, and you may forfeit some of your shareholder rights, such as privatization bonuses or other shareholder perks. And the latest proposals for a new settlement system seem likely soon to make it Hobson's choice: either you accept a nominee account or you pay more and may suffer other disadvantages.

Nominee accounts coupled with faster settlement may also mean you have to have a deposit account with your broker. Some are likely to link this with a facility for 'margin trading', whereby you only need to put up part of the money involved in a deal. This whole area was still in flux when we went to press. So check out recent developments and whether your broker is competitive in this area.

Last but not least, don't let your portfolio be used as a rubbish dump. Brokers might be tempted to see private clients as a useful dumping ground for their in-house unit trusts, share placings, or issues they have underwritten. Make it plain that you want to see details before any such investments go into your portfolio.

Finding a broker

IN A NUTSHELL

1. Stockbrokers offer three main types of share dealing service – execution only, dealing with advice and portfolio management. In anything apart from execution only, the quality of advice is as important as the level of charges.

2. Execution only broking is a pure deal for a (low) commission. Dealing with advice is more expensive, the amount of advice varies between firms and on the value of your business.

3. Portfolio management divides into two types – advisory and discretionary. With advisory the broker suggests investments to you. Discretionary dealing means that you give the broker power to invest on your behalf.

4. When choosing a broker look out for the minimum portfolio size the firm will handle, the size of commission, and any other management fees or charges.

5. Also check on any other services the broker provides, such as overseas shares, PEPs, in-house unit trusts and personal financial planning.

6. Find out how experienced your broker is, and try to find out how he is paid. Some 'half-commission men' still exist; the more often they make you deal, the more they are paid.

7. Make sure your portfolio doesn't become a dump for your broker's poor investments, and make sure that cherished shares are not sold because they do not appear on a house list.

PRIVATE CLIENT BROKERS: DEALING ONLY

Name/Telephone Number	Minimum Commission £	Commission on bargain of £5,000 £	£25,000 £	Minimum Bargain Size £	No of Clients	Comments
Adams & Nevile 071-512 0410	20	92.50	260	no min	2,000	
Allied Provincial Securities Ltd 0590 671112	29.50	97.50	211.50	no min	150,000	Small sales commissions available
Arnold Stansby 061-832 8554	18	90	225	no min	not given	
Astaire & Partners Ltd 0242 251000/071-332 2600	30 (£15 for sales under £500)	90	240	no min	not given	
Barclays Stockbrokers 071-403 4833	20	75	260	no min	15,000	Custody fee of £4 per stock a quarter (min £100 a year) payable quarterly advance
M D Barnard & Co Ltd 081-534 9090	20	75	185	no min	3,000	
Barratt & Cooke 0603 624236	18	82.50	240	no min	20,000	
BCP Dublin 6684688	20	50	175	1,000	1,000	
Bell Lawrie 031-225 2566	20	50	100	no min	not given	
Blankstone Sington Ltd 051-707 1707	25	103.37	221.37	no min	1,000	
Bloxham Dublin 6771341	30	82.50	290	2,000	not given	
HRE Bradshaw 071-600 7281	40	100	234	2,000	100	
Branston & Gothard 071-250 1180	28	92.50	187.50	no min	7,000	
James Brearley & Sons 0253 28686	6 (sales)	82.50	213.50	no min	not given	£22 minimum on purchases. Offices Blackpool, Kendal, Southport, Carlisle and Stockport
Brewin Dolphin 071-248 4400	30	97.50	290	no min	250	Concessionary rates can apply with directors' approval and for bargains under £200
Broadbridge 0532 422211	20	87.50	216.50	no min	25,000	£2.50 contract charge
Brown Shipley 071-726 4059/0534 67557	30	90	216	no min	not given	£5 compliance charge
Burrough Johnstone Ltd 0432 344244	40	*82.50 **50	*277.50 **182.50	no min	not given	*UK equities **Gilts
BWD Rensburg 0484 608066	30	104.25	256	no min	52,000	
Capel-Cure Myers Capital Management Ltd 071-488 4000	10	87.50	302.50	no min	22,000	£20 admin charge per bargain
Cave & Sons 0604 21421	22	80	147	no min	not given	
Cawood, Smithie & Co 0423 530035	20	101	287	no min	not given	
Central Stockbrokers Ltd 061-832 2924	20	50	125	no min	not given	Postal service: £10 for privatisation sales £15 min on others up to £1,500, then
Charles Stanley & Co Ltd 071-739 8200	20	50	112.50	no min	8,000	£35 max commission for the "Gold Pl
Charles Schwab Ltd 071-495 7444	$39	$101.50	$182.50	$1	Over 1m	Introduces clients to Charles Schwab & Co Inc to deal in US Securities. Al accounts are US dollar denominated
Charterhouse Tilney 051-236 6000	40	115	245	no min	5,000	
Cheviot Capital Ltd 071-377 8888	50	90	255	1,000	not given	
Christows Ltd 0392 210510	30	92.50	neg	no min	not given	
City Merchants Investment Management Ltd 071-929 5269	55	85	260	no min	not given	
Davy Dublin 679 7788	30	82.50	287	500	10,000	
G R Dawes & Co Ltd 021-643 7877	25	95	241	no min	2,500	
Dunbar Boyle & Kingsley Ltd 071-247 8898	20	70	233	no min	not given	
Durlacher & Co 071-628 4306	25	neg	neg	no min	not given	
Fidelity Brokerage Services 0800 222 190	25	50	85	no min	15,000	Dealing on UK, US and European markets

Key to non-Stock Exchange investments: a=bullion, b=cash, c=commodities, d=futures, e=options, f=life insurance, g=unit trusts, h=offshore funds, i=Peps. Costs brokers based in the Republic of Ireland are given in Irish punts.

PRIVATE CLIENT BROKERS: DEALING ONLY

Name/Telephone Number	Minimum Commission £	Commission on bargain of £5,000 £	£25,000 £	Minimum Bargain Size £	No of Clients	Comments
Firstdirect 0800 222 000	20	75	184	no min	not given	Orders taken 24 hrs, 365 days a year
Fyshe Horton Finney Ltd 021-236 3111	25	82.50	187	no min	7,000	
Gall & Eke Ltd 061-228 2511	10	45	45	no min	not given	Clients referred to "Sharemarket" (see below): a division of Gall & Eke Ltd
Gerrard Vivian Gray 071-831 8883	24	97.50	271.25	no min	35,000	
Goodbody Dublin 667 0400	40	82.50	315	no min	not given	
Greig Middleton & Co Ltd 071-247 0007	25*	82.50	240	no min	40,000	+£6 transaction charge *There is a sliding scale commission for very small bargains below £150
Griffiths & Lamb 021-236 6641	15	25	225	no min	not given	
Hargreave Hale & Co 0253 21575	25			10,000	not given	*By negotiation
Hargreaves Lansdown Stockbrokers Ltd 0272 741309	25	75	225	250	2,500	
Harris Allday Lea & Brooks 021-233 1222	22	82.50	180.50	no min	40,000	£5 bargain charge
Hedley 0254 699333	25	82.50	231.50	no min	not given	
Henderson Crosthwaite 071-283 8577	25	92	282	no min	30,000	£10 bargain charge
Henry Cooke, Lumsden 061-834 2332	25	95	241	no min	40,000	
Hill Osborne & Co 0522 513838	24	87.50	212.50	no min	not given	
Hoare Govett 071-601 0101	0*	50*	175.50†	nil (sales) 500 (lump sum purchases)	not given	*Low cost dealing service (postal) open to all for some companies †Telephone service open to employees of corporate clients only
Hoodless Brennan & Partners Ltd 0344 845888	25	78.75	188.75	no min	not given	
WH Ireland, Stephens & Co 061-832 6644	15	90	242	no min	not given	
Keith Bayley Rogers 071-378 0657	25	87.50	221.50	no min	10,000	
Killik & Co 071-589 1577	10*	10*	10*	no min	not given	*Postal service (071-515 0398) sales only
Llewellyn Greenhalgh & Co 0204 21697	15	87.50	127.50	no min	not given	Negotiable rates for deals over £50,000
Laing & Cruickshank Investment Management Ltd 071-588 2800	50	97.50	285	no min	23,600	£250 fee offsettable against commission
Midland branches	20	75	199	no min	not given	Midland account holders only
Midland Goldline 071-260 5831	20	75	184	no min	not given	Midland Gold Card holders only
Midland Shareshops	20	75	150	no min	not given	Open to all
Philip J Milton & Co 0271 44300	21	75	250 neg	no min	not given	
NatWest Stockbrokers 071-895 5000	25	75	212.50	no min	not given	Service called Brokerline. £1 compliance charge on all bargains. Concessionary rates for NatWest Gold Plus members
NCB Stockbrokers Ltd Dublin 6614977	40	82.50	277.50	no min	not given	Special dealing facility to intermediaries
NCL Investments Ltd 071-600 2801	40	92.50	275	no min	not given	
Neilson Cobbold Ltd 051-236 6666	25	103.75	266.25	no min	not given	
Neilson Cobbold 0962 852362	25	by neg	by neg	no min	not given	
Nicholson Barber 0742 755100	20	87.50	175	no min	not given	Bargains under £10,000 max comm £100
Olliff & Partners 071-374 0191	50	87.50	250	5,000	not given	
Pilling & Co 061-832 6581	20	62.50	162.50	no min	not given	Postal service only
P H Pope & Son 0782 202154	20	82.50	205.50	no min	not given	
I A Pritchard Stockbrokers Ltd 0202 297035	22.50	90	190	no min	7,000	Special commissions on privatisations: 1% (buy & sell) + £7.50
Quilter Goodison Co Ltd 071-600 4177	37	95	255	no min	not given	£3 contract charge per bargain
Redmayne-Bentley 0532 436941	17.50	82.50	203	no min	40,000	
Rowan Dartington & Co Ltd 0272 253377	20	75	225	no min	not given	
Jefferson Seal Ltd 0534 74725	40	82.50	255	no min	not given	
Seymour Pierce Butterfield Ltd 071-814 8700	30	90	270	500	not given	
SGST 071-638 5699	50	97.50	249	no min	not given	
Shakespeares 021-632 4199	25	75	225	no min	50	
Share Centre 0442 890800	10	44	106.50	no min	not given	
Sharelink 021-200 2242	20	56.25	76.25	Purchases 100: no min sales	300,000	US equity dealing min $38
Sharemarket 061-237 9443	10	45	45	no min	not given	Commission as follows: up to £1,000, £10 (flat rate); £1,000 to £1,667: £15 (flat rate); £1,667 to £45,000: 0.9% (max £45); over £45,000: £22.50 + 0.05%

Key to non-Stock Exchange investments: a=bullion, b=cash, c=commodities, d=futures, e=options, f=life insurance, g=unit trusts, h=offshore funds, i=Peps. Costs for brokers based in the Republic of Ireland are given in Irish punts.

PRIVATE CLIENT BROKERS: DEALING ONLY

Name/Telephone Number	Minimum Commission £	Commission on bargain of £5,000 £	Commission on bargain of £25,000 £	Minimum Bargain Size £	No of Clients	Comments
Albert E Sharp & Co 021-200 2244	30+1.25%	92.50	197.50	no min	55,000	
John Siddall 061-832 7471	25	95	239	no min	30,000	
Sobhag Stockbroking Ltd 081-446 1913	16	50	112.50	250	500	
Southard Gilbey McNish & Co 071-638 6761	20	82.50	209.50	no min	not given	
Standard Bank Stockbrokers CI Ltd 0534 67557	40	90	216	no min	not given	International dealing service (overseas stocks +£50 per bargain)
Stirling Hendry & Co 041-248 6033	25	90	255	no min	not given	
R L Stott & Co (sponsored by Standard Bank Stockbrokers (CI) Ltd) 0624 662400	25	91	225	no min	2,500	
Teather & Greenwood 071-256 6131	25	82.50	209.50	no min	not given	
Townsley & Co 071-377 6161	40	82.50	209.50	no min	3,500	
Walker Crips Weddle Beck (Investorlink) 0800 289 600	15	50	100	no min	25,000	
Waters Lunniss 0603 622265	17	55	75	no min	not given	
Westons Securities 071-283 8466	20	50	125	no min	3,000	Joining fee £15+VAT (refundable)
Wilkinform Stockbrokers 0580 754488	25	50	212.50	no min	not given	
Williams de Broë 071-588 7511	75 buy 50 sale	95	340	5,000	not given	
Wilshire Baldwin 0533 541344	20	80	neg	none	not given	
Wise Speke 091-201 3800	30 buy 20 sale	97.50	270	no min	not given	

PRIVATE CLIENT BROKERS: DEALING WITH ADVICE

Name/Telephone Number	Minimum Commission £	Commission on bargain of £5,000 £	Commission on bargain of £25,000 £	Minimum Bargain size £	Other charges	Dealing in overseas shares?	In-house unit trusts?	Personal financial planning?	Non-Stock exchange investments	No of private clients	Comments
Campbell O'Connor & Co Dublin 6771773	15	75	195	no min		yes	no	yes	f,g	not given	
Chambers & Remington Ltd 021-236 2577	25	82.50	165	no min		yes	no	no	*g,i	not given	*Through Lloyds Bank
Charlton Brett & Boughey 0282 422042	14	82.50	209	no min		restricted	no	no	e,g	not given	
Derivative Securities 071-253 5835	50	92.50	335	no min		yes	no	yes	d,e,h	not given	
Ellis & Partners Ltd 0293 517744	30 (below £1000 £15)	92.50	237.50	no min	Compliance fee £3 up to £7000 £5 thereafter	yes	no	no		900	Specialises in smaller company shares
Farley & Thompson 0202 556277	20	75	235	no min		yes	no	yes	b,e,f,g,h,i	not given	
R N McKean & Co 0234 351131	17	80	180	no min		yes	no	no	e,g,i	not given	Also BES investment
D M Wright & Partners 0504 263344	19	87.50	216.50	no min		yes	no	yes	—	1,500	

Most brokers offer a dealing with advice service, often at the same rates as their dealing only service. This table includes only firms which do not offer a portfolio management service.

PRIVATE CLIENT BROKERS: PORTFOLIO MANAGEMENT

Name/Telephone Number	Minimum Portfolio Size		Minimum Commission £	Commission on bargain of		Annual Fee	
	Discretionary £	Advisory £		£5,000 £	£25,000 £	Discretionary	Advisory
Adams & Nevile 071-512 0410	no min	no min	20	92.50	260	0.5% up to £1m	none
Allied Provincial Securities Limited 0590 671112	no min	no min	29.50	50	160	Min: £250; Max: £2,500; First £250,000 0.5%	Min: £250; Max: £2,500; First £250,000 0.5%
Angel SP 071-623 3427	no min	no min	22.50*	82.50	277.50	none	none
Arnold Stansby 061-832 8554	no min	no min	18	90	225	none	none
Astaire & Partners Ltd 0242 251000	no min	no min	30 (sales under £500:25)	90	nego-tiable	1% up to £150,000, 0.5% above	1% up to £150,000, 0.5% above
MD Barnard & Co Ltd 081-534 9090	10,000	no min	30	82.50	209.50	none	none
Barclays Stockbrokers 071-403 4833	50,000	50,000	20	75*	260*	0.85% up to £100,000, 0.65% on next £150,000, 0.55% on next £250,000 (min £425)	0.85% up to £100,000, 0.65% on next £150,000, 0.55% on next £250,000 (min £425)
Barratt & Cooke 0603 624236	—	25,000	18	82.50	240	—	none
BCP Dublin 6684688	10,000	2,000	30	75	250	none	none
Bell Lawrie 031-225 2566	50,000	no min	30	97.50	290	250	none
Blankstone Sington Ltd 051-707 1707	no min	no min	25	103.37	221.37	Min £300	none
Bloxham Dublin 6771341	50,000	50,000	30	82.50	290	negotiable	negotiable
HRE Bradshaw 071-600 7281	10,000	10,000	40	100	234	none	none
Branston & Gothard 071-250 1180	—	no min	28	92.50	187.50	none	none
James Brearley & Sons 0253 28686	10,000	no min	22	82.50	213.50	0.5%	none
Brewin Dolphin 071-248 4400	no min	no min	30	97.50	290	250	none
Broadbridge 0532 422211	20,000	20,000	20	87.50	216.50	none	none
Brown Shipley 071-726 4059/0534 67557	15,000	no min	40	90	216	Optional fee with discounted commissions	As discretionary
Burrough Johnstone Limited 0432 344244	no min	no min	40	82.50 UK equities; 50 gilts + fixed int	277.50 182.50	0.75% up to £250,000	£150 portfolio fee
Butler & Briscoe Dublin 6777348	—	20,000	25	82.50	239.50	—	none
BWD Rensburg 0484 608066	no min	no min	25 – fee based 30 – comm based	25 – fee based 104.25 – comm based	25 – fee based 256 – comm based	First £10,000 £250; next £240,000 0.5%	Min £50; max £150
BZW Portfolio Management 071-623 2323	250,000	250,000	50	82.50	240	0.75% on first £1m, 0.6% on next £2m	1% on first £1m, 0.7% on next £2m
Capel-Cure Myers Capital Management Ltd 071-488 4000	no min	no min	10	87.50	302.50	Minimum £1,250; 1% on first £250,000	Minimum £150; 0.1% on first £250,000; 0.5% thereafter
James Capel 071-626 0566	100,000	250,000	45*	†55.50	†210	Min £750; up to £500,000:0.6%; next £500,000: 0.3%; thereafter 0.15%	£250
Carr Sheppards Ltd 071-378 7000/7050	100,000	100,000	30*	102.50 (inc. admin. charge)	295	Up to £250,000: 0.75%; on next £250,000: 0.5%; thereafter: 0.25%; min £350: less if nominee account used	£150 (£100 if nominee account used)

Key to non-Stock Exchange investments: a=bullion, b=cash, c=commodities, d=futures, e=options, f=life insurance, g=unit trusts, h=offshore funds, i=Peps. Costs for brokers based in the Republic of Ireland are given in Irish punts.

PRIVATE CLIENT BROKERS: PORTFOLIO MANAGEMENT

Other charges	Dealing in overseas shares?	In-house unit trusts?	Personal financial planning?	Non-Stock Exchange Investments	No of private clients	Comments	Name Telephone Number
Contract charge: £20 per nominee bargain; £25 per own name bargain	Yes	Yes	Yes	a,b,c,d,e,g,h,i	2.000		**Adams & Nevile** 071-512 0410
Bargain charge £3; nominee charge £5 per holding each year	Yes	No	Yes	a,b,c,d,e,f,g,h,i	150.000	Advisory commission: £62.50 (£5,000), £185 (£25,000)	**Allied Provincial Securities Limited** 0590 671112
*Includes £7.50 bargain charge	Yes	No	No	e	2.000-2.500		**Angel SP** 071-623 3427
PEP £35 pa	Yes	No	Yes	b,f,g,h,i	not given		**Arnold Stansby** 061-832 8554
£10 transaction charge (from 1-9-93)	Yes	No	Yes	a,b,c,d,e,g,h,i	not given		**Astaire & Partners Ltd** 0242 251000
	Yes	No	No	g,i	200		**MD Barnard & Co Ltd** 081-534 9090
Portfolio admin service: £3 per stock (min £36 pa); Advisory service: £4 per stock (min £100 pa) – both payable quarterly in advance	Yes	Yes	No	g,h,i	13.400	*Advisory commission: £62.50 (£5,000), £245 (£25,000)	**Barclays Stockbrokers** 071-403 4833
	No	No	No		1.000		**Barratt & Cooke** 0603 624236
	Yes	No	Yes	b,d,e,f,g,h	8.000		**BCP** Dublin 6684688
£5 per bargain, £10 per nominee holding each year	Yes	No	Yes	a,b,e,f,g,h,i	not given		**Bell Lawrie** 031-225 2566
	Yes	No	Yes	a,b,e,g,h,i	1.000		**Blankstone Sington Ltd** 051-707 1707
	Yes	No	No	f	not given		**Bloxham** Dublin 6771341
£10 administration	Yes	No	No		300		**HRE Bradshaw** 071-600 7281
Service charge nil to £500; £4 on £500 to £3,000; £6 on £3,000 to £10,000; £12 on £19,000 plus; £5 per nominee holding	Yes	No	Yes	e,g,h,i	7.000		**Branston & Gothard** 071-250 1180
	Yes	No	Yes	b,e,f,g,h,i	not given	Offices Blackpool, Kendal, Southport, Carlisle & Stockport	**James Brearley & Sons** 0253 28686
£10 per bargain	Yes	Yes	Yes	b,d,e,g,h,i*	30.000	*advisory (discretionary b,i)	**Brewin Dolphin** 071-248 4400
£2.50 contract charge	Yes	No	No	b,e,g,h,i	25.000		**Broadbridge** 0532 422211
£5 compliance charge; £100 for a nominee account each year	Yes	No	No	g,h	not given	Will also deal in Eurobonds	**Brown Shipley** 071-726 4059/0534 67557
Choice of one-off £20 per nominee holding, or annual charge on sliding scale up to £150 each year for 20+ holdings	Yes	No	Yes	b,g,h,i	not given		**Burrough Johnstone Limited** 0432 344244
	Yes	No	Yes	b,d,e,f,g,h	10.000		**Butler & Briscoe** Dublin 6777348
	Yes	Yes	Yes	b,e,f,g,h,i	52.000		**BWD Rensburg** 0484 608066
	Yes	No	Yes	b,c,e,f,g,h,i	not given	Minimum fee £1,500 discretionary, £2,000 advisory	**BZW Portfolio Management** 071-623 2323
£20 admin charge per bargain	Yes	Yes	Yes	b,f,g,h,i	22.000		**Capel-Cure Myers Capital Management Ltd** 071-488 4000
	Yes	Yes	No	b,d,e,g,i	not given	*Minimum commission for purchases £55; †Advisory commissions £92.50, £350. Also offers unit trust management service, min £25,000	**James Capel** 071-626 0566
£10 admin charge per bargain	Yes	Yes	Yes	b,d,e,f,g,h,i	17.000	*Minimum commission for purchases £35. Also offers self-invested pension scheme	**Carr Sheppards Ltd** 071-378 7000/7050

Key to non-Stock Exchange investments: a=bullion, b=cash, c=commodities, d=futures, e=options, f=life insurance, g=unit trusts, h=offshore funds, i=Peps. Costs for brokers based in the Republic of Ireland are given in Irish punts.

PRIVATE CLIENT BROKERS: PORTFOLIO MANAGEMENT

Name/Telephone Number	Minimum Portfolio Size		Minimum Commission £	Commission on bargain of		Annual Fee	
	Discretionary £	Advisory £		£5,000 £	£25,000 £	Discretionary	Advisory
Cave & Sons Ltd 0604 21421	—	no min	22	80	147 nego-tiable	—	negotiable
Cawood Smithie & Co 0423 530035	50,000	no min	20	101	287	none	none
Central Stockbrokers Ltd 061-832 2924	25,000	25,000	30	87.50	212.50	none	none
Charles Stanley & Co Ltd 071-739 8200	50,000	—	25	92.50	219.50	0.75%	By arrangement
Charterhouse Tilney 051-236 6000	50,000	50,000	40	109*	239*	none	none
Cheviot Capital Ltd 071-377 8888	50,000	30,000	50	90	255	negotiable	negotiable
Christows Ltd 0392 210510	25,000	no min	30	92.50	neg	1%	none
City & International Securities Ltd 0624 627134	50,000	50,000	27	95	251	0.5%	none
City Merchants Investment Management Ltd 071-929 5269	100,000	100,000	55	55	125	0.6%	0.6%
Cunningham Coates Ltd 0232 323456	50,000	10,000	26	87.50	212.50	0.75%	0.5%
Davy Dublin 679 7788	50,000	50,000	30	82.50	287	0.5% pa	0.25% pa
GR Dawes & Co Ltd 021-643 7877	25,000	no min	25	95	241	none	none
Dunbar Boyle & Kingsley Ltd 071-247 8898	10,000	10,000	20	105*	302*	none	none
Durlacher & Co 071-628 4306	50,000 – stocks; 25,000 – options	50,000 – stocks; 25,000 – options	25	87.50	250	1.5% minimum £800; over £250,000 negotiable	0.9%
Fleming Private Asset Management Ltd 071-377 9242	100,000	100,000	50	92.50	335	£200	£200
CCF Foster & Braithwaite 071-588 6111	50,000*	—	20	92.50	267.50	1% on first £25,000 reducing thereafter	—
Fyshe Horton Finney Ltd 021-236 3111	20,000	no min	25	82.50	187	£0-£250,000: 0.425%; balance to £500,000: 0.3%; balance 0.2%	none
Gall & Eke Limited 061-228 2511	25,000	25,000	12.50	87.50	212.50	0.25%	0.25%
Gerrard Vivian Gray 071-831 8883	50,000	no min	24	97.50	271.25	Up to £200,000: 0.25%; next £300,000: 0.2%; thereafter 0.15%. Commission rebated against fee at 75%	As discretionary: rebate at 50%
Goodbody Cork 270828/Dublin 667 0400	100,000	50,000	40	82.50	315	£500+VAT	£150+VAT
Greig Middleton & Co Ltd 071-247 0007	25,000	25,000	28*	96.25	290	none	none
Griffiths & Lamb 021-236 6641	25,000	5,000	20	92.50	170	none	none
Hargreave Hale & Co 0253 21575	25,000	25,000	25	87.50	237.50		
Harris Allday Lea & Brooks 021-233 1222	no min	no min	22	82.50	180.50	none	none

Key to non-Stock Exchange investments: a=bullion, b=cash, c=commodities, d=futures, e=options, f=life insurance, g=unit trusts, h=offshore funds, i=Peps. Costs f brokers based in the Republic of Ireland are given in Irish punts.

PRIVATE CLIENT BROKERS: PORTFOLIO MANAGEMENT

Other charges	Dealing in overseas shares?	In-house unit trusts?	Personal financial planning?	Non-Stock Exchange Investments	No of private clients	Comments	Name/Telephone Number
	Yes	No	Yes	e,f,g,h,i	not given		Cave & Sons Ltd 0604 21421
	Yes	No	Yes	b,e,f,g,i	not given		Cawood Smithie & Co 0423 530035
	Yes	No	Yes		not given		Central Stockbrokers Ltd 061-832 2924
£7.50 compliance charge; £3 per nominee holding each year	Yes	No	Yes	b,e,f, g,h,i	21,000		Charles Stanley & Co Ltd 071-739 8200
	Yes	No	No	b,e,g,h,i	20,000	*Advisory commissions: £115, £245; investment trust management service	Charterhouse Tilney 051-236 6000
Compliance and nominee charges negotiable	No	No	Yes	b,h,i	not given		Cheviot Capital Ltd 071-377 8888
	Yes	No	Yes	e,f,g,h,i	4,000		Christows Ltd 0392 210510
	Yes	Yes	No	b,e,g,h	not given		City & Intern[t]ional Secukities Ltd 0624 627134
£5 regulatory charge	Yes	No	Yes	a,e,g, h,i	1,005		City Merchants Investment Management Ltd 071-929 5269
	Yes	No	Yes	b,d,e,f, g,h,i	12,000	No commission charged on discretionary client transactions	Cunningham Coates Ltd 0232 323456
Nominee charge, depending on level of dealing	Yes	Yes	No		2.000		Davy Dublin 679 7788
£5 contract	Yes	No	Yes	b,e,g,h,i	2.500		GR Dawes & Co Ltd 021-643 7877
£20 bargain charge	No	No	Yes	b,f,g,h,i	not given	*Advisory commission £113, £318	Dunbar Boyle & Kingsley Ltd 071-247 8898
£7 administration; £2.50 per nominee holding each quarter	Yes	No	Yes	e,g,h,i	not given		Durlacher & Co 071-628 4306
£10 contract charge	Yes	Yes	No	e,h	5,850		Fleming Private Asset Management Ltd 071-377 9242
	Yes	Yes	No	b,e,g,h,i	5.000	*£10,000 for an investment trust portfolio	CCF Foster & Braithwaite 071-588 6111
Nominee charge for some advisory clients	Yes	No	No	b,g,h,i	7,000		Fyshe Horton Finney Ltd 021-236 3111
	Yes	No	No	b,e,g,h,i	not given	*Up to £1,000: £10 flat rate; £1,000-£1,667: £15 flat rate; £1,667-£45,000: 0.9% (max £45); over £45,000: £22.50 + 0.05%.	Gall & Eke Limited 061-228 2511
£10 compliance; £10 per nominee holding each year, for advisory clients	Yes	No	Yes	a,b,d,e, g,h,i	35,000	Also offers unit trust and investment trust management service	Gerrard Vivian Gray 071-831 8883
	Yes	No	No		not given		Goodbody Cork 270828/Dublin 667 0400
£6 administration charge	Yes	Yes	Yes	a,b,c,d, e,f,g,h,i	40.000	*There is a sliding scale commission for very small bargains with a value below £150. Nominee service is provided free of charge.	Greig Middleton & Co Ltd 071-247 0007
	Yes	No	Yes	No	not given		Griffiths & Lamb 021-236 6641
£2.50 bargain charge	No	No	Yes	b,e,f, g,h,i	20,000		Hargreave Hale & Co 0253 21575
£5 bargain charge	Yes	No	No	b,g,i	40,000		Harris Allday Lea & Brooks 021-233 1222

Key to non-Stock Exchange investments: a=bullion, b=cash, c=commodities. d=futures, e=options, f=life insurance, g=unit trusts. h=offshore funds, i=Peps. Costs for brokers based in the Republic of Ireland are given in Irish punts.

PRIVATE CLIENT BROKERS: PORTFOLIO MANAGEMENT

Name/Telephone Number	Minimum Portfolio Size		Minimum Commission £	Commission on bargain of		Annual Fee	
	Discretionary £	Advisory £		£5,000 £	£25,000 £	Discretionary	Advisory
Hedley & Co 0254 699333	25,000	no min	25	82.50	231.50	none	none
Henderson Crosthwaite 071-283 8577	100,000	40,000	40	*62	*200	0.35% first £150,000; 0.25% next £150,000	same in London:£200 outside London
Henry Cooke, Lumsden 061-834 2332	40,000	40,000	25	95	241	0.4% first £100,000; 0.3% next £150,000; 0.2% next £250,000	same
Hill Osborne 0522 513838	25,000	no min	24	87.50	212.50	none	none
Hoodless Brennan & Partners 0344 845888	—	no min	25	78.75	188.75	—	none
WH Ireland, Stephens & Co 061-832 6644	no min	no min	15	90	242	none	none
Roy James 021-200 2200	25,000	25,000	25	90	202.50	none	none
Keith Bayley Rogers 071-378 0657	10,000	no min	25	87.50	221.50	none	none
Killik & Co 071-589 1577	25,000	25,000	40	82.50	240	none	none
Kleinwort Benson Private Bank 071-956 6600	no min	no min	50 sell; 75 buy	82.50	315	*Min £1,500: 0.9% on £1m, 0.5% on next £2m, thereafter 0.25%	*Min £1,800: as discretionary
Laing & Cruickshank Investment Management 071-588 2800	100,000	50,000	50	97.50	285	none	none
Laurence Keen 071-489 9493	50,000	50,000	25	102.50	280	Admin charge: min £100. max £250	Portfolio service fee: £100
Llewellyn Greenhalgh & Co 0204 21697	no min	no min	no min	—*	—	1.5% min £200	1.5% min £200
Magennis 0693 64314	—	no min	15	82.50	209.50	—	none
Midland Personal Asset Management 0703 229929	100,000	100,000	20	82.50	219.30	1% – negotiable on large portfolios	1% – neg on large portfolios
Philip J Milton & Co 0271 44300	10,000	no min	no min	50	250	1.5%	0.7%
NatWest Stockbrokers 071-895 5000	100,000	100,000	35	97.50	307.50	none	none
NCB Stockbrokers Ltd Dublin 661 4977	100,000	20,000	40	82.50	277.50	min £500	min £300
NCL Investments 071-600 2801	no min	no min	40	92.50	275.00	First £100,000: 0.4%; next £100,000: 0.3% and reducing	same
Neilson Cobbold Limited 051-236 6666	no min	no min	25	75	206.25	1st £50,000 1%, next £200,000 0.5%. Thereafter 0.125%. Minimum £250	same
Neilson Cobbold 0962 852362	no min	no min	25	103.75	266.25	none	none
Nicholson Barber 0742 755100	no min	no min	20	87.50	175	none	none
Olliff & Partners 071-374 0191	—	no min	50	87.50	250	—	none
Panmure Gordon 071-638 4010	200,000	200,000	35	110	322	£300	£300
P H Pope & Son 0782 202154	no min	no min	20	82.50	205.50	none	none
I A Pritchard Stockbrokers 0202 297035	no min	no min	22.50	90	190	none	none
Quilter Goodison 071-600 4177	30,000	70,000	30.00	60*	172.50*	min £300	min £400
Raphael Zorn Hemsley Ltd 071-628 4000	no min	no min	30	97.50	125	none	none

Key to non-Stock Exchange investments: a=bullion, b=cash, c=commodities, d=futures, e=options, f=life insurance, g=unit trusts, h=offshore funds, i=Peps. Costs for brokers based in the Republic of Ireland are given in Irish punts.

PRIVATE CLIENT BROKERS: PORTFOLIO MANAGEMENT

Other charges	Dealing in overseas shares?	In-house unit trusts?	Personal financial planning?	Non-Stock Exchange Investments	No of private clients	Comments	Name/Telephone Number
	Yes	No	Yes	e,g	not given		**Hedley & Co** 0254 699333
	Yes	Yes	Yes	a,b,d,e, f,g,h,i	30,000	*Higher commissions for advisory	**Henderson Crosthwaite** 071-283 8577
Sometimes, £17.50 per nominee holding each year	Yes	Yes	Yes	e,f,g,h,i	40,000	Alternative charging structure available	**Henry Cooke, Lumsden** 061-834 2332
	Yes	No	Yes	b,e,g,h,i	not given		**Hill Osborne** 0522 513838
	Yes	No	Yes	f, g, h, i	not given		**Hoodless Brennan & Partners** 0344 845888
	Yes	No	Yes	b,e,g,h,i	not given		**WH Ireland, Stephens & Co** 061-832 6644
£3 compliance charge	Yes	No	Yes	e,g,i	8,000		**Roy James** 021-200 2200
£4 admin charge; £5 per nominee holding each year	Yes	No	Yes	d,e,f, g,h,i	10,000		**Keith Bayley Rogers** 071-378 0657
	Yes	No	No	No	10,000		**Killik & Co** 071-589 1577
£50 per bargain transaction charge	Yes	Yes	Yes	b,d,e,g, h,i	not given	* Fees offsettable by commissions.	**Kleinwort Benson Private Bank** 071-956 6600
£15 contract charge	Yes*	Yes	Yes	b,f,g,h,i	23,600	*Additional charge for overseas securities	**Laing & Cruickshank Investment Management** 071-588 2800
£10 per nominee holding each year, maximum up to £250 depending on amount invested, for advisory clients; £12.50 per nominee holding each year for other investors	Yes	Yes	Yes	b,e,f, g,h,i	15,000		**Laurence Keen** 071-489 9493
Performance fee: 0.25% for each 5% growth above 10% each year	Yes	No	No	e,h	not given	Flat annual 1.5% fee includes all management and dealing costs	**Llewellyn Greenhalgh & Co** 0204 21697
Nominee charge if client inactive	Yes	No	No		4,000		**Magennis** 0693 64314
	Yes	Yes	Yes	g,h,i	15,000		**Midland Personal Asset Management** 0703 229929
	Yes	No	Yes	e,f,g,h,i	500	After initial fee, other full commission rebated to client	**Philip J Milton & Co** 0271 44300
£1 compliance charge on all bargains	Yes	No	Yes	b,g,h,i	not given		**NatWest Stockbrokers** 071-895 5000
	Yes	No	Yes	b,f,g,h	not given		**NCB Stockbrokers Ltd** Dublin 661 4977
	Yes	No	No	a,b,c,d, e,f,g,h,i	not given		**NCL Investments** 071-600 2801
	Yes	Yes	Yes	e,g,i	not given		**Neilson Cobbold Limited** 051-236 6666
	Yes	No	Yes	a,b,e,f, g,h,i	not given		**Neilson Cobbold** 0962 852362
	Yes	No	Yes	b,d,e,g, h,i	not given	Bargains under £10,000 max commission £100	**Nicholson Barber** 0742 755100
£10 per nominee holding every six months	Yes	Yes	Yes		not given		**Olliff & Partners** 071-374 0191
	Yes	No	No	a,b,e,g, h,i	2,000		**Panmure Gordon** 071-638 4010
	Yes	No	Yes		not given		**P H Pope & Son** 0782 202154
£7.50 compliance charge	Yes	No	Yes	b,e,f,g, h,i	1,000		**I A Pritchard Stockbrokers** 0202 297035
£3 contract charge per bargain	Yes	Yes	No	a,b,e,g, h,i	not given	*Commissions on advisory bargains: £5,000 = £70 £25,000 = £192.50	**Quilter Goodison** 071-600 4177
£12.50 compliance charge	Yes	No	No		2,500		**Raphael Zorn Hemsley Ltd** 071-628 4000

Key to non-Stock Exchange investments: a=bullion, b=cash, c=commodities, d=futures, e=options, f=life insurance, g=unit trusts, h=offshore funds, i=Peps. Costs for brokers based in the Republic of Ireland are given in Irish punts.

PRIVATE CLIENT BROKERS: PORTFOLIO MANAGEMENT

Name/Telephone Number	Minimum Portfolio Size		Minimum Commission £	Commission on bargain of		Annual Fee	
	Discretionary £	Advisory £		£5,000 £	£25,000 £	Discretionary	Advisory
Rathbone Investment Management 071-630 5611	100,000	—	no min	67.50	210	up to £250,000 – 0.5% next £1,250,000 – 0.25% over £1,500,000 – 0.125%	
Redmayne-Bentley 0532 436941	100,000	20,000	17.50	82.50	203.00	none	none
Robson Cotterell 0202 557581	25,000	10,000	20	90	215	none	none
Rowan Dartington & Co Ltd 0272 253377	10,000	10,000	20	75	225	(1) Commission and no fee. (2) 1% fee up to £500,000 portfolio and 0.5% on balance and no commission (3) 0.75% fee up to £500,000 portfolio and 0.5% on balance and half commission rate	
Jefferson Seal Ltd 0534 74725	no min	no min	40	82.50	255	none	none
Seymour Pierce Butterfield Ltd 071-814 8700	30,000	40,000	25	95	280	0.5%	0.5%
SGST (Investment Advisers) 071-638 5699	50,000	50,000	50	97.50	249	none	none
Shakespeares 021-632 4199	50,000	50,000	25	75	225	0.2%	0.2%
Albert E Sharp 021-200 2244	20,000	no min	30 + 1%	80.00	170.50	£400	none
James Sharp & Co 061-764 4043	50,000	no min	22	82.50	205.50	none	none
Shaw & Co Limited 071-638 3644	75,000	25,000	25	92.50	233	none	none
John Siddall & Son 061-832 7471	no min	no min	25	95	239	1%	none
Southard Gilbey McNish 071-638 6761	no min	no min	20	82.50	209.50	none	none
Standard Bank Stockbrokers (CI) Ltd 0534 67557	100,000	—	40	90	216	none	none
Stirling Hendry & Co 041-248 6033	no min	no min	25	120 90*	352.50 255*	none	£50
RL Stott & Co (Sponsored by Standard Bank Stockbrokers (CI) Ltd) 0624 662400	50,000	25,000	25	91	225	0.5% on first £200,000 0.25% on balance	£100
Teather & Greenwood 071-256 6131	10,000	10,000	25	82.50	209.50	1%	none
Townsley & Co 071-373 2212	no min	no min	40	82.50	209.50	none	none
Walker Crips Weddle Beck 071-253 7502	no min	no min	25	87.50	250	none	none
Waters Lunniss 0603 622265	50,000	50,000	20	92.50	240.50	none	none
Wilkinform Stockbrokers 0580 754488	10,000	10,000	25	75	262.50	£50 for portfolios up to £50,000 and £100 for portfolios over £50,000	
Williams de Broë 071-588 7511	100,000	250,000	50 sell 75 buy	95	340	£500	£750
Wilshere Baldwin 0533 541344	no min	no min	20	80	175	none	none
Wise Speke 091-201 3800	25,000	15,000	31	97.60	270	Clients may choose either a commission or fee structure Fees: up to £250,000: 0.5%, on next £75,000: 0.3%, over £1m: by arrangement	

Key to non-Stock Exchange investments: a=bullion, b=cash, c=commodities, d=futures, e=options, f=life insurance, g=unit trusts, h=offshore funds, i=Peps. Costs for brokers based in the Republic of Ireland are given in Irish punts.

PRIVATE CLIENT BROKERS: PORTFOLIO MANAGEMENT

Other charges	Dealing in overseas shares?	In-house unit trusts?	Personal financial planning?	Non-Stock Exchange Investments	No of private clients	Comments	Name-Telephone Number
	Yes	No	Yes	b,f,g,h,i	2,500+	Similar service offered in Liverpool.	**Rathbone Investment Management** 071-630 5611
£25 annual charge for nominee service	Yes	No	Yes	b,e,g,h,i	40,000		**Redmayne-Bentley** 0532 436941
	Yes	No	No	e,i	not given		**Robson Cotterell** 0202 557581
£25 for half yearly valuations*	Yes	No	Yes	b,e,g,h,i	not given	*Valuations free to clients using nominee account	**Rowan Dartington & Co Ltd** 0272 253377
	Yes	No	No	a,e,f,g,h	not given		**Jefferson Seal Ltd** 0534 74725
	Yes	No	No	b,e,g,h,i	not given		**Seymour Pierce Butterfield Ltd** 071-814 8700
£20 per nominee holding each year, max £200	Yes	No	No	e,g,i	not given		**SGST (Investment Advisers)** 071-638 5699
	Yes	No	Yes	a,b,f,g,h,i	400	Fee based option: 1% with dealings at 0.3%	**Shakespeares** 021-632 4199
	Yes	Yes	Yes	a,e,f,g,h,i	55,000		**Albert E Sharp** 021-200 2244
Nominee charge by negotiation	Yes	No	No	b,g,h,i	not given		**James Sharp & Co** 061-764 4043
£10 service charge	Yes	Yes	Yes	b,d,e,g,h,i	25,000		**Shaw & Co Limited** 071-638 3644
£4.50 contract charge	Yes	No	Yes	b,d,e,f,g,h,i	30,000	Commission on contracts reduced for discretionary clients	**John Siddall & Son** 061-832 7471
	Yes	No	No	e,g	8,200		**Southard Gilbey McNish** 071-638 6761
£5 per nominee holding each quarter	Yes	Yes	No	b,e,g,h	not given	Also discretionary offshore fund management services: min £30,000; fee 1% pa	**Standard Bank Stockbrokers (CI) Ltd** 0534 67557
£3 compliance charge; £10 pa per nominee holding: * non-nominee service	Yes	No	Yes	e,f,g,i	not given		**Stirling Hendry & Co** 041-248 6033
	Yes	No	No	a,e,g,h	2,500	Discretionary clients receive 30% discount commission & free nominee service	**RL Stott & Co (Sponsored by Standard Bank Stockbrokers (CI) Ltd)** 0624 662400
	Yes	No	Yes	a,b,c,d,e,g,h,i	not given		**Teather & Greenwood** 071-256 6131
£10 admin charge	Yes	No	No	a,b,d,e,g,h,i	2,500-3,500		**Townsley & Co** 071-373 2212
Nominee services £8 per stock per annum basic charge	Yes	No	No	g,i	not given		**Walker Crips Weddle Beck** 071-253 7502
	Yes	No	No	e,g,i	not given	Personal financial planning through associated company	**Waters Lunniss** 0603 622265
	Yes	No	Yes	b,e,f,g,h,i	not given		**Wilkinform Stockbrokers** 0580 754488
	Yes	No	No	b,g,h,i	not given	Annual fee is offset by commission	**Williams de Broë** 071-588 7511
	Yes	No	No	e,g,h,i	not given		**Wilshere Baldwin** 0533 541344
Nominee service: £10 per investment per year	Yes	No	Yes		not given		**Wise Speke** 091-201 3800

Key to non-Stock Exchange investments: a=bullion, b=cash, c=commodities, d=futures, e=options, f=life insurance, g=unit trusts, h=offshore funds, i=Peps. Costs for brokers based in the Republic of Ireland are given in Irish punts.

Glossary

Accepting house: One of a breed of top-level merchant banks whose credit guarantees *commercial bills*.

Account: The current method of settling equity deals on the Stock Exchange. Account periods are normally for two (though sometimes three) weeks, running from Monday to the Friday eleven days hence. All deals done in that period are settled at the same time on the Monday ten days following. This system has the flexibility to allow traders to *go short*, but gives rise to worries about credit. When *Taurus* dealings are introduced, transactions are likely to move to rolling five day settlement, with all deals being settled five business days after they are struck.

Account dealing: If an investor buys and sells the same shares within an *account*, he only pays his broker the difference between the buying and selling price, plus any commission. Also known as **netting** a deal.

ACT: Advance Corporation Tax. The basic rate tax paid on dividends by a company to the Revenue on behalf of shareholders. It counts as part payment of a company's corporation tax bill.

ADR: American Depository Receipt. American investors are restricted in their purchases of foreign shares so banks package overseas shares into depository receipts which American investors can buy.

Advisory client: Here a broker gives investment recommendations to a client, but it is the client who takes the decisions. The other types of relationship are *discretionary* where the broker takes investment decisions, and *execution-only* where the client takes decisions but receives no advice from the broker.

Analysts: Employees of stockbroking firms whose job is to research into companies' prospects and try to predict their investment performance. This research is then provided to investment institutions (along with any investment recommendation).

Arbitrage: Seeking to exploit price differences between different markets in similar instruments. An early arbitrage was between the dollar/sterling market in New York and that in London. Because prices in the two markets sometimes differed, traders could occasionally buy dollars or pounds in one market, and sell them immediately in the other for a profit. With satellite communications such geographical arbitrage is now rare. Modern arbitrage is frequently between cash and futures markets or involves options. It is a purely professional occupation since most opportunities are only available for a few seconds. Arbitrageurs can either be viewed as vultures, or traders who help keep markets efficient, according to taste.

Backwardation: Known as a 'back' for short, this refers to a situation where one market maker is offering securities at a lower price than another is bidding for them. As with *arbitrage* an investor could buy from one and sell to the other immediately making a risk-free profit. However in the politeness of English society, making money by getting between professionals in the same market is regarded as a little tacky, and is banned by the Stock Exchange. Also used more obscurely in the commodity markets when the cash price is higher than the *forward* or *futures* price.

Balance sheet: The statement of the capital position of a company, showing what it owns (its assets) and what it owes (its liabilities). Normally companies produce a balance sheet once a year in their annual report. The usefulness of these balance sheets can depend on the level of creative accounting involved. See also *P&L*.

Bargain: The stockmarket term for a deal. Not all bargains are real bargains!

Bear: An investor who thinks a market will fall. Also used to refer to a *short* position held by a market maker. A **Bear market** is one where prices are falling over an extended period. Investors are **bearish** if they think the market will fall, and will sometimes use the American jargon that the market is **going south**.

Bearer security: A bond or share whose ownership is not recorded on a register. Possession of a bearer stock proves ownership, so they are the capital markets' equivalent of cash. See also *registered securities*.

Bed and breakfast: Selling stock one night and buying it back the next morning for tax purposes.

Beneficial owner: The person who really owns a security, rather than some *nominee* used to hide his real identity. These can be crucial in takeover bids.

Bid: 1) An attempt by one company to take over another. 2) The price at which a *market maker* is prepared to buy shares. The price at which he will sell is known as the *offer* or *ask*. Naturally enough this is higher than the bid. The difference between them is called the **bid-offer spread**.

Big Bang: The deregulation of the London Stock Exchange which abandoned minimum commissions, *single capacity* and allowed foreign members to join. This led to the modern integrated securities houses. Less importantly the term also refers to the origins of the universe.

Blue chip: Shares in a well established, large and highly regarded company. Named after the highest value chip in poker.

Book: Very similar to the set of bets which a bookmaker has taken, in finance a book refers to the set of positions which a *market maker* owns. It comprises a set of shares which he owns (his *longs* or *bulls*) and some he has sold but does not own (his *shorts* or *bears*). *Market makers* in bonds run similar books. Because this information would be useful to other *market makers*, it is guarded carefully.

Bull: An investor who thinks a market will rise. Also used to refer to a *long* position held by a *market maker*. A **bull market** is one where prices are on a rising trend. Investors who think a market will rise are **bullish** or think the market is **heading north**.

Bulldog: UK domestic security – particularly a bond – held by overseas investor.

Bullet: A bond which has a single redemption date. It travels straight from issuance to maturity with no possibility of either the issuer or the investor redeeming the bond early.

Call: An option to buy a share or commodity.

Cash flow: The amount of money which flows in to and out of a business. The difference between the two being the important number. If more money flows into a business than out of it it is **cash positive**, if more flows out it is **cash negative**.

Cash market: Normally used to contrast with *forward* or *futures* markets, the cash market refers to the market in the underlying security, or the market for immediate delivery. See also *spot*.

Certificate of Deposit: CD for short, this is a tradeable bank deposit. Instead of having to put their money with a bank for three months, institutional investors can put their money with the bank and get a three month CD instead. Then if their circumstances change, the institution can sell the bill in the money market. Because they are *negotiable*, CDs tend to pay a slightly lower rate of interest than conventional deposits.

Charting: See *technical analysis*.

Chinese walls: These are the regulations which are supposed to prevent conflicts of interest arising in integrated securities firms. *Market makers* who buy and sell for the firm, salesmen who advise investors, *analysts* who study companies and markets and corporate financiers who advise companies, may at some times have information which might cause a conflict of interest if it was known to one of the other groups in the firm. Chinese walls are supposed to keep them apart at those times. Frequently Chinese walls have proved paper thin.

Commercial bill: In trade finance such bills are used as an international payment system. The bill guarantees to pay for the exported goods, when they are delivered some months hence. To ease the exporter's cash flow, he sells this bill to a merchant bank – often an *accepting house* – at a discount to its total value. The bank then guarantees the bill and sells it on at a higher price (the bill is worth more because of the bank's creditworthiness). The **discounted bill** is then traded as a money market instrument.

Consolidated accounts: The accounts of a group of companies or subsidiaries amalgamated to give an overall picture.

Contango: Deferring settlement of an *equity* deal from one account to the next for an extra fee. One way of extending a *short* position.

Convertible: A bond or share which has the option to convert into another bond or share at a fixed date or set of dates and under fixed terms.

Cost of carry: The difference between the cost of borrowing money and the yield which the investment offers. If a *market maker* can borrow money at 12 per cent to buy shares yielding five per cent, then the cost of carrying those shares is the difference between the two –

seven per cent. The *market maker* must be confident that the shares will rise more than seven per cent in a year for him to break even. (Of course most *market makers* take a much shorter term view than this.) In periods of very high interest rates, the high cost of carry is a disincentive to *market makers* holding shares. In *futures* markets cost of carry is used to describe the difference between the yield available when holding the underlying investment and the interest earned leaving the money in the bank and buying futures on *margin*. Cash and futures prices are supposed to adjust to make investors indifferent to which type of transaction they choose – buying cash or futures.

Coupon: The amount of interest which a bond pays, on its **nominal** value, but not the same as its *yield*, which is the rate of interest the bond pays at the market price. The coupon refers to the fact that bonds have historically had detachable interest payment coupons attached to them.

Cum: Normally seen in the context cum-dividend, it means that the shares are being traded with the dividend still included. Without the dividend is called **ex-dividend**.

Cumulative preference shares: Prefs which have the right to accrue any dividends which have been missed.

Debenture: A loan secured on assets of a company.

Depreciation: The accounting convention whereby firms write down the value of their assets – for example the cost of a new machine might be written down over its life of ten years. Important not least because it has implications for reported profits and tax.

Discount houses: Middlemen in the money market who stand between the Bank of England and other banks.

Discretionary: A discretionary account with a stock-broker is one where the broker has the discretion to buy shares he thinks will suit you, rather than the other way around. Clients can put limits on discretionary accounts –

banning the purchase of media shares for example. See also *advisory* and *execution-only*.

Dividend: The proportion of profits which is paid out to shareholders in a company – it often comes in two slugs, interim and final.

Dividend cover: The number of times a company could pay its annual dividend from its earnings.

Dual capacity: The current system of stockmarket dealing where a firm can act both as agent advising clients on investments, and as principal, dealing for its own account. To prevent conflicts of interest *Chinese walls* have been established. See also *Single capacity*.

Ecu: The European currency unit – a basket currency containing fixed percentages of European currencies. At present these percentages are renegotiated every five years, with the weighting of each currency in rough proportion to the size of its economy. Because of Germany's economic strength the Ecu is dominated by the mark.

EMS: The European Monetary System. This is a package of proposals designed to make the EC's economies move closer together or **converge**. It includes the *Ecu* and the *ERM*.

Equity: Commonly used to mean the **ordinary shares** of a company. The equity holders are a company's owners.

ERM: The Exchange Rate Mechanism of the *European Monetary System (EMS)*. The ERM ties European currencies together by confining them within set bands. If any currency starts to move outside the bands, the European central banks must take action to oppose the movement.

Euromarket: An international market which exists outside of the jurisdiction of any one government. Euro-investors are investing in bonds, shares or currencies abroad. The Euromarket's unofficial headquarters is London.

Execution-only: Here a broker simply executes his client's orders, without giving any advice. This is the cheapest form of stockbroking and is often done by phone. Known in America as **discount brokerage**.

Exercise: If an investor chooses to take up an *option* he is said to exercise it.

Federal Reserve: The American central bank.

Forward: In the foreign exchange market, this is a tailor-made deal where an investor agrees to buy or sell an agreed amount of currency at a future date. The deal is calculated from the current or *spot* price, with an adjustment for the cost of interest between when the deal is struck and when it is completed. Forwards are good for investors who need unusual deals, but have limitations because they are not *negotiable*.

FRN: Floating rate note. A type of Eurobond which resets its interest rate in line with money market rates every three or six months.

Fundamentals: The underlying business or economic conditions of a company or country. Used by economists and analysts to assess the investment prospects of a business, country or currency. Usually contrasted with *technical analysis*.

Futures: Contracts to buy or sell standardised amounts of a commodity or financial instrument at a specific date in the future. Unlike *forwards*, futures are *negotiable*, and because they are standardized they approximate to what many investors want. The aim of this is to make futures markets *liquid*, so dealing is easy. Futures prices are related to the current price of the commodity, adjusted for the *cost of carry*.

Gearing: Any situation where the swings between profits and losses can be caused by quite small changes in underlying conditions. 1) In futures and options, deals are executed on *margin*, and an investor can make or lose large amounts, relative to his original investment. 2) A company is said to be **highly geared** if it has high borrowings relative to its share capital or turnover. Under those conditions, profits can be dramatically affected by small changes in interest rates. Americans call gearing **leverage**, hence **leveraged buy-outs**.

Gilts: British government bonds.

Go short: Sell shares one does not own in the hope of buying them back more cheaply later. Some speculators go short within an *account*, hoping for a rapid fall in a share price so that they can buy back quickly. If this does not happen the speculator has a problem. *Market makers* can get round this by borrowing shares from money brokers in order to deliver the shares they have sold, and give themselves longer before buying them back. Also known as **setting a bear**.

IDB: Inter dealer broker. A broker who acts between market makers, smoothing out the flow of stock in bond and equity markets. IDBs charge very small commissions but deal in huge volumes.

IMF: International Monetary Fund. One of the institutions set up after the **Bretton Woods agreement** at the end of the second world war. (Another is the World Bank.) The IMF's job is to lend to governments and help them sort out budget and monetary problems.

Index linked: A security whose value and/or interest payments are linked to inflation. Particularly index linked gilts.

Indication-only: A *market maker's* idea of what the price of a security may be, but on which he is not prepared to deal.

Institutions: The bane of British life. In finance, this normally refers to the investing institutions who handle large sums of money – primarily the insurance companies and pension funds. Sometimes also applied to the Bank of England, Stock Exchange and even banks.

Interim: Formal statement of trading results for the first half of a company's financial year. If things are going well, there may also be an interim dividend. Perversely, a full year's results are known as *preliminary*.

Introduction: A way of launching a share issue on the stockmarket without raising any money. Shares are normally widely held before the introduction and trading is simply put onto an official footing.

Investment trust: A company which exists to invest in the equity of other companies. Used by small investors to gain a wide spread of investments easily. Some 200-odd trusts are quoted on the stockmarket. See also *unit trusts*.

LIBOR: London Inter-Bank Offered Rate. The rate at which banks lend to one another. A 'fixing' of these rates is taken at 11am every day, and is used as the benchmark to determine the interest rate on many large international loans.

Liquid: A market where there are many buyers and sellers (and consequently it is easy to deal) is described as liquid. Investors who hold cash are said to **be liquid**, and those who have sold their securities for cash have **gone liquid**.

Liquidation: What happens when a **liquidator** (an accountant) is appointed to wind up a company.

Listing: For shares (or bonds) to be traded officially on a stockmarket they need to get a listing, which is really an endorsement from the market authorities that the securities and their issuer meet certain criteria. On the Stock Exchange, listed shares are those which have a quote on the main market (as opposed to the *USM*) and their transactions appear in the daily **Official List**.

Long: A gilt or other bond with more than 15 years to go before it is *redeemed*.

Margin: The thing which makes futures markets risky. Securities where only part of the money has to be paid in advance are said to be dealt on margin. Investors get the full profit or loss from any move in the price of the security, but as they only put up a part of the cash, their percentage profit or loss is greatly increased. See also *gearing*.

Market maker: Someone who offers to buy and sell securities for his own account, acting as a *principal*. This contrasts with a **broker** who acts as an agent for the investor. Market makers in integrated firms who advise clients face a conflict of interest, since shares they think investors should hold are also those which the securities house wishes itself to hold. See also *Chinese walls*.

Maturity: Another word for *redemption*.

Medium: A bond with between five and fifteen years to redemption.

Merchant bank: A specialist bank which arranges deals (unlike clearing banks which make money by taking deposits and making loans). Merchant banks have low capital and make money by advising on takeovers, flotations, bond issues and other complex transactions.

MMC: The Monopolies and Mergers Commission. The body responsible for preventing companies operating monopolies or cartels in Britain. Also safeguards the public/national interest in takeover bids.

Multiple applications: Putting in several applications for a new issue of shares used to be standard practice. In privatizations it is now illegal. So it goes.

NAV: Net asset value. The total assets of a company, less its liabilities, debentures and loan stocks. Essentially the amount that would come to ordinary shareholders if the business was wound up. A measure of value most used when companies fall on hard times, or with specialist businesses like property companies or *investment trusts*.

Negotiable: A security which can be bought and sold is said to be negotiable. A bank loan is not negotiable, because it is made to one individual or firm, and cannot be transferred to another. A share (or a ten pound note) can be transferred between people and so is negotiable. Negotiable instruments are more flexible investments because the holder is not committed to owning them for their full term.

Nominee: Legal agreement where one person or firm holds shares on behalf of another, hence **nominee account**.

Offer: The price at which a *market maker* is willing to sell shares. Also known as the **ask**. Market makers quote two prices – a *bid* where they buy and an offer where they sell; the full bid-offer quote is known (unimaginatively) as a **two-way price**.

Offer document: Often quite entertaining, this is the official document sent by the **predator** to the defending company's shareholders in a takeover battle. Such documents sometimes verge on Stalinist denunciations of an incumbent management's record.

Offer for sale: A way of launching a new issue on the stockmarket which allows anyone to apply for shares. See also *placing* and *introduction*.

Offshore: This frequently carries tainted overtones as it refers to arrangements outside the jurisdiction of an investor's tax authorities.

Option: The right but not the obligation to buy or sell a security. This limits an investor's risk, since he can simply walk away from his option if things go badly, and only lose the premium he has paid. See also *writing options* and *warrants*.

Over-the-Counter market: A place where securities are traded outside a recognized exchange. They range from the small and spivvy, to the largest market of them all – foreign exchange.

Partly paid: Shares or bonds may be issued partly paid, meaning that the full value of the investment will be paid in several instalments, only the first of which is required at issue. Because of this partly paid shares are *geared*.

Pass: As in Mastermind it means 'give up and go on to the next one'. If a company is doing very badly it may pass on its dividend – a nice way of saving that shareholders aren't going to collect that year. Preference shareholders will get the dividend which has been passed later if the company returns to health. Ordinary shareholders won't.

Pension funds: Most people save in occupational pension schemes, and these large sums are administered by pension funds. As a result these funds have become powerful investors in the equity market.

PE ratio: Price-earnings ratio. A relative measure of how cheap or dear a company's shares are. It measures the number of years' earnings required to equal the current share price.

P&L: Profit and loss. Along with the *balance sheet* the P&L is the main financial report which appears in a company's annual report. It describes the current trading conditions of the company – what it has sold (turnover), and what it has paid out in raw material costs, salaries etc. It is intended to complement the *balance sheet*. P&L is also a term used by *market makers* to refer to their own trading profits (or losses).

Placing: A issue of shares which is sold privately to a group of investing institutions. This can be a way for a new company to join the stockmarket, or in place of a *rights issue* to raise additional equity finance or a way for a major shareholder to dispose of his holding. However, rules for either type of placing are quite restrictive.

Preference shares: As known as **prefs**. These are really debt issues by a company, which (usually) pay a fixed dividend, but carry some voting rights and rank ahead of ordinary shares in the creditors' pecking order, but behind *debentures* or loan stocks.

Preliminary: The statement of a full year's results which a company makes to the Stock Exchange. This contains the headline information on the company's trading position which is fleshed out in the annual report some six weeks later.

Premium: 1) The amount paid to buy an option. 2) If one share is valued more highly than another it can be said to be **at a premium**.

Primary dealer: A gilt market maker who can deal with the Bank of England on privileged terms, in return for agreeing to provide a *liquid* market in UK *gilts*.

Principal: 1) Someone who deals for his own account. 2) The lump sum lent in a loan (or bond).

Put: An option to sell shares, bonds or a commodity.

Real: The amount after taking account of inflation. So, for example, the 'real' rate of interest is the interest rate with inflation deducted, similarly the real rate of growth is growth after accounting for inflation.

Redemption date: The date on which a bond will be repaid. Some bonds can be redeemed early or **called** by the issuer. If the investor is entitled to redeem the bond early he has the right to **put** the bond. Those bonds which are never repaid are known as **irredeemables** or **perpetuals** (War Loan is an example). Some preference shares and convertibles also have redemption dates.

Registered securities: Share or bonds whose ownership is recorded on a central register, as opposed to *bearer securities*.

Retained earnings: The proportion of profits which a company does not pay in tax or dividends but retains for investment, working capital or growth.

Rights issue: An issue of new shares to raise further equity finance for a company, where existing shareholders are given rights to the new shares in proportion to their existing holdings.

RPI: Retail prices index. A measure of consumer inflation.

Samurai: Japanese domestic security held by non-resident.

Scrip issue: A share issue which raises no new money for a company, but simply gives new shares to existing holders. It has the effect of cutting the effective share price. Also known as a **capitalization issue**.

SEAQ: Stock Exchange Automated Quotations. The new stockmarket dealing and price service introduced at *Big Bang*.

Securities: Tradeable financial instruments.

Shell: A moribund company whose main value lies in its stockmarket quote. These can be taken over by entrepreneurs who inject their own business interests into the company and use the stockmarket quote to raise equity finance via a series of rights issues or takeover bids. Those shells which do well can make spectacular gains, those which fail, fail badly.

Short: 1) A bond with less than five years to maturity. 2) Selling securities one does not own in the hope that they will fall in price and so can be bought back at a profit.

SIB: The Securities and Investments Board. The chief regulator under the Financial Services Act, it oversees the **Self Regulatory Organisations, or SROs**.

Single capacity: The old stockmarket dealing system, where to avoid conflicts of interest, dealers could act as brokers advising clients or jobbers who bought and sold shares for their own account, but not both.

Spot: Used in a variety of areas to mean good for 'immediate' delivery, though the definition of immediate varies between markets. Spot in the foreign exchange market means dealing for settlement two days hence. In the gilt market it is for settlement the next day.

Spread: The difference between a maker maker's *bid* and *offer* prices, which ranges from less than one per cent of the value of the shares in the case of large companies, to 20 per cent-plus in some small shares.

Stag: An investor who applies for shares in a new issue believing them to be under priced, and intending to sell them in the market (at a profit) as soon as dealings begin.

Stop loss: A limit placed by an investor on the amount he is prepared to lose on an investment. Typically placed eight to ten per cent behind the purchase price. A **trailing stop loss** moves up with the share price so the stop is activated when the share falls by the set amount below its highest price. Sometimes people set stops according to *chart* values.

Straddle: Buying a put and a call option so that the investor makes money if the share rises or falls by more than the combined **premium**. Known as a **double** in traditional options.

Straight: A bond which pays a fixed rate of interest. Normally used to contrast with *FRNs*.

Strike: Price at which an option can be *exercised*. A 120p June call, gives an investor the right to buy shares at 120p before June. In this case 120p is the strike price.

Swap: An agreement between two borrowers to swap interest payments with each other in the belief that both will gain. The two most common types are swaps of fixed interest payments for floating, and swaps of interest payments in one currency for interest payments in another.

Takeover Panel: The unofficial City institution which overseas takeover bids for quoted companies.

Tap: A continuous supply of stock available to a market – most often seen when the Bank of England has gilts available to sell. Small taps are known quaintly as **taplets**.

Taurus: The new electronic share register which has been about to be introduced for as long as anyone can remember. See also Advanced Passenger Train.

Technical analysis: Also known as *charting*, this is a way of trying to predict future price movements from past movements in prices **only**. It depends on mass psychology and predictable crowd behaviour. Whether it is in any way valid is hotly disputed. Normally seen in contrast to *fundamental analysis*.

Touch: The highest bid and lowest offer between a bunch of competing market makers' two way price quotes. It gives an idea of the best terms an investor could deal on in the market.

Underwriter: Institutional investor who effectively insures a new issue (or rights issue) by agreeing to buy all shares which are not sold to interested investors. Naturally the underwriter earns a fee for his trouble.

Unit trust: A form of collective investment where investors' money is pooled and then invested in a spread of shares to reduce risks. It is **open ended** because more units can be created or destroyed, depending upon demand from investors.

USM: The Unlisted Securities Market. This is London's second-tier stockmarket, where companies can raise money and have their shares traded under less onerous requirements and with lower costs than with a full listing. Companies only need a two year trading record to be admitted to the USM.

Warrant: Essentially a long-term *option* to buy a company's shares.

Withholding tax: Tax deducted from dividends on investments which are paid to investors who are non-residents. This can often be claimed back if there is a **double taxation agreement**.

World Bank: Institution set up at the end of the second world war to help countries finance development projects. See also *IMF*.

Writing options: A way to get poor quickly. In return for receiving a *premium*, investors grant others the right to buy or sell shares. The only conditions under which small investors should even consider this is writing **covered calls** – selling other investors the right to buy shares they already own.

Yankee: American domestic security held by non-US resident.

Yield: The annual rate of income on a share or bond which an investor would earn from the security at the current market price. Two common measures of bond yields are the **current** or **interest yield** which measures immediate returns, and the **yield to maturity** or **yield to redemption** which measures the total return over the life of the bond.

Bibliography

Brett, M., (1991) *How to Read the Financial Pages*, London: Hutchinson

Burrough, B., and J. Hellyar, *Barbarians at the Gate*, London: Jonathan Cape

Chamberlain, G., *Traded Options*, Cambridge: Woodhead-Faulkner

Coggan, P., (1989) *The Money Machine: How the City Works*, London: Penguin

Ellinger, A.G., *The Art of Investment* (out of print but available from Investment Research – see below.)

Emmott, W., and R. Pennant-Rea, *Pocket Economist*, Oxford: Blackwell

Galbraith, J.K., *The Great Crash*, Harmondsworth: Penguin

Gann, W.D., *Forty five years in Wall St*, Washington: Lambert-Gann Publishing

Gifford, E., *Making Money Matters* (Investment Research, 28 Panton St, Cambridge, 0223 356251)

Hexton, R., (1989) *Dealing in Traded Options*, New Jersey: Prentice Hall

Holmes, G., and A. Sugden, (1990) *Interpreting Company Reports and Accounts*, Cambridge: Woodhead-Faulkner

International Stock Exchange, (1991) *The Book of Traded Options*, London: Heron

Lefevre, E., *Reminiscences of a Stock Operator* (Books of Wall St, Box 494, 309 South Willard, Burlington, Vermont 05402)

Lipsey, R., *Positive Economics*, London: Weidenfeld and Nicolson

Mackay, C., *Extraordinary Popular Delusions and the Madness of Crowds*, New York: Harmony Books

McRae, H., and F. Cairncross, (1991) *Capital City*, London: Methuen

Maguire, S., (1990) *The Handbook of Convertibles*, Cambridge: Woodhead-Faulkner

Masey, A., (1988) *Investment Trusts*, FTBI

Millard, B.J., (1991) *Profitable Charting Techniques*, Qudos

O'Shea, D., (1991) *Investing for Beginners*, FTBI

Redhead, K., (1990) *Introduction to Financial Futures and Options*, Cambridge: Woodhead-Faulkner

Reid, M., (1988) *All Change in the City*, London: Macmillan

Rutterford, J., (1983) *An Introduction to Stock Exchange Investment*, London: Macmillan

Sampson, A., (1981) *The Money Lenders*, London: Coronet

Slater, J., *Return to Go*, London: Weidenfeld and Nicolson (out of print)

Soros, G., *The Alchemy of Finance*, London: Weidenfeld and Nicolson

Stapely, N., *The Stock Market,* Cambridge: Woodhead-Faulkner

Stigum, M., *The Money Market,* Dow Jones Irwin

Stopp, C., (1988) *Unit Trusts,* FTBI

Train, J., *The Money Masters,* New York: Harper and Row

Valentine, S., *International Dictionary of the Securities Industry,* London: Macmillan

Wolfe, T., (1988) *Bonfire of the Vanities,* London: Jonathan Cape

Index

INVESTORS
CHRONICLE

A Financial Times Magazine

If you enjoyed this book, why not try a subscription to the weekly Investors Chronicle?

The weekly Investors Chronicle magazine is designed to help private investors compete on equal terms with the investing institutions. The magazine's clear and structured format makes it easy for you to get information you want fast.

Each week the magazine begins with general issues and gets progressively more specific:-
*broad news coverage and business analysis
*investment and stockmarket strategy and sample
  portfolios
*personal financial planning and current best buys
*regular and comprehensive coverage of the top 1000
  UK companies' results with tips, news and statistics
  on the smaller companies
*reports on the top 400 European companies.

If you are interested in investment, can you afford to be without the Investors Chronicle each week? Turn to the next page for details of our special trial offer, which gives you four free issues.

INVESTORS CHRONICLE SUBSCRIPTION FORM

Please return to:
FT Magazines,
Subscription Department,
1st Floor, Central House,
27 Park Street, FREEPOST
Croydon CR9 1WZ England

☐ **YES,** Please enrol me in your trial subscription
offer to Investors Chronicle.
I understand that I will receive my first four issues
absolutely free. Thereafter, I will receive my first year's
subscription at the normal rate.

If I cancel within 4 weeks any money I pay out will be
refunded in full.

Please enrol me as below

☐ £80 UK (inc. N. Ireland)
☐ £96 Europe (letter rate) Eire
   (or local currency equivalent)
☐ £115 Rest of World
☐ I enclose a cheque payable to
   F.T. Business Enterprises Ltd.
☐ I wish to pay by credit card.
   Please debit my account.
☐ Visa   ☐ Access   ☐ Amex   ☐ Diners

Card No ☐☐☐☐☐☐☐☐☐☐☐☐☐☐☐☐☐☐

BLOCK CAPITALS PLEASE

Mr/Mrs/Miss/Ms_____

Job Title_____

Company/Private Address_____

_____

_____ Country_____

Nature of business_____

604116

FT Business Enterprises Ltd
Registered office: Number One Southwark Bridge
London SE1 9HL. Registered in England No. 980896
INVESTORS CHRONICLE is a Trademark of the Financial Times Group.

FIMBRA
A
MEMBER